LITIGATING IN AMERICA

Civil Procedure in Context

LITIGATING IN AMERICA

Civil Procedure in Context

Stephen N. Subrin

Professor of Law
Northeastern University School of Law

Margaret Y. K. Woo

Professor of Law
Northeastern University School of Law

ASPEN

PUBLISHERS

111 Eighth Avenue, New York, NY 10011
http://lawschool.aspenpublishers.com

© 2006 Aspen Publishers, Inc.
a Wolters Kluwer business
http://lawschool.aspenpublishers.com

Aspen Publishers
Attn: Permissions Department
111 Eighth Avenue, 7th Floor
New York, NY 10011-5201

Printed in the United States of America.

1 2 3 4 5 6 7 8 9 0

ISBN 0-7355-5266-5

Library of Congress Cataloging-in-Publication Data

Subrin, Stephen, 1936-
   Litigating in America: civil procedure in context / Stephen N. Subrin, Margaret Y. K. Woo.- 1st ed.
      p. cm.
   ISBN-13: 978-0-7355-5266-5
   1. Civil procedure — United States.   I. Woo, Margaret Y. K. II.   Title.

   KF8840.S83 2006
   347.73'5 — dc22   2006002725

Cover photos:
The United States Supreme Court, Washington, D.C. © iStockphoto.com/Mark Hurlburt. Used with permission.
Ontario County Courthouse, Canandaigua, N.Y. Courtesy of www.visitfingerlakes.com.

About Aspen Publishers

Aspen Publishers, headquartered in New York City, is a leading information provider for attorneys, business professionals, and law students. Written by preeminent authorities, our products consist of analytical and practical information covering both U.S. and international topics. We publish in the full range of formats, including updated manuals, books, periodicals, CDs, and online products.

Our proprietary content is complemented by 2,500 legal databases, containing over 11 million documents, available through our Loislaw division. Aspen Publishers also offers a wide range of topical legal and business databases linked to Loislaw's primary material. Our mission is to provide accurate, timely, and authoritative content in easily accessible formats, supported by unmatched customer care.

To order any Aspen Publishers title, go to *http://lawschool.aspenpublishers.com* or call 1-800-638-8437.

To reinstate your manual update service, call 1-800-638-8437.

For more information on Loislaw products, go to *www.loislaw.com* or call 1-800-364-2512.

For Customer Care issues, e-mail *CustomerCare@aspenpublishers.com*; call 1-800-234-1660; or fax 1-800-901-9075.

Aspen Publishers
a Wolters Kluwer business

DEDICATION

---

*I dedicate this book to H.S., Milt, and Bert, who chose law, and
Joan, Elisabeth, Julie, Jennifer, and Dennis, who have
preferred stories; humanity needs both.*

— Steve Subrin

To Andrew, Katie, Alex, and my parents — who make it all worthwhile.

— Margaret Woo

SUMMARY OF CONTENTS

TABLE OF CONTENTS

CHAPTER 4

AN AMERICAN CIVIL LITIGATION FROM BEGINNING TO END   59

CHAPTER 5

DIVIDED POWER: JURISDICTION, VENUE, NOTICE, AND CHOICE OF LAW   71

CHAPTER 6

THINKING LIKE AN AMERICAN LAWYER: BURDENS OF PROOF, PLEADINGS, AND A LAWYER'S OBLIGATIONS   103

CHAPTER 7

DISCOVERY AND JUDICIAL CASE MANAGEMENT   129

CHAPTER 8

ADJUDICATION WITHOUT TRIAL: DISPOSITIVE MOTIONS   155

CHAPTER 9

JOINDER AND CLASS ACTIONS   181

CHAPTER 10

PUBLIC ADJUDICATION, PRIVATE RESOLUTION, AND THE ALTERNATIVE DISPUTE RESOLUTION MOVEMENT   213

CHAPTER 11

TRIALS AND JURIES	239

CHAPTER 12

THE QUEST FOR FINALITY: PRECLUSION, APPEALS, AND ENFORCEMENT OF JUDGMENT	259

PREFACE

Our Introduction explains the genesis, purpose, and major themes of this book, so little is required here. This book provides "local knowledge" to understanding American civil procedure and civil litigation. It is neither a civil procedure casebook nor a civil procedure treatise. It is background reading for law students, lawyers, and judges from other countries; beginning American law students; undergraduates interested in law; and others who want to learn about our civil litigation system, including the procedures that judges and lawyers use in such litigation. We present American civil procedure from several vantage points: the procedural doctrine that has evolved over time; the practical implications of that doctrine; the social context in which the doctrine grew, is used and abused; the recent efforts to contain procedure, and the global context of how other systems may have made different choices. We hope we have captured the character of American civil litigation and procedure at this very critical juncture of retrenchment.

We thank Professor Jiang Wei of Renmin University, Beijing, China, whose wisdom and courage have provided insight and inspiration – and his students and colleagues, who asked such probing questions. Of course, we are appreciative of the Ford Foundation, which encouraged and supported this project. We thank literally dozens of Northeastern University School of Law students (especially Ethan Eddy) and the school's librarians who during all stages of this book have provided countless hours of much appreciated help. We are grateful to the Dean, Emily Spieler, for granting research funds and giving encouragement.

We also thank the many at Aspen Publishers who have aided and guided us throughout, including Jessica Barmack, Melody Davies, Eric Holt, and Dana Wilson. We hope Carol McGeehan at Aspen knows that we know that she made this book happen; we truly appreciate her combination of energy, intelligence, experience, humor, and graciousness.

We learned so much writing this book, and thank each other for pushing the other on. Our ever-changing civil litigation system is markedly different from, and yet similar to, those in the rest of the world. We sincerely hope that we have been able to describe accurately American institutions, values, lawyers, procedure, and litigation to students and lawyers from other countries, undergraduates, and novice American law students trying to make sense of litigating in America.

Please write Steve at s.subrin@neu.edu or Margaret at m.woo@neu.edu with corrections and ideas for improving this book.

Steve Subrin
Margaret Woo

Boston, January, 2006

Introduction

Clifford Geertz, the noted anthropologist, wrote, "[l]ike sailing, gardening, politics, and poetry, law and ethnography are crafts of place: they work by light of local knowledge." [1] By this, Geertz meant to emphasize that law is embedded in the culture of place and time. Laws and legal systems do not descend from heaven. In order to understand them, one must not simply know the rules, but also their derivation, the choices they represent, the policies behind them, and how they actually operate in practice.

This book provides "local knowledge" to understanding American civil procedure and civil litigation. It is neither a civil procedure casebook nor a civil procedure treatise. It is background reading for law students, lawyers, and judges from other countries; beginning American law students; under-graduates interested in law; and others who want to learn about our civil litigation system, including the procedures that judges and lawyers use in such litigation. The law school course for which this book is most relevant is of course civil procedure, but we think it will also help law students in their other courses. The book provides context about American legal institutions, legal culture, and the legal profession that often falls between the cracks, but without which learning becomes unnecessarily rarefied and abstract.

This book also looks at American civil procedure in a comparative context. In this era of globalization and transnational disputes, the American civil justice system is but one of many options. As international economic transactions invariably lead to complex legal problems without borders, a lawyer must not only negotiate complex cross-border transactions; she must also be able to resolve complex cross-border disputes. Where appropriate, then, we also note differences and similarities between American civil procedure and that of other nations. Ultimately, we examine American civil procedure comparatively in order to highlight the assumptions within our own system, rather than to teach the intricacies of another's legal system.

By "civil," in the phrases "civil litigation" and "civil procedure," American lawyers and we mean "not criminal." (We sometimes use the word "America" or "American" to refer to the United States, fully aware that "America" can also refer to other geographical areas.) One way of dividing up the law cases that are brought in United States courts is to distinguish between "criminal" and "civil" cases. Criminal cases refer to when the government, either that of the United States or one of the states, seeks to convict a person for breaking the criminal law.

"Civil" cases, then, are those that are not criminal. Typically, a civil case involves one or more people suing another person or people for causing harm. This might be because one person thinks another did not fulfill a contract, unreasonably drove an automobile in a way that caused the claimant harm,

---

1. Clifford Geertz, Local Knowledge: Fact and Law in Comparative Perspective in the Interpretation of Culture: Selected Essays 168-234 (Basic Books 1973) [hereinafter Geertz].

or illegally discriminated in employment based on race or for some other prohibited reason. Sometimes Americans sue their own government in civil cases, or the government sues a person for civil remedies, rather than seeking the criminal sanctions of imprisonment or fine.

"Civil," when used in a legal context, also has another meaning. Some legal scholars divide up legal systems between "civil law" and "common law" countries. By civil law countries, they mean those countries in which the law is primarily written in codes, such as Germany and France. By common law countries, they mean those, such as the United States and England, in which much of the law has been developed on a case-by-case basis through judicial opinions, rather than in codes. Even though much of the law in the United States is now in written statutes and rules, it is still considered a common law country because of its heavy reliance on judicial opinions in both the development of court-made law and the interpretation of statutes. But in the terms "civil procedure" and "civil litigation," the word "civil" denotes "noncriminal" as opposed to distinguishing between common law and civil law countries.

"Litigation" refers to a contest initiated in a tribunal, usually a formal court, typically for the purpose of enforcing a right guaranteed by law. By "procedure," American lawyers mean to denote the rules by which a lawsuit is conducted. "Substantive" rules describe such matters as what conduct is illegal, the relationships between people (such as marriage or adoption), and the relationships between people and property (such as leasing an apartment). There are substantive rules about what constitutes a breach of contract, negligence, discrimination, or ownership of property.

By contrast, "procedural" rules prescribe how litigation is to be conducted. Procedural rules and procedural statutes cover matters such as which court can hear what type of case, what pieces of paper must be filed, what information has to be in the papers, how many people can join in the same law suit, how one side of the litigation can get information from the other side, what cases can be disposed of without a full trial, what goes on at the trial, and other such questions in processing the case. Rules governing procedure are found in statutes and in written rules that have been authorized by legislative statutes, state constitutions, or the United States Constitution. Increasingly, however, in the United States, parties to a dispute are deciding among themselves what procedures they choose to follow.

The line between "substance" and "procedure" is not an iron-clad one, and some legal questions fall between the two. For example, there are statutes called "statutes of limitations" that prescribe that one must bring a law suit within so many years — such as three years — of one's being harmed. It is not clear whether this is a substantive or procedural rule. In general, though, it is usually fairly easy to determine whether one is talking about a rule for the processing of cases — procedural — or a rule that describes proper and improper conduct in everyday life — substantive.

"Civil procedure," then, is the field of law that covers the rules for the processing of noncriminal cases. Civil litigation and its accompanying procedure are the topic of this book.

Your initial impression might be that procedure concerns boring, technical stuff that is not nearly as interesting as the substantive rules. In fact, civil procedure and civil litigation raise many of the most interesting issues in law, government, social thought, history, literary criticism, economics, anthropology, and culture generally. As observed by C.J. Hamson, legal procedure is

> a . . . ritual of extreme social significance. If we can appreciate the meaning of this ritual in the case of our own and even one other community, we obtain a remarkable insight into the fundamental and largely unformulated beliefs accepted by, and acceptable to, these societies; we begin to understand their collective and perhaps contrasted social sense of what is just and fair.[2]

Five years ago, we taught American civil litigation and procedure in Beijing to two dozen young Chinese civil procedure scholars. In having to explain the American system to a distinctly different cultural audience, we realized something that we should probably have known all along. Many American law students, as well as foreign lawyers, judges, and law students, would also crave the same background information about civil procedure as these young Chinese law professors. They would want historical background for our system and our procedures and want to know how lawyers actually use the system and what remedies clients are apt to receive and not receive. They, too, would want to know what we have learned empirically about the profession and the procedures.

In fact, nothing reminds us more of the importance of placing legal process in a cultural context than when we step out before a class of new law students to explain some technical rule of civil procedure. While such topics as torts or criminal law have resonance in everyday life, civil procedure, more than any other first-year course, is imbued with its own legal language and culture, one with which we (as teachers) are entrusted to translate and reveal the realm to novices. Understanding civil procedure does not simply mean reading the rules and applying them in a literal way to facts; the facts are more malleable and the law is less defining than law students expect. True understanding requires an understanding of the history of the procedural rules; the values they contain; and how they have been used, and on occasion abused, in practice.

It is not easy to understand a procedural system. Litigation has multiple interrelated steps, and one does not truly understand any one step without exposure to the whole or understand the whole without the composite steps. But on the positive side, there is a somewhat predictable flow to civil litigation. One learns over time a sense of coherence in the various litigation steps as they proceed. We will try to convey that coherence to you from chapter to chapter. There is also a good deal of conceptual coherence that underlies both the procedural steps and the system as a whole.

A handful of major themes and questions run throughout the whole of American civil procedure and litigation, and hence, this book. These same themes and questions probably underlie dispute resolution in most countries. The four themes relate to (1) the culture in which the litigation system evolved and currently takes place; (2) the ways in which the litigation system and its

---

2. C.J. Hamson, *In Court in Two Countries: Civil Procedure in England and France*, The Times of London, November 15, 1949.

procedures distribute power amongst the various participants; (3) the tension in the procedural system between rigorous rules and less structured narrative; and (4) the ultimate question of whether the country's litigation system and its procedures are considered legitimate by those who live and dispute there: Does the system work well in the sense of enhancing the values of the society and are those values admirable?

First, as we have suggested, litigation and the outer culture are reciprocal: A litigation process is both a reflection and an integral part of the larger culture. Culture, in the way we are using the term, includes the major ideology — the philosophic-political outlook — that supports the society. For example, in the United States, the "rights revolution" of the 1950s and 1960s shaped, and was shaped by, American culture as one that persistently turned to courts for remedies from social ills and litigation as a vehicle for orderly social change.

The process of disputing and dispute resolution unveil "the meaning participants attach to going to court, [as well as] social practices that indicate when and how to escalate disputes to a public forum."[3] As will be discussed throughout this book, the administration of justice in America typically involves a judgment on legal facts that are "socially constructed by everything from evidence rules, courtroom etiquette, and law reporting traditions, to advocacy techniques, the rhetoric of judges and scholasticism of law school education."[4] In the American context, procedural rules are often intertwined with changing cultural attitudes towards litigation and the substance of the litigation itself (for example, expansion and contraction of class actions, in which groups of unnamed people sue in the same law suit, fluctuated with the changing attitudes towards litigation and civil rights litigation).[5] Adding legal culture to the picture, then, is "like winding up a clock or plugging in a machine. It sets everything in motion."[6]

Second, issues of power abound. Procedures inherently carry with them decisions about power distribution. In determining who has the obligation to do what in a litigation, procedural rules and statutes in the United States distribute power among parties, lawyers, judges, experts, lay community, different branches of government, state and national governments, rich and poor, corporations and individuals. Try as rule-makers may, procedural rules tend to yield nonneutral results. Understanding the role of courts then must also mean understanding the effect (intended or otherwise) of the procedural rules and statutes on power distribution.

A third theme is simultaneously literary and utilitarian. In many ways, litigation is drama and a literary form, from the storytelling inherent in a complaint to the final theatrical staging of a trial. At least in the American society, litigation is less one of deciphering an objective reality and more a judgment on legal facts that are socially constructed and circumscribed by rules and language of the courtroom.

In making choices of what to include and exclude from the litigation, procedural rules are pulled in separate directions. In the name of efficiency

---

3. Sally E. Merry, *Disputing Without Culture*, 100 Harvard L. Rev. 2057, 2063 (1987).
4. Geertz, *supra* note 1, at 173.
5. Class actions are discussed in Chapter 9.
6. Lawrence M. Friedman, Law and Society: An Introduction 76 (Prentice Hall 1977).

and predictability, some rules constrict the number of variables and exclude more of the underlying story. In the name of overall justice or mercy, there are also pulls in the opposite direction, resulting in rules that include more of the underlying story. Telling more of the story will often take more time and cost more money, but may also, in an individual case, lead to a fairer result. These differing pulls have variously been described as the tension between rule and narrative, efficiency and fairness, law and equity.

Finally, the fourth theme, related to the other three themes of culture, power, and efficient story-telling, involves assessing whether the litigation system and its procedures work well. Is the litigation system, including the procedures underlying it, deemed to be legitimate by the society? Is the system beneficial to those who live within the society? Do folks trust and admire their litigation system?

This theme of legitimacy is related to, and often equated to, the concept of "rule of law." Many people, even within the same country, ascribe different meanings to the phrase "rule of law."[7] There seems to be general consensus, though, that the concept includes the idea that those in power are bound by rules, rather than their own arbitrary wishes. Most think that the concept includes the notion that laws will be applied and enforced by neutral dispute resolvers who will apply laws that are known in advance to the events that actually happened, thereby affording society some degree of predictability.[8] In the United States, what is called "due process" includes the right to be notified of a law suit brought against you and the right to "be heard" in the sense of presenting evidence and making legal arguments. Such procedural rights are included in most people's meaning of the rule of law.

A dictator or an apartheid regime could accept and follow the procedural incidents of rule of law, but the laws could be cruel to minority citizens or dissenters. In the United States, rule of law probably also includes substantive values of democracy, such as freedom of speech and religion and the protection of minority rights. It probably also includes substantial limitations on government power, the protection of property, and the enforcement of contracts. For some, the key to rule of law is the enhancement and protection of human dignity, including economic security. Dignity itself may be enhanced by the procedural aspects of rule of law, such as the right to be heard. Whatever is meant by rule of law, it is important to consider whether the litigation system and its procedures advance or impede the values implied by the phrase by those who use it.

This fourth theme has become particularly important not only in the United States but in the broader world as well. Along with market forces, rule of law is now the favorite export of developed countries to developing countries.[9] That export consists of law reform projects by such institutions as the World

---

7. *See, e.g.*, Michael Rosenfeld, *The Rule of Law and the Legitimacy of Constitutional Democracy*, 74 S. Cal. L. Rev. 1307 (2001), Berta Esperanza Hernandez-Trual, *Human Rights Commitments in the Americas: From the Global to the Local – The Rule of Law and Human Rights*, 16 Fla. J. Int'l L. 167 (2004).

8. *See, e.g.*, John Rawls, A Theory of Justice 235 (Belnap Press 1971).

9. *See e.g.* Alan Watson, Legal Transplants: An Approach to Comparative Law (2nd ed., University Press of Virginia 1993); Thomas M. Franck, *The New Development: Can American Law and Legal Institutions Help Developing Countries?*, 1972 Wis. L. Rev. 767.

Bank, International Monetary Funds that equate economic development with free markets and the rule of law. [10]

The rule of law theme has renewed relevance for the United States. Much dispute resolution in recent years is increasingly governed by contracts entered into by parties and less according to rules of the court. [11] Parties to a dispute are negotiating, in advance or at the time of disputes, the location of where the law suit will take place, who will be the decision maker, and even what procedures they will follow. This privatizing of dispute resolution, the taking of certain disputes out of the public realm, highlights the need to revisit questions of when, whether, and how a country's overall litigation system is legitimate and fair for disputants and for the society at large.

Our book begins by giving you the needed context in a number of ways: historical background and a description of our system of government (Chapter 1), an exposition of the legal profession and the adversary system (Chapter 2), the historical background of American civil procedure (Chapter 3), and a summary of one law suit from beginning to end (Chapter 4). We then explore various aspects of the civil litigation system in greater contextual and doctrinal detail: jurisdiction, venue, and notice (Chapter 5), burden of proof and pleadings (Chapter 6), discovery (Chapter 7), adjudication without trial (Chapter 8) and joinder and class actions (Chapter 9). Next we turn to settlement and alterative dispute resolution (Chapter 10), trial and juries (Chapter 11), and finality (Chapter 12). We end with an epilogue that highlights some of the current pressing issues confronting American civil litigation and procedure.

One or several of the four themes of culture, power, rule and narrative, and legitimacy are interwoven in each chapter. Throughout, we attempt to explain the legal language of civil procedure, bearing in mind not simply the primary meaning of words and rules, but also layers of nuance built up as a result of the historical context in which the words and rules have been used. Remember, this is not a casebook, nutshell summary book, or a treatise. Our intent is not to teach you the intricacies of civil procedure, although we will expose you to much of the doctrine and many of the issues covered in civil procedure courses. Many of you will be taking a full course on civil procedure as you are reading this book or soon afterwards. It is our intent that this book will deepen your understanding of American civil procedure and civil litigation deepen that your enjoyment of the topic will be materially enhanced. This is a distinctively "American story" but you will find that it has within it universal themes.

---

10. *See* Legal Institutions and the Rule of Law, in World Development Report 1996, From Plan to Market (Published for the World Bank, Oxford University Press, 1996); Law and Development at the Asian Development Bank (Asian Development Bank 1998). For a good critique of some aid programs in the United States, *see* Thomas Carothers, Aiding Democracy: The Learning Curve (Carnegie Endowment for International Peace 1999).

11. *See* Judith Resnik, *Procedure as Contract*, 80:2 Notre Dame L. Rev. 593 (2005).

CHAPTER
1

The American Legal System:
Distrust and Dispersing Power

Ambition, avarice, personal animosity, party opposition, and many other
motives not more laudable than these, are apt to operate as well upon those
who support as those who oppose the right side of a question.[1]
  Alexander Hamilton, The Federalist Papers, No. 1, 1787

AMERICAN LEGAL CULTURE

One way to begin examination of American legal culture is to read any United
States newspaper. Much of the news centers on civil litigation. People injured
by asbestos, smoking, or medicines sue manufacturers and doctors. Shareholders sue management for misdeeds and brokers and accountants for
misrepresentation. Employees sue employers for discrimination, and companies sue each other for unfair competition and patent infringement. Parents
sue schools to gain admission for their children and churches and priests for
clergy sexual abuse. American litigation, as we will later discuss, is not as
extensive or pernicious as it first appears. But it is sufficiently prevalent to
support the conclusion that law, lawsuits, and lawyers play a dominant role in
American society. It is to civil litigation that Americans frequently turn for
redress of social ills; and it is a rights-based culture that has shaped and is
reshaped by the process of litigation.

This chapter examines some of the early reasons for the importance of
law in America, and two themes pervade it: the relationship of civil litigation
to American culture as a whole and the ways in which issues of power and
control infiltrate the United States legal system. Each of these in turn raises the
question of a third theme: whether the choices made enhance or impede the
legitimacy, real and perceived, of the country's dispute resolution processes.

The historic American distrust of concentrated power, authority, and government has led to a governmental structure that relies on the principle of a
separation of powers among the executive (the President at the federal level and
the Governor at the state level), legislative, and judiciary, as well as on a federal

---

1. Alexander Hamilton, James Madison, & John Jay, The Federalist Papers 34 (A Mentor
Book, The New American Library 1961).

system of government. The 50 states that comprise the United States share much of the power that in other countries resides in the central government of the nation. The same distrust of concentrated power has also led to the persistent retention of a lawyer-dependent and jury-based adversary system of adjudication. Juries, more prevalent in the United States than anywhere else in the world, act as a brake on government and corporate power. These characteristics — separation of powers, federalism, heavy reliance on lawyers, and jury trials — are central to understanding American civil litigation and procedure.

Also critical to our civil litigation system and its evolution is the autonomy, pragmatism, and entrepreneurial spirit of American culture, which has resulted in continual experimentation and change of the system. Unlike lawyers in other countries who might see themselves as officials and bureaucrats of the state, American lawyers pride themselves in pragmatic thinking and creative problem-solving and view themselves as actors in bringing social change. This attitude is not a new phenomenon. To trace the origin of this culture of pragmatism and distrust of power, one needs to look historically at the roots of American law.

DIVERSITY, DISTRUST, AND THE EMBRACE OF LAW

In discussing American legal history, it is traditional to focus on English antecedents, because undeniably the American legal tradition drew heavily on lessons learned from England. It is true that the first permanent English settlers arrived in today's state of Virginia in 1607, and when the colonies declared their independence in 1776, it was to England that all 13 of them owed allegiance. In the writings that preceded the Declaration of Independence (1776), in which the American colonies proclaimed themselves independent from England, and in speeches given and pamphlets written during the Revolutionary War (1775-1783) between the 13 colonies and England, the former colonists repeatedly claimed the rights of Englishmen. After the colonies won the Revolutionary War, the newly formed states proclaimed the common law of England to be the operative law in the absence of state statutes or applicable federal law.

But it would be a mistake to concentrate only on the English roots of the American experience or to treat the colonists as homogeneous in background or thought. By 1790, the year after the United States Constitution was adopted, it is estimated that only 60 percent of those living in the states and territories were of English origin. Scotch, German, and Irish nationalities each represented over 8 percent of the population. There were also large numbers of settlers of Dutch, French, and Swedish origin. [2] One historian put it this way: "Multiple origins, ethnic diversity, and social heterogeneity have produced discomforting strains."[3] The United States began and remains a nation of

2. Encyclopedia of American History 653 (Richard B. Morris et al eds., Harper & Row 1976) [hereinafter Encyclopedia].

3. Michael Kammen, People of Paradox–An Inquiry of the Origins of American Civilization 113 (Vintage Books 1973). We rely heavily on Kammen's evidence and analysis in our description

immigrants, a fact to be remembered when trying to understand the country's legal institutions and traditions.

These early settlers brought with them diverse and often divisive religions. An estimate of the religious affiliation of American settlers in 1775 shows varied faiths: Congregationalists (575,000); Anglicans (500,000); Presbyterians (410,000); Dutch Reformed (75,000); German Churches (200,000); Quakers (40,000); Baptists (25,000); Roman Catholics (25,000); Methodists (5,000); Jews (2,000).[4] The bulk of the colonists were Christian, many of whom had come to the New World to escape religious persecution, and they took their particular tenets of Christianity very seriously. As one prominent historian of early America summarized: "[t]he Revolution released torrents of popular religiosity and passion into American life, and everywhere ordinary white folk as well as black openly revealed their religious feelings as never before. . . . Nowhere else in Christendom was religion so fragmented. Yet nowhere else was it so vital."[5]

As a result, the American Revolution was not "born from a Pentecost of mutual understanding, but from a Babel. That is why one of the best students of America, Thomas Pownall, had predicted in the 1760s, that no force but massive stupidity in England could draw the colonies together."[6] Each colony had its own distinct history; many of the colonies were over 150 years old at the time of the Revolutionary War, considerably older than most countries today.

What the colonists did share was personal experience with, or at least the witnessing of, some form of democracy, albeit limited to the white propertied class. Free white men who owned 50 or more acres of land typically had the right to vote. As the "least taxed territories on earth,"[7] the colonists balked when England tried to collect taxes from colonists in an aggressive manner. Taxation without colonial representation in the English parliament was a major impetus to the rebellion.

The huge amount of unsettled land to the west of the continent and an unprecedented ability to earn money and obtain land as the result of hard work, added to the white colonists' sense of entitled personal freedom and social mobility. Yet, despite a shared respect for personal freedom and independence of action and thought, there were strikingly unresolved contradictions that remain within American society even today. Michael Kammen, an astute writer on the historical background of the American experience, in his seminal book *People of Paradox — An Inquiry of the Origins of American Civilization,*[8] noted a number of unreconciled tensions in the beliefs of many leading colonists. They believed that one's destiny was preordained by God, but at the same time that the individual should work feverishly to improve his or her own circumstances; they believed in individualism and simultaneously had a deep desire to join groups and form communities. The

---

of the contradictions in the lives and ideology of the colonists, paradoxes that remain in tensions in contemporary America.

4. Encyclopedia, *supra* note 2, at 824.

5. Gordon S. Wood, The American Revolution–A History 134-135 (Modern Library Chronicles 2002).

6. Gary Wills, Inventing America–Jefferson's Declaration of Independence 47 (Mariner Books 1978).

7. Paul Johnson, A History of the American People 108 (Harper Perennial 1997).

8. Michael Kammen, *supra* note 3.

colonists valued the individual but battled with a deep distrust of the population at large; and they believed in equality of opportunity but held antagonism to the desirability of universal economic, social, and intellectual equality.

More closely relevant to the establishment of courts and the legal order was the contradiction between the desire for security and order and the desire for individual freedom of action. Colonists professed the dignity and liberty of each human being but they oppressed and murdered natives, and they owned and humiliated slaves. Although they believed in law, they also pushed the boundaries of old law and old solutions and engaged in lawlessness. Along with the recognized need for courts, they held a deep distrust of courts and judges.

The paradoxes of these American beliefs may lie inherent in the human condition. Which of us does not want freedom but at the same time crave security, desiring individual rights as well as a sense of community? But Professor Kammen points out that many aspects of life in pre-Revolutionary America deepened the contradictions within the belief structure and lives of the colonists, leaving them in a state of unrest, uncertainty, and disorder. From their unsettled relationship with England and Native Americans to the ambiguous boundaries between forest and farm, nature and civilization, these colonists opted for a governmental design that reflects an inherent tension but contains the potential for stability.

After peace was made with the British, the 13 colonies (now states) were left with the problem of forging one nation. Notwithstanding the idealism often attributed to the colonists and their leaders, the drafters of the constitution who met in Philadelphia in 1787 were deeply skeptical of the inherent goodness of human beings. They took as a given that self-interest was at the heart of much, if not most, human behavior. Alexander Hamilton,[9] in the first of The Federalist Papers, designed to convince the voting public to endorse the newly drafted constitution, wrote: "Ambition, avarice, personal animosity, party opposition, and many other motives not more laudable than these, are apt to operate as well upon those who support as those who oppose the right side of a question."[10]

A year after the Declaration of Independence was signed, representatives of the colonies drafted Articles of Confederation that governed the colonies until the United States Constitution was adopted in 1789. The Articles proved deficient in a number of ways, notably, in failing to establish a national government. The Articles created no central authority strong enough to impose and collect taxes or to impose a coordinated tariff policy among the colonies themselves or with respect to other countries. There was no court at a national level that could decide disputes among citizens of the different colonies or between the colonies themselves.

9. Hamilton was born in the British West Indies in 1755, but moved to New York as a teenager. He served in the Continental Army, the Continental Congress, and the 1787 Philadelphia Constitutional Convention. He practiced law in New York and was the first Secretary of the Treasury in President Washington's cabinet. Michael Nelson, The Presidency A to Z: A Ready Reference Encyclopedia, Vol. 2 200-01 (Congressional Quarterly Inc. 1994).

10. Alexander Hamilton, James Madison & John Jay, The Federalist Papers 34 (A Mentor Book, The New American Library 1961).

In designing a central authority, James Madison, [11] duly credited as the major architect of the United States Constitution, had to balance one more contradiction. He had witnessed the Shays's Rebellion, an armed insurrection of "distressed debtor farmers" in western Massachusetts, and was horrified that after the rebellion was quelled the insurgents were elected to public office and passed "pro-debtor" legislation in their own self-interest. [12] For Madison and other patricians who drafted the U.S. Constitution, a pure democracy was apt to lead to a tyranny of the masses, which would trample on the property or rights of others. And so these constitution makers were faced with the dilemma — they distrusted both human nature and the monarchy, yet they needed to instill a democratic form of government and ratify a constitution that mandated the granting of power to ordinary citizens who would have the power of the ballot, some for the first time.

So where did the drafters of the constitution turn? They did not trust human nature. They did not trust the people. They did not trust the centralization of power in the few. Further, the states did not trust each other. But the drafters knew that the people clamored for some representation in their own government, and they knew a nation of states with some shared sovereignty would be necessary. In an unformed nation with great diversity among the people and extreme paradoxes in their thinking, some order and balance was desperately needed. An astonishing 34 of the 55 delegates, representing 12 states, who attended the Philadelphia Convention in the summer of 1787 were lawyers. [13] Perhaps reflecting their training, these delegates turned to a written constitution and a system of laws as the primary method of bringing order and boundaries to a people largely lacking in common traditions.

RESTRAINING POWER: FEDERALISM AND SEPARATION OF POWERS

What the Constitution drafters were forced to trust was their own ability to construct a system that would control the passions of the mob and demagogue as well as the warring instincts of the 13 states. As a result of cheap or even "free" land, those who owned property were more numerous in the new nation than in older countries. The drafters believed that the self-interest of those who owned property would instill a desire to protect that property from government and from nonowners' intrusion. [14] So the drafters focused on

---

11. Madison, born in Virginia in 1751, participated in the framing of the Virginia Constitution in 1776, served in the Continental Congress, and was a leader in the Virginia Assembly. At age 36 Madison was an active delegate in the Constitutional Convention in Philadelphia, was later referred to as the "Father of the Constitution," and helped frame the Bill of Rights. He served as President Jefferson's Secretary of State and was elected as the fourth President of the United States in 1808. Michael Nelson, The Presidency A to Z: A Ready Reference Encyclopedia, Vol. 2 293-295 (Congressional Quarterly Inc. 1994).

12. Wood, *supra* note 5, at 152.

13. Wood, *supra* note 5, at 153.

14. "During the eighteenth century the British electorate made up only a tiny portion of the nation; probably only one in six British adult males had the right to vote, compared to two out of three in America." Wood, *supra* note 5, at 39.

property and designed a series of checks and balances and divisions of power to protect property — and thereby citizens — from the tyranny of the masses as well as from the tyranny of the few. This focus on property included white, male property owners, but excluded blacks, Native Americans, and women at the time.

The framers made two essential choices, each of which dispersed power: a unique two-tiered, federal and state governmental and court system (called *federalism*), and a separation of power between the three branches of the government (the legislature, executive, and judiciary). These constitutional ideas were not invented by the framers. The drafters of the Constitution borrowed from philosophical and political thinkers past and present. They looked "to the legacy of British constitutionalism, to the teachings of the Enlightenment, and to the lessons of history."[15]

These two major methods to disperse power remain in the United States to this day, as preserved by the U.S. Constitution. Under the Constitution, the states are separate political entities, each with its own citizens and its own government, but a citizen of a state is also a citizen of the nation as a whole. The federal government is given specific powers, particularly in the areas of the military, international affairs, interstate commerce, patents and copyrights, bankruptcy, and the coining of money. Where the federal government can constitutionally act, usually through federal legislation, this legislation is the supreme law of the land. Each state, in a sense, is not only kept in check by the existence of other neighboring states but also by the national government. Each state, however, maintains much of the lawmaking and every day governing power that in other countries is given to the national government, such as regulation of contracts, domestic relations, inheritance, and education.

The United States Constitution also lays out the "separation of power" principle, with Article I of the Constitution prescribing the federal legislature and its limited powers, Article II granting limited powers to the executive branch of government, with a president at its head, and Article III describing the limited power of the federal judiciary, with a mandated Supreme Court and whatever inferior courts Congress chooses to establish. Within each branch of government there are checks and balances. This set of checks and balance is replicated at the state level for the 50 state governments.

The federal legislature is divided into the Senate and House of Representatives. Each state, no matter how small, has two Senators elected for a term of six years, now elected by the voters in the state. Citizens of each state elect members of the House of Representatives for a term of two years, with the number of representatives for each state based on the population of that state.

15. A.E. Dick Howard, *The Values of Federalism*, 1 New Eur. L. Rev. 143, 143 (1993). The principle of checks and balances is most frequently said to owe its origin to Montesque (1689-1755). *See* Baron de Montesquieu, The Spirit of Laws 151-52 (Thomas Nugent trans. The Colonial Press vol. 1 1899). The English system of separation of powers, and the writings of John Locke (1632-1704) were also influential. The idea of federalism was influenced by the history of ancient and modern federations, such as found in early Greece and the Holy Roman Empire, as well as by thinkers as diverse as Plato (427-347 B.C.), Polybius (203-120 B.C.), and once again, Montesquieu. Gottfried Dietze, The Federalist: A Classic on Federal and Free Government 303, 326-327, 290-292 (The Johns Hopkins University Press 1999).

There is no limitation on the number of terms either Senators or Representatives may serve. Legislation is enacted only with the approval of both the Senate and the House, and signed by the President. Although the President can veto a congressional bill, the legislature can override a presidential veto by a two-thirds vote of both the House and the Senate. It is important to note that this is "representative democracy," that is, adult citizens of the United States have the right to vote for their representatives and not directly for the legislation itself.

The Executive Branch is headed by a President, elected by an Electoral College system in which citizens vote for representatives who in turn will vote for the President.[16] Each state has the same number of Electoral College votes as the total number of its members of the Senate and the House of Representatives. (This in effect gives the less populous states a power disproportionately greater than their size to elect a president.) The President cannot make treaties with foreign countries without the approval of two-thirds of the Senate. The President can be impeached and removed from office by articles of impeachment voted by the House of Representatives and after a trial, by a two-thirds vote of the Senate. And while the President can appoint his own cabinet (with the advice and consent of the Senate), and is supported by an increasingly large bureaucracy of agencies and bureaucrats, the Executive Branch is checked by Congress's power to control appropriation of money and to tax.

The federal judiciary is composed of judges of the Supreme Court and judges of federal trial courts and courts of appeals. The bulk of state judges are appointed or elected for fixed terms, depending on the state constitution. By contrast, federal judges are appointed with life-long tenure by the President, but only with the consent of the Senate. Their pay is set by Congress, although it cannot be reduced during their tenure. Their power is limited to specific types of cases described in Article III and authorized by Congress. For implementation of their decrees, the judiciary relies on the executive branch, which in turn relies on the legislature for its funds. But the courts have the power of "judicial review," that is, the power to rule on the constitutionality of enacted federal and state statutes, as well as the constitutionality of activity of state and federal officials. The decrees of federal judges are almost always enforced, often through the sanction of contempt, rendering federal judges enormous power.

Government in the United States is further limited by the first ten amendments to the Constitution, called the Bill of Rights. These amendments, which became law in 1791, spell out inalienable rights of individual Americans, to be protected from incursions by the federal government, in such areas as freedom of speech and religion. The Fourteenth Amendment, ratified in 1868 after the Civil War between the northern and southern States, further protects similar rights of people from infringement by state governments.

The American jury is another method of dispersing power.[17] The right to jury is protected in federal trial courts by Article III of the Constitution, the

16. "Electors" are now elected by popular vote and agree in advance to vote for specific presidential candidates. Earlier, they were elected by state legislatures and had independent choice in casting their vote for President, again keeping the "masses" one step away from actual power.

17. Chapter 11 centers on the jury trial.

Sixth Amendment (in criminal cases), and the Seventh Amendment (in civil cases). The jury, composed of lay people, reflects the historic American distrust of unbridled governmental authority. Just as the branches of government check the power of each other, the jury acts as a restraint on judges within the judicial branch. But, as will be discussed later, American judges, through the years, have evolved and developed procedures to severely restrain the power of juries.

It is through these many ways — federalism, separation of powers, Bill of Rights, representative democracy, and jury trials — that the Founding Fathers, true to their fears of both the masses and of centralized power, attempted to circumscribe governmental authority and to protect private property and the rights of individuals from mass tyranny and abusive government intrusion.

THE EMERGING ROLE OF THE JUDICIARY

Article III of the United States Constitution establishes the Supreme Court as the highest court in the United States with the power to be the final interpreter of federal law, including the Constitution. Most significantly, the Supreme Court, as established by *Marbury v. Madison*, even has the power to void federal and state statutes as unconstitutional[18] The President of the United States appoints the nine members of the United States Supreme Court, but the President can only do so with the approval of the United States Senate. Members of the Supreme Court serve for their lifetime, unless they choose to retire before they die. When a vacancy occurs, the sitting president has the power to make an appointment to fill the vacancy, but only if the then sitting Senate concurs with the President's choice. Given its important role in shaping American social policy, Supreme Court appointments have frequently drawn the ammunition and battle cries of multiple interest groups, making the judicial appointments process the most contentious and divisive process of any presidential appointments.

Under Article III, the federal legislature was given the power to establish a system of federal courts below the Supreme Court. Congress established such federal trial courts, called federal district courts, of which there are 94, as well as federal courts of appeals, which hear appeals from the district courts. The country is divided into regions called circuits, and 12 out of the 13 circuit courts hear appeals coming from the district courts within the circuit. The thirteenth court of appeals, called the Court of Appeals for the Federal Circuit, has the exclusive power to decide cases appealed from the Court of Federal Claims, which hears contract claims against the United States, as well as other specialized appeals.

Federal statutes prescribe what kinds of cases can be heard by the Federal District Courts. Generally these courts hear cases arising under federal law,

18. The opinion was authored by John Marshall (1775-1835), who was Chief Justice of the Supreme Court from 1801 to 1835.

cases in which the litigants are from different states, or cases in which the United States is a party. The Federal District Court judges and the judges of the Federal Courts of Appeals are also appointed for life by the president in the same manner as the United States Supreme Court judges. By February 2004, there were 651 Federal District Court judges and 161 judges in the United States Courts of Appeals.[19] There are also specialized federal courts, such as the Bankruptcy Court and the Court of Claims. With the growth of the federal government and hence, federal legislation, federal judges have increased in number and authority over the years, causing a present movement by more conservative groups to rein back the power of the federal courts.

A litigant who loses a case at the District Court level can appeal as a matter of right to the appropriate Circuit Court. The Supreme Court, on the other hand, controls its own docket, and decides which appeals it desires to hear from the Circuit Courts and from the highest court in the states, when a federal issue is involved. A losing litigant who wants the Supreme Court to hear a case must file what is called a writ of certiorari to seek review. Of the thousands of writs filed with the Supreme Court each year, the justices grant appellate review in only a fraction. In 2002, for example, the Supreme Court decided 84 cases, disposing of 79 by full opinions.[20]

The drafters of the United States Constitution thought it was important that the federal judiciary be independent from the political pressures of the other two branches. This is especially critical because federal judges now have the power to strike down federal and state executive and legislative action. The Constitution ensures judicial independence of federal judges through a vigorous appointments process as well as by the provision of life tenure. Life tenure is thought to insulate judges from political and partisan pressures in their decision-making.

Unlike civil law countries as in most of Europe, judges in America are lawyers, either appointed or elected, but usually only after substantial experience in practice, rather than part of a bureaucracy that one can select to enter directly out of law school. For federal district and appellate judgeships, the President of the United States nominates judicial candidates. Each nominee must be confirmed by the Senate of the United States. Judicial applicants at all federal court levels are usually experienced attorneys with excellent professional and personal credentials. Federal judges are generalists — that is, they hear both criminal and civil cases of different kinds. To date, however, there is some lack of racial diversity in both the state and federal bench.[21]

19. As of February 2004 there were 29 Federal District Court Judge vacancies and 29 United States Court of Appeals Judge vacancies. U.S. Department of Justice Office of Legal Policy, Judicial Nominations, *available at* www.usdoj.gov/olp/judicialnominations.htm (last updated Feb. 20, 2004).

20. Supreme Court of the United States 2003 Year-End Report on the Federal Judiciary *available at* www.supremecourtus.gov/publicinfo/year-end/2003year-endreport.html (released Jan. 1, 2004). The other three opinions were *per curiam*, meaning an opinion by the Court as a whole, rather than an opinion attributed to any one judge.

21. According to a study of the Alliance for Justice, the federal bench is over 73 percent white, with African Americans comprising 10.4 percent, Asian Americans 8 percent, and Hispanic Americans 6.6 percent, with 3.6 percent vacancy. Alliance for Justice, Demographic Portrait of the Federal Judiciary, *available at* http://www.allianceforjustice.org/judicial/judicial_selection_resources/selection_database/byCourtRaceGender.asp (last accessed Nov. 12, 2004).

Critics have argued that since the Reagan years, the increased politicization of the federal nomination process has resulted in federal appointments based more on a political "litmus" test than on legal experience. Historically, committees of the local, state, and national bar associations have an active role in judicial nominations. Thus, for example, since the presidency of Dwight Eisenhower, the American Bar Association, through its Standing Committee on Federal Judiciary, had been given an opportunity to evaluate candidates for the federal bench before their names were announced publicly. Scrutiny by a bar's diverse membership is an attempt to make the federal judge appointment process less political, and a nominee who receives a highly qualified rating from the American Bar Association is more likely to receive bipartisan support in the Senate. Nonetheless, presidents obviously want to appoint federal judges who generally share their political inclinations, and the George W. Bush presidency, in recent years, limited the role of the ABA to the post-nominations period, when a name had already been formally nominated and publicly announced by the president. Given the highly contentious climate of the post-nomination period, this latest approach can dilute the ABA's input on the assessment process.[22]

To ensure judicial independence but at the same time prevent abuse of powers, federal judges may be removed from office only by impeachment for serious misconduct, never for unpopular decisions. The Constitution specified the misconduct as "High Crimes and Misdemeanors." The Circuit Council, a group of district and appellate judges who operates at the circuit level, may also discipline federal judges.

The judicial impeachment process originates in the House of Representatives, where a Bill of Impeachment is drafted and passed, often based on a criminal conviction. The Bill is then sent to the Senate for prosecution and hearing where designated members of the House of Representatives act as prosecutors and members of the Senate serve as the jury. Historically, only a small number of judges have been impeached. As of 2004, only 13 federal judges had ever been impeached, and only 7 had been convicted.[23] Though this small number of impeached judges does speak to the integrity and rigor of the judicial confirmation process in screening out corrupt applicants, it should also be recognized that most judges have resigned when faced with impeachment.

Not to be ignored in the federal system are specialized "judges," notably magistrates and bankruptcy judges, who are said to be "statutory" judges — that is, their authority is granted by federal statute, rather than originating from Article III of the Constitution. Appointed for fixed, renewable terms, magistrate judges and bankruptcy judges were originally conceived as

---

22. Furthermore, the Judiciary Committee under Orin Hatch had also eliminated the ABA's special status in his Committee hearings processes, but the Committee Democrats continue to insist on receiving the ABA evaluations before proceeding with a nominations hearing on a candidate. Sheldon Goldman, Elliot Slotnick, Gerard Gryski, and Sara Schiavoni, *W. Bush's Judiciary: The First Term Record*, Judicature, May-June 2005 at 254.

23. Federal Judicial Center, Federal Judicial History: Impeachments of Federal Judges, *at* www.fjc.gov/history/home.nsf/page/topics_ji_bdy (last visited Mar. 22, 2004).

subsidiary to life-tenured judges and thought of as largely administrative officers. Magistrate judges are appointed by district court judges and bankruptcy judges are appointed by appellate judges of the circuit.[24] Magistrate judges handle most of the pretrial matters as well as some minor cases in federal court, while bankruptcy judges hear bankruptcy cases. In recent years, however, both the number and the scope of authority of these magistrate and bankruptcy judges have grown to meet increased demands of civil litigation, thereby blurring somewhat the roles between life-tenured Article III judges and statutory judges.

American civil procedure is primarily taught through examining the procedure in federal courts, rather than trying to understand the frequently similar but not identical civil procedure of the 50 state court systems. Otherwise, civil procedure teachers would not know which state procedure to teach; students will end up practicing in many different states. We, too, concentrate on federal procedure in this book. But the fact is that 90 percent of the civil lawsuits in the United States take place in state, not federal, courts. Although each state has its own procedural system, many of the procedures are similar to those used in federal court and the underlying civil litigation concepts are similar in most American courts, state or federal. Most states have a judicial branch that is set up in much the same manner as their federal counterparts. Most states have a system of trial courts, intermediate appellate courts, and a state supreme court. The number of supreme court judges in any one state, however, is usually fewer than the nine at the federal level.

Each of the original colonies had its own judicial history that preceded the federal court system, but one can make some observations about the colonial judicial experience relevant to today's state court systems. Throughout American history, there have been movements at the state level to make the judiciary more democratic and responsive to popular opinion. Some states, particularly in what are called the Populist and Progressive Eras (approximately 1890-1925), have experimented with using the vote of citizens to recall judges and alter judicial opinions.

Further, unlike the federal system, state judges in four-fifths of the states are subject to some kind of election, rather than appointment. About half of the states (some 28 states but 47.9 percent of the judges) provide for some form of partisan or nonpartisan election of state trial judges for the initial term. Of the remainder states, 18 states (but 52.1 percent of the judges) provide for gubernatorial appointment or merit appointment through a nominating committee, with 4 more states varying in their method of selection.[25]

If appointed, state judges normally serve set terms that are likely to range between 6 and 14 years for state appellate judges. These terms are generally automatically renewed, absent misconduct. Only the state of Rhode Island offers appellate judges lifetime appointments, although some states do have

24. Appointment of Bankruptcy Judges, 28 U.S.C. § 152(a) (1994); Appointment and Tenure, 28 U.S.C. § 631(e).

25. David B. Rottman et al., State Court Organization 1998 ix, 19, Department of Justice, Bureau of Justice Statistics (June 2000). As for appellate judges, 21 of the 50 States selected their appellate judges through a gubernatorial appointment and 3 by legislative appointment in 1998. An additional 14 states used nonpartisan elections, 8 used partisan elections, and 4 used retention elections. *Id.*

appointments that last until a specific retirement age, without periodic elections.

About 80 percent of the state judges (including some who were appointed for the initial term) face periodic elections for subsequent terms.[26] Their elected terms also generally range from 6 to 14 years. While some of these judges run in uncontested elections or retention elections, many run in contested elections that increasingly look like mayoral, congressional, or gubernatorial elections. The contests for judicial election have become extremely heated in some states, with large amounts of money expended supporting and opposing incumbents. Advertisements applaud and condemn specific judges and their judicial decisions, particularly in cases involving controversial social issues, such as abortion, discrimination, and the treatment of criminals.

Recent literature points out the problem of partisanship on the part of state judges facing periodic elections. This is a particularly troubling issue because the state judiciaries resolve some 100 million cases each year, in contrast to the federal judiciary, which decides only about 300,000 cases each year. With judicial candidates involved in "full-scale partisan battles, with lots of money, television advertising, and campaigning[, i]ncreasingly, we are seeing special interests, sometimes from outside the state, running issue ads. We hear that these advocates are seeking to reshape a court to be sympathetic to a particular interest."[27]

Like the federal system, most states traditionally used only impeachment to remove judges prior to their next election. In 1960, though, California instituted a Commission on Judicial Performance to deal with accusations of judicial corruption, disablement, or injudicious behavior. About two-thirds of the states now have such commissions, composed of judges, attorneys, and often lay people. Their recommendations "almost always . . . [go] to the state supreme court, which is empowered to take final action. When a complaint is lodged against a [state] supreme court justice, lower court judges, often chosen by lot, consider the recommendation."[28]

Most states have a number of different types of trial court. They have courts of general subject matter jurisdiction, which have authority to hear every type of civil or criminal case except those reserved for a specialized trial court. Such general trial courts are often called Superior Court, Court of Common Pleas, County Court, or District Court; the names differ depending on the state. States typically have specialized courts that deal with matters such as housing, family, juveniles, land, and wills. As at the federal level, a litigant who loses at the trial court usually has a right to appeal to the state intermediate appellate court. But, again like the federal system, appeal from the intermediate court of

---

26. *Id.* at 19.

27. Alfred Karlton, *The American Judiciary Cornerstone of Society*, Judges' Journal (Spring 2002). A noteworthy report published by the American Bar Association's Standing Committee on Judicial Independence gets at the issue of partisanship among state judges. Standards on State Judicial Selection, Report of the Commission on State Judicial Selection Standards (June 2000), *available at* http://www.abanet.org/judind/downloads/reformat.pdf.

28. Bradley C. Canon, *Comments on Professor Burbank's Essay*, 76 Ky. L.J. 643, 701 (1987-1988).

appeals is normally a matter of discretion, not of right, within the state's highest court.

Since the United States Constitution and federal statutes are the "supreme law of the land," courts at both the state and federal levels frequently apply federal law. But it is the United States Supreme Court, not the state supreme courts, that has the final say in interpreting federal law. A loser at the supreme court of a state can only ask the Supreme Court of the United States to overturn a state verdict if there has been a mistake in the interpretation of federal law or if the state verdict violates the federal constitution. Federalism in the United States, with this overlapping system of state and federal courts, as well as state and federal law, leads to a good deal of complexity that will be explored further in this book.

The complexity does not stop with multiple courts. Since the mid-1930s, there has been the expansion of an administrative bureaucracy in the federal and state governments that partakes of attributes of all three branches of the government, fulfilling executive, legislative, and judicial functions. Some of the functions of the federal and state governments, such as deciding who can broadcast on the airways, under what circumstances one can sell stocks and bonds, and who is entitled to what welfare benefits, required some government agency to act on a day-by-day basis in a manner that cuts across the branches of government. Administrative agencies, authorized by the federal or state legislatures, often administer programs (acting for the executive), promulgate regulations (that are similar to statutes), and hold hearings to decide disputes (looking like a judicial function).

PRAGMATISM AND COMPROMISE

The habits of mind of the drafters of the constitution are not distant from those of the current American lawyer. The types of tensions faced by constitutional drafters are strikingly close to those that confront today's lawyers and their clients in the daily practice of law or to those confronted by current procedural reformers. It is fair to say that there would not have been a constitution, nor would there have been a United States, without anguishing compromises by the drafters. The most glaring was the acceptance of the institution of slavery, largely through silence in the Constitution, in contradiction to the high ideals of equality espoused in the Declaration of Independence. Additionally, the idea of proportionate representation, so important to the ideology that led to the Revolutionary War, was violated by the equal representation (two senators per state) in the Senate, but which was necessary to achieve ratification from those states with smaller populations.

The Nationalists, called "Federalists" at the time, disagreed with the enormous authority left to the states and with the enumeration of powers as a method of limiting federal legislative and executive authority. By contrast, Republicans, those associated with Thomas Jefferson and who had a more states-rights and individual liberty orientation, were discomforted by the centralized power in the new Union, particularly those powers residing in the president. The compromises between the Federalists and Republicans were not only among different drafters; they existed within the minds and hearts of many colonists.

Pragmatism, as a full-blown philosophy developed after the Civil War (1861-1865), has an impact reaching back to the Founding Fathers. It would be difficult to describe the Founding Fathers, just as it would be difficult to describe the American lawyer, in words that do not include "pragmatic." While one can trace antecedents to their thoughts and political actions to such philosophers as Hobbes, Locke, Hume, Montesquieu, and Scottish economists, when push came to shove, the constitution-makers acted pragmatically: They compromised their ideals and preferred solutions and acted in a practical manner to achieve the best that they could under the circumstances. Perhaps it is even more accurate to say that they tried to accommodate a number of competing values and goals, some out of self-interest and some of a more exalted nature.

To a remarkable degree, the Founding Fathers, although operating in part from self-interest, were also able to meet the needs of diverse populations. They created a federal system with multiple states of conflicting interests that has endured and thrived, although admittedly, the success was in part tragically built on the backs of Native Americans, African-Americans, and women. From the 1954 Supreme Court decision in *Brown v. Board of Education of Topeka*,[29] which addressed the desegregation of the races in public schools, to the 2003 case of *Grutter v. Bolinger*,[30] which examined racial preferences in university admissions, one can see that the American courts and judiciary have been and still are forced to confront issues of equality, race, and the needs of a diverse population. Descendents of those who were systematically denied voting rights, equal access to education, and even their own freedom still face disadvantages in the United States. To a remarkable degree Americans still face conflicting desires and tensions in today's society. The responses to these tensions are often compromises that are evocative of the past. These are the compromises that balanced the need to reach practical accommodations of competing values and competing claims for power, and they are compromises that pervade the American litigation process and its procedures to this day.

29. 347 U.S. 483 (1954).
30. 539 U.S. 306 (2003).

CHAPTER
2

The Adversary System and the Legal Profession

> In the United States the lawyers constitute a power which is little dreaded and hardly noticed; it has no banner of its own; it adapts itself flexibly to the exigencies of the moment and lets itself be carried along unresistingly by every movement of the body social; but it enwraps the whole of society, penetrating each component class and constantly working in secret upon its unconscious patient, til in the end it has molded it to its desire.
> Alexis de Tocqueville[1]

Something about de Tocqueville's observation remains true today. Lawyers still occupy a unique role in American society. Not the least of this is because America is a law-dependent polity based on the adversary system, a system dependent on lawyers for its implementation. Reviled as "ambulance chasers" and yet idolized as crusaders of social change and protectors of fundamental rights, lawyers are simultaneously embraced and rejected by American society.

In truth, lawyers dominate many arenas in America from the legislature and government bureaucracy to the corporate, financial, and commercial worlds. No longer unnoticed, lawyers have and will continue to have influence on how America deals with the great issues of our time. This chapter gives a picture of the American adversary system and the turbulent changes in the legal profession in American society today. Changes in a profession that is so integral to American society in turn illuminate changes in American society itself.

In the study of American civil procedure, two topics are often taken for granted. The first is the philosophy or outlook that underlies American civil litigation: the adversary system of dispute resolution, in which opposing lawyers and their clients do most of the heavy lifting rather than judges or other government personnel. The second unexplored topic is the nature and development of the legal profession. Who are the lawyers who work within the system? How many? How do they organize their practices? How are they trained? These two topics are intertwined, and together they help inform the contours of American civil litigation.

1. Alexis de Tocqueville, Democracy in America 270 (George Lawrence trans., J.P. Mayer ed., Doubleday Anchor 1969).

Certainly, the adversary system and the dominance of lawyers are critical components of American culture and reflect values inherent in that culture. Together, lawyers and the adversary system contribute to the legitimacy, or in the minds of some, the illegitimacy, of the American dispute resolution system. And lawyers and the adversarial manner in which they represent clients are intimately related to a number of power issues inherent in any legal system: power for the legal profession, more power within the legal profession for some groups than others, power for classes of clients, power and counterweights to power for the executive and legislative branches of government. In some ways, lawyers and their adversariness are even counterweights to judicial power. It is lawyers and their "rule of law" that have checked abusive government powers, serving as the cornerstone of American democracy.

THE AMERICAN ADVERSARY SYSTEM

The basis of American litigation is the adversary system. Under the adversary system, the litigation process is party-initiated, party-controlled, and party-driven. The major engines that propel the adversary system are the lawyers for the litigants (plaintiffs and defendants) who bear responsibility for investigation and presentation of evidence and argument. When disputes are not settled out of court, they are typically resolved by a judge or jury, passive decision makers who (in theory) are neutral and impartial, and who listen to both sides and decide based on what the litigants present. The judge acts as referee, trying to make certain that the lawyers obey the procedural rules. The entire litigation is, in this sense, party-controlled or more specifically, lawyer-controlled. However, as will be discussed later, judges in relatively recent times have increased their control over civil litigation.

The adversary system is often contrasted with the "inquisitorial system," used in civil law countries such as France and Italy. Under the "inquisitorial system," the decision maker, the judge, takes more of an active role in unearthing the facts through investigation and trial. Today, however, there is no pure form of either system, as there has been convergence in some respects of the two systems. Judges are taking a more active role in the adversary system and parties are taking more control in the inquisitorial system.

The underlying premise of the adversary system is individual autonomy and initiative. Individual litigants or their lawyers have the responsibility for developing the facts and presenting the case to the court. This reflects the belief that the people most interested in the dispute — the litigants themselves — have the greatest incentive to investigate facts thoroughly in order to muster their strongest case. With both sides having a personal interest in the outcome, the presumption is that all the relevant facts will be presented, and "truth" will be unearthed.

Supporters of the adversary system also find ammunition in the psychology of decision making that argues against having a fact finder who is also the fact investigator. The concern is that if the decision maker actively participates in developing the evidence, she would have also developed a preliminary mindset that would not be easily changed and would likely become the basis of her final decision. She may favor one party over another and may begin to decide the issues even before all the evidence is presented. She may also unconsciously discount certain information that discredits her initial impression and search out information that supports that impression. It is therefore better, adversarial system proponents argue, to have different hypotheses presented by the parties so the decision maker can keep an open mind in assessing the evidence. Under the adversary system, the decision-making judge or jury is supposed to know nothing about the case until it is packaged and presented by the individual parties.

The adversary system has deep roots in the Anglo-American legal and political tradition. Its predecessor is often said to be the Norman trial by battle, in which issues were resolved by the outcome of a duel. Today, duel in combat is replaced by verbal contestation in the courts. But the adversary system is not simply a method of dispute resolution; it reflects the Anglo-American political theory that sees the legal system as an important limit on governmental powers. Historically, certain key elements of the adversary system, such as the right to choose one's own counsel and the right to present evidence, evolved from seventeenth century England as legal controls on arbitrary government action. Once again we witness the historic American values of individuality, autonomy, competition, and disdain for government.

Under the United States Constitution, all litigants in both criminal and civil cases are guaranteed certain basic rights, including the right to due process, the right to equal protection of the law, and in many cases, the right to a jury trial. "Due process" includes the idea that all cases should not be decided without notice and an opportunity to be heard, and decided according to basic rules of evidence and procedure that are uniformly, objectively, and consistently applied. The Supreme Court has increasingly equated due process with the adversarial trial in the determination of legal rights. "Equal Protection" means that all litigants should be treated the same under law regardless of race, religion, ethnicity, or sex; regardless whether the litigant is an individual, the state, or big business; regardless whether the litigant is wealthy or poor, politically powerful or weak. In upholding due process and equal protection, the adversary process provides the opportunity for individual citizens to challenge governments on an equal footing and to assert democratically secured rights in court.

The adversary system is also consistent with, and bolsters, the substantive rights of freedom and open competition inherent in a market economy. First, the adversary system depends on and promotes an active market of private lawyers. Aggrieved litigants are free to pick and choose a lawyer and negotiate the appropriate fee. Just as the freedom of speech and "marketplace of ideas" have a prominent place in American basic rights, freedom and open competition in the presentation of evidence and argument similarly are pillars in the American legal system. Indeed, the ability to present one's side of the story to decision makers is a due process right in itself, a right that is said to add to one's dignity and make individuals fuller members of society. And open competition in the presentation of evidence, it is argued, is the best way to ensure that truth will be unearthed. The American adversary system in this sense is as entrepreneurial and subject to supply and demand as other consumer services and goods; it is also spurred by the same market spirit to creativity and innovation.

The adversary system is not without its critics. While defenders of the adversary system maintain that it is the best method for finding the truth, critics counter that the adversary system distorts the truth. Critics point to the bias and motives of the parties who, in desiring to win, might hide or distort unfavorable facts and evidence. The adversary process, they say, feeds the contentious nature of lawyers such that litigation becomes an argument for arguments' sake and a debate over procedural niceties, rather than conceding what should be conceded. Critics also point out that the system is costly and unwieldy as contentiousness breeds unnecessary wrangling over issues and procedures.

More problematically, the adversary system is potentially unfair. As a system dependent on private lawyers for implementation, the adversarial process can and does benefit wealthier litigants who are able to afford more investigation and a more skilled and also more expensive lawyer. Those who cannot afford a lawyer must represent themselves in court or utilize the increasingly limited free legal services. Others fail to assert their rights at all because they lack access to lawyers.

Once in court, the imbalance in resources is answered somewhat by rules of pretrial discovery, a mechanism whereby each side may obtain relevant information from each other. The most recent set of reforms has also taken the form of requiring voluntary disclosures in pretrial discovery to the other side of certain information about the dispute. Proponents argue that pretrial discovery offsets the withholding of relevant facts and evidence and helps to make up for disparity in resources of particular attorneys. By contrast, opponents note that pretrial discovery itself has become a site for skillful and, at times, contentious lawyering. Moreover, discovery can be so expensive as to dissuade the economically poor from suing or to force them into disadvantageous settlement.

It is also an important part of the adversary system that once a case is filed and is ongoing, the litigants can only communicate with the decision maker by formal documents filed into the public record and by evidence and arguments presented in open court when both sides are present. Outside influences or one-sided communications to the decision maker are considered improper and can lead to sanctions against the offending party or lawyer. These formal protections help to ameliorate somewhat the dark side of the adversary process, reducing possibilities of corruption in an attorney's zeal in representation and ensuring a transparent and open legal system.

Theorists have speculated that the growth of markets and modernization necessarily result in more complex transactions and a more mobile population. Complex transactions bring increasingly more complicated disputes. A mobile population means that social norms previously relied on to resolve disputes are no longer used as the glue in holding society together. It may be an inevitable aspect of markets and modernization that we see greater reliance on laws and the legal system for normative guidance as well as for dispute resolution. Between strangers, absent warfare, there could be no common authority other than law and no commonly accepted umpire other than the judge.

The question, however, is whether this necessarily compels the adoption of an adversary process, as some countries are presently considering. One can argue the contrary may be true, with the civil law, inquisitorial system as the leading contender. Certainly, one can take the position that a government financed, judicial controlled litigation system such as that in civil law countries may result in greater access to courts and lawyers than the United States form of market-based, entrepreneurial adversary system. It may also be true that the distinctions between civil and common law countries are lessening.

American legal scholars are increasingly predicting the convergence of legal practice for the twenty-first century. As technology and the global economy lead to complex legal problems without borders, legal systems may drop their barriers, resulting in greater exchanges and the merging or fading of some of the distinctions between legal systems. Writings on "mixed jurisdictions" that highlight the convergence of civil and common law systems and argue for the creation of a new third legal family are proliferating.[2]

Whether or not there is convergence, the classic distinctions between civil law and common law countries — from the role of the judge, remedies, juries, legal fees, evidentiary standards, and burdens of proof — have eroded somewhat.[3] There are notable changes taking place, as will be discussed later in greater detail, in the American legal system. The managerial judge has replaced the passive, neutral judge of the adversary system; less than 1.8 percent of the civil cases in the federal courts progress to trial; and civil discovery has, in some instances, become more forthright and voluntary.[4] Today, the American adversary system itself is in flux.

PROFILE OF THE LEGAL PROFESSION

The lawyer is central to adjudication under the adversary system, because it is the lawyer who determines the theory of the case, investigates the facts, and controls the presentation of evidence. By and large, because of the procedural technicalities present in the American adversary system and compounded by complicated substantive laws, lawyers are needed to represent most litigants in American courts. Parties in civil litigation in the United States can represent themselves in court (called "pro se" representation, from the Latin, "for yourself"), and although pro se litigation is said to be on the rise, it remains relatively infrequent.[5] In ten Federal District Courts, pro se cases comprised 21 percent of all federal cases filed from 1991-1994, with most of these being

---

2. *See, e.g.*, Alain Levasseur & Jackie M. McCreary, *Mixed Jurisdictions Worldwide: The Third Legal Family, by Vernon V. Palmer, ed.*, 18 Tul. & Euro. Civ. L.F. 117 (2003) (book review).

3. Linda S. Mullenix, *Lessons from Abroad: Complexity and Convergence*, 46 Vill. L. Rev. 1 (2001).

4. As of 2002, less than 1.5 percent of cases filed in the federal courts go to trial before a jury, and only 1.8 percent of the filed cases go to trial at all. Edward Wood Dunham, *A Rare but Scary Thing: More on Franchise Jury Trials*, 21 Franchise L.J. 179 (2002).

5. Pro se representation is evidently on the rise in torts claims as well as family dispute litigation. There is much discussion about the reasons for this in recent literature. *See, e.g.*, Margaret Graham Tebo, *Self-Serve Legal Aid*, 88 A.B.A.J. 38 (Aug. 2002).

cases brought by prisoners.[6] For the most part, it is only in small cases, such as those in small claims court for which the amount involved is very low, that lawyers are absent from the litigation.

Once a lawyer is involved in a case, the technicalities of the system mean that the lawyer dominates. Legal scholars have tried to point out the power imbalance between lawyer and client and advocate returning more control to clients. Nevertheless, it is still the lawyer who will make the decisions about what papers to file, how to argue, and what and how evidence will be presented. While decisions to settle must ultimately rest with the client, this decision is usually heavily influenced by the recommendation of the lawyer.

As civil litigation has grown, so have the numbers within the legal profession. One may argue that the causal relationship is the reverse: that as the numbers of lawyers have grown, so has the amount of civil litigation. If the increase of doctors in a community often results in an increase in surgery; then more lawyers similarly may have led to an increase in litigation. Whether it is the nature of complex economies to have high numbers of civil disputes or that the adversary system breeds more lawyers and in turn more litigation, these high numbers have unquestionably earned the United States the reputation as the most litigious country in the world.

The number of lawyers in America is undisputedly large. Between the years 1966-1997, the number of lawyers tripled from 313,500 to 946,500.[7] It is estimated that there were over a million lawyers in America in 2002 or about 1 in 279.[8] Although the number of American lawyers may be the highest in the world, this number may not be substantially greater than legal workers in civil law countries. In the United States, lawyers perform much of the drafting, debt collection, and other out-of-court activities that may be done by non-lawyers who are legally trained but not bar certified in other countries.

Historically, the legal profession was primarily white and male, and remains so today. Since the civil rights movement of the 1960s and 1970s, however, women and minorities have joined the legal profession in America in greater numbers. This development is important because lawyers work on issues of great social significance and so it is useful for the profession to reflect the society and population at large. It seems inevitable that over time, the addition of large numbers of women and minorities to the legal profession will change how law is practiced and the clients who are served. Scholars, such as Carrie Menkel-Meadow, voiced the hope that the "growing strength of women's voice in the legal profession may change the adversarial system into a more cooperative, less war-like system of communication between disputants in which solutions are mutually agreed upon rather than dictated by an outsider,

6. Federal Judicial Center 1996 Annual Report of the Federal Judicial Center (Federal Judicial Center 1996).
7. Daniel J. Meador, *A Perspective on Change in the Litigation System*, 49 Ala. L. Rev. 7, 13 (Fall 1997).
8. According to the ABA statistics for 2003, the total number of active attorneys in the United States was 1,058,662. Memorandum from A.B.A., Market Research Department, *National Lawyer Population Trends* (June 16, 2003), <http://www.abanet.org/barserv/lawyerpopulation98-03.pdf>(accessed Sept. 15, 2005). The lawyer-to-population ratio took into account the 2003 population estimate of 290,809,777 from the U.S. Census Bureau. *See* <http://quickfacts.census.gov/gfd/states/00000.html> (accessed Sept. 15, 2005).

won by the victor, and imposed upon the loser."[9] At a minimum, the entry of women and minorities has challenged the image of the profession as an elite club limited to white men.

According to an American Bar Association (ABA) study, women represented 48.7 percent,[10] while minorities represented 20.6 percent of law school enrollment in 2003.[11] This seemingly optimistic number may face future setbacks, however, as affirmative action programs implemented to increase diversity are being challenged in the courts. Furthermore, recent changes in the profession may not be keeping pace with changes in the population. Despite the projection that the United States population will be almost 60 percent minority by the year 2050, total minority representation in the profession in 1999 remained at about 10 percent.[12]

Additionally, these impressive numbers have to be placed in context. Even though minorities and women are enrolling in law schools, they are still less likely to enter the potentially more lucrative private practice. Minorities and women lawyers are more likely to work for the not-for-profit sector including the government, and continue to be underrepresented in top legal positions, such as partnership in large law firms.[13] A 2001 *New York Times* survey of the 12 highest grossing law firms in the United States revealed that minority lawyers constituted only about 5 percent of the new partners at the seven firms that supplied that data.[14] Absent a mentor or advocate, few minority associates rise to law firm partners; the top echelon of the profession remains substantially closed.

Similar barriers to the profession faced women, although by comparison, women by far have made the greatest gains. Yet, although differences have narrowed, women lawyers are still twice as likely to practice in the public as opposed to the private sector.[15] Pay and opportunity disparities continue to

9. Carrie Menkel-Meadow, *Portia in a Different Voice: Speculations on a Women's Lawyering Process*, 1 Berkeley Women's L.J. 39, 54-55 (1985).

10. Memorandum from A.B.A., Section of Legal Education and Admission to the Bar, to Deans of A.B.A.-Approved Law Schools on Fall 2003 Enrollment Statistics (January 14, 2004), *available at* <http://www.abanet.org/legaled/statistics/enrollment2003statistics.pdf> (accessed Sept. 22, 2005). *See also* Terry Carter, *It's Not Just a "Guy Thing" Anymore*, 85 A.B.A.J. 18 (April 1999) (noting that, in 1999, women represented "46 percent of law school enrollment, up from 44 percent in 1996, 42 percent in 1992-93, and 23 percent in 1975-76").

11. *Id.* In 2003, the A.B.A. experienced its first African-American president. Joan E. Lisante, *No Quick Fix*, 90 A.B.A.J. 61 (Jan. 2004). Nonetheless, the number of minorities attending law school is still "disturbing," especially where minorities make up less than 10 percent of the U.S. lawyer population. James Podgers, *Progress Hits a Wall*, 86 A.B.A.J. 94 (Sept. 2000). While the A.B.A. has implemented a number of programs in order to increase diversity in the profession, including providing scholarships and training programs, bringing minorities into the fold is still slow. Robert A. Stein, *Building a Better Profession*, 87 A.B.A.J. 96 (April 2001).

12. Elizabeth Chambliss, A.B.A. Comm'n on Racial & Ethnic Diversity in the Profession, Miles to Go 2000: Progress of Minorities in the Legal Profession (2000), Executive Summary *available at* <http://www.abanet.org/minorities/publications/milesummary.html> (accessed Sept. 22, 2005).

13. A.B.A. Comm'n on Opportunities for Minorities in the Profession, Miles to Go: Progress of Minorities in the Legal Profession tables 12-14, 19 (1998) (the category of "minorities" includes African Americans, Hispanics, Asian Americans, and Native Americans).

14. Podgers, *supra* note 11, at 94.

15. Nat'l Ass'n for Law Placement, Inc., Employment Patterns — 20-Year Trends (Aug. 2003), *available at* <http://www.nalp.org/content/index.php?pid=169> (accessed Sept. 22, 2005). ("Compared to men, women from the Class of 2002 were less likely to enter private practice and more likely to accept positions in government or public interest organizations or as judicial clerks. Although this pattern is similar to those of prior years, the differences in how many

exist — male lawyers continue to have higher average income, to have more years of experience than female lawyers, and to stay in the practice longer.[16] In 2002, female lawyers' median weekly salary was 76 percent of male lawyer's salary and of the Fortune 500 corporations, only 43 women ranked the title of general counsel.[17] Only 27 percent of female attorneys surveyed are partners in private practice, compared to 40 percent of male attorneys.[18] Sandra Day O'Connor's appointment to the United States Supreme Court in 1981 represented the major breakthrough for women in the judiciary. Today, of the 700 or so active federal judges, about 201 are women.[19]

Of greatest concern is the perception that the increasing demand in billing expectation may push back any gains women have made in terms of flexible time schedules, part-time work, or day care benefits. Women lawyers continue to face problems balancing work with family responsibilities. Retaining flexible work schedules to accommodate family responsibilities can result in a second tier and lesser status "mommy track" for women lawyers in private law firms.[20]

Bearing the brunt of race *and* gender bias, minority female lawyers face even greater barriers. Minority female lawyers in top positions numbered in the single digits. As of 2000, there was only one minority female general counsel in the Fortune 500 companies, only six minority female federal appellate judges, and only two minority female law school deans.[21] Attrition rate for minority women from law firm practice is higher than any other group, at 12.1 percent within the first year of practice and over 85 percent by the seventh year of practice.[22]

In short, many gains have been made for women and people of color in the legal profession in the United States. Yet, a "glass ceiling" still exists such that the top echelon of the legal profession remains stubbornly closed to women and minorities. America continues to grapple with power imbalances inherent in its legal system as evidenced by the profile of its legal profession.

---

women take jobs in private practice, government, and clerkships have narrowed. Women, however, remain about twice as likely as men to take public interest jobs").

16. According to an American Bar Association Journal poll in April and May 2000, the average pay for male lawyers surveyed was $155,000 and the average time in practice was 17.6 years, while the average pay for women was $113,000 and average time in practice was 12.4 years. Hope Viner Samborn, *Higher Hurdles for Women*, 86 A.B.A.J. 30, 31-32 (Sept. 2000). For statistics on average career lengths and reasons for entry and re-entry into law by women, *see* Joe G. Baker, *The Influx of Women Into Legal Professions: an Economic Analysis*, (Aug. 2002). Monthly Lab. Rev. 14, *available at* <http://www.bls.gov/opub/mlr/2002/08/art2full.pdf> (accessed Sept. 22, 2005).

17. *See* A.B.A. Comm'n on Women in the Profession, A Current Glance of Women in the Law (2003), *available at* <http://www.abanet.org/women/glance2003.pdf>; *see also*, Martha Fay Africa, *Glass Ceiling: Darwin's Daughters Hit the Glass Ceiling*, 19 A.B.A. 18 (September 1993).

18. Samborn, *supra* note 16, at 31-32. According to a 2003 Equal Employment Opportunity Commission study, the number of women and minorities in the legal profession has increased substantially since 1975, but white men are still more likely to become partners in major law firms. *See* U.S. Equal Employment Opportunity Commission, Diversity in Law Firms 27-33 (2003), *available at* <http://www.eeoc.gov/stats/reports/diversitylaw/lawfirms.pdf> (accessed Sept. 22, 2005).

19. Adam Liptake, *O'Connor Leap Moved Women Up the Bench*, N.Y. Times, July 5, 2005, at 1. In 1977, there were only 10 women on the federal bench. The first woman to serve on the federal bench was Florence Ellinwood Allen, appointed by Franklin D. Roosevelt in 1934 to the federal appeals court, followed by Harry S. Truman's appointment of Burnita Shelton Matthew to the trial bench in 1949.

20. A.B.A. Comm'n on Women, *supra* note 17.

21. Chambliss, *supra* note 12.

22. *Id.*

LEGAL TRAINING AND PRACTICE

Just as the composition of lawyers has changed, so too has their training, although not as drastically. Lawyers were initially trained by the apprentice method by which young lawyers studied and practiced under the tutelage of a more experienced lawyer. Today, lawyers are trained in law schools as an advanced professional educational degree program. Unlike their counterparts in civil law countries, American lawyers begin their legal training only after four years of college and often after some work experience, rather than as part of their undergraduate education.

When law schools were first established and up until the mid-twentieth century, gaining entry to an American law school was relatively easy. There were no prerequisites and almost everyone was admitted. Some citizens even eluded the law schools and educated themselves in law. The most famous of such is Abraham Lincoln, America's Civil War President, who was reputed to have taught himself law in a small log cabin in Illinois and later served as an apprentice to a practicing lawyer. Many lawyers were ordinary citizens and in important respects, represented the voice of everyday community life. It is this prevailing frontier spirit of early America and informality that shaped the idealistic image of American lawyers as the egalitarian crusader of social justice.[23]

After World War II, the influx of returning soldiers changed American higher education and created greater competition among applicants for law school seats. Applications to law school again rose dramatically in the 1970s as women and minorities joined the field. Today, the study of law remains popular because the law degree is seen as a route to personal and professional advancement with the increased status and income that the degree can provide.

In order to be enrolled in a law school, one must first complete and obtain a four-year college degree and then apply and be admitted into one of approximately 190 nationally accredited law schools or to an unaccredited law school.[24] Between 2001 and 2003, applications to accredited law schools nationwide jumped nearly 28 percent. The fluctuation in applications tracks the ebb and flow of the nation's economy, so that a downturn in economy is often matched with an upswing in law school enrollment.[25]

---

23. Richard Marcus, *Reining in the American Litigator*, 27 Hastings Int'l & Comp. L. Rev. 3, 5 (Fall, 2003) (citing Thomas Burke, Lawyers, Lawsuits and Legal Rights 48 (University of California Press 2002)).

24. *See generally* A.B.A. Section of Legal Education and Admissions to the Bar, *ABA-Approved Law Schools*, <http://www.abanet.org/legaled/approvedlawschools/approved.html> (accessed Sept 22, 2005).

25. William Young, *Guess What? Mad Rush to Become Attorneys*, 12 N.J. Law. (Sept. 15, 2003). For example, when the technology sector began creating jobs out of thin air, the numbers of those applying to law school began to shrink. In 1994, according to the Law School Admissions Council, 84,300 people applied to law school. That number fell the following year to 76,700 before stabilizing in the mid to low 70,000s the remainder of the decade and into 2000 when the technology boom incinerated in April. There was a modest 3.6 percent bump in applications in 2001 as the first wave of victims of newly downsized companies began to reassess their possibilities. There was a huge 17.7 percent leap in 2002 when 90,900 applied to law school. As

The law school curriculum is a standard three-year curriculum, composed of traditional substantive and procedure law courses. Civil procedure is usually taught in the first-year curriculum. There are also clinical training courses, in which law students work on cases under the supervision of a clinical teacher. If law students receive any practical experience as a lawyer, they generally do so by taking a clinical course in law school and by working in a legal setting during summers.[26] Notoriously, American-based law schools are only beginning to explore a more international curriculum and what it means to prepare lawyers for practice in the global marketplace.

On completion of law school, the law student must take and pass a written bar exam administered by and in the state in which she wants to practice. Unlike other countries that have instituted national bar exams, such as China or Japan, the new lawyer in America, having passed the bar exam of a particular state, is sworn in and becomes authorized to practice in that state only. Lawyers are expected (and in some states, such as New Hampshire, required) to keep up in their fields by taking continuing legal education courses, usually provided by the bar associations.

An American lawyer can be admitted to practice in more than one state so long as she takes and passes the bar exam in each state. Some states will "waive" admission for attorneys who have passed the bar examination of another state and achieved a high score. Other states permit a lawyer from another state who has practiced for a certain length of time to be admitted to the bar of the second state. Once a lawyer has been admitted to the "bar" of a particular state, it is usually automatic that she can represent clients in that state's federal and state courts.

The principle employment setting for lawyers in this country continues to be private practice, constituting about 57.8 percent of first-year lawyers in 2004.[27] About 60.5 percent of men and 58.2 percent of women initially go to work in the private sector.[28] American lawyers, however, often move from the private to the public sector and vice versa. This is unlike lawyers abroad, who must choose their track at law school, enter that track upon graduation, and remain there — be it prosecutor, judge, or lawyer.

While most American lawyers do not spend the bulk of their time at trial, the category of "litigator" (those lawyers involved in litigation rather than business transactions) is nevertheless substantial. For example, the Section of Litigation boasts the largest section of the American Bar Association with 60,000 members, reflecting the residual importance of litigation in the Association and the bar generally. Although trials in America appear to be a vanishing phenomenon, many lawyers nevertheless spend much of their

---

for 2003, approximately 98,800 people applied to American Bar Association-accredited law schools. *Id.*

26. *See e.g.*, Daniel J. Givelber, Brook K. Baker, John McDevitt, Robyn Miliano, *Learning Through Work: An Empirical Study of Legal Internship*, 45 J. Legal Educ. 1, 4 (March 1995).

27. Nat'l Ass'n for Law Placement, Inc., Class of 2003 Summary Findings, *available at* <http://www.nalp.org/assets/45_ersini.pdf> (accessed Sept. 22, 2005). *See also* Clara N. Carson, The Lawyer Statistical Report: The U.S. Legal Profession in 1995 3 (American Bar Foundation 1999).

28. *Id.* However, an American Bar Association poll shows a slightly higher number with 71.5 percent female and 75.2 percent of male lawyers work as solo practitioners or in law firms as partners or associates. Terry Carter, *Paths Need Paving*, 86 A.B.A. J. 34, 35 (Sept. 2000).

time anticipating litigation and preparing cases for settlement or the occasional trial.[29]

In private practice, American lawyers who represent clients in civil cases are privately engaged and paid for by the client. The so-called American rule is that the parties pay for their own attorney's fees. This is in contrast to other countries, as those in the European Union, which to discourage litigation, impose a requirement that the losing party must pay the other party's attorney's fees.

The client and lawyer usually agree on a fee arrangement in advance. Lawyers representing defendants will agree to an hourly rate to be paid for the lawyer's work, whether in preparation of a case, at trial, or on appeal. Perhaps uniquely American, lawyers representing plaintiffs, particularly in personal injury cases, will normally use what is called a "contingency fee" arrangement — that is, the lawyer receives a percentage of the plaintiff's recovery, whether by settlement or by trial, and nothing if the case is lost. Typically, the percentage is one-third of the recovery, so that if a plaintiff wins $100,000 in a lawsuit, the plaintiff's lawyer would receive $33,333. In some geographic areas, the contingency fee is as large as 50 percent of the recovery.

The argument for contingency fee is that this sharing of risks between lawyer and client helps the impoverished litigants to proceed with litigation. Other countries, however, view the idea of contingency fees with distain, arguing that lawyers should not have a financial stake in the outcome of the case. Only a few nations, such as Italy, Luxembourg, and Portugal, permit fees that are based to some extent on results.[30] By and large, other countries, such as Germany, prefer to rely on statutory tariffs and fee shifting (allowing winning parties to recover fees from the losing side) to keep costs down and to finance litigation.[31]

Apart from attorney's fees, the winning litigant in an American civil case can recover some minor costs such as docket fees and photocopying costs from the losing party,[32] and in certain kinds of cases, there are statutory exceptions that would allow the recovery of attorney's fees by the winning party, as a form of fee shifting. These are primarily cases involving civil rights and other social issues in which the government wants to encourage enforcement through private litigation. In those cases, there is considerable litigation about what constitutes a reasonable fee.

In America, legal assistance in civil cases is not a constitutional guarantee. In fact, it was not until the 1960s that substantial legal assistance was provided by the government for indigent litigants in civil cases. During the 1960s and the civil rights movement, legal aid offices were established with the support of tax dollars and evolved into a government supported but independent

---

29. A recent study of the A.B.A. Litigation Section focuses on the "crisis" of the vanishing trial. *See, e.g.*, Patricia Lee Refo, *The Vanishing Trial*, 30 A.B.A.J. Sec. Litig. 2 (Winter 2004), *available at* <http://www.abanet.org/litigation/journal/winter2004/LTM30no2-OS.pdf> (accessed Sept. 22, 2005).

30. Herbert M. Kritzer, *Fee Arrangements and Fee Shifting: Lessons from the Experience in Ontario*, 47 Law & Contemp. Probs. 125, 130 (1984).

31. France and England prohibit a straightforward contingent fee arrangement, but France would allow a supplemental payment based on results and England would allow a lawyer to seek payment only if successful. W. Kent Davis, *The International View of Attorney Fees in Civil Suits*, 16 Ariz. J. Int'l & Comp. L. 361, 383-384 (1999).

32. *See* Taxation of Costs, 28 U.S.C. § 1920, for a list of the costs that are recoverable.

corporation called the Legal Services Corporation. In the 1980s, the Reagan administration tried to terminate funding for the Legal Services Corporation in an effort to curb the more progressive lawsuits brought by legal aid lawyers.

Since then, there has been substantial retrenchment of funding for legal services for the poor and limitations set on the range of activities that these legal services can address. Other than the Legal Services Corporation, there are also a number of nonprofit and nongovernment organizations that provide legal assistance, such as American Civil Liberties Union (ACLU) and Now Legal Defense and Education Fund (NOW renamed Legal Momentum) and on the conservative side, the Institute for Justice and Center for Individual Rights, who engage in civil litigation focused on far-reaching social and economic issues. Bar organizations of the different states also have stepped in to establish legal aid funds collected as part of the bar membership fees, voluntary contributions, or from interest from escrow accounts opened by lawyers in charge of client funds.

By and large, the American system relies on the contingency fee structure and private lawyers to finance litigation. In some kinds of cases, the contingency fee arrangement does mean that even clients with no resources can afford legal services. In personal injury cases in which the plaintiff's recovery can be quite substantial, lawyers have the economic incentive to take on these cases even when plaintiffs are poor. But the contingency fee does not assist indigent defendants or those meritorious cases with small recoveries.

Many American lawyers, be they in corporate practice or litigation, view the judiciary as the final, pinnacle point of a legal career. Rather than moving within a career bureaucracy of an hierarchical civil service system as in most civil law countries, judges in the United States are lawyers who come from private practice and have accumulated many years of experience as lawyers. Similar to the private sector, the judiciary has also grown substantially in recent years. The number of judges of general jurisdiction in state courts had risen to 11,390 in 2002.[33] At the federal level, as of September 2003, there were 179 authorized Circuit Court of Appeals judgeships for the 13 appellate circuit courts (plus 91 senior appellate judges), 680 authorized district court judgeships (plus 275 senior judges), and 491 full time magistrate judges at the federal district court level.[34] This is a dramatic increase from 1966, when there were only 343 federal judges and the position of magistrate judge did not even exist.[35] As of 1997, 1387 administrative law judges were assigned to federal agencies.[36] Certainly, the growth in judgeships as well as lawyers renders the legal profession a formidable presence in American society.

33. Nat'l Center for State Courts, Overview: Examining the Work of State Courts 9-16 (2003), *available at* <http://www.ncsconline.org/D_Research/csp/2003_Files/2003_Overview.pdf> (accessed Sept. 22, 2005).

34. Administrative Office of the United States Courts, Judicial Facts and Figures, table 4.6, *available at* <http://www.uscourts.gov/judicialfactsfigures/table4.06.pdf> (accessed Sept. 22, 2005).

35. Meador, *supra* note 7, at 9.

36. Judith Resnik, *Trial as Error, Jurisdiction as Inquiry: Transforming the Meaning of Article III*, 113 Harv. L. Rev. 924, 953 n. 101 (Feb. 2000) (citing to U.S. Office of Personnel Management, Federal Civilian Workforce Statistics, Occupation of Federal White-Collar and Blue Collar Workers as of September 30, 1997, at 97-98 table W-E (1998) (copy on file with the Harvard Law School Library)).

Such professionalism within the judiciary, and the institutional emphasis on judicial independence has served to bolster the legitimacy of the American legal system. According to a 1999 study of the American Bar Association, public confidence in the judicial system is high, with the greatest confidence ratings awarded to the United States Supreme Court.[37] This is somewhat astonishing given the controversial social issues that are often brought to the Supreme Court and that will inevitably result in resolutions dissatisfactory to some constituency. Indeed, the fact that the Court has not shirked from its responsibility has drawn fire (from both the right and the left) asserting that the Supreme Court and other courts have become an overly active judiciary that is undermining the legislature and the democratic process.

TRANSFORMATION OF THE PROFESSION

Rosco Pound, former dean of Harvard Law School and a respected legal scholar, once exalted legal practice as not only a means of livelihood, but a profession to be pursued in the spirit of "public service." In the ideal, law was an art as well as a proud craft, a learned and liberal profession.[38] Yet, the last 30 years has seen a significant shift in how American lawyers have practiced law and how lawyers view their role in American society.[39]

Until the 1970s, the legal profession was relatively stable, and the practice of law was in some respects exalted. The practice held itself out as a "gentlemen's profession," not to be associated with ordinary business. However, the nature of legal work changed in the 1970s and 1980s as did the environment in which the work was done. As you will read in our chapter on pre-trial discovery, some of these changes may well be related to what has been called a "discovery revolution." But perhaps the changes are more related to demographics, technology, and the global market. With the advent of the global market and a larger legal labor pool, the profession became increasingly competitive and driven by economics. Technology such as word processing, faxes, and e-mail pushed legal work to be faster paced, more routinized, and more adversarial. These developments led critics to bemoan the change in the legal profession from an honorable calling to an ordinary craft.

The latter part of the twentieth century saw the rise of multi-national corporations and the global economy. Mega-law firms accompanied mega-corporations and became both national and international in scope, with rising

37. Of the 1,000 respondents, only 17 percent were minorities. The confidence ratings for the U.S. Supreme Court, other federal courts, judges, and state and local courts among whites were 51 percent, 35 percent, 32 percent, and 28 percent respectively. Corresponding ratings among non-whites were 42 percent, 26 percent, 30 percent, 23 percent respectively. Symposium, *American Bar Association Report on Perceptions U.S. Justice System*, 62 Alb. L. Rev. 1307, 1319-1327 (1999).

38. Roscoe Pound, The Lawyer from Antiquity to Modern Times 5 (West Publishing Company 1953).

39. Michael Dorf, *Americans Believe Lawyers to be Necessary but Dishonest, Survey Finds, available at* <http://www.archives.cnn.com/2002/LAW/04/columns/fl.dorf.lawyers.04.17> (accessed Sept. 22, 2005).

profits of 13 percent or more increase in gross revenue on average per year. [40]
By 2000, at least 20 American law firms have stationed more than 10 percent of
their lawyers in overseas offices. [41] Almost all of these law firms report that
their global work accounts for an increasing percentage of the firm's gross
revenue. Law practice has become increasingly global in nature to a point
where law firms are outsourcing — sending some of the work traditionally
done by new lawyers overseas where labor is cheaper. [42]

Law firms as mega-business also meant increased pressures on lawyers to
bring in more money to cover the larger overhead. Often, the bigger the firm,
the higher the expectation for associates to produce profits. As Mary Ann
Glendon has noted in her study of American lawyers, the pressure to produce
profits can result in associates billing around 1800 hours a year for an average
size law firm, and between 2000 to 2500 hours a year for a large law firm. [43]
Since billable hours do not include time eating, taking a break, or acquiring
new clients, the actual time spent at work was likely substantially higher. In
reality, then, a lawyer would have to spend at least 60 hours per week at work to
actually bill 2000 hours per year and take no more than two weeks vacation a
year. [44]

The high expectation for billable hours is further exacerbated by the up and
down turns of the economy. After the economic boom of the 1980s, law firm
revenue began to drop by the late 1980s and layoffs of highly paid associates
were commonplace. A 1991 survey of 104 of the country's largest firms
found that 93.4 percent had dismissed associates in the preceding 18 months
and that 86 percent expected to make similar layoffs within the next year
and half. [45] By 1993, almost half of the 250 largest firms reported they had
downsized. Even partnership ceased to be a lifelong relationship, with law
firms replacing seniority-based compensation with a productivity based
system rewarding "rainmakers" (those lawyers who bring in the business).
This tightening of the business means that associates and partners have to
work even longer hours to justify their high compensation. The economic
pressures and demands of long billable hours in large firm practice have led
some to conclude that lawyers in big firms are among the least happy. [46]

As the size of law firms has grown, the practice of law concomitantly became
specialized and more focused on short-term client goals. Many American

---

40. Jim Schroeder, *The Am Law 100: An Overview*, The Am. Law. July 7, 2002, *available at*
<http://www.law.com/jsp/article.jsp?id=1024078929507> (accessed Sept. 22, 2005).

41. Alison Frankel, *Who's Going Global?*, The Am. Law. November 2000.

42. *See* Renee Deger, *Model Behavior*, The Recorder Dec. 1, 2003, *available at* <http://
www.law.com/jsp/article.jsp?id=1069801652626> (accessed Sept. 22, 2005).

43. Mary Ann Glendon, A Nation Under Lawyers: How the Crisis in the Legal Profession is
Transforming American Society 30 (Farrar, Straus & Giroux 1994).

44. Patrick J. Schiltz, *On Being a Happy, Healthy, and Ethical Member of an Unhappy, Unhealthy,
and Unethical Profession*, 52 Vand. L. Rev. 871, 894 (May, 1999). Billing by time worked may also
be attributable to the expended utilization of discovery. George B. Shepherd and Morgan Cloud,
Time and Money: Discovery Leads to Hourly Billing, 1999 U. Ill. L. Rev. 91, 92.

45. Glendon, *supra* note 43, at 30.

46. Schiltz, *supra* note 44, at 886-888; *see also*, Marcia Pennington Shannon, *Charting a Course
for Satisfaction and Success in the Legal Profession*, A.B.A. Report on Law Practice Management 57
(March 2000). Shannon addresses the issues of the depression syndromes predicted and then
seen among lawyers and raises the question of whether lawyers practicing in the current climate
"have" to be unhappy.

lawyers must specialize to meet the needs of their clients — big companies who increasingly want outside, specialized lawyers to perform one-shot transactions. These big companies also seek zealous representation in this one-time hire, resulting in less enduring relationships between lawyers and clients and between lawyers and other lawyers. This has subsequently been reflected in the manner lawyers treat each other and the way they litigate. Lawyers in one-shot transactions are more likely to be pressured to be more zealous and less civil in their representation.

Modern technology may also have fueled the increased incivility among lawyers, because technology can speed the pace of litigation and add to its overall competitiveness. New technology, such as e-mail and faxes, demands that lawyers respond almost immediately (and hence, must work more hours a day) to requests and inquiries. Xerox machines and computers enable massive discovery, more filings with the court, and more potential abuses of the litigation process. Modern technology made work more routine, and in the legal context, increased the repetition and drudgery that have always been present in legal work. [47]

Technology also blurs the line between work and home. Increasingly, everything one might need in litigation (research information or document retrieval, for instance) is accessible through the portable laptop. This technology has benefited the profession, in narrowing the divide between large firm and small firm practices. Computer technology expands a small firm's capacity to litigate; small law firms can now tackle cases that previously were the exclusive arena of big firms. At the extreme, there are even "e-lawyers," whose offices are no more than an on-line legal site on which legal advice is rendered for a fixed fee. [48] But by expanding a law firm's capacity, technology has also extended law practice beyond the office and into the home. According to the Center on Law and Computers, close to 92 percent of the law firms surveyed have computer programs that allow attorneys to tap into the office computer from home. [49] Lawyers can now work seamlessly and endlessly in the office and at home, day and night [50]

There is widespread belief that civility in law practice has declined and adversarial tactics increased. Scholars observe that "[m]ore competitiveness and economic pressure have led to less loyalty all around from clients towards their lawyers, from partners towards each other, and from lawyers towards

---

47. On the issue of changes in the profession brought about by clients, technology, and ever-evolving law, *see* Mitch Orpett, *The View from the Chair, Change: Clients, Careers, and Chaos,* 30 Winter ABA Brief 2 (2001).

48. *See* Scott Brede, *Lawyers Nervously Eyeing 'Net-Based Legal Advice,* 26 The Connecticut Law Tribune, May 8, 2000.

49. *Symposium, The Development and Practice of the Law in the Age of the Internet,* 46 Am. U. L. Rev. 327, 331 (Dec. 1996); *Symposium, Courtroom 2000: Technology and the Legal System,* 25 Ohio N. U. L. Rev. 523 (1999). Ambivalence towards the impact that technology has had on legal practice continues. *See* David Beckman and David Hirsch, *Communication Power Tool, The Internet Can Improve Lawyers' Efficiency, But It's Not Always the Answer,* 84 A.B.A. J. 92 (Aug. 1998).

50. *See* Jeffrey M. Allen, *How to Be a Mobile Lawyer and Avoid an Aching Back,* 18 4 G.P. Solo 6 (June 2001) (writing on mobile lawyering and amplifying this point and those discussed below about new forms of lawyering practice) *available at* <http://www.abanct.org/genpractice/magazine/june2001/june01_16.html> (accessed Sept. 24, 2005).

notions of collegiality."[51] Based on survey data, the Court of Appeals for the Seventh Circuit recently concluded that, "Lawyers no longer appear frequently against the same opponent or before the same judge, thereby reducing the opportunity for building mutual respect and learning the ethics of an honored profession from seasoned hands.... The incentive to retain cordial relationship often dies because the relationship will not likely become an ongoing one."[52]

In response, courts, as well as state bars, have adopted codes of civility to encourage lawyers to be more conscious of uncivil conduct. For example, the U.S. Court of Appeals of the Seventh Circuit has established civility standards.[53] The Supreme Court of the State of Georgia and the Supreme Court of the State of Texas also established standards of conduct for lawyers in their respective jurisdictions and will impose sanctions for rude and abusive conduct and unnecessary contentious practices ranging from "benign incivility to outright obstruction." The American Bar Association has proposed model rules and developed programs and publications to assist lawyers and judges to confront the problem of incivility among lawyers. Whether these codes of conduct can actually alleviate abusive conduct is highly questionable; one underlying problem may be overall lawyer dissatisfaction with the practice.

As a result of changing practice norms, being a lawyer may have become less satisfactory. According to a 1990 American Bar Association survey of lawyer satisfaction (a follow-up to a prior national survey in 1984), there was a close to 20 percent drop, from 41 percent to 33 percent, in lawyers who say they are "very satisfied" with private practice. Correspondingly, the number of lawyers who say they were "very dissatisfied" rose slightly from 3 percent to 8 percent.[54] This same survey found that twice as many women expressed dissatisfaction as men. In the corporate legal departments, the dissatisfaction was even greater, and it was highest among new lawyers and women and minority lawyers. Encouragingly, this trend may be changing as a later survey of lawyers in Chicago, Illinois, showed that 84 percent of lawyers were "satisfied" or "very satisfied" with their jobs.[55] Others, meanwhile, may have found satisfaction by using their law degrees in work other than as a practicing lawyer, adding to the growing legal culture in the general population even if not to the profession at large.[56]

51. Committee on Civility, Interim Report of the Committee on Civility of the Seventh Federal Judicial Circuit 392-393 (Marvin E. Aspen, Chairman & Cornelia E. Tuite, Reporter, 1991); Final Report of the Committee on Civility of the Seventh Federal Judicial Circuit 392-93 (Marvin E. Aspen, Chairman & Cornelia E. Tuite, Reporter, 1992).
52. Id.
53. The U.S. Court of Appeals for the Seventh Circuit Standards of Professional Conduct, 143 F.R.D. 441 (1992).
54. A.B.A. Young Lawyers Division, The State of the Legal Profession 1990 51-52 (American Bar Association 1991). A Michigan law practice found that only 29 percent of those working in private practice were "quite satisfied" with the balance of their family and work life, as compared to 35 percent of those working in corporations, 45 percent of those working for the government, and 50 percent of those doing public interest work. Schiltz, *supra* note 44.
55. John P. Heinz, Kathleen E. Hull & Ava H. Harter, *Lawyers and Their Discontents: Findings from a Survey of the Chicago Bar*, 74 Ind. L.J. 735, 736 (Summer 1999); *see also* John P. Itein, Edward Laumann, and Robert Nelson, Study of American Lawyers (American Bar Foundation 1995).
56. Helen Lavan, *Dissatisfied Attorneys Have Plenty of Options*, Wall St. J. (May 25, 2004). In 1994, 18 percent of California 145,000 lawyers were listed as inactive. In Massachusetts, the

ROLE OF CIVIL LITIGATION IN AMERICA

The role of civil litigation in America is somewhat different perhaps from its role in other countries, and it defines the character of our legal system. Rather than simply seeking courts to resolve private disputes (the conflict resolution model), Americans have relied on relatively open access to court and private civil litigation to be at the heart of a great deal of the enforcement of our public laws (the behavior modification or social control model).[57] With a mistrust of big government and intrusive states, the American public has (probably more than most other countries) relied on private civil litigation rather than solely on state-controlled litigation or state regulatory agencies to enforce our public values.[58]

This role for our courts was particularly entrenched with the civil rights movement of the 1960s and its burst of litigation that placed the federal courts at the center of many of the nation's pressing social issues. Rightly or wrongly, "activists, perhaps naively and certainly optimistically, viewed the federal courts as the ultimate protectors of individual rights and, under the appropriate circumstances, arbiters of social change."[59] While the federal docket remained relatively small around the turn of the century, federal filings grew four-fold from 71,000 civil cases in 1966 to 269,999 in 1996.[60]

More significantly, not only has the number of civil lawsuits increased but the nature of civil lawsuits in federal courts has also changed dramatically during the last 60 years. As pointed out by Daniel Meador, federal cases in the 1930s were primarily commercial and contract disputes, but by the 1990s included substantial numbers of product liability, environmental, and civil rights cases. The predominance of cases enforcing market relationships gave way to make room for cases enforcing public values, such as civil rights, tort liability, and other public law. According to the Administrative Office of the United States Courts, between 1974 and 1998, more than 470 new federal causes of action were created.[61]

Civil cases filed in the federal courts reached an all time high in the mid-1990s. While environmental and product liability cases were not even listed as separate categories of cases in federal court in 1966, they numbered 1,131 and

---

number of attorneys paying the annual state licensing fee has dropped to 38,355 this year from 39,612 three years ago. Lisa Gubernick and Joshua Levine, *Make Lox, Not Law (Lawyers Drop Out of the Profession)*, 118 Forbes 68 (Nov. 4, 1996).

57. Martin Shapiro, Courts: A Comparative and Political Analysis 24 (University of Chicago Press 1981).

58. "Calibration of discovery is calibration of the level of enforcement of the social policy set by Congress." Patrick Higginbotham, *Forward to Symposium on the Evaluation of the Civil Justice Reform Act*, 49 Ala. L. Rev. 1, 4-6 (Fall 1997).

59. Martha F. Davis, Brutal Need: Lawyers and the Welfare Rights Movement, 1960-1973 1 (Yale University Press 1993).

60. Meador, *supra* note 7, at 7. In 1993, federal courts saw 939,935 filings and 962,333 terminations. Administrative Office of the United States Courts, Federal Judicial Workload Statistics 5-7 (Government Printing Office 1993).

61. Judith Resnik, *Statement and Testimony, The Senate's Role in the Confirmation Process: Whose Burden?: Hearings Before the Senate Comm. on the Judiciary, Subcommittee on Administrative Oversight and the Courts*, 107th Cong. 1st Sess. 179 (Sept. 4, 2001) (arguing that the Senate ought to take an active role in assessing the appropriateness of nominations), reprinted in 50 Drake L. Rev. 511, 539-552 (2002).

32,856 in 1997 respectively. Civil rights cases grew from 1,300 in 1966 to 43,278 in 1997 and prisoner's petitions from 8,500 to 62,966. [62] In response to recent amendments in the civil procedural rules as well as substantive legislation aimed at raising the hurdles to civil litigation, the total number for all such categories of cases dropped in 2003. [63] But for the years between 1960 and 1990, the federal courts were the site for redressing the nation's wrongs from desegregation of the nation's schools; improving the conditions of or, in the alternative, closing the nation's prisons; cleaning-up massive toxic sites; and dismantling and reorganizing large industries (such as the telephone and computer industries).

Not to be ignored are the state courts where the majority of civil litigation is filed. State courts handle 90 percent of the country's civil litigation. [64] Most civil litigation in state courts involves modest sums of money. In a study of five jurisdictions, it was found that these ordinary cases often involve an individual plaintiff suing an organizational defendant, with the exceptions being domestic relations and debt collection cases. The vast bulk of litigation involves routine matters such as accidental injury, contracts, and dissolution of marriage. While tort filings rose steadily at 9 percent a year from 1978 to 1984, scholars such as Marc Galanter have argued that this growth was not disproportionate to the population. [65] In 1993, tort filings constituted only about 10 percent of the civil cases filed in state courts of general jurisdiction. [66]

Civil cases have become increasingly more complex. Civil cases are now often multi-partied and multi-claimed and involve millions of dollars and complicated social, scientific, and ethical issues. The most controversial civil cases are class actions in which one named plaintiff can represent the legal rights and interests of thousands of people. Entire government programs, agencies, or corporations are brought into court, and the legality of their operations is questioned and determined. [67]

The penchant for litigating public issues in the courts has undoubtedly been aided by the procedural rules that were enacted in the last hundred years or so. As will be discussed in Chapter 3, procedural rules moved from rigidity to

62. Civil rights cases were 3.1 percent of the filings in the district courts in 1960, but grew to constitute 34.7 percent of the filings in 1995. Richard Posner, The Federal Courts: Challenge and Reform 57, 60-61 (2d ed., Harvard University Press 1996).

63. For the total number of cases by the nature of the suit, see charts for federal civil and criminal cases, *available at* <http://www.uscourts.gov/judicialfactsfigures/table2.02.pdf> and <http://www.uscourts.gov/judicialfactsfigures/contents.html#tables>.

64. Brian Ostrom and Neal Kauder, Examining the Work of State Courts 11 (1993 reprint, National Center for State Courts 1995). The range is quite varied from a high of 20,321 filings per 100,000 persons in the District of Columbia to a low of 1,267 per 100,000 in the state of Tennessee. *Id.* at 12.

65. Professor Galanter also pointed out that in the 1981 to 1984 period, tort filings actually decreased in eight of the seventeen state courts with tort data. Marc. S. Galanter, *The Day After the Litigation Explosion*, 46 Md. L. Rev. 3 (1986).

66. Neal Kauder, National Center for State Courts, Caseload Highlights, Examining the Work of the State Courts (August 1995), *available at* <http://www.ncsconline.org/D_Research/csp/Highlights/vol1no1.pdf> (last accessed Nov. 12, 2004). The document reflects that by 1993, an "estimated 1 million tort cases were filed in state courts of general jurisdiction, which represented about 10 percent of the cases filed in upper level trial courts." *Id.*

67. We cover class actions in Chapter 9.

flexibility, away from the confining ways of the common-law tradition toward equity's aspiration for more perfect and complete justice. One important shift was the relaxed limitation on who could become a party to a lawsuit — what are called "standing" requirements, making it easier for ordinary citizens affected by government action to bring "public law" litigation that asserts constitutional or related claims. More liberal joinder of parties and claims rules also allowed multiple parties to join together in a single lawsuits that can affect large numbers of people in a myriad of ways. The 1966 amendment of the federal class action rule further enabled the size of litigation to expand to cover classes of amorphous interests, so that civil litigation represented by class actions came to hold a more vigorous presence than in earlier eras.

Not only joinder rules, but pleading was also liberalized to allow for more general allegations of the facts constituting a claim, without requiring specific pleading of a legal theory or cause of action. These liberal pleading rules facilitated the filing of multiparty, multi-claim lawsuits involving complex social and economic problems. Finally, the discovery revolution enabled litigants with limited resources to challenge those with greater might, but also permitted more prosperous litigants to engage in discovery that was massive and potentially crippling. In sum, the framers of the 1938 federal rules fashioned a package of unprecedented breadth and flexibility, expanded by subsequent amendments, that as a whole helped to render civil litigation, particularly in the federal courts, a highly accessible vehicle for enforcing public norms.

The growth of civil litigation is not without its critics. Some critics point to chronic and serious problems such as increased costs, delays, and greater incivility; others focus on the inability of courts to deal effectively with multi-party, multi-claims lawsuits crafted under liberal pleading and joinder rules. Starting in the 1980s, the perception of American society as overly litigious, with a civil justice system run amuck, led to a series of significant civil procedure reforms, this time, away from the 1938 liberalization. Taken together, these later reform measures represent a tightening of procedure and the raising of the barriers to access to court.[68]

While the details of these reforms will be discussed in later chapters, it is helpful to outline here the course of the reforms. The 1980s and 1990s brought civil justice reforms characterized by greater judicial management of cases. Beginning in 1984, the America Bar Association adopted goals for reduction of civil litigation delay — that 90 percent of all cases be completed within one year and that all be cleared within two.[69] In 1990 Congress passed the Civil Justice Reform Act (CJRA), one of the major steps in civil litigation reform, requiring each of the 94 federal districts to devise and implement plans to reduce expense and delay in civil litigation.

The CJRA was an important endorsement of increased judicial management of cases, a trend that had already begun in the early 1980s and originated from the district courts themselves. Specifically, the CJRA noted that an effective litigation management plan should include: different treatment of cases that

68. *See, e.g.,* Jack Weinstein, *After Fifty Years of the Federal Rules of Civil Procedure: Are the Barriers to Justice Being Raised?*, 137 U. Pa. L. Rev. 1901 (1989).
69. American Bar Association, Defeating Delay: Developing and Implementing a Court Delay Reduction Program 1 (American Bar Association 1986).

provides for individualized and specific management; early involvement of a judicial officer in planning the progress of a case; regular communication between a judicial officer and attorneys during the pretrial process; and utilization of alternative dispute resolution programs in appropriate cases. [70]

In particular, the discovery process received special attention from civil procedure reformers. For example, in 1993, the Advisory Committee on Civil Rules passed a set of revisions that included the controversial initial disclosure requirement (discussed in greater detail in Chapter 7), requiring each side to disclose initial information relevant to the dispute. This proposal was so controversial that it was passed over the objection of some members of the Supreme Court, and initially only in a compromised fashion, allowing federal districts to "opt out" of this national rule and permitting lawyers to opt out by agreement. This opt out provision has since been rescinded, but other amendments remained. These included numeric limits on depositions and interrogatories, stricter standards on conduct during depositions, and sanctions that would exclude materials if they were not turned over when they should have been.

In sum, the late twentieth century is characterized by reforms to the civil procedure rules and changes to civil litigation in an effort to contain litigation. In the procedure area, amendments were passed to further clarify the initial disclosure requirement, narrow the scope of discovery, and impose a presumptive limit on the duration of a deposition, all in an effort to curb abuses in the discovery process. Continuing procedural reforms include a focus on the class action, to limit its scope but at the same time, to regulate its use in settlements and arbitrations and to curb attorney misconduct. [71] These revisions often attempt to match pace with the changing practice to include, for example, measures to regulate electronic discovery.

Not only procedural law, but substantive law was also revised in an attempt to meet the perceived infirmities of the litigation system. Mass torts have received quite a bit of attention. For example, some states require professional malpractice claims to be first reviewed by a board of experts before the litigation can move forward to filing in court. Other changes attempt to put caps on recovery for pain and suffering or empower judges to review and cut back on jury awards. Limits on prisoner's rights suits and securities fraud actions were adopted with the passage of the federal Private Securities

70. *Civil Justice Reform Act of 1990*, Pub. L. No. 650, 101st Cong., 2d sess. (Dec. 1, 1990). The CJRA has a "sunset provision" ensuring the automatic expiration of this act.

71. *See, e.g.*, Deborah R. Hensler, *Revisiting the Monster: New Myths and Realities of Class Action and Other Large Scale Litigation*, 11 Duke J. Comp. & Int'l L. 179 (2001); Deborah R. Hensler and Thomas D. Rowe, Jr., *Beyond "It Just Ain't Worth It": Alternative Strategies for Damage Class Action Reform*, 64 Duke Law & Contemp. Probs. 137 (2001). *See also* Alan S. Kaplinsky, Ballard Spahr Andrews & Ingersoll, LLP, Videoconference: Consumer Financial Services Litigation 2004 Arbitration and Class Actions: A Contradiction in Terms (The Practicing Law Institute, New York City, March 11-12, 2004; San Francisco, May 6-7, 2004; Beverly Hills, Videoconference, May 6-7, 2004; Los Angeles Videoconference, May 6-7, 2004; Costa Mesa Videoconference, May 6-7, 2004).

Litigation Reform Act of 1995[72] and the Prison Litigation Reform Act of 1995.[73]

Assessments of these reform efforts are ongoing and the data so far is inconclusive. Yet, attributable to civil justice reforms or not, America's image as an overly litigious nation may not be entirely accurate today, or at least, it may not be the entire picture. Admittedly, filings of federal cases continue to increase; there are five times as many federal lawsuits as four decades ago — 258,876 in 2002 compared to 50,320 in 1962. However, the rate of cases going to trial has decreased dramatically in recent years. Cases are not fought to the bitter end. As noted earlier, less than 1.8 percent of civil cases filed in federal court resulted in trials (judge or jury),[74] representing a decline of almost 800 percent in the rate of trial from the pre-1938 period, prompting an ABA commissioned study on this phenomenon of "vanishing trials."[75] The RAND Corporation's Institute for Civil Justice concluded that in the years between 1980-1993, two-thirds of all civil cases were closed within one year of filing.[76] A majority of the civil cases, then, are disposed of early in the process. To the extent that trials are an important component of the American democracy, as a signpost to future cases, as a method for educating and empowering lay jurors, and as means of providing a training ground for new lawyers who will become articulate public figures, the "vanishing trial" phenomenon is a troubling development.[77]

Certainly, the upswing in alternative dispute resolution needs acknowledgement.[78] From mediation to arbitration, alternative dispute resolution methods can be found prospering inside as well as outside the formal legal system. Increasing options for private justice mechanisms are carving a new and important voice in the American legal system. While some have touted the benefits of having a quicker, less costly, gentler, and more creative method of dispute resolution, others have criticized the reduction of the public role of civil litigation. When private settlements are agreements between the parties and are sometimes even sealed as secret, private settlements, they do not

72. This act provided a heightened pleading standard, an elaborate notice procedure upon filing of action to ensure that the person "most capable of adequately representing the interests of the class members" be appointed lead plaintiff, and bars discovery if defendant files a motion to dismiss, unless the motion is denied. *Private Securities Litigation Reform Act of 1995*, Pub. L. No. 104, 104th Cong., 1st sess. (Dec. 22, 1995).

73. This act imposes limits on the remedies available in prison conditions litigation, limits on *in forma pauperis* suits and expands grounds for dismissing suits by prisoners. *Prison Litigation Reform Act of 1995*, Pub. L. No. 104, 104th Cong., 2d sess. (Apr. 26, 1996).

74. Administrative Office of the United States Courts, 2003 Annual Report of the Director: Judicial Business of the United States Courts 150, table C-4. U.S. District Courts — Civil Cases Terminated, by Nature of Suit and Action Taken, During the 12-Month Period Ending September 30, 2003. (Washington, D.C.: U.S. Government Printing Office 2004).

75. Stephen Yeazell, *The Misunderstood Consequences of Modern Civil Process*, 3 Wis. L. Rev. 631, 633 (1994).

76. Terence Dunworth & James S. Kakalik, *Symposum on Civil Justice Reform: Preliminary Observations on Implementation of the Pilot Program of the Civil Justice Reform Act of 1990*, 46 Stan. L. Rev. 1303, 1311 (1994).

77. *Studies Show Fewer Cases are Going to Trial* (Dec. 13, 2003), <http://www.rednova.com/news/stories/6/2003/12/14/story120.html.> The A.B.A. report (litigation division) was prepared for the symposium on The Vanishing Trial, sponsored by the Litigation Section of the American Bar Association (Dec. 12-14, 2003). See the overview of the meeting at <http://www.abanet.org/media/dec03/120803.html. (The report includes an especially useful updated (2001 data) appendix regarding types of cases going to (jury and non-jury trials)).

78. Alternative Dispute Resolution and settlement are discussed in detail in Chapter 10.

publicize the determination of right and wrong nor serve as legal precedent for future cases. Private settlements rather than open court-initiated and decided judgments may signal the reduced public role of litigation as a vehicle of social change.

In the 1830s, Tocqueville saw the American lawyer as the key to American democracy. He found that members of the legal profession have "made a special study of the laws..., have derived there from habits of order, something of a taste for formalities, and an instinctive love for the regular concatenation of ideas."[79] From this, Tocqueville concluded that the legal spirit is the most promising as "a useful antidote to popular government's tendencies towards present-mindedness, disorder, and majoritarian oppression."

It is unclear whether lawyers today are meeting Tocqueville's prediction and assessment. Yet, it is true that American lawyers and private civil litigation have been, and continue to be, a major force in defining and enforcing a wide array of social policies. Procedural rules have been an engine, or at least provided the framework, for driving this force.[80] As you will see in the remainder of this book, changes to procedure have both direct and ripple effects on the legal profession and litigation and in turn on social policies and the distribution of power within the society. Far from being simply a technical tool, procedure continues to inform our understanding of the values and priorities of how our society resolves its disputes.

79. Tocqueville, *supra* note 1, at 264.
80. Higginbotham, *supra* note 58, at 4-5.

CHAPTER
3

The Historical Background of American Civil Procedure:
Rule and Narrative; Law and Equity

[E]quity was not a self-sufficient system, at every point it presupposed the existence of common law . . . [I]f the legislature said, 'Common Law is hereby abolished,' this decree if obeyed would have meant anarchy. . . . Equity without common law would have been a castle in the air, an impossibility.
Frederic W. Maitland [1]

Behind every litigation is a messy story. Civil procedure, by regulating what can be included or excluded, shapes this messy story to fit within the contours of the legal system. Simply put, a dispute resolution system decides, implicitly or explicitly, how much of the litigant's story will be admissible and relevant to the ultimate result. Running through civil procedure are the tensions between its literary, ethical, cognitive, and pragmatic dimensions.

In the United States, part of the decision of inclusion or exclusion is borne by substantive law. That law describes what events and mental states the plaintiff must prove to prevail. The term *cause of action* or *claim upon which relief can be granted* is a shorthand title for the totality of what the plaintiff must prove. The term *elements* is used for the subparts of a cause of action or claim. Part of the exclusion/inclusion burden is also borne by procedural rules that determine who can participate and how in any litigation, as well as when and where that litigation can take place. These rules, in balancing the need for efficiency, can often leave out other parts of the story underlying the dispute.

Take the cause of action, "battery," as an example. If a defendant is found to have intentionally caused an unwanted touching — Sally hits Susan on purpose without permission — then this would make Sally liable to Susan for the damage caused to Susan, and it would also be a crime. The possible civil cause of action is "battery," or the intentional causing of an unwanted touch, and its elements are: (1) defendant acted and (2) she intended to cause either (a) a harmful or offensive contact or (b) imminent apprehension of

---

1. Frederic W. Maitland, Equity Also the Forms of Action at Common Law, Two Courses of Lectures 19 (A. Chaytor & W. Whittaker eds., A. Hamilton 1920).

such contact (3) with (a) the plaintiff or (b) a third person (4) and harmful contact with the plaintiff directly or indirectly results.

But think of how much is left out of this story. What was Sally doing during the rest of the day? Had she slept the night before? What was her upbringing? Did her childhood contribute to a violent temper? Did Susan subtly provoke Sally? Are they sisters who have always played around with each other by boxing? Was Sally mentally unstable and not in control of herself? There is always more information that may be offered, and sometimes those additional facts may be relevant and shed important light on the incident.

The scope of lawsuits — that is, the permissible topics to be covered and appropriate evidence to be admitted — is linked to human cognition. We try to make sense out of the myriad of messages that reach our senses in any situation by turning the disparate information into a meaningful story. As the eminent psychologist, Jerome Bruner, suggests, the narrative is what "gives shape to things in the real world and often bestows on them a title to reality."[2] How much of the litigants' stories is permitted can add fairness or unfairness to the ultimate decision, and can make the process more or less costly. Consequently, how the lawsuit can or must be sculpted will add or detract power from the current litigants and future ones.[3]

Rigorous civil procedure rules confine the litigation, but these rules are sometimes in tension with the equity and desire of hearing more of the underlying story. This tension between rule and narrative drives the evolution of American civil procedure, as it does in any legal system. Awareness of this tension helps one to appreciate the daunting task of creating a fair and at the same time, efficient procedural system.

American civil procedure was historically a rule bound, confining system. Since 1938, this system has gradually evolved to a more permissive, flexible one in which the parties, particularly plaintiffs, could tell expansive stories involving greater numbers of parties in whatever narrative style they chose. Blending in ancient equity procedure, this more flexible procedural system facilitated new causes of action, creative theories of recovery as well as the means of discovering facts needed to win, and flexible types of relief, all in a single lawsuit. But this wide-open system added to the costs in money, time, and inconvenience of the litigation, and its negative impact on defendants has led to current attempts to put restraints on the procedure and to seek less formal means of resolution.[4]

2. Jerome S. Bruner, Making Stories: Law, Literature, Life 8 (Farrar, Straus & Giroux 2002).
3. The question of what facts to include and exclude is important to most disciplines. For example, novelists, poets, historians, physicists, engineers, and architects all have to deal with how much of an almost unlimited reality, including a myriad of potential variables, to include in their work. The Legal Imagination by James B. White (Little, Brown and Company 1973) has greatly influenced the authors of this book. Steve Subrin thinks he first saw the Maitland quote that starts this chapter in White's book.
4. In this chapter, we draw heavily upon Stephen N. Subrin, *How Equity Conquered Common Law: The Federal Rules of Civil Procedure in Historical Perspective*, 135 U. Pa. L. Rev. 909 (April, 1987); Stephen N. Subrin, *David Dudley Field and the Field Code: An Historical Analysis of an Earlier Procedural Vision*, 6 Law and History Rev. 311 (Fall, 1988); Stephen N. Subrin, *Federal Rules, Local Rules, and State Rules: Uniformity, Divergence, and Emerging Procedural Patterns* 137 U. Pa. L. Rev. 1999 (June, 1989).

LAW AND EQUITY

By the time of the American Revolution, the leaders of the colonists, many of whom were lawyers,[5] were aware that formal litigation in England, especially those involving land, took place in a two-court system. First, there were the three Common Law courts: King's Bench, Exchequer, and Common Pleas. Second, one could sometimes resort to the Chancery or Equity court. The Law Courts and Equity Court had distinct outlooks and procedures, each informative of what is needed for a desirable procedural system. A merging of these two distinct systems, but with equity procedure as its foundation, is what later formed the basis of contemporary American civil procedure.

All three of the English Law courts had the major identifying characteristics: the writ system, single issue pleading, and the jury. If a subject of the king desired royal aid, he or his lawyer would come to the Chancery in London, the business office of the Chancellor, the king's adviser, secretary, and agent. The aggrieved or his lawyer would ask that a royal order be drafted authorizing a court to hear the dispute and instructing a sheriff to compel the attendance of the defendant. The Chancellor's staff organized complaints into categories, each requiring its own allegations and procedures. Plaintiffs could not go to one of the three great Law Courts unless their story fit the confines of one of the known royal orders, otherwise known as writs. These writs, with their requirements, in time would become the foundation of modern day causes of action.

A second characteristic of the Law Courts was the jury trial as the prime method of deciding facts. Before the development of the jury, parties at common law were tested by ordeal, battle, or by the swearing under oath of "compurgators" as a way to discern God's judgment as to who was telling the truth and who should win. In 1215, Pope Innocent III withdrew church approval of these trials by ordeal, spurring a replacement method of fact-finding.[6] After much improvisation, the compulsory 12-man jury became entrenched in the English Law Courts.

The Law Courts were also characterized by an elaborate system of technical pleading, initially done orally but later in writing, that was designed to reduce cases to a single issue for resolution. The parties pleaded back and forth, eliminating extraneous issues or issues in agreement, until they reached a single disputed issue to be decided, by judges in London if the issue were of law or by a jury where the parties or the disputed land was located if the issue were of facts.

A homey example illustrates how this might work in modern day. The authors each have children; the children in each home have, on occasion, bickered. Assume that one of the author's daughters, Elisabeth, lent her favorite sweater to her sister, Julie, and has now complained to her parents that Julie did not return it promptly. Elisabeth's complaint to their parents

---

5. Almost 20 percent of the signers of the Constitution were trained in the Middle Temple. *American History Legal Profession, available at* http://www.bucklinsociety.net/legal_profession.htm (last visited April 11, 2004).

6. Lloyd E. Moore, The Jury: Tool of Kings, Palladium of Liberty 52 (W. M. Anderson Company 1973).

would have been called a "declaration." Julie might issue a "dilatory plea" saying their parents had no jurisdiction over this dispute, or a "demurrer," stating that returning a sweater late is not a known cause of action in this household. The parent judges would then have to decide the questions raised by the "dilatory plea" or the "demurrer." If instead Julie "answered," by claiming that Elisabeth gave her permission to wear the sweater; this would be a "confession and avoidance." Elisabeth could then issue a "replication" which included her own "confession and avoidance": "I did give her permission to wear the sweater, but only for a day." Julie might then issue a "rejoinder" in the form of a "traverse" denying that there was any time limitation given on the right to wear the sweater. The parents would then have to decide the pure factual issue of whether there was a time limitation put by Elisabeth on the permission given to wear the sweater. You might rejoice at this point that: (a) your parents were not lawyers or (b) if they were, they did not engage in trials with their children or (c) if they did create a procedural system for the resolution of civil disputes, it did not include single issue pleading.

It is not difficult to see how the combination of the writ and single issue pleading system could become rigid and impractical. Plaintiffs could only use one writ at a time. This severely limited the joining of multiple claims or additional parties. In order to escape the technicalities that developed, lawyers resorted to fictions, alleging multiple theories under the same writ, or responding with general denials, which kept open multiple factual issues. As these evasions grew, the Law Court system became less rational. Lawyers became adept at beating the system for the benefit of their clients. The writ, single issue pleading system began to look like a technical game, barely related to the merits of the case.

Historic common law courts, though, did have lofty aspirations and formidable achievements. They replaced an unfathomable God as arbiter with rational and more predictable substantive and procedural law. Single issue pleading attempted to focus disputes to a limited question so that if it was a law question, judges could more easily decide the question, thus assisting growth of logical substantive law. If the single issue was a fact question, the jury could decide, thereby permitting lay jurors to participate in the affairs of their neighborhood. As jury participation added legitimacy to verdicts, the likelihood of voluntary compliance with the verdict also increased.

By the beginning of the fourteenth century,[7] an observer to formal litigation in England would have noted that in addition to the three branches of Law Courts there was another court with substantially different procedures. In unusual circumstances, aggrieved parties could petition the Chancellor for royal justice even if there was no writ. When the petitioner was aged, ill, or had been defrauded by the defendant, petitions to the Chancellor, unlike the common law writ, allowed more complete stories. At Equity Court, petitioner could persuade the Chancellor to relieve the petitioner from the injustice of the more rigorous common law.

In the Law Courts, the parties could not testify, but in the Equity Court, the Chancellor, usually a bishop, could compel the defendant to come before him to answer under oath questions attached to the petitioner's bill. This form

7. Edward Jenks, A Short History of English Law 80 (Little, Brown, and Company 1913).

of oral questioning became the precursor to modern day discovery. While remedies were usually limited to monetary damages in the law courts, the Chancellor could issue injunctions, that is, ordering the defendant to perform an act or cease performing it.

In Equity, the Chancellor tried to resolve the entire larger controversy rather than breaking it up into smaller units through writs and single issue pleading. He could compel a significantly greater number of parties to appear and permit substantially more issues to be heard and resolved than was typical at common law. These joinder methods utilized in the Equity Courts became the antecedent to modern joinder of party and claims rules of American civil procedure. As a means of easing some of the harsh results from the more rigorous and formalized common law system, the Equity Court developed expertise and new law in cases involving fraud, mistake, and fiduciary relationships. Such equity doctrine formed the basis for much of today's contract and trust law in America.

The jury was usually excluded from equity cases, with the Chancellor remaining as the sole decision maker. Equity cases often became unwieldy, time-consuming, and costly as a result of their multiplicity of issues and parties. Their complexity ultimately meant the need to have the decision rendered by the sole Chancellor, rather than by a disparate jury. Some thought the Chancellor had too much discretion, leading to arbitrary decisions.

Hence, one sees two quite different procedural systems: the more formal Common Law courts with their writs, single issue pleading, and juries, emphasizing confinement of the breadth of the dispute, focus, and predict-ability; and the Equity court, with its more flexible procedures and its emphasis on comprehensiveness, conscience, and discretion. We find one court having the burdens and benefits of rigorous rules and the other having the burdens and benefits of wide-open narrative.

But the systems were complementary. One could not go to equity if there was an adequate remedy in the law courts. Equity grew interstitially, filling in only where there were gaps in the common law. One can now understand what the great nineteenth-century English legal historian, Frederic W. Maitland (1850-1906), meant when he said that "[e]quity without common law would have been an impossibility, a castle in the air." A castle in the air lacks substance; it falls to the ground for lack of structure and support. Equity needed the companion foundation of the common law in order to be a plausible, working procedural system.

THE AMERICAN EXPERIENCE BEFORE 1848

The early colonists could not bring across the Atlantic the whole package of formal law court procedure. They did not have the experience, education, books, court personnel, desire, or time to replicate such a formulaic rule-laden system, a system that relied so heavily on a coterie of professionals. Moreover, particularly in the Northern colonies, many settlers deeply distrusted equity courts, which to them represented royal power, uncontrolled discretion, and extreme delay and expense. Instead, many colonists, and in turn the courts they developed, showed great faith in jurors, who were permitted to decide issues that in England were reserved for the Chancellor or for common law judges.

Issues of power and politics played a significant role in the development of American courts and procedure, just as they had in England. In England, the King's forcing the adjudication of important land issues into the common law courts was an important mean of legitimizing the central authority in London. With the jury trial seen as an enlightened step, the public at large was encouraged to bring disputes to the Law Courts and accept royal justice and authority. Within the English court system itself, there were numerous power struggles between parliament and the courts, the equity court and the law courts, jurors and judges, the court bureaucracy in London and the sheriffs in the counties.

In the American colonies, and later when they became states, the power issues surfaced in the profound distrust of judges displayed by much of the population and the corresponding embrace of juries as an important and integral part of democracy. The American legal historian, William Nelson, reminds us that to the colonist "the jury was viewed as a means of controlling judges' discretion and restraining their possible arbitrary tendencies."[8] Much of the political struggle in the court system revolved around the question of how much discretion judges should have to control juries and whether equity, admiralty, and patent jurisdiction could be extended to eliminate the use of juries. On achieving statehood, all 13 colonies, and later the federal government, provided citizens with the right to jury trial in both criminal and common law cases.[9]

The earliest colonial courts were unstructured and combined executive and legislative functions with their judicial business. These courts had jurisdiction over types of disputes that in England would have fallen to the different courts of common law, equity, manor, and county. But from the late seventeenth century until about 1820, there was a gradual movement from the more informal and nontechnical procedural solutions of the early colonists to an increased reliance on common law forms and procedures. After all, the Revolution was fought, it was said, to achieve the rights of Englishmen. Though the writ and single issue pleading system never developed to the same degree of sophistication as they did in England, the common law restrictions on joinder, a single form of action, and precision and detail in pleadings were all integrated into early American court procedure.

1848: THE FIELD CODE

By the end of the 1830s, there were many critics of the common law procedural system as well as of the dual courts of law and equity that had

---

8. William E. Nelson, Americanization of the Common Law: The Impact of Legal Change on Massachusetts Society 20-21, 347-348 (University of Georgia Press 1994).
9. Lysander Spooner, An Essay on the Trial by Jury (1852) (criminal).

developed in some states. There was concern that common law procedure, and the resultant methods designed to circumvent it, obscured facts and legal issues. Some complained that common law procedure was so inflexible that it impeded legal evolution required to meet the needs of an increasingly industrialized society. It was often difficult to determine in which court, law or equity, to commence suit, which resulted in wasteful dismissals. Furthermore, the entire controversy often could not be decided in one court. For some, it did not make sense for a new democracy to borrow the antiquated methods of the defeated England.

In 1846, the State of New York passed a new Constitution that eliminated the court of chancery and mandated the creation of a single court "having general jurisdiction in law and equity." Another provision provided for the legislature to appoint a commission of three members to "revise, reform, simplify, and abridge" the procedural law and report back.[10] David Dudley Field (1805-1894), one of the preeminent American trial lawyers of the nineteenth century, became the dominant member of the New York drafting commission.

David Dudley Field believed passionately in the importance of freedom for each individual, with as little interference from government as possible. As Field explained his political philosophy: "It is not the business of government to take care of the people. The people must and will take care of themselves. This is the law of nature, which is the law of God."[11] Field thought that all law, both substantive and procedural, should be the product of democratically elected legislatures and that the power of authorities, especially judges, must be limited. Here is quintessential Field:

> No Judge should have power to decide a cause without a rule to decide it by, else the suitor is subject to his caprice.[12]

> It may be first observed, that flexibility, in its ordinary sense, is one of the worst qualities which a law can have, or rather that it is inconsistent with the idea of law. As the law is a rule of property and of conduct, it should be fixed...[13]

Field helped draft codes for all substantive law (except criminal), in addition to the New York procedural code. His goal was to define precisely what activity was prohibited, leaving as much room for independent and uncontrolled human action as possible, while still preserving a society of individuals living together. The substantive law was to identify precisely which acts would lead to what legal consequence. The procedural law was to force the plaintiff to identify the facts that would permit recovery, and defendants to admit or deny these facts, leading to settlement or a focused case on limited facts for the jury to decide. Pleadings were to be verified as true under oath. Although Field had

10. N.Y. Const. (1846) art. XIV, § 5, art. VI, § 3, & art. VI, § 27 (1846).
11. David Dudley Field, Municipal Officers, Address to the Young Men's Democratic Club of New York, March 13, 1879, reprinted in Classics in Legal History: Speeches of David Dudley Field, Volume 2, 176, 183 (A. Sprague ed. 1884, reprint, D. Appleton, 1890) [hereinafter Field, Speeches].
12. *Id.* at Volume 1, 349, 354.
13. Field, Speeches, *supra* note 11, at Volume 1, 323.

often sought and won equitable injunctions, he favored jury trials and did not approve of the discretion afforded equity judges.

One problem for Field and the Commissioners was to create a pleading requirement that would work for both law and equity cases in the now merged court. The code that Field drafted required plaintiffs to allege in their initial document "facts constituting a cause of action," rather than the traditional "form of action." Field was drawn to the word "facts" for he thought the system should try to determine objective reality, as in the sciences, which he admired. He did not want to use the words "form of action" because he sought to escape the common law formulary system and its writs. Also, the increasing complexity of fact patterns did not fit "the forms of action" that had previously been adjudicated in the law courts.

The Field Code expanded somewhat the limited joinder provisions of the common law, but parties and issues could not be joined unless they belonged to a single cause of action. The Field Code provided very limited methods to discover information before trial from the opposing side or other witnesses. Full discovery must wait until 1938 and the promulgation of the Federal Rules to make its appearance. The Field Code was adopted in about half of the states, covering well over half of the country's population, with the other half of the states retaining common law procedures. The federal courts, from 1789 until 1938 (with one brief hiatus), followed state procedure as prescribed by federal process acts.

The Field Code was a half-way step between common law procedure and the modern American procedure introduced by the Federal Rules of Civil Procedure of 1938. Merging law and equity cases, rejecting the writ and single-issue pleading, and expanding the ability to join claims and parties and discovery were all forward-looking steps. But the goals of David Dudley Field and his code were in some ways quite close to the common law mentality. He wanted to limit and confine litigation. He wanted rigorous rules that gave judges little discretion. He disliked flexibility in law. In keeping with the nineteenth-century *laissez-faire* philosophy, he wanted to let citizens do all activity that was not specifically forbidden by the written law. Field wanted the limitations on governmental action to be strong and those on citizen activity to be minimal. It was a period of economic expansion for America, and the owners and managers of the large corporations, whom he represented and who paid him handsomely, agreed with him.

1934-1938: THE RULES ENABLING ACT AND FEDERAL RULES OF CIVIL PROCEDURE

By the end of the nineteenth century, many criticisms were levied against the Field Code. Lawyers and judges tend to practice their craft largely influenced by what they learned at law school or early in their careers. Notwithstanding the Field Code, many courts persisted in treating law and equity as distinct. Lawyers continued to draft and interpret the pleadings in a way that replicated the technicalities of the common law. They argued that a single theory of recovery was all that the plaintiff could have in one complaint.

Commentators wrote about the hyper-technicality that had developed around the Field Code. Arguments had developed over such technicalities as whether the pleader had pled evidence or conclusions, rather than the bare facts, or whether the pleader had more than one theory within his cause of action. These technical disputes diverted attention from the merits of the case. Furthermore, the legislatures, driven by petty politics, frequently amended the codes in ways that made them too long, too complicated, and too technical.[14]

"Simplicity" and "flexibility" became the rallying cries for reform. Complaints about procedural complexity and legislative rule-making were particularly strident at the federal level. The federal Process Act of 1789 and subsequent acts prescribed that federal courts should apply the procedural law of the state that housed the federal court.[15] But this conformity solution, critics alleged, led to great uncertainty of what procedural law to apply in federal courts. There was the state procedure of the state in which the federal court sat. There were federal statutes that covered some areas of procedure. And there were occasions when federal judges refused to apply state procedure at all, arguing that a state rule interfered with their inherent rights to make procedure. Federal judges particularly protected their right to regulate judge-jury relations and methods of enforcing judgments for debts.

By 1912 the American Bar Association (A.B.A) had taken up the cause of civil procedural rules reform. By the time the Rules Enabling Act (Enabling Act) was passed in 1934 by Congress, the pro-Enabling Act arguments were multifold. Critics lobbied for new federal procedure rules that would be uniform, simple, and flexible. The new rules, the critics urged, should give judges a good deal of discretion to do justice and give lawyers a good deal of latitude as to how to frame their cases so that cases could be decided on the merits. Further, it should be the Supreme Court Justices who make the procedural rules because of the respect in which they were held and because of their expertise. Legislatures, so the argument went, acted too politically and too much on the whims of the moment. Finally, critics expressed the hope that new federal rules would be so simple and useful that the states would soon adopt the same rules. There were to be three types of procedural uniformity: the same rules for all federal district courts (inter-federal district court uniformity), the same procedural rules within the state (intrastate uniformity), and the same procedural rules for all types of cases regardless of their substance (trans-substantive uniformity).

The A.B.A. at the time was largely controlled by conservative lawyers who often represented wealthy individuals and large corporations. It joined with

14. The initial Field Code in New York had 392 provisions; by 1897, it had 3441 provisions and was called the Throop Code. In comparison to the Field Code, the Throop Code was "not general, but detailed, not brief but voluminous, not flexible but iron-clad." Furthermore, the Throop Code re-established the procedural law and equity distinction. Michael Joseph Hobor, *The Form of the Law: David Dudley Field and the Codification Movement* 379 (unpublished Ph.D. dissertation, The University of Chicago 1975).

15. Prior to the passage of the famous Conformity Act of 1872, a similar statute was adopted in 1842 "to cover states admitted between 1828 and 1842." Charles Alan Wright & Mary Kay Kane, Law of Federal Courts 427-428 (West Group 6th ed. 2002).

Republican members of Congress in the attempt to have the Rules Enabling Act passed, as part of an overall program to give the judiciary, and in particular, federal district court judges, more authority and discretion, not less, as favored by progressives at the time. Those who favored a Rules Enabling Act joined the theme of strengthening the judiciary with the idea that modernity required simple, flexible, uniform federal procedural rules.

It was the Democrats on the Senate Judiciary Committee, led by Senator Thomas Walsh, a progressive Democrat from Montana, who kept the Enabling Act from being passed for over 20 years. Walsh also argued that the Field Code worked quite well in his state. He thought the proposed Enabling Act would handicap the vast majority of local trial lawyers in order to help the relatively few lawyers who tried cases in more than one federal district court. In contrast to A.B.A. proponents who cited the Federal Court Equity Rules of 1912 as a good template for modern, simplified procedure, Walsh argued that these equity rules were a great deal more cumbersome than the proponents allowed. Finally, Walsh argued that the Supreme Court, too conservative in nature and too distant from the workings of trial courts, was an inappropriate body for promulgating procedural rules for the trial courts.[16] Rather, such a task would require legislative hearings, and therefore — reminiscent of Field's position — the legislature was the more appropriate body for procedural rule making in a democracy.

During the 1920s, a different group of voices joined the A.B.A. in supporting the Enabling Act and the establishment of uniform federal procedure. These were academics who wrote about civil procedure. Central to this group was Charles E. Clark, who in 1929 became Dean of the Yale Law School. Clark endorsed Field's merger of law and equity, but thought the Field Code stopped short of adopting flexible equitable procedure that relied on the discretion of judges. Clark's 1928 treatise suggested several reforms, most of which were borrowed from equity, and most of which ultimately ended up in the Federal Rules of Civil Procedure ten years later. These included freedom in pleading, alternative pleading, broader joinder of parties and issues, ease of counterclaim, intervention, ease of jury waiver, ease of amendment, declaratory judgment, summary judgment, and flexible relief (all discussed in later chapters).

Clark was part of what was called "the Legal Realist movement," which focused on what lawyers and judges actually did, as opposed to what one could learn about doctrine in law books that covered primarily appellate cases. In contrast to Field, Clark rejected "fact-based" pleadings because he believed that one could not distinguish what was a fact, evidence, or ultimate fact. He concluded that such words were best seen as a continuum, without logical cutoff points.

Most importantly, Clark wrote: "One of the most important recent developments in the field of the law is the greater emphasis now being placed upon the effect of legal rules as instruments of social control of much wider import than merely as determinants of narrow disputes between individual litigants."[17] In other words, while Field wanted to use law to control

16. S. Rep. No. 892, 64th Cong., 2d Sess., pt. 2, at 6 (1917).
17. Charles Clark, *Fact Research in Law Administration*, 1 Miss. L.J. 324, 324 (Jan. 1929).

government, Clark saw the need for law and expansive government to play a more active role in society. Toward this end, he and other Legal Realists thought that a sensible procedure would permit the amassing of all relevant information so that experts, like judges, could then decide the best legal resolution for disputes.

Clark's ideas were complemented by Edson Sunderland of the University of Michigan Law School, who extolled the virtues of equity procedure and of the English liberalized procedure. In the 1930s, Sunderland wrote about the importance of expanding pre-trial discovery as part of modern, flexible, simple civil procedure. This fit well with the idea of accumulating all relevant information in order to make wise decisions, and as we will later see, discovery became an important part of modern federal civil procedure.

By 1932, a severe economic depression in the United States led to the presidential election of Franklin Delano Roosevelt, a Democrat who promised to experiment with more active government in an attempt to jar the country out of its economic woes. Roosevelt initially picked Senator Thomas Walsh, an opponent to the Enabling Act, to be his first Attorney General, the highest ranking legal position in the executive branch. But Walsh died on the way to the presidential inauguration in 1933, and in an ironic twist of history, Roosevelt then appointed Homer Cummings, who became a key Democratic liberal spokesman for Roosevelt's expansive "New Deal" program. Echoing the need to leave behind technical rules in order to assist the government in drafting and implementing legislation to solve the nation's economic ills, Cummings personally sponsored legislation in 1934 that led to the swift passage of the Rules Enabling Act in that year.[18]

One can disentangle four different viewpoints and agendas that joined together to result in the Enabling Act of 1934, and later led to the Federal Rules of Civil Procedure in 1938: the conservatives who wanted to give more discretionary power to judges; liberals who wanted law, lawyers, and judges to help government play a more active role; lawyers, judges, and law professors who in fact thought that code procedure and the Conformity Acts were defective and inefficient; and lawyers who wanted to play pivotal and profitable roles in the emerging New Deal of President Roosevelt.

The Enabling Act authorized the Supreme Court to promulgate rules of civil procedure for law cases in the federal district laws, so long as they did not alter substantive rights. If they chose, the Supreme Court Justices could also make the rules apply to equity cases, thus merging law and equity as under the Field Code. However, such merger rules must first be presented to Congress, and if Congress did not intervene, these rules would become law by congressional inaction.

In 1935, Clark and Sunderland were appointed by the Chief Justice of the Supreme Court to serve as members of a 14-person Supreme Court Advisory Committee to draft procedural rules that would cover both law and equity cases. Three additional law professors and nine lawyers were also appointed to the committee. Most of the lawyers were associated with what was then considered large firm practice or were active participants in the A.B.A., and, in

---

18. Act of June 19, 1934, Public Laws No. 73–415, 48 Statute 1064 (current version is 28 U.S.C. § 2072).

most cases, both. Clark was named to be the Reporter, or chief draftsman, of the Rules.

Clark, with major help from Sunderland, presented drafts for consideration by the rest of the Committee. The drafts reflected positions that Clark and Sunderland had previously taken: merger of law and equity procedure, relaxed pleading requirements, ease of amendments, expansive joinder of parties and causes of action (now called claims entitling one to relief), expansive discovery, flexible remedies, summary judgment, waiver of jury trial unless specifically claimed by a party, and pretrial conference. These rules were drafted in an open-textured way, leaving a great deal of flexibility for lawyers and discretion for judges. In short, the equitable model of broad narrative, broad joinder, and broad judicial discretion largely supplanted the common law and Field Code model of rigorous rules designed to control and mold substance. The new model was predicated on a philosophy that was the antithesis of David Dudley Field's ideals. Where Field wanted to limit the discretion of judges and to codify the law in a manner that limited change, Clark wanted to expand judicial discretion and to permit more rapid expansion of the law and of government.

The Rules that the Advisory Committee drafted, largely accepted by the Supreme Court, were presented to Congress, and became effective as the procedural rules for all federal district courts on September 1, 1938. The Federal Rules of Civil Procedure, although since amended many times, still remain as the rules that govern civil cases in the federal trial courts today. Twenty-two states, plus the District of Columbia have judicially adopted civil procedure rules that are substantially modeled after the Federal Rules of Civil Procedure, with four additional states doing the same, but through legislative rather than judicial enactment. In total, there are 26 out of 50 states whose procedure is closely modeled on the Federal Rules. However, all of the states were influenced by the Federal Rules. Features such as liberal pleading, broad joinder, and expansive discovery are now the norm not only in the federal court system but also throughout most of the state court systems.

THE FEDERAL RULES OF CIVIL PROCEDURE AND PROCEDURAL ISSUES IN AMERICA TODAY

Civil procedure and litigation, of course, do not act in a vacuum. They interact within social and economic and political currents, rendering the exact influence of any one variable difficult to pinpoint. It is fair to conclude, however, that the equity-based flexible, permissive, expansive Federal Rules, and their counterparts at the state level, gave force to other currents to permit an enormous growth of legal rights and civil litigation, an increase in the amount of discovery and hence, the expense of litigation. One can also point to the Federal Rules as giving rise to the number of lawyers in the country and the fees paid to lawyers who conduct litigation. The combination of factors, coalescing with a conservative political turn in the country, has led to the recent 25 to 30 years of retrenchment to reign in the original Federal Rule system and in the alternative, to avoid courts altogether. As we write this book, the United States is probably in the midst of a fifth type of procedural regime: informal during the colonial period; common law-based until the mid-nineteenth century; mixed common law and equity as result of Field Code-like procedure (1848-1938); equity-based Federal Rules from 1938 until about 1980; and today, Federal Rule based but since 1980, with a mass array of containment methods and growing amounts of privatization. It is perhaps inevitable that the equity-based Federal Rule system, with so few methods of containing the number of parties, issues, and costs, would incite the present day attempts to control that system and in the alternative, to avoid it and its consequences.

And so, what has happened since the Federal Rules were adopted? While later chapters will provide more detail about the rules and their amendments, a few points are worth highlighting here. Starting in about 1928, America suffered a severe economic depression and responded with the federal government's passing a large amount of legislation regulating the economy and providing federally protected rights, such as minimum wage, the right to organize unions, and social security. World War Two (1941-1945 in the United States) brought an enlarged national economy with more federal law and greatly enlarged federal government. The Civil Rights movement, following the end of the World War and accelerating from about 1960 to 1975, brought another increase in federal law and the expansion of legal rights generally. Professor Judith Resnik summarizes:

> Congress authorized litigants to bring lawsuits aimed at enforcing civil rights, environmental rights, consumers' rights, and workers' rights, and Congress enlarged the power of federal prosecutors to pursue criminal actions. Between the 1960s and the 1990s, caseloads within the federal system tripled, as hundreds of new statutory causes of action were enacted. In terms of budgets, Congress provided substantial resources to the federal courts, whose budgets grew from about $250 million in the early 1960s to its current $4.2 billion.[19]

Since World War II, the types of lawsuits permitted by American tort law, with the liberalization of negligence and products liability doctrine, have greatly expanded. And the Federal Rules of Civil Procedure have made these lawsuits possible. Amendments in 1966 made class actions, in which thousands of plaintiffs could join in one suit, more available. Standing and jurisdictional requirements were loosened, enabling entry to the courts with greater ease. State law has often followed the liberalization of federal procedure. In 2003, state courts reported the filing of 5,367,096 civil actions in their trial courts of general jurisdiction (courts that can hear nonspecialized types of cases), and this excludes domestic relation cases.[20]

---

19. Judith Resnik, *Procedure as Contract*, 80 Notre Dame L. Rev. 593, 603 (Jan. 2005). The federal budget comparison has been adjusted to 1996 dollar values.

20. For the total number of cases by the nature of the suit, see charts for federal civil and criminal cases, *available at* <http://www.uscourts.gov/judicialfactsfigures/table2.02.pdf> and <http://www.uscourts.gov/judicialfactsfigures/contents.html#tables>.

Starting in the mid-1970s, there has been a multi-pronged backlash against the perceived growth of litigation in America and the leniency of the Federal Rules. Interestingly, many of these steps take the form of revisions to the procedure rules, rather than the more visibly controversial substantive laws. There have been numerous attempts, by rule and case law, to require more factual support and precision in complaints and less discovery. The courts have used what are called motions for summary judgment in large measure to dismiss the cases of plaintiffs prior to trial. The United States Congress, dominated by Republicans who are antagonistic to large civil actions against corporate entities, and at the urging of conservative lobbyists, passed statutes making it considerably harder to bring and win securities cases, prisoners' rights cases, and class actions. The United States Supreme Court too has joined in the fray to greatly encourage arbitrations and enforce the decisions of arbitrators. The Supreme Court has also used procedural rulings to increase the difficulty of winning civil rights cases.

As you have read, when the Federal Rules of Civil Procedure finally became law it was as the result of a liberal, Democratic, New Deal mentality; many of the new rights were made possible by a Democratic controlled Congress and a liberal Supreme Court. In some ways, the backlash has been the opposite, partially the result of laissez-faire, conservative, Republican political powers that seek smaller government and less litigation.

Most significantly, the Federal Rules of Civil Procedure have also been amended to encourage the settlement of cases, as we will discuss later. Lawyers throughout the country have increasingly turned to mediation in order to facilitate settling cases. In 1940, the percentage of federal civil cases terminated during or after trial was 15.2 percent. By 1962, the figure had dropped to 11.5 percent. In 2002, only 1.8 percent of federal cases were tried. Trying to sort out the reasons has proven difficult, but the federal court trial rate has dropped over eight fold since the Federal Rules became law.

Increasingly lawyers in America have turned to private contracts in order to regulate where and how lawsuits are litigated. Corporate lawyers, in particular, who largely represent defendants have resorted to putting clauses in their contracts (including tickets and warranties) requiring agreement to arbitration or declaring in which court and where cases can be commenced. A large percentage of cases now end with settlements, often negotiated under the auspices of a judge or a private mediator. The courts are increasingly called on to interpret settlement agreements, some of which are incorporated into formal court dismissals but many of which do not show up in court records. Judith Resnik of Yale Law School, in her provocative article, entitled "Procedure as Contract," argues that contracts between private parties have so frequently replaced or accompanied due process law as the underlying norm for civil litigation that we are in a new civil procedure world. If courts continue to encourage and sponsor settlement, she points out, new law will be needed to regulate what is permitted by private contracts that control and terminate civil litigation.

Thus, expansion and contraction characterized the course of American civil litigation in the twentieth century. It is unclear what the twenty-first century will bring, but one thing is clear: American civil procedure continues to be in flux. The liberal, flexible Federal Rules of Civil Procedure model will continue to be altered by amended rules, statutes, and judicial decisions designed to control and constrict their flexibility and plaintiff-friendly nature. Lawyers are finding ways to avoid the risks of trial in traditional courts. We seem to have gone from a common law procedural mentality, to an equity-dominated regime, to a nontrial mentality.

Maitland may have been right, that equity standing alone is a castle in the air that cannot be sustained without a more rule-bound structure by its side. But Maitland could not have foreseen the potential of private contractual ordering superimposed on formal adjudication that is occurring today. Constriction of more flexible rules can come from private negotiations as well as more formally defining procedures. And it is as yet unknown what the effects may be of subjecting public disputes to private ordering resolution.

CHAPTER

4

An American Civil Litigation From Beginning To End

No truth about our subject is more profound than its unity; what happens in the beginning depends mightily on what we expect to happen in the middle and at the end.

Paul D. Carrington and Barbara Allen Babcock[1]

To understand a procedural system requires looking in some detail at each segment of the litigation process and discovering how each is inexorability linked with the other. Before taking you on that journey, we introduce you to one American lawsuit from beginning to end. As you go through this book, you may find it useful to return to this chapter periodically; this will remind you of the relationship of each piece to the whole. We occasionally refer to this lawsuit in later chapters when we think it is illustrative. This chapter is just an introduction. You will learn a good deal more about each litigation step in the remainder of the book.

Assume you are a lawyer in a private law firm in Boston, Massachusetts, in the United States.[2] It is August of this year. Because of your reputation as a successful lawyer in personal injury cases, a new potential client has come to your office. Mr. Albert Lee and his wife, Mabel Lee, reside in Springfield, Massachusetts. Mr. Lee owns a gardening and lawn service company, and Mrs. Lee works part-time as a secretary at Springfield Central High School.

What follows is Mr. Lee's story as he told it. Lawyers learn, though, that what a client tells them does not always conform with what actually happened or

---

1. Paul D. Carrington and Barbara Allen Babcock, Civil Procedure 3 (3d ed. Little, Brown & Co. 1983)

2. This case is adapted from a real case that a lawyer in Boston, Massachusetts shared with us. We also used this case when we taught American civil procedure to Chinese civil procedure professors in Beijing. We changed the names and some of the facts in the case to fit the purposes of this book. The events and the lawsuit took place in Massachusetts, which is also the state in which we practiced law and teach. Massachusetts has adopted the Federal Rules of Civil Procedure in most relevant respects, so it is a good state to use for an illustrative procedural case. We return to this case throughout the book with the hope that having one repeated fact pattern will make it easier for our readers to begin to internalize the interrelated steps in an American civil litigation. We doubt that the case would have been handled much differently by skilled lawyers in another state or another court.

what a fact finder later believes. According to Mr. Lee, on June 6 of this year, he drank a can of Cherryum soft drink that contained, among other things, the toxic chemicals Lindane and Dimethoate, commonly used in insecticides. According to Mr. Lee, on the day of the incident, he opened the can of Cherryum, heard the usual "pop" of the seal breaking, and took a long drink. After he swallowed, Mr. Lee immediately knew that something was wrong. Not only did the soft drink taste terrible, but there was also a milky white substance inside the can. Mr. Lee began to feel dizzy and weak within one minute after drinking the Cherryum. He began to perspire and took a shower as a result. Although this helped a bit, Mr. Lee still felt nauseous and weak.

Mr. Lee then drove to a nearby job site, thinking that he just needed some air. Once there, he became extremely dizzy and asked one of the employees to drive him home. When they arrived, Mr. Lee collapsed on his front lawn. His wife called an ambulance and Mr. Lee was transported by ambulance to the Springfield General Hospital. Since the poisoning, Mr. Lee has suffered many severe medical complications. Mrs. Lee had to take several weeks off from work in order to care for Mr. Lee.

You tell Mr. Lee that you are very interested in his case, but you want to do a little investigation of your own before you begin representing him, if he decides he wants you to be his lawyer. Mr. Lee says he is quite sure he wants you to be his lawyer. You explain your fee arrangement to Mr. Lee — that if you end up representing him, your fee will be one-third of his total recovery, whether through settlement or winning at trial. Mr. Lee will also have to pay all additional expenses of litigation, such as filing fees, the hiring of experts to testify, the copying of documents, the price of stenographers for depositions, and similar expenditures. This attorney fee arrangement is called a contingent fee arrangement, and is generally used by plaintiff's counsel in tort cases. As discussed in Chapter 2, the contingent fee arrangement has allowed even poor plaintiffs to hire proper counsel because under this arrangement, plaintiffs need to pay attorneys' fee only if they win. However, the client is responsible for other expenses (but not for attorneys' fees) even if he loses the case. Sometimes, a client cannot even afford to pay these expenses, and the lawyer often ends up having to pay all of the expenses even though he or she received no fee payments.

You have learned from previous experience to do a good deal of research, in order to assess the strength of your case, before agreeing to take a case. Other lawyers often take cases quickly, and look for the proof later. After Mr. Lee leaves, you ask your paralegal to assist you with some initial investigation about the case by getting you a copy of the hospital records, doctor's reports, the names of the ambulance driver, the names and addresses of Cherryum's corporate headquarters, and where Mr. Lee purchased his bottle of Cherryum. You also ask your paralegal to find out if any of the potential defendants have insurance coverage, although you will probably have to wait until a later stage of litigation to receive that information.

When you receive the hospital report, you find out that when Mr. Lee arrived at the hospital, he was in a state of cardiogenic shock. His cardiac rhythm was unstable, and he experienced arterial fibrillation, which continued for several days. Mr. Lee vomited continuously for some time and was in extreme pain. The doctors felt that Mr. Lee's condition was serious enough to require him to remain in the Intensive Care Unit for three days and in the hospital for two days after that.

Conversations with the ambulance crew revealed that the crew had saved some of Mr. Lee's vomit and delivered it to the hospital for testing. The crew also saved the Cherryum can, which was later delivered to a lab for testing. The crew reported feeling sick and dizzy because of the odor from the Cherryum can and Mr. Lee's vomit. Witnesses at the hospital also reported that the can contained a small amount of white fluid and gave off an unusual odor.

Lab results from Mr. Lee's stomach sample indicated the presence of phorodithioicacid (which is consistent with Dimethoate) and Lindane. As mentioned earlier, both Dimethoate and Lindane are commonly found in insecticides and are highly toxic. Mr. Lee's stomach sample was subsequently tested at another lab. That test revealed a Dimethoate level of 9mg/ml liquid and a Lindane level of 7mg/ml liquid. According to toxicologists you consult, these levels are surprisingly high, indicating that the amount of poisons in the Cherryum consumed by Mr. Lee was large. The remaining contents of the Cherryum can were also tested. These tests revealed that the contents of the can matched Mr. Lee's stomach sample and also contained traces of Dimethoate and Lindane. According to hospital records, the hospital staff initially assumed that Mr. Lee had ingested a herbicide because, as a gardener, Mr. Lee works with such chemicals and had actually sprayed a herbicide the day before the incident.

You meet with Mr. Lee again, and you agree to represent him. You have been greatly influenced in this decision by the following facts: First, you believe that Mr. Lee's poisoning was not the result of herbicide poisoning. The herbicide Mr. Lee was working with does not contain either Dimethoate or Lindane. Second, Mr. Lee did not spray any herbicide on the date of his poisoning. Third, the levels of Dimethoate and Lindane consumed are far too high to have come from any accidental drops from containers. According to the manufacturer, a small amount of the herbicide ingested directly would not have made Mr. Lee as sick as he was. Fourth, the herbicide used by Mr. Lee the previous day was never inside the cab of his truck, and the can of Cherryum was never in the truck, and it could not have come into contact with any herbicide accidentally. Fifth, the herbicide was never spilled in the cab of the truck, because Mr. Lee's workers would have noticed the strong chemical odor. Sixth, Mr. Lee drank the soda immediately after opening it and did not leave the can lying around.

Mr. Lee is interested in holding the appropriate parties responsible for his poisoning. The can of Cherryum carries the trademark of Cherryum, Inc., and says the bottler is the Cherryum Bottling Company. Mr. Lee believes it is likely that the Cherryum Bottling Company and Cherryum, Inc., use insecticides in their bottling plants to control insects. Mr. Lee purchased the drink from Miller's Market, a local convenience store. Cherryum, Inc., and Cherryum Bottling Company, Inc., are each incorporated outside of Massachusetts and their principal places of business are outside of Massachusetts. Miller's Market is a Massachusetts corporation with its principal place of business in Springfield, Massachusetts.

After taking the case, you have a lot of decisions to make. First, whom should you sue? Under Massachusetts law, which will apply whether you choose to commence suit in a Massachusetts state or federal court, a manufacturer of food or beverage for human consumption owes a duty to the ultimate purchaser to exercise reasonable care in its preparation and delivery to the consumer in order that the product not cause injury to the consumer. The degree of care required is one of ordinary negligence. The elements of such a negligence cause of action are (1) duty to the plaintiff (which there is here); (2) unreasonable care (or breach of the duty to act reasonably); (3) cause in fact of harm to the consumer; (4) which harm is reasonably foreseeable (often called "proximate cause"); and (5) damages.

Massachusetts law also provides that a manufacturer of a product and a seller of a product owe an implied warranty to the buyer that it is fit for the ordinary purposes for which such goods are used, and for those purposes that are reasonably foreseeable. Under Massachusetts implied warranty law, the court will not look to the conduct of the seller, but only whether the product was "fit for the ordinary purposes for which such goods are used."[3]

One Massachusetts case states the policy behind this implied warranty cause of action:

> [T]he public has the right to and does expect, in the case of products which it needs and which it is forced to rely upon the seller, that reputable sellers will stand behind their goods; that public policy demands that the burden of accidental injury caused by products intended for consumption be placed upon those who market them, and be treated as a cost of production against which liability insurance can be obtained . . . [4]

The elements of the implied warranty cause of action are: (1) a sale of a product; (2) the product is not fit for the ordinary purpose for which it is ordinarily used; (3) the product causes; (4) a foreseeable harm; and (5) damages.

Finally, under Massachusetts common law, a spouse may sue for her own pain and suffering under what is called "a loss of consortium" cause of action if as a direct and proximate result of the breach of warranty and negligent action of defendants, a spouse suffered the loss of expected protection and care, assistance, and services and consortium and income of his or her spouse for a substantial period of time.

One defendant you want to sue is Cherryum, Inc., because they are a large corporation and probably the defendant who can most pay a judgment. Since Mr. and Mrs. Lee are Massachusetts residents, and Cherryum, Inc., is an out-of-state corporation with an out-of-state principal place of business, you have what is called "diversity of citizenship," which is a type of subject matter jurisdiction that would allow you to go to a federal court if the amount of

---

3. M.G.L. c. 106, § 2-314.
4. *Correia v. Firestone Tire & Rubber Co.*, 388 Mass. 342, 355 (1983) (quoting § 402A of the Restatement (Second) of Torts, Comment c (1965)).

recovery you seek is more than $75,000, which it is, considering the amount of injury sustained by Mr. and Mrs. Lee.

You could also sue Cherryum Bottling, Inc., in federal court because there would still be complete diversity of states between plaintiffs (Massachusetts) and the defendants (both are out-of-state corporations). You have not yet decided to sue Miller's Market, but you might add Miller's Market later. Note that if you decided to sue Miller's Market, a Massachusetts business, you could no longer choose a federal court. In that instance, adding Miller's Market would destroy diversity of citizenship because the plaintiffs and Miller's Market are Massachusetts domiciles (resident and intent to stay) and hence, Massachusetts citizens. If there were a federal cause of action arising out of any federal statute regulating the purity of food products, then you could get into federal court under the federal question subject matter jurisdiction and in that event would not need diversity between the parties. You could demand a jury in this case in federal court, because you seek damages and not an injunction (more on this and most topics in this chapter as the book progresses).

You may decide, though, that you would rather be in state court. Each state has a court of general subject matter jurisdiction, which can hear all types of cases. Massachusetts has a trial court of general subject matter jurisdiction called the Massachusetts Superior Court. One is also permitted to make a jury claim in Superior Court. So if you decide to sue all the defendants, including Miller's Market, you can sue in Massachusetts Superior Court and ask for a jury trial. Massachusetts has procedural rules identical to the Federal Rules of Civil Procedure in most respects.

Assume that you decided not to sue Miller's Market. If you only sue Cherryum, Inc., and Cherryum Bottling Co., you can stay in federal court. You can file a complaint with the federal district court in Massachusetts. Massachusetts has one federal judicial district, with judges sitting in Boston and in Springfield. The federal courts follow the Federal Rules of Civil Procedure. One rule is called Federal Rule of Civil Procedure 20 (abbreviated as Fed. R. Civ. P. 20), and it is a joinder of parties rule. It says that you can join multiple plaintiffs and defendants in one lawsuit if the cases arise from the same transaction or occurrence and if there is a common question of law or fact. In this instance, the same transaction is the ingestion of a toxic Cherryum soda, and the common question of fact will revolve around how the incident happened. There is, therefore, a "transaction" and "questions of fact" that will be common to all plaintiffs and defendants. Under Rule 20, you can bring a lawsuit that joins Mr. and Mrs. Lee as co-plaintiffs, and Cherryum, Inc., and Cherryum Bottling Co. as co-defendants.

There is another preliminary matter that you, as a plaintiff's attorney, must address – personal jurisdiction. You cannot sue a defendant in a state unless the defendant has sufficient contact with that state such that it is fair to sue in that state. For instance, if the accident had happened in California (e.g., Mr. Lee brought the drink with him to California and drank it there), and Cherryum does not sell its sodas in California, then you may not be able to bring a suit against Cherryum, Inc., in California, unless you can somehow argue that Cherryum has some contacts in California to justify jurisdiction over it in California. This is called a question of personal jurisdiction. In this case, Cherryum, Inc., markets and sells its sodas in Massachusetts. It is therefore fair to sue Cherryum, Inc., as well as Cherryum Bottling Co. in a court in Massachusetts. Indeed, Massachusetts has a statute, called a "long arm" statute that permits plaintiffs to sue a nonresident of Massachusetts in a Massachusetts court if the nonresident allegedly acted in Massachusetts in a way that caused harm to the plaintiff in Massachusetts or under certain conditions, acted in such a way outside of Massachusetts that caused harm in Massachusetts. The Massachusetts federal court will also apply this state long arm statute.

Once you decide to join the parties, and you decide to sue the defendants in the federal district court in Massachusetts, you still have a problem called "venue." The federal venue statute tells you which of the various jurisdictionally possible federal judicial districts you can sue in. Venue is provided for by federal statute (there are similar state venue statutes for state court systems to distribute cases throughout the counties within the state) and generally considers where the defendants reside and where the events occurred. Because the incident happened in Massachusetts, and Massachusetts has only one federal judicial district, you will be able to sue all the defendants in the Federal District Court of Massachusetts.

In order to sue in an American court you always need at least one cause of action. A cause of action describes the circumstances under which one party is liable to another. For instance, an old cause of action, existent even in early English legal history, is a battery. You read about this cause of action in Chapter 3. To win in the tort of battery the plaintiff must show an intentional unwanted touching. Probably the most frequent cause of action in American tort law is negligence. As we stated earlier, to win a negligence suit, the plaintiff must show: (1) that the defendant owed a duty to act reasonably with respect to the plaintiff; (2) that the defendant breached the duty to act reasonably or engaged in unreasonable care; (3) that the defendant's unreasonable action or inaction in fact caused harm to the plaintiff; (4) that the harm caused was reasonably foreseeable; and that (5) there was a harm. The numbered items above are called the "elements" of the negligence cause of action. Sometimes, these elements of the negligence cause of action are simply referred to as duty, unreasonable care, cause in fact, proximate cause, and harm.

In this lawsuit, you will probably allege that both defendants acted negligently with respect to the plaintiffs: Cherryum, Inc., in producing and Cherryum Bottling Co. in bottling the soft drink in a negligent way such that toxins got in the drink. You will also allege a breach of implied warranty of fitness, that the soft drink was not fit for normal consumption. If you join Mrs. Lee as a plaintiff, you would also want to allege a count of loss of consortium. Thus, there may be multiple legal theories on which to base your lawsuit. You can join multiple causes of action against the same party, allowable by Fed. R. Civ. Pro. 18, which allows such joinder of theories and causes of action, although it calls it "joinder of claims," which we will discuss later.

Now that you have picked a court, decided on your plaintiffs and defendants, and know your causes of action, how do you actually start the lawsuit? Fed. R. Civ. P. 8 provides that you commence a lawsuit by filing a complaint in a courthouse. Rule 8 tells you what you must include in a valid complaint. The main language in the rule is that you must state "a claim for which relief may be granted," which is another way of saying you must state a legally recognized cause of action. We will discuss in Chapter 6 why the language "a claim for which relief may be granted" is now in the rule instead of the language, "facts constituting a cause of action," which was in many nineteenth century American procedure codes.

In American law, you are required to give notice of the right to be heard to a defendant under the Due Process Clause of the United States Constitution.[5] Similar clauses in state constitutions require that plaintiffs formally tell the defendant that he or she or it is being sued, so that the defendant can come and defend herself in court. Most typically, pursuant to Fed. R. Civ. P. 4, an official of the court will serve (deliver) a copy of the complaint on the defendant, along with a summons telling the defendant how and when to respond. Your complaint will probably have one cause of action in negligence against each of the defendants. Typically, you would just describe the parties, tell briefly what happened, and then allege a "count" that states why the circumstances add up to negligence and what relief you seek. In this instance, your complaint will have at least two counts, one against each defendant in negligence. If an implied breach of warranty cause of action is applicable as against the defendants, then you will have an additional two counts against Cherryum, Inc., and Cherryum Bottling Co. Adding Mrs. Lee's claim for loss of consortium would bring your complaint to a total of six or eight counts, depending on whether you include both negligence and breach of implied warranty counts in her portion of the complaint. If you want a jury, you will also make a written jury claim.

Let's say you have now filed the complaint. There is a nominal filing fee, which your clients will pay back if you win for them. Let's also say that both defendants have been officially served. (The corporations will probably be served by handing a copy of the complaint to an official of the corporation or mailing it to them in an official way.) Something would be filed in court to show that the defendants have been served, usually an affidavit by the person who did the service called a "return of service." Now it is up to the defendants to act. If the defendants do not answer within 20 days of receipt of the copy of the complaint and the summons, unless the court gives them an extension of time, they will be considered in default and lose automatically.[6]

What do the defendants have to do in order to respond appropriately? The answer that a defendant will want to file will raise any preliminary arguments it may have to try to dismiss the case. If applicable, each defendant could attack the plaintiffs' case for being brought in the wrong court or because the defendant did not have enough connection to the state in which the case is brought, called the "forum state," to constitutionally permit that state to have personal jurisdiction over it. A defendant might, in some cases, be able to say that the plaintiffs did not correctly state a claim for which relief can be granted.

In addition, the defendants will have to admit or deny each allegation in the plaintiffs' complaint. Then the defendant will have to list any affirmative defenses. Affirmative defenses are those defenses that say, in effect, that even if defendants are liable, the plaintiff has done something that makes it

---

5. The Fifth Amendment to the United States Constitution places that limitation on the federal government, while the Fourteenth Amendment brings due process to bear on the states.

6. See Fed. R. Civ. P. 12(a) and 55(a).

impossible for the plaintiff to win. You may recall from Chapter 3 that at common law, this defense was a "confession and avoidance." For example, if the plaintiffs did not bring suit until too much time had passed from the time of their injury (which is not true in this case), then the defendant could successfully assert the affirmative defense of statute of limitations. In an automobile accident case, if the plaintiffs were required to wear safety belts, and they did not, then their failure would be a basis for the defendants to assert an affirmative defense of contributory or comparative negligence.

The defendant can also make cross-claims against other defendants. They can also bring counterclaims against a plaintiff if the defendant believes that the plaintiff in turn caused the defendant harm. Under Fed. R. Civ. P. 14, defendants can also bring in any third party on a derivative liability basis to defend the claim. In this case, Cherryum, Inc., for instance, may want to bring in Miller's Market, on the argument that if Cherryum, Inc., is liable to the plaintiffs, then Miller's Market is also negligent, and may be liable to the defendants and contribute to Cherryum, Inc.'s losses. As we will discuss later, this impleading of a third party (in this instance, a party from the same state as the plaintiff) adds to the jurisdictional complexity of the case, and there are rules governing how courts should deal with the subject matter and the personal jurisdiction issues relating to this third party claim.

As the plaintiff's lawyer in this case, you would have to know about burdens of proof. In general, the plaintiff has the full burden of proof as to every element of any cause of action it alleges and the defendant has the burden of proof as to any affirmative defenses. The "burden of proof" normally has two parts: the burden of production and the burden of persuasion. At trial, the plaintiff must present enough evidence to permit reasonable people to find that every element of its cause of action is true. This is called the plaintiff's burden of production. The plaintiff also has the burden to convince the fact finder, whether judge or jury, that each element is in fact true. This is called the plaintiff's burden of persuasion. In general, the party with the burden of proof also has the obligation to plead her claims appropriately. Therefore, as to affirmative defenses, the defendant (and not the plaintiff) usually has the pleading burden to properly plead the defense. The defendant will also have both the production and persuasion burdens as to each element of the affirmative defense.

After the defendants file their answers, there will probably be a period of discovery. You may want to begin the discovery by sending written questions to any of the opposing parties, which they will have to answer under oath. These are called "interrogatories," and the defendants' answers to them will also be available for your use at the trial. You, as the plaintiffs' lawyer, may wish to take the oral deposition of company executives and workers at Cherryum, Inc., and Cherryum Bottling Co., to inquire about the method of production and bottling of the drinks. This means that these witnesses will have to appear before a stenographer, who will administer an oath to them, and they will have to answer your questions under oath. You will be able to use their answers at the trial in accordance with Fed. R. Civ. P. 32.

After discovery, the defendant may wish to ask the court for a ruling (that is, file a motion) that will summarily decide the case without trial.[7] This motion,

7. *See* Fed. R. Civ. P. 56.

called a motion for summary judgment, might ask the court to decide, from looking at the pleadings (the complaint, answer, cross claims, counterclaims, etc.), the discovery materials, and any affidavits (sworn written statements under oath), that the party with the burden cannot win because the party will be unable to produce any proof as to at least one element. For example, if discovery or plaintiffs' affidavits did not show any potential evidence that Cherryum, Inc., acted unreasonably or caused the harm, then Cherryum could move for a summary judgment on the negligence count. The motion would be granted, because the plaintiffs could not win at a trial anyway. In this case, however, it would be almost impossible for Cherryum, Inc., or Cherryum Bottling Co. to win a summary judgment. Mr. Lee can testify that he did in fact drink a Cherryum drink that contained toxins, which would at least permit a fact finder to infer that the drink was manufactured or bottled negligently.

What often happens next in a lawsuit, or sometimes even before the completion of discovery, is that the parties try to settle the case. This means, that the lawyers for the parties, with their client's permission, try to reach an agreement of how to dispose of the case without a trial. The insurance company for Cherryum, Inc., may offer each of your clients $100,000 (a total of $200,000, the insurance policy limit) in exchange for your agreement to drop the case against it. If you settle the case on those terms, then you will have a trial only against Cherryum Bottling Co.

If you settle with only Cherryum, Inc., you will move forward to trial as to the remaining defendant, Cherryum Bottling Co. Since you have asked for a jury trial, the judge will have to impanel a jury. Many people will be called to appear at the courthouse to serve as potential jurors. There are laws requiring citizens to show up for jury duty, unless a judge excuses them for good cause. From the large jury pool (those potential jurors who show up) a lottery system will pick names in order to end up with six or twelve people (depending on the court) who will sit as jurors in the case.

There will then be a *voire dire*, in which the judge, and sometimes the lawyers, ask the potential jurors questions. A lawyer can request that a person be excluded from the jury for cause, for example, if the potential juror was a relative or friend of a party or otherwise biased or prejudiced. The parties also have a certain number of peremptory challenges to potential jury members, whereby they can have a person excluded without giving any reason. Ultimately, a full jury will be chosen and sworn in to hear the case.

At the trial, you will present your evidence, including any witness testimony as well as relevant documents and photographs, and the Cherryum can, — that will be entered by the court clerk as exhibits. You question each witness of your choice by direct examination, and the opposing lawyer or lawyers will ask questions of your witnesses, called cross examination. Each opposing lawyer may make evidence objections to any question, such as that the question is irrelevant. The judge will rule on the objections by sustaining the objection (the question is impermissible) or overruling the objection (the witness must answer).

When you are finished with your presentation of evidence (which is "resting" your case), the lawyer for the defendant may move for a directed verdict. A directed verdict motion usually asks the judge to rule that even if the jury believes your evidence as true, you did not meet your burden of production.

This means that as to one or more of the elements of the cause of action you are relying on, you did not offer sufficient evidence to permit a jury to find that element true. If the judge agrees with the defendant, then she will grant a directed verdict. A directed verdict in effect takes the case away from the jury and awards the defendant a victory. In federal court, the directed verdict is now called "judgment as a matter of law."[8]

If you survive the directed verdict motion, then the defendants can then put in their evidence. They will then rest. Each party may ask for directed verdicts, which would likely be denied in this case. Each party will next give a closing argument to the jury. Usually the side with the burden of proof, which is normally the plaintiff, is permitted to argue last. At the closing arguments, the lawyers review the law and the evidence and try to persuade the jury as to why their side should win (that is, that they have met their burden of persuasion). The judge will then give the jury instructions, usually orally, about the law they should apply and tell them that they are bound by oath to apply that law.

The judge usually gives the jury foreperson (one of the jurors the judge has picked to be chairman of the deliberations) a slip of paper for each defendant, called "general verdict" slips. For instance, as to Cherryum Bottling Co., the general verdict slip would simply say "for the plaintiff" or "for the defendant" with a line for each count. Some jurisdictions would have a separate general verdict slip for each count. The jury would be instructed by the judge either to put an "x" next to "for the defendant" or an "x" next to for the plaintiff, and in the case of "for the plaintiff," to also fill in an amount of damages awarded. In some cases, the judge would give the jury specific questions to answer.

Once the jury comes in with their verdict or verdicts, the parties have ten days to request a new trial if they have grounds for such a motion or to renew their request for directed verdicts. This is called a motion for judgment n.o.v. or judgment notwithstanding verdict.[9] A motion for judgment n.o.v. asks the court to enter a judgment in spite of the jury verdict. Later in the book, we will describe these motions in greater detail. If the outcome of the case is not changed by these motions, then the jury verdict will become a final judgment.

The procedural rules regulating the appeals process will give the parties a certain number of days to appeal the case to a higher court on questions of law. For example, assume the plaintiff won at trial, and that the jury was permitted inappropriately to hear some evidence, over the objection of the defendants' lawyers that the evidence was irrelevant or hearsay. Defendants' lawyers could appeal to the federal Court of Appeals for the First Circuit arguing that the evidence was not only inadmissible, but that the erroneous admission of such evidence caused material error — that is, that the jury might well have found for the defendants except for this mistake of wrongly admitted evidence.

If the Court of Appeals for the First Circuit agrees with the defendants' lawyers, they will reverse the case and send it back to the trial court for a new trial. If they do not think there was a material error at the trial level, the appellate court will affirm the verdict of the trial court. The losing party or parties at appeal may petition the U.S. Supreme Court to review the case

---

8. *See* Fed. R. Civ. P. 50(a).
9. *See* Fed. R. Civ. P. 50(b), which again calls the motion one for "judgment as a matter of law."

once again. However, the losing party from an intermediate appellate court ordinarily does not have an automatic right of appeal to a supreme court. The United States Supreme Court and most state supreme courts decide which cases to hear on appeal.

Once the case reaches final judgment, with no further chance to appeal, then the final judgment will be given a *res judicata* effect. Plaintiffs will not be permitted to bring the same claim or claims against these defendants again. [10]

Once you achieve such a final judgment for your plaintiffs, you will hope that the defendants will simply pay you and your clients the money owed. Since there is insurance, there is a good chance you will collect on the judgment promptly. If the defendants do not voluntarily comply with the final judgment, you will have to take formal legal steps to collect on the judgment, which is called "executing the judgment" or "levying on the judgment." This can result in the forceful seizing of the defendants' property and having it sold for your clients' benefit at a public sale.

Most cases in America settle before or during trial, because it takes so many steps to win a case and, even if you win, you may have trouble collecting the judgment. There is also the consideration that a trial is expensive, and there is a risk the jury may not find for your clients after a trial. The damages that a judge or jury will award are also frequently unpredictable.

Having presented a picture of a civil litigation from beginning to end, we will now discuss in greater detail the rules governing the major steps in an American lawsuit. We begin the next chapter with considerations of jurisdictional requirements and related matters.

---

10. We will discuss the preclusion doctrine in Chapter 12.

CHAPTER
5

Divided Power: Jurisdiction, Venue, Notice, and Choice of Law

[D]ue process requires only that in order to subject a defendant to a judgment in personam, if he be not present within the territory of the forum, he have certain minimum contacts with it such that the maintenance of the suit does not offend "traditional notions of fair play and substantial justice."

Chief Justice Stone[1]

Except in matters governed by the Federal Constitution or by Acts of Congress, the law to be applied in any case is the law of the State. And whether the law of the state shall be declared by its Legislature in a statute or by its highest court in a decision is not a matter of federal concern.

Justice Brandeis[2]

ADVERSARINESS, POWER, AND FAIRNESS

The two quotes at the beginning of this chapter are from cases decided within a short span of seven years. One emphasizes fairness and the other federalism. Both these issues lie within the heart of the rules that confront any American lawyer at the commencement of suit. At the initiation of any litigation, a lawyer must consider where to bring suit and what law to apply. The rules outlining what subject matter a court may hear, when a court may assert power over the defendant, which location of the court is proper, and what law of which jurisdiction should apply all fall within the ambit of jurisdiction, venue, notice, and choice of law.

Rules regulating where to file suit and what law to apply necessarily involve individual as well as institutional considerations. In the United States, two themes underlie this body of legal doctrine: they are the concern for fundamental fairness to the litigants and the appropriate distribution of

1. *International Shoe Co. v. Washington*, 326 U.S. 310, 316 (1945) (quoting *Milliken v. Meyer*, 311 U.S. 457, 463 (1940).
2. *Erie Railroad v. Tompkins*, 304 U.S. 64, 78 (1938).

71

power (between different branches of government as well as between the federal and state government). Rules laying out parameters of a court's authority wrestle with balancing fairness to the litigants and preserving the structure of the legal system and, in America, the federal structure of government.

One parameter of any court's power is the subject matter it is authorized to hear. In the United States, states vie with other states and with the federal government on jurisdiction and choice of law questions. Classes of litigants in this power battle have tried both to shape and use jurisdictional choices to enhance their overall strategic advantage in the litigation. Concerns with distribution of power between the state and the federal government pervade subject matter jurisdiction rules for the federal courts in the United States.

Courts are further constrained by personal jurisdiction rules — rules that prescribe when a court can assert power over the person, thing, or relationship at issue to adjudicate the dispute. Unlike other countries, American personal jurisdiction rules (and subject matter jurisdiction rules) flow from the Constitution. Our litigation process has codified concepts of fairness as a constitutional right in the Due Process Clause of the Fourteenth Amendment of the United States Constitution. Protecting a defendant's due process right as well as protecting the sovereignty of individual states lies at the heart of the personal jurisdiction doctrine. Insisting that litigants have the right to be notified and to be heard as a constitutional due process right, even as against the state, lies at the heart of our "notice" requirement.

Imagine you are an American lawyer talking to a potential client about a grievance, such as a broken contract, employment discrimination, or medical misdiagnosis. What must you consider before commencing suit? There are a few obvious issues: Did the client tell a story that can be translated into a known cause of action, could this be quickly settled out of court without litigation, and how will you (the lawyer) get paid? Less obvious perhaps are the questions relating to where suit must be brought and other jurisdictional choices that must be confronted early on.

One way to understand these jurisdictional prerequisites may be to think in terms of a game with four squares on it, squares that must be appropriately filled in to succeed at this game. In this game, unlike bingo or monopoly, the squares are not filled by random selection. The lawyers make calculated choices, trying to optimize the odds of victory for their clients. The four squares are: "personal jurisdiction" (judicial power over people and things); "notice" (usually through service of process); "subject matter jurisdiction" (judicial power to hear the subject matter of the dispute); and "venue" (which of the courts with subject matter and personal jurisdiction bears the most sensible relationship to the claims asserted or to the parties and hence, should hear the claim). The plaintiff's lawyer normally has to correctly satisfy all four squares in order to commence her suit. Every American lawyer learns, or at least is taught, how to fill in all four squares during the first year civil procedure course.

Each of these four prerequisites relies on geography — that is, the lawyer must get something accomplished in a permissible location. And because the United States is such a large country, geography can make a big difference to the litigants. After all, it is as far from Boston, Massachusetts on the east coast of the United States to Los Angeles, California on the west coast as from Boston to Dublin, Ireland. A related geographic dimension is provided by the United

States federal system of government. Modern technology may reduce the sense of distance and lead one into the false sense that state boundaries are unimportant. But in civil litigation, the boundaries between states often take on deep significance, as does the less tangible boundary between all of the states and the federal government. Although the four squares in the above game share a geographic element, it is very important, in order to understand these prerequisites, to treat each of them as a separate compartment of knowledge.

PERSONAL JURISDICTION: JURISDICTION OVER PEOPLE AND THINGS

As a lawyer for a potential plaintiff in a lawsuit, you want to make sure that you can force the potential defendant to answer to suit in a court that has the power to bind the defendant by the judgment. The American lawyer would say that she has to make sure that she (or actually the court she has filed in) has "personal jurisdiction," often called *in personam* jurisdiction, as against the defendant or at least some kind of jurisdiction as against the defendant's property. This simply means that the court must have power over the person, thing, or relationship[3] at issue to adjudicate the dispute.

If personal jurisdiction exists in the forum state, then the case may be tried in that state, and the judgment issued will be respected, enforced, given "full faith and credit" by every other state in the union. If the plaintiff's lawyer is unable to achieve personal jurisdiction over the defendant or her property in the lawyer's home state, the lawyer will usually have to recommend that the potential plaintiff client sue in a state that does have personal jurisdiction over the defendant or the property. Usually, this will also mean finding a new lawyer in the other state. Most lawyers ordinarily practice law only in a state in which they have passed a bar exam and been formally admitted into practice by the supreme court of that state, and absent special permission, they can only represent clients in that state.

American personal jurisdiction jurisprudence has its roots in the due process of the Constitution. This is unlike civil law European countries, in which personal jurisdiction is prescribed by statutory provisions that specify precisely the factual conditions for finding personal jurisdiction — such as where the contract was formed or the place of the harm. By contrast, the United States courts applied the Constitution and developed more amorphous requirements such as "minimum contacts with the forum state," and "traditional notions of fair play and substantive justice" in determining the limits of a court's personal jurisdiction reach.

The earliest foundation case for personal jurisdiction is *Pennoyer v. Neff*,[4] decided by the U.S. Supreme Court in 1877.[5] *Pennoyer* was a case challenging the enforcement of a judgment obtained in a prior litigation. In the prior lawsuit,

3. There are a group of jurisdiction cases called "status" cases in which it is the site of the relationship, such as marriage, adoption, or guardianship that permits the forum state to have personal jurisdiction.
4. 95 U.S. 714 (1877).
5. The majority opinion was authored by Justice Stephen Field, a younger brother of David Dudley Field, author of the Field Code reforms to civil procedure discussed in Chapter Three.

Mitchell v. Neff, John Mitchell, a lawyer, obtained a default judgment against Marcus Neff in a state court in Oregon. Neff, who had moved to California, was never served with a complaint in Oregon nor was he ever actually notified of the commencement of suit. Not surprisingly, Neff did not answer the complaint and a default judgment was awarded against him. Armed with the judgment, Mitchell sought to enforce the judgment by "attaching" land in Oregon that was acquired by Neff after the commencement of the lawsuit and selling the land in a sheriff's sale; Pennoyer was the eventual buyer. To gain back the land, Neff sued Pennoyer in a federal trial court in Oregon, claiming that the sale of his land was invalid because the underlying judgment was invalid. Neff won and the case made its way to the U.S. Supreme Court and laid the basis for over a hundred years of Supreme Court opinions on personal jurisdiction.

For the majority, Justice Field spelled out three conditions for a court to render power over a defendant quasi in rem, in rem, and in personam. First, if Neff had in fact owned the land at the time of commencement of the prior suit and the land had been so attached, this would have given the Oregon trial court what is known as *quasi in rem* jurisdiction — jurisdiction based on the attached land, even though the land was not the subject of the litigation. Quasi in rem jurisdiction, now a defunct concept, would have given the court jurisdiction to determine a defendant's personal rights through assertion of jurisdiction over his property. If the land were the reason for the initial litigation between Mitchell and Neff, then the court would have what is called *in rem* jurisdiction over the land.

The Supreme Court also reasoned that the Oregon courts did not have *in personam* power over Neff at the time of the initial litigation. Neff was not a resident[6] of Oregon when the case was commenced, nor was he served in hand with court papers in Oregon at the beginning of the case, nor did he consent to the jurisdiction of the court. Any one of these possibilities would have permitted an Oregon court to exercise jurisdiction over Neff. In their absence, the Oregon trial court did not have what is called *in personam* or personal jurisdiction over him. Therefore, the initial lawsuit between Mitchell and Neff was a nullity, and Mitchell had no valid judgment to enforce.

Two parts of the majority opinion influenced law in this area to this day. First, the opinion emphasized ancient notions of geographic boundaries, explaining that each state still retains some aspects of sovereignty within its territorial boundaries. This understanding of jurisdiction seems to have been derived from ancient notions of feudalism. Whoever ultimately owns real estate, such as the King, has jurisdiction over what is found physically within or on that real estate. If at the commencement of the suit, Neff was in Oregon and served with court papers in Oregon or the land he owned there was put under the control of the court at the commencement of the first litigation, the Oregon court would have had valid jurisdiction over Neff or his property to render a judgment against it.

Second, the majority cited to the then-new Due Process Clause of the Fourteenth Amendment of the United States Constitution, which protects the "privileges and immunities of citizens of the United States" and also states:

---

6. American courts usually define "resident" for this purpose in terms of the "domicile" or "citizenship" of the individual defendant. Domicile is usually interpreted for this purpose as the place in which the person resides with the intent to remain for the indefinite future. A law student or vacationer may reside in a state without being a domiciliary of the state.

"nor shall any State deprive any person of life, liberty, or property without due process of law."[7] Personal jurisdiction statutes enacted by the states must meet the Due Process Clause commands. American courts today routinely measure personal jurisdiction statutes enacted by forum states against the Due Process Clause of the Constitution. Such statutes are deemed unconstitutional if they go beyond what is permitted by due process.

Finally, the United States Constitution preserves the sovereignty of state governments by enforcing Article IV, Section I, which provides: "Full Faith and Credit shall be given in each State to the public Acts, Records, and judicial Proceedings of every state." The *Pennoyer* opinion recognizes that a judgment from a trial court in one state may be negated in a court in another state or in federal court, but only if the first court's exercise of jurisdiction exceeded its permissible reach under the Due Process Clause. In effect, fairness considerations of the Due Process Clause are joined with sovereignty considerations of the "Full Faith and Credit" clause of the Constitution.

Considerations of federalism also underlie the *Pennoyer* opinion. While each state is held to have retained a portion of its sovereignty prior to joining the Union of states and is not permitted to interfere with the sovereignty of the other 49 states,[8] *Pennoyer* stands for the proposition that all courts (state as well as federal) must follow what the federal Constitution dictates. In personal jurisdiction disputes, the United States Supreme Court must consider the balance of power between the states, as well as questions of fairness and due process rights to the defendant.

After *Pennoyer v. Neff*, probably the other most important case in this area of law is *International Shoe Co. v. Washington*.[9] *International Shoe* dealt with the question of how to handle personal jurisdiction over corporations, and in the process, laid the foundation for modern day personal jurisdiction concepts. Corporations are unlike people in the sense that their presence is manifest through their business activities, which can extend their physical presence to many states. *Pennoyer v. Neff* and its progeny, based on a "physical presence" conception of jurisdiction, had said that if a person is physically found and served in hand within a forum state, then his physical presence in the forum state could serve as the basis for assertion of personal jurisdiction by that state. Yet when is a corporation sufficiently present in the forum state by virtue of its doing business there? The courts had no trouble finding jurisdiction when the corporation was incorporated or maintained its principal place of business in the forum state. It was instances in which a

---

7. U.S. Const., Amend. XIV, § 1. The Fifth Amendment has similar language forbidding the United States from committing such deprivations without affording due process.

8. For those cases that are commenced in federal court, Congress could grant a much broader scope for reaching nonresident defendants in the forum state than is afforded the state courts, because the federal courts are part of the national government. Congress has chosen to do this in some instances, but Congress has normally made the reach of personal jurisdiction subject to the law of the state in which the federal court sits. When Congress chooses to reach further, there is still the limit of the Fifth Amendment Due Process Clause; there is very little law on this, but most commentators think that the Fifth Amendment Due Process Clause as applied to personal jurisdiction is a good deal narrower than when the Fourteenth Amendment is applied to the states; in other words, Congress could probably mandate a broad reach that spans beyond an individual state without violating the Constitution.

9. 326 U.S. 310 (1945).

corporation was incorporated and had its principal place of business in some other state but did a little business in and was sued in the forum state that gave courts reason to pause.

In *International Shoe*, the State of Washington passed a statute taxing employers for contributions to an unemployment compensation fund[10] if such employers had employees in Washington. Pursant to the statute, the state of Washington can bring suit against out-of-state employer corporations to collect the tax, by serving the employer with process by certified mail. The International Shoe Company was incorporated in Delaware and had a principal place of business in St. Louis, Missouri. It had no manufacturing plants in Washington but it did have 13 salesmen in Washington, who were supervised from St. Louis. These employees had no authority to finalize sales or make contracts in Washington.

The State of Washington sued International Shoe in Washington state court to collect the tax. In response, International Shoe raised several defenses, including the defense of lack of personal jurisdiction. The case made its way to the U.S. Supreme Court. In finding *in personam* jurisdiction, the unanimous opinion of the Supreme Court declared that courts could no longer engage in fictions such as pretending that corporations are physically present in the forum state in the same manner that humans are present. Instead, "[w]hether due process is satisfied must depend rather upon the quality and nature of the activity in relation to the fair and orderly administration of the laws which it was the purpose of the due process clause to insure."[11] Due process, the Court held, requires that an absent defendant, such as International Shoe, have such "minimum contacts" with the forum state that the jurisdiction in the forum state's court does not offend "traditional notions of fair play and substantial justice." The "minimum contacts" test, as amorphous as it is, has remained the test to this day.

The Supreme Court in *International Shoe* did provide some guidance in laying out a spectrum of contacts that would satisfy this test. It said that the strongest case for personal jurisdiction is when the cause of action sued upon arises out of defendant's activity in the forum state and when such activities of the corporation in the forum state have been "continuous and systematic" and "substantial." The weakest and constitutionally unjustified case for jurisdiction is when there is only a little defendant activity in the forum state and the cause of action is unrelated to that activity. But the forum state could also find personal jurisdiction if the defendant activity in the forum state (even if the activity is a single occurrence) gives rise to the cause of action or if the defendant does so much in the forum state (continuous, systematic, substantial activity) that it can be sued there on an unrelated cause of action.

After *International Shoe*, most states passed personal jurisdiction statutes, called "long-arm statutes" reaching out to nonresident defendants whose activity in the forum state gave rise to the alleged cause of action in the lawsuit. An example would be a Texan driving negligently in the state of Arizona and thereby causing harm in Arizona. Even if the Texan never returns to Arizona,

---

10. Unemployment compensation funds give money for a limited period to employees who have lost their job through no fault of their own.

11. *International Shoe*, 326 U.S. at 319.

the person injured in Arizona could sue the Texas driver in Arizona under such a statute. Such jurisdiction is called "specific jurisdiction," because the jurisdiction is only for the cause of action specific to the activity in the forum state.

More problematic are the cases in which the defendant's alleged tortuous activity is outside the forum state, but the impact or harm is within the forum state (e.g., the boiler manufactured in State A blows up in the forum state, State B). Some members of the Supreme Court believe that the manufacturer has to have done something else in addition to just putting the manufactured goods into the stream of commerce before the forum state can assert specific jurisdiction over the defendant.

If the jurisdiction is based on a corporation doing so much business in the forum state (persistent, systematic, substantial) that the defendant can be sued on an unrelated cause of action, this category has been called "general jurisdiction." A majority of the court believes that in such cases one does not have to analyze whether the cause of action is related to activity in the forum state. General jurisdiction in the context of personal jurisdiction means that a court has power over the defendant to adjudicate any lawsuit against him. Traditional methods of asserting personal jurisdiction also suffice for general jurisdiction, such as service on individuals while they are in the forum state or because the defendant resides, is incorporated, or has consented to be sued in the forum state. Most states have passed statutes that spell out the basis for general personal jurisdictional, in addition to specific jurisdiction.

The field of personal jurisdiction law has remained convoluted in the United States. Because human beings can engage in so many different types of activity with such variations of relationships to a forum state, lawyers frequently can make plausible arguments for or against personal jurisdiction based on fairness grounds and/or state sovereignty arguments. Rather than spelling out a state's own requirements for personal jurisdiction (permissible so long as they are within the parameters of the federal constitution), some states have passed long-arm statutes that merely say that the state chooses to reach out to nonresident defendants to the extent permitted by the United States Constitution. This renders every personal jurisdiction case a matter of constitutional due process law.

To further compound the confusion, the Supreme Court has not been altogether consistent in this area. One recent rendition of the "minimum contacts" and "traditional notions of fair play and substantial justice" test resurrected traditional notions of "physical presence." It held that service of process on a defendant on a brief visit to the forum state is sufficient to give constitutional personal jurisdiction to the forum state over the visitor, even on a claim unrelated to the purpose of the in-state visit. [12] At the same time, the Supreme Court has also held that a pure quasi in rem case, that is, "physical presence" of property in the forum state, is insufficient to serve as basis for personal jurisdiction over a defendant for a cause of action unrelated to the property. [13]

---

12. *Burnham v. Superior Court of California*, 495 U.S. 604 (1990).
13. *Shaffer v. Heitner*, 433 U.S. 186 (1977).

Finally, in a case called *Asahi*, involving a manufacturer from abroad whose valve allegedly caused harm in California, eight of nine Supreme Court Justices held that in some cases, even if there are sufficient minimum contacts under the usual tests, a defendant can successfully defeat jurisdiction. The defendant can ask the court to weigh the interests of the plaintiff, the defendant, the forum state, and interstate policies of judicial administration and law application, and find that personal jurisdiction fails. [14] But the unique facts of the *Asahi* case (only foreign corporations remained in the suit by the time the appeal had reached the Supreme Court), rendered its future applicability questionable.

Reflecting the mood of the country to limit litigation (see Chapters 2 and 3), the Supreme Court has also upheld "forum selection clauses" in contracts in which the parties pre-select a single forum where a law suit can be brought. This was true in the case of *Carnival Cruise Lines, Inc. v. Shute*, [15] even though the defendant corporation had total control over the wording of the "forum selection clause," the plaintiff could not negotiate with respect to it, the forum selection was in small print, and the plaintiff had not read the clause. Dissenting Justices, as well as legal commentators, thought this was grossly unfair to unsuspecting consumer plaintiffs. It was, they thought, insensitive to the unequal bargaining power of the respective parties and disregarded the public interest in deterring negligent conduct.

As a final note, in order to maintain consistency within the legal system, federal courts are usually obligated to follow the personal jurisdiction statutes of the state in which the court sits. While federal courts differ from state courts regarding subject matter jurisdiction, they match state courts in the area of personal jurisdiction. Apart from certain kinds of federal subject matter cases (for example, antitrust), federal courts will have the same personal jurisdiction reach as the state courts in that state. For example, Massachusetts federal court would usually have the same personal jurisdiction reach as Massachusetts state courts.

Think once again about the *Cherryum* case that we described in Chapter 4. You, the plaintiff's lawyer, decide that you want to bring the case in the Federal District Court for Massachusetts. That court, applying Federal Rule of Civil Procedure 4(k)(1)(A), would look to the Massachusetts long-arm statute and any other relevant Massachusetts personal jurisdiction statutes in order to see whether Albert Lee and his wife, as plaintiffs, could get personal jurisdiction in Massachusetts over Cherryum, Inc., the manufacturer of the soft drink in question, and Cherryum Bottling Company, the bottler of the drink. Both of these corporations were incorporated outside of Massachusetts and had their principal places of business outside of Massachusetts. Had they been Massachusetts corporations, Massachusetts courts would have easily obtained personal jurisdiction over these defendants; the corporations would have been treated like ordinary people who live in Massachusetts.

Massachusetts has a typical long-arm statute permitting jurisdiction, if among other grounds, the cause of action arises out of the defendant's

---

14. *Asahi Metal Industry Co., Ltd. v. Superior Court of California, Solano Country*, 480 U.S. 102 (1987).
    15. 499 U.S. 585 (1991).

transaction in the forum state or commission of a tort in the forum state. The statute also permits jurisdiction over a defendant whose tortuous activity outside the state caused injury to a person within the state if the defendant also engages in a persistent course of conduct or derives substantial revenue from goods consumed in the state.[16] Using this "specific jurisdiction" statute, the plaintiff Lees could undoubtedly get specific personal jurisdiction in Massachusetts over the two foreign corporations because of the alleged negligent manufacturing or bottling outside of Massachusetts resulting in injury to the Lees in Massachusetts; and because defendant corporations derive substantial revenue from large amounts of Cherryum consumed in Massachusetts.

It is also possible that Cherryum, Inc., and Cherryum Bottling Company had so many of their drinks sold in Massachusetts that the court would consider the corporations' activities to be continuous, systematic, and substantial in Massachusetts. This would give the court general personal jurisdiction, within the meaning of *International Shoe,* regardless of where the injury occurred. In that case, the court would probably rely on an older Massachusetts statute subjecting corporations to personal jurisdiction in Massachusetts for "doing business" within the state.

To contest a court's assertion of personal jurisdiction, the defendant has some options. The most risky is to default (fail to appear) in a forum state court and later attack the validity of an adverse judgment in a subsequent action to enforce the judgment in another state. This is called a "collateral attack." By not protesting a lack of personal jurisdiction in the initial case and instead relying on a collateral attack, the defendant is taking a huge chance. If the second court finds that the first court had jurisdiction over the defendant, the defendant will not then be able to put in evidence on the merits and will be bound by the first verdict. The defendant can also directly challenge jurisdiction in the initial case by raising the defense in her answer or pre-answer motion. This is called a "direct attack." If the defendant loses on that issue, she can still defend the underlying merits of the claim. A defendant will be deemed to have waived the "lack of personal jurisdiction" defense if she did not raise the issue in either her answer or pre-answer motion.

You might well wonder why this issue of personal jurisdiction is so important to litigants and why the Supreme Court has had such limited success in providing clarification. The lack of clarification by the Court may be a function of the diverse goals of fairness, predictability, and state sovereignty, as well as the multiplicity of potential fact patterns that resist classification. "Due process," like fairness, is itself a bit amorphous and it is difficult to know in advance how to apply it in complicated cases.

It is easier to ascertain why personal jurisdiction is so important to the litigants. It is considerably more convenient to try a case in one's home state than having to travel to another state and find a lawyer who practices there. It is also easier to be closer to home in conducting pretrial discovery and in showing up for trial, if that becomes necessary. One's lawyer will be more

---

16. The court does not make the plaintiff prove the tort in deciding this jurisdictional issue; a good faith allegation suffices. Otherwise, personal jurisdiction would depend on first proving the merits of the case.

familiar with the judges and their practices in her own state, and there may be a "home court" bias on the part of judges and juries. Perhaps most importantly, particularly in large litigation, plaintiffs' lawyers seek to sue defendants in a state with more favorable substantive law. Although "conflicts of law" doctrine dictates what law to apply, the forum court judge, when in doubt, is more likely to end up applying her own state's law. The fact that such law may be favorable to the plaintiff is exactly what the plaintiff's lawyer may be seeking in choosing a particular forum, even if the defendant has very little contact or relationship with that forum state.

It is this type of "forum shopping" that many foreign countries and their legal commentators find offensive in the American law of personal jurisdiction. Applied in transnational litigation, the American "minimum contacts" test and the concept of general personal jurisdiction places the American legal system apart in the breadth of choice it offers plaintiffs as compared to other countries' personal jurisdiction laws. This has resulted in acrimonious accusations of American domination because it allows American courts to adjudicate claims against foreign corporations based on very little contact on American soil.[17]

One foreign model, the European Convention on Jurisdiction and the Enforcement of Judgments (known as the Brussels Convention), applies to suits between domiciliaries of the original Common Market countries. A European Court of Justice provides rulings when cases fall within this Convention. The Lugano Convention adopted the same jurisdictional and enforcement provisions for member states of the European Free Trade Association, but without review by the European Court of Justice.[18] A primary goal of the Brussels and the Lugano Conventions is to limit the number of potential forum countries for any given lawsuit.

By contrast to the American court's focus on due process and the relationship of the defendant to the forum state, these European conventions tend to look at the relationship of the dispute to the forum country. American courts tend to ask what the defendant has done to bring itself into the forum state (such as, did it seek benefits from the forum state?). The European Conventions concentrate on what aspects of the transaction or occurrence in question happened in the forum state. As a result, European lawyers find our "tag" jurisdiction (jurisdiction based solely on serving the defendant in the forum state) offensive, and also object to the "doing enough business in the forum state to permit general jurisdiction" category in *International Shoe*.[19] Note that each of these American bases of jurisdiction adds unpredictability to the process, as a defendant can be served in any of the 50 states in which he is found, resulting in the possibility of personal jurisdiction asserted by any of the

17. Article 17 of the Hague Draft Convention does not acknowledge specific jurisdiction based on transacting business as a ground of jurisdiction. Rather, it is included within the so-called grey list of Article 17. Peter Gottwald, *Jurisdiction Based on 'Business Activities' in the Hague Draft Convention on Jurisdiction and Foreign Judgments in Civil and Commercial Matters*, 4 Eur. J. L. Reform 199-217 (2002).

18. For a good brief description of the European jurisdictional law, see Linda J. Silberman & Allan R. Stein, Civil Procedure: Theory and Practice 213-216 (Aspen 2001).

19. The Hague Draft Convention of October 30, 1999, Article 18(e) excludes jurisdictional basis solely of commercial or other activities of the defendant in the forum state, except where the dispute is directly related to such proceedings. *See* Gottwald, *supra* note 17.

50 states. It is this unpredictability and forum shopping that the Europeans are seeking to limit.[20]

DUE PROCESS NOTICE AND SERVICE OF PROCESS

The Due Process Clause of the Fourteenth Amendment puts limitations on how far a state can reach in binding out-of-state defendants.[21] But the Due Process Clause also requires fair "notice" to the defendant so that the defendant knows of the litigation and is given an opportunity to "be heard," before judgment is rendered. Appropriate notice is usually fulfilled by properly serving process papers (a complaint and summons, which tells the defendant where and by when to answer the complaint) on the defendant, physically in his hand, leaving it at his home, or mailing it to him.

At the time of *Pennoyer v. Neff,* notice was typically satisfied by the "physical presence" of either defendant's person or thing in the forum state. At the time, the typical way to commence suit was to serve the defendant, while he was in the forum state, in hand with the requisite court papers. Consequently, the basis of personal jurisdiction, service in hand while the defendant was physically present in the forum state, overlapped with notice to the defendant. The defendant automatically receives notice at the same time jurisdiction is asserted. In such a way, *Pennoyer* conflated the requirements of personal jurisdiction and notice.

Subsequent to *Pennoyer,* however, the Supreme Court has made clear that the due process underpinnings of personal jurisdiction and notice to the defendant are quite distinct. With *International Shoe* and the "minimum contacts" test — that is, whether the defendant or the defendant's property has a sufficient due process nexus with the forum state, courts may assert power over out of state defendants not physically in the forum state. Personal jurisdiction evolved into a quite different issue from whether the defendant has been fairly notified of the commencement of suit.

Notice as a separate constitutional requirement rests on the Supreme Court case *Mullane v. Central Hanover Bank & Trust Co.*[22] Written by Justice Robert Jackson, one of the last Supreme Court Justice to be trained by the apprentice method in a law office and a former chief counsel for the United States at the

20. In some respects, the European Conventions and the law of individual European countries expand the reach of personal jurisdiction beyond what is permitted by the American due process clause. It is the multiple choices given American plaintiffs and what is perceived as pro-plaintiff substantive law that troubles Europeans. *See, e.g.,* Linda Silberman, *Comparative Jurisdiction in the International Contest: Will the Proposed Hague Judgments Convention be Stalled,* 52 DePaul L. Rev. 319, 320, 322 (Winter 2002).

21. The idea of "due process of law" stems from the Magna Carta, enacted in 1215 by King John of England while under duress from rebellious nobles. Chapter 39 of the Magna Carta states: "No free man shall be taken, imprisoned, disseised, outlawed, exiled, or in any way destroyed, nor will We proceed against or prosecute him, except by the lawful judgment of his peers and by the *law of the land.*" In 1354, the English Parliament used the phrase "due process of law" for the first time in interpreting Chapter 39 of the Magna Carta. A.E. Dick Howard, Magna Carta Text and Commentary 43 (U. Press of Virginia 1964) (emphasis added). For the American colonists reliance on rights based on the Magna Carta, *see* Sources of our Liberties 17 (Richard L. Perry ed., American Bar Foundation 1959).

22. 339 U.S. 306 (1950).

Nuremberg criminal trials of Nazi war criminals after WWII, the *Mullane* opinion challenges the practical as well as the philosophical.[23] Jackson was known for his down-to-earth, practical views of life, law, and decision making.

In *Mullane*, beneficiaries of a common trust fund (similar to today's mutual funds that pool assets for investment) challenged the notice provided by the bank of its accounting process. The New York statute required that in the event of an accounting, the bank must publish a notice for four consecutive weeks in a newspaper designated by the court. The notice, according to the statute, "may" name the estates, trusts, or funds that had deposited funds with the common bank fund. The newspaper notice actually provided in the *Mullane* case, however, did not in fact list the names of the donors and beneficiaries of the smaller funds. The Surrogate's Court of New York, to which the Bank had petitioned for an accounting, appointed Mullane as a guardian and attorney to protect the beneficiaries of smaller funds who were entitled to receive income from the property invested in the common trust fund accounts.

Mullane raised two objections to the process. One was the failure of due process notice to the income beneficiaries who would be affected, a topic to which we will soon turn. The other objection was to a lack of "jurisdiction of people or things.[24] What the *Mullane* case has become more known for is the due process obligation to notify those parties who will be bound by the decision so that they have an opportunity to be heard.

In setting out the appropriate guidelines, Justice Jackson applied his common sense and practical wisdom to explain how notice was to be given. Many of the beneficiaries who would be bound by the decision were unknown to the bank. Trust instruments frequently provide for different beneficiaries at different times; for instance, births, marriage, or reaching the age of 21 may result in a new set of beneficiaries unbeknownst to the bank. This, however, did not excuse the bank from giving actual notice to those beneficiaries whose names and addresses it did know. Jackson reasoned that as long as the known beneficiaries were realistically notified, they could be expected to represent and protect the interests of those who were not, because those notified were similar in motivation and knowledge as the others.

What Justice Jackson made clear was that perfunctory notice, such as an ad in a newspaper, does not pass due process muster when there are known people with known addresses who will be bound by the judgment; they must be given notice that is likely to actually reach them:

> An elementary and fundamental requirement of due process in any
> proceeding which is to be accorded finality is notice reasonably calculated,

23. He did attend Albany Law School for one year. The Oxford Companion to the Supreme Court of the United States 443 (Kermit L. Hall ed., Oxford U. Press 1992).

24. As to the personal jurisdiction issue, Justice Jackson could not figure out how the case fit any known category of jurisdiction. But he decided, in his typically pragmatic way, that it did not matter that the case did not perfectly fit any of the known categories of personal or in rem jurisdiction; it was obvious to him that New York was the state most suitable to administer periodic accountings and to patrol the activity of its own Bank. Courts in no other state could constitutionally assert jurisdiction over all of the beneficiaries. Some commentators think that perhaps Justice Jackson found a new basis for jurisdiction: necessity. *See* 339 U.S. 306. There are occasional cases when one state has the most connection, although attenuated, with all those who will be bound by the decision.

under all the circumstances, to apprise interested parties of the pendency of the action and afford them an opportunity to present their objections.[25]

Reasonableness is the key, and in the circumstances of this case, Justice Jackson could "find no tenable ground for dispensing with a serious effort to inform [the known beneficiaries] personally of the accounting, at least by ordinary mail to the record addresses."[26] Of course, the notice can be accomplished by other means than the mail. In a typical case, if the defendant is found in the forum state, he or she can be notified the old fashioned way, by having him or her served with a complaint and summons.[27]

In the *Cherryum* case, you would have no trouble providing constitutional due process notice to the two corporate defendants. Massachusetts, like most states, would undoubtedly have some kind of "doing business" statute requiring out-of-state corporations to register within the state and to list an address where they could be served with process either within the state or through mail delivery in their own state.[28] Moreover, the long-arm statute would also include notice provisions, permitting, among other methods, certified mail notice to the offices of each corporate defendant.[29] Each of these methods provides actual notice to the defendants in keeping with the constitutionally mandated requirement of *Mullane*.

Why are notice and the right to be heard the keystones of procedural due process? As we saw in Chapter 2, American procedure assumes that the self-interest of parties acting in an adversary system will come closer to successful law and fact ascertainment than other systems. In order to gain such party participation, those to be bound by the decision have to be notified and given a chance to be heard. Due process protects this right.

But it is not simply the actual benefits in fact and law ascertainment that come from notice and the right to be heard. Supreme Court justices have pointed out the importance of both the reality and the perception of fairness. Justice Felix Frankfurter put it this way:

> No better instrument has been devised for arriving at truth than to give a person in jeopardy of serious loss notice of the case against him and opportunity to meet it. Nor has a better way been found for generating the feeling, so important to a popular government, that justice has been done.[30]

25. *Id.* at 314-315 (internal citations omitted).
26. *Id.* at 318.
27. Fed. R. Civ. P. 4(d) provides an elaborate scheme for federal court cases by which the plaintiff can seek a waiver of the need to give formal notice from the defendant. Under some circumstances, if the waiver is not given, the defendant will have to pay the cost of more formal service.
28. For this obligation, as well as others imposed on foreign corporations, *see* M.G.L. c. 181, § 4 (2004). For requirements regarding service of process to foreign corporations, *see* M.G.L. c. 181, § 15 (2004).
29. The Massachusetts long-arm statute can be found at M.G.L. c. 223A, § 3 (2004).
30. *Joint Anti-Fascist Refugee Committee v. McGrath*, 341 U.S. 123, 171-172 (1951) (Frankfurter, J., concurring). The case arose when the Attorney General labeled several charitable organizations "Communist" and furnished their names to the Loyalty Review Board of the United States Civil Service Commission. The charities that were not given due process notice and the right to be heard alleged harm, including diminution in contributions and membership and loss of tax-exempt status.

As Frankfurter writes, "generating the feeling...that justice has been done" also underlies the Due Process Clause. In a democracy, it is critical that individuals be afforded the sense of individual dignity and autonomy. For a legal process to be considered legitimate, such that its judgments will be obeyed, process should be provided to those who will be bound by the judgment. Empirical data and literature in the United States, broadly covered by the label "procedural justice," have demonstrated the importance parties place on having a realistic chance to be heard, either themselves or through their chosen representative; otherwise, they feel unjustly treated.[31]

The idea of "due process" received added impetus with the 1960s and 1970s civil rights movement (also known as the "due process revolution"). During this period, plaintiffs, unable to secure government social benefits as a constitutional right, took the procedural route to complain that the government, acting through officials, courts, or agencies, could not constitutionally take these social benefits away from them without first giving notice and the right to be heard. Repeatedly during this period, the Supreme Court held that due process notice and the right to be heard had to be given prior to the deprivation of these rights. The Due Process Clause, which provides that the state cannot deprive one of property without due process of law, was held to mean that when there was a legally protected expectancy in one's right to such social or welfare benefits, the government could not terminate absent the constitutional due process protections. In such a way, the definition of property and procedural safeguards are inextricably linked.[32]

SUBJECT MATTER JURISDICTION

A plaintiff's lawyer who is thinking about commencing litigation in an American court has now considered two of the four criteria: personal jurisdiction and notice or service of process. The lawyer still has to consider in which particular court to commence suit. There will be many state courts in the state in question, and there will also be at least one federal court in that state. This issue of picking a court that will have jurisdiction to hear the particular type of case in question is called "subject matter jurisdiction."

In the *Cherryum* case, the Lees, Massachusetts citizens, want to sue the manufacturer and the bottler of Cherryum, out-of-state corporations, for their negligence, causing harm in Massachusetts. As we have seen, you, as their lawyer, could commence suit in Massachusetts on the theory of specific

31. For a good review of the procedural justice literature, *see* Nancy A. Welsh, *Making Deals in Court-Connected Mediation: What's Justice Got to Do With It?*, 79 Wash. U. L.Q. 787, 820-830 (Fall 2001).

32. One of the authors of this book and his then-student, wrote about this due process revolution and the connection between property and due process protection in Stephen N. Subrin & A. Richard Dykstra, *Notice and the Right to be Heard, The Significance of Old Friends*, 9 Harv. C.R.-C.L. L. Rev. 449 (1974). The Supreme Court has in some cases applied a balancing test, including the cost to the government, in determining whether due process requires a pretermination hearing. *See, e.g., Mathews, Secretary of Health, Education and Welfare v. Eldridge*, 424 U.S. 319 (1976).

personal jurisdiction; you might also achieve general personal jurisdiction. Either way, Cherryum, Inc., and Cherryum Bottling Company are subject to suit in Massachusetts.

Massachusetts has several state courts and a federal district court. The Lees could sue in a state court or, as you will later see, in the federal court based on diversity of citizenship subject matter jurisdiction. This is because the plaintiffs and the defendants are citizens of different states and the amount in controversy is in excess of $75,000. If the Lees wish to remain in the state court system, they could bring their claims to the Massachusetts state trial courts; because the stakes are large and they probably want a jury, they would probably bring the case in Massachusetts Superior Court.[33] If the case involved title to land, they could bring it in Massachusetts land court. If it involved marriage, divorce, guardianship, or the probating of a will, they would ordinarily bring the case to Massachusetts probate court.

The trial court in Massachusetts (called the superior court) is called a court of "general subject matter jurisdiction"; it can hear almost every type of case. Other state courts, such as the land court and probate court, are called courts of "limited subject matter jurisdiction." They can hear only cases of a limited type as prescribed either in the state constitution or legislative enactments.

The trial courts at the federal level are called federal district courts. Each state has at least one federal district court, and some large states have as many as four. Federal district courts are also courts of limited subject matter jurisdiction; that is, they can only hear disputes involving selected people or subjects that the U.S. Congress permits them to hear. By contrast, state courts have "general subject matter jurisdiction" and can hear even federal matters unless the U.S. Congress gave exclusive jurisdiction to hear the matter to the federal courts, such as bankruptcy, copyright, or patent cases. In most lawsuits that can be heard by a federal district court, then, there is concurrent jurisdiction with a state court of general jurisdiction. The plaintiff's lawyer in such cases, as in the *Cherryum* case, has her choice of state or federal court.

In order to understand what types of cases the federal district courts are permitted to hear it makes sense to return once again to the founding of our country and issues of federalism. The nationalists (later called Federalists), primarily from the larger states, wanted a strong federal government with a separate, independent federal judiciary that would decide all cases involving federal law. The anti-Federalists (later called Republicans or Jeffersonians), often from smaller states, feared a large federal government and argued against the expense of a federal trial court system and proposed that all trials could commence and be heard locally in state trial courts. Both sides agreed that a supreme court was needed to decide some cases, particularly those cases involving conflicts between two or more states or between a state and other nations. Their compromise was to establish a United States Supreme Court, but to give the United States Congress, in Article III of the Constitution, the power to establish a system of lower federal courts, which could, if Congress so decided, hear a limited number of kinds of cases.

---

33. Massachusetts has recently passed a statute allowing the state district courts to utilize juries in 2004 (M.G.L. c. 218 § 19B) but it is in our opinion that a case with severe injuries and potentially large damages will likely still be brought in superior court (the level of state court above the district courts).

Article III, Section 2 of the Constitution describes two general types of cases that if lower federal courts are established, can be heard by those courts to the extent Congress permits. The first category describes jurisdiction based primarily on subject matter: cases arising under the federal constitution, laws, and treaties; cases affecting ambassadors, other public ministers, and consuls; and cases of admiralty and maritime jurisdiction. The second category describes jurisdiction based on party status: cases involving the United States as a party; controversies between two or more states; controversies between a state and citizens of another state; controversies between citizens of different states; controversies between citizens of the same state claiming lands under grants of different states; or controversies between a state or its citizens, and foreign states, citizens, or subjects.

Pursuant to Constitutional authorization, the first United States Congress passed the Judiciary Act of 1789,[34] establishing circuit and district courts; originally, district courts had trial jurisdiction and the circuit courts had both trial and appellate jurisdiction. The federal district courts subsequently became the federal courts of original or trial jurisdiction, with the circuit courts becoming predominantly the intermediate courts of appeal. The original circuit courts, now an anomaly, were to meet twice a year and be composed of one district court judge and two Supreme Court justices. Today, there are 13 different circuit courts of appeals and the U.S. Court of Appeal for the federal circuit, which hears appeals from specialized federal courts dealing with matters such as claims against the United States government, customs, and patents.

Initially, Congress chose not to give these trial courts the full breadth of subject matter jurisdiction as permitted by Article III. One surprising aspect of the First Judiciary Act was its failure to grant the new federal trial courts jurisdiction to hear cases arising out of the United States Constitution, Laws, and Treaties. It was not until 1875 that Congress granted the federal district courts subject matter jurisdiction over federal question cases, a topic we will return to later. Prior to 1875, cases involving federal questions were ordinarily heard first in state trial courts and only reached the Supreme Court of the United States after being ruled on by the state appeals courts, ordinarily the state supreme court.

DIVERSITY OF CITIZENSHIP

One of the first grants of subject matter jurisdiction to the new federal trial courts was jurisdiction over cases involving citizens of different states.[35] From the very beginning, this grant of what is called "diversity of citizenship jurisdiction" required that the litigation involve a minimum monetary

---

34. The Judiciary Act of 1789, 1 Stat. 73.
35. Initially, under the First Judiciary Act, this jurisdiction was limited to cases between a citizen of the forum state and a citizen of another state, but later Congress enlarged the grant to citizens of different states, even if none were citizens of the forum state.

amount, set initially at above $500 but increased today to "in excess of $75,000."[36]

Historians have been unable to recover much information about why Article III included diversity of citizenship jurisdiction as proper subject matter jurisdiction for federal courts. Probably the major reason for the inclusion of diversity jurisdiction was the quite realistic potential for local prejudice. The 13 colonies, later to become states, had their own lengthy histories, cultures, and different religious beliefs. A plaintiff from Boston, Massachusetts, could by no means feel assured of a fair hearing in Baltimore, Maryland. Moreover, the antagonism of many to Britain would mean that a British citizen might be exposed to extreme prejudice in a state court. Diversity jurisdiction included cases involving citizens and subjects of other countries. The founders must have assumed that a federal court with judges appointed through a federal process would provide a more level playing field than state courts in cases in which one or more of the parties were from out of state but another of the parties was a citizen of the forum state.[37]

A second reason for diversity jurisdiction involves a subset of the "fear of prejudice" rationale. Creditors would usually have to go to the state of the debtor, which could be another state, in order to sue to collect the debt. After the Revolutionary War, some of the states and their citizens reacted in an aggressively anti-creditor manner. Jurors in state courts often refused to enforce debt collection. The nationalists in particular thought it was vital that creditors be able to collect their debts, because the future of the country was dependent on the ability of the national government, states, and entrepreneurs to borrow money. Money would not be lent or lent only at prohibitive rates if collection through litigation was too risky. Finally, the Alien Tort Statute, enacted as part of the First Judiciary Act, permitted foreign citizens to sue in a federal trial court. The fear of prejudice to foreign creditors in state courts may have been another important consideration in the inclusion of diversity jurisdiction in Article III and in the decision of the first Congress to establish federal trial courts and to invest them with diversity jurisdiction.[38]

Yet, since its inception, diversity jurisdiction has been limited by both Congress and the federal courts. Congress has always included a necessary minimum monetary amount as a requisite for commencing a diversity case in a federal trial court. And in *Strawbridge v. Curtiss*,[39] decided in 1806, the Supreme Court interpreted the language "between a citizen of a state where the suit is brought, and a citizen of another state" to require "complete diversity" – that is, no plaintiffs can be of same citizenship as any of the defendants. Early Supreme Court decisions also excluded federal courts from

---

36. The grant of diversity jurisdiction is now found in 28 U.S.C. § 1332.

37. Also, under the First Judiciary Act, a decision in the federal district court in which the controversy exceeded $50 could be appealed to a circuit court. Circuit courts at the time were composed of a district court judge and two Supreme Court justices and were therefore likely to provide judges who were citizens of a variety of states.

38. It is true that in federal court a creditor could still have to deal with jurors, but other considerations meliorated against the potential prejudice: the jurors might come from a wider geographic area, the judges would more likely have a federal outlook, and the federal judges could use federal procedures to attempt to control the outcome.

39. 7 U.S. 267, 3 Cranch 267 (1806).

hearing cases involving domestic issues, such as divorce and guardianship, and the probating of wills, even if there was diversity of citizenship.

On the other hand, the First Judiciary Act expanded the potential of diversity jurisdiction. That Act permitted defendants to remove a case to federal court under certain conditions, such as the defendant's being an alien or citizen of another state, when sued by a plaintiff who was a citizen of the state where the suit was filed.[40] Variations of this removal provision have remained to this day. Although there are exceptions, a defendant can usually remove to federal district court a case that could have originally been brought in federal court.[41]

Choice of multiple forums is important to lawyers and their clients, and practical considerations guide their selections. A lawyer may prefer her state or federal judges for a number of reasons; perhaps most importantly are familiarity and previous success or failure. Federal judges have life tenure, while judges in most states are elected, rendering them more prone to political pressure. The procedural rules in federal court are often different from state procedure. Proximity of the respective courthouses to the lawyer and her client can also be a factor, as well as the potential for delay — the time from commencement to termination — in each court. The jury pools in federal court are ordinarily drawn from a wider area than those used in the local state courts.

Factors leading lawyers and their clients to prefer federal to state court, or vice versa, are so strong that one can detect a pattern for certain types of cases during specific time periods. In the 1960s and 1970s, federal courts were favored by plaintiffs' lawyers especially in civil rights cases. That was not always the case. From 1890 to 1910, it was defendants' lawyers for railroads and insurance companies who systematically removed cases from state court to federal court.[42] Federal courts were usually far distant from the home and office of the plaintiff and her lawyer, increasing dramatically the costs of litigation, and delays in the federal courts were notorious. Defendants were often railroads and insurance companies who could afford the expensive defense and delay far more readily than impoverished plaintiffs could afford a lack of recovery. At the time (before 1938), the substantive law applied in federal court was also frequently less favorable to plaintiffs than that applied in most state courts.[43] Moreover, the federal judges were themselves often thought to be considerably more conservative and pro-defendant than their state counterparts.

40. The Judiciary Act of 1789 § 13, 1 Stat. 73, 80-81.

41. 28 U.S.C. § 1441. Removal is "to the district court of the United States for the district and division embracing the place where such action is pending." Federal question cases, which we will soon discuss, can be removed regardless of the citizenship of the defendant; diversity cases can only be removed if none of the defendants "is a citizen of the State in which the action is brought." All defendants must agree to the removal.

42. Edward A. Purcell, Jr., Litigation and Inequality; Federal Diversity Jurisdiction in Industrial America, 1870-1958 (Oxford U. Press 1992). This section relies extensively on Professor Purcell's book.

43. Under the Supreme Court decision in *Swift v. Tyson*, discussed at the end of this chapter, federal courts were permitted to craft their own federal common law in diversity cases and had developed what most observers felt was pro-defendant laws, which would apply in federal court diversity cases, but not if the same case had remained in the state court. Purcell, *supra* note 42, chapter 3, *The Federal Common Law*, at 59-86.

When one calculates all of the benefits for defendants that accrued from removal to federal court with all the detriments to plaintiffs, perceived and real, one can see why the bulk of plaintiffs' cases settled for a good deal less once they were in the federal courts. Over time, members of the plaintiffs' bar developed their own methods to keep their cases in state court – by either joining nondiverse defendants or keeping the amount in controversy low. The use of removal from 1890 to 1910 is an apt example of the many considerations that influence choice of forum and the ways that jurisdictional issues can alter the results in tried or settled cases — and even those cases not commenced at all.

Although diversity jurisdiction has existed for well over 200 years, there have been persistent attempts to reduce its use and even to eliminate it. Congress has consistently raised the monetary amount needed to bring a diversity case. In 1958, Congress also amended the diversity of citizenship jurisdiction statute to make corporations citizens of both the state where they are incorporated *and* where they have their principal place of business. [44] Some courts have even held that a corporation can have more than one state of incorporation. The more states in which a corporation is a citizen, the more likely that a plaintiff will also be a citizen of one of the states of a defendant corporation's citizenship. This, of course, makes it less likely that there is complete diversity and jurisdiction in federal court.

More dramatic than curtailment is the persistent attempt by some, including many prominent jurists, to eliminate diversity jurisdiction completely. Diversity cases account for about one-fourth of the civil cases filed and one-half of the civil cases tried in the federal trial courts. [45] The Federal Judicial Center, the research arm of the federal judiciary, estimated that diversity jurisdiction costs the federal government about $131 million annually and recommended abolishing this type of federal subject matter jurisdiction in large part because it accounts for 10 percent of all of the expenditures in the federal judicial system. [46]

In addition to the expense, opponents of diversity jurisdiction argue that there is no evidence that present day state courts are biased against litigants from a different state. Proponents counter that such prejudice against out-of-state litigants still exists and that even the appearance of such bias is pernicious. Moreover, proponents of diversity jurisdiction see benefits for interstate commerce in having a federal trial court system with uniform procedural rules to accommodate interstate commercial litigation. Proponents also argue that the interplay of state and federal law in both state and federal courts encourages the improvement of law. The argument for cost savings projected by its elimination, proponents argue, is superficial because

44. The current version is 28 U.S.C. § 1332(c).

45. For the twelve-month period ending September 30, 2003, of 252,962 cases commenced in the federal district courts, approximately 24 percent were diversity of citizenship cases, 56 percent were federal question cases, and in 20 percent subject matter jurisdiction was based on the United States or an agency or officer thereof being a party. Annual Report of the Director Leonidas Ralph Mecham, Judicial Business of the United States Courts 2003, Administrative Office of the United States Courts, at table C-2, *available at* http://www.uscourts.gov/judbus2003/appendices/c2.pdf (accessed Sept. 27, 2005).

46. These statistics are cited in Erwin Chemerinsky, Federal Jurisdiction 288-289 (3d ed., Aspen 1999). This book provides a good summary of the issues surrounding diversity jurisdiction in § 5.3.

the states will merely have to pick up the costs of those cases that would have been tried on diversity grounds in federal court.

The truth of the matter is that litigators always like options and will always try to get better results for their clients in one tribunal rather than another. As a result, the organized bar, particularly the litigation section, continues to support diversity of citizenship jurisdiction in federal court. With the weight of history behind it, as well as supporters in Congress, diversity jurisdiction is likely to remain in place for a long time.

FEDERAL QUESTION JURISDICTION

One important type of federal court jurisdiction is based on the United States, or an officer or agency of it, being a party to the lawsuit.[47] This is usually straightforward and easy to determine. Considerably more complicated is another major type of subject matter jurisdiction in federal court called "federal question" jurisdiction.

At America's inception, the nationalists at the Constitutional Convention in Philadelphia argued that federal trial courts should have exclusive original subject matter jurisdiction to hear all litigation arising out of the federal Constitution, treaties, and laws, thus providing a consistency of federal law application that could not be achieved merely through United States Supreme Court appellate review. States' rights proponents did not want any federal trial court system to exist, let alone one that could hear all cases involving federal law exclusively. The resultant compromise was the establishment of a U.S. Supreme Court empowered with review over the federal law decisions of state courts.[48] Consequently, since 1789 the Supreme Court has had the last say, if it desired to hear the case, on state court decisions in which the losing party relied on the United States Constitution, treaties, or the exercise of federal authority.

Except for a brief period between 1801 and 1802, the grant of power to the federal district courts to hear what are called "federal question" cases — cases arising under federal law — awaited the completion and aftermath of the Civil War (1861-1865) fought between the northern states and southern states.[49] After the northern states won the Civil War, between 1865 and 1868 the Thirteenth, Fourteenth, and Fifteenth Amendments were passed. These

47. 28 U.S.C. § 1345, § 1346. *See* Mecham, *supra* note 45 *supra* for the numerical breakdown of types of cases in federal court.

48. Under Section 25 of the 1789 Judiciary Act (1 Stat. 73, 85-87), the Supreme Court was granted authority to review final judgments and decrees of the highest state courts in which the decision is against federal law or authority; where state law or authority is challenged on the basis of federal law, and the decision is in favor of the state law or authority; or where a provision of federal law or treaty is drawn in question, and the decision is against a federal right or exemption. The current statute covering Supreme Court review of state decisions on federal law permits review of the same three categories, but further extends its appellate power regardless of whether the state court decision is protective or limiting of federal law or authority. 28 U.S.C. § 1257.

49. Although volumes have been written about the Civil War, there is little doubt that important causes included the abolition or extension of slavery and issues relating to the disparate economic development between the north and south.

amendments respectively abolished slavery and gave citizenship to slaves and others born or naturalized in the United States; prohibited the states from denying citizens the equal protection of the laws and due process; and forbid any state from depriving a citizen of his vote because of race, color, or previous condition of solitude.

But racism itself was not laid to rest. The Ku Klux Klan, founded in Pulaski, Tennessee in 1866, grew in power as it aimed to reverse the rights granted former slaves and to establish white supremacy.[50] In response, Congress passed the Civil Rights Act of 1871, which provided a civil cause of action by private individuals to enforce the rights granted by the Fourteenth Amendment. This was the predecessor statute to 42 U.S.C. § 1983, which currently makes liable any person who under the color of state law[51] deprives a citizen or other person within a state, territory, or the District of Columbia "of any rights, privileges, or immunities secured by the" United States Constitution or other federal laws. A companion statutory provision permitted causes of action brought under this Civil Rights Act of 1871 to be brought in federal court.[52]

Yet, it was not until 1875 that Congress went even further and at last granted the federal district courts subject matter jurisdiction over all civil cases "arising under" federal law, provided that such cases, along with diversity cases, sought damages in excess of $5,000. In 1980, the monetary amount provision was eliminated for federal question cases, but not for diversity cases.[53] The "federal question" statute is the most commonly utilized basis for asserting federal subject matter jurisdiction.

Historians make clear that the grant of federal question jurisdiction to the federal district courts in 1875, along with the other civil rights legislation, heralded an enormous potential shift of power from the states to the federal government and from state courts to federal courts. Plaintiffs could now go to federal court to force persons operating under the shield of state law to obey federal law, including the equal protection and due process provisions of the Fourteenth Amendment.[54]

The statutory language authorizing federal courts jurisdiction to hear cases "arising under" federal law has proven difficult to interpret. At some attenuated level, all cases can be said to arise from federal law, because the Constitution is the foundation of the States, protector of contract and property and the right to due process. But the Supreme Court settled on a more narrow reading of "arising under federal law" that works in the vast majority of cases. The appropriate inquiry is whether the plaintiff's cause of action in a

---

50. The Klan and other racist groups were all too willing to use violence and lawlessness to return African-Americans to their pre-war status. A 600-page U.S. Senate Report in 1871 "detailed the unwillingness or inability of Southern states to control the activities of the Klan." See Chemerinsky, *supra* note 46, at 454.

51. "Under color of state law" is not easy to define, but basically the courts find that it exists when the violation of federal law has been committed by a state or municipal official acting in an official capacity, the defendant's activity is authorized or supported by the state, or a private person is acting jointly with a state official. Chemerinsky, *supra* note 46, at 458-466 (§ 8.3).

52. The current version of this statute, providing jurisdiction for § 1983 actions in the federal court, is found at 28 U.S.C. § 1343.

53. Federal question jurisdiction in the federal court is currently found at 28 U.S.C. § 1331.

54. Although § 1983 was used sparingly before 1961, the growth of § 1983 litigation in federal courts grew from 287 civil rights suits against state and local governments and their officials in 1960 to 20,000 such suits in 1977 and over 57,000 in 1995. Chemerinsky, *supra* note 46, at 456.

well-pleaded complaint arises under federal law — that is, whether it is federal law that grants authority to sue and defines the cause of action.[55] If there were a federal statute that granted the Lees in our *Cherryum* case the right to bring a private federal cause of action for violation of federal pure food standards, then that lawsuit could be brought in federal court on federal question grounds as well as on diversity of citizenship grounds.

Note that although defendants can waive their defenses to personal jurisdiction, notice or service of process, and venue (a concept we soon discuss), they cannot through waiver or consent gain federal subject matter jurisdiction when it is not permitted by a constitutional statute. Federal judges are generally quite vigorous on their own in dismissing cases that lack federal subject matter jurisdiction, regardless of what the parties want. Federal judges want to be very sure that they do not overstep their jurisdictional power to hear cases, as they do not want the other branches to worry that federal judges are usurping power. Nonetheless, legislators, presidents, and the public often accuse federal judges of overstepping their legitimate power and of "judicial activism."

You may wonder what considerations might draw Congress to place federal question cases in federal trial court. It is by no means self-evident that federal courts are better equipped to decide such cases than the state courts. After all, state court judges also take an oath to uphold the United States Constitution. Under the "Supremacy Clause," Article VI, of the U.S. Constitution, all judges in this country must apply all federal law (assuming the law is constitutional) when it is meant to apply to a case. Furthermore, if the state courts misapply federal law, the losing party can ultimately seek review to the United States Supreme Court to make the final, and thereby by definition, "correct," determination of that law.

There are several lines of argument in support of federal trial courts having federal subject matter jurisdiction. One is that federal judges, unlike most state judges who are elected, have life tenure. Therefore, federal judges are protected in a way that permits them to courageously apply federal law, even when their decision will be politically unpopular. Moreover, they are appointed to a federal official position through a rigorous nation-wide appointment process. Fewer than a thousand, these federal district court judges are arguably better trained and more capable than their state court counterparts. They continue their training through federal judicial meetings and federal continuing education courses. Arguably, federal judges are more likely to have a national outlook and a special awareness of the sanctity of federal law, enhanced by their repeated need to apply federal law in federal question cases.

While state judges do apply federal law on occasion, most state judges do not regularly hear such federal claims and may lack expertise in federal law. Finally, even though the Supreme Court can review state court applications of federal law, the Supreme Court hears and decides fewer than 100 cases a year.

---

55. As usual, we have to qualify a statement of doctrine with "ordinarily." In a case that has bedeviled federal courts students and teachers for decades, the Supreme Court held that a federal question can be sufficiently and inextricably entangled with a state cause of action to support the federal question jurisdiction of a federal district court. *Smith v. Kansas City Title & Trust Co.*, 255 U.S. 180 (1921). But the case has been rarely followed.

In practicality, most state court mistakes about federal law will not be reviewed, yet alone overturned, and erroneous factual decisions are usually not reviewable by the United States Supreme Court in any meaningful sense. Thus, it is argued, litigants need the option to have federal question cases heard in federal trial courts.

Those with a more states' rights orientation, and that includes the current majority of the present sitting Supreme Court Justices, think that there is greater "parity" between state and federal courts and judges than was previously suggested. They argue that there is no evidence that state judges are less willing or less capable of applying federal law than federal judges. Further, in most states, the procedural law is not so dissimilar from federal procedure as to make that a major consideration. The election of state judges, it is argued, helps to insure that they are responsible rather than undercut their judicial independence. Finally, those who assert state-federal court parity point out that there is so much applicable federal law now, as a result of ever-expanding federal statutes and rights, that state judges are apt to have a great deal of experience in interpreting federal law. Despite the debate, there is in fact very little impetus from any quarter to remove federal question jurisdiction from the federal district courts, although some would resurrect a monetary amount requirement much like that in diversity jurisdiction.

SUPPLEMENTAL JURISDICTION

There is one more complication wrought by our system of federalism. Especially given the broad joinder provisions provided by the Federal Rules of Civil Procedure, a topic we will address in a later chapter, it is not unusual for a plaintiff to join a state law cause of action with what is clearly a federal law cause of action. One can sue a defendant for violating federal employment discrimination law and join a state cause of action for breach of contract, defamation, or even violation of a state discrimination statute. The lawsuit can get even more complicated. What if an accident occurs and two individuals are at fault, and the plaintiff sues one defendant on a federal cause of action but a co-defendant on a state cause of action?

The broad joinder provisions of the Federal Rules of Civil Procedure, as you will soon learn, permit a wide variety of methods of expanding the parties and claims by defendants in a case well beyond what the initial plaintiff envisioned. Defendants can bring counterclaims against the plaintiff that arise out of the same fact situation as the initial case, or assert a cross-claim against a co-defendant, or even under some circumstances bring in a new party altogether (called an "impleader," which is described in Chapter 9).

Doctrines that used to be called "pendent" and "ancillary jurisdiction," now codified in 28 U.S.C. § 1367 as "supplemental jurisdiction," sometimes permit such claims to piggy-back on claims that are allowed in federal court. The test is generally whether the claims that stand alone can be in federal court and the claims that cannot but are attached to them (such as a state cause of action joined to a federal cause of action) arise from a "common nucleus of operative fact." The constitutional question is whether the additional causes of action are part of the same "case or controversy" that federal courts are permitted to hear within the meaning of Article III of the United States Constitution.

The statute also makes clear that whether to permit supplemental jurisdiction is a discretionary matter to be determined by the trial judge. The trial judge is to consider such matters as whether the state claims raise novel or complex issues and whether the state claims "substantially predominate" over the initial federal claim. If the initial diversity of citizenship or federal question are terminated prior to trial by settlement or otherwise, then the Federal District Court judge is obligated to dismiss the supplemental state claims from federal court, but will give a 30-day grace period for the claim to be refiled in state court.[56]

VENUE

The final requirement, "venue," is also intimately related to geography. Let us assume that you, as an American lawyer, have chosen to bring your case in a state trial court of general subject matter jurisdiction, say a Massachusetts trial court having personal jurisdiction over the defendant and subject matter jurisdiction over the claim; in this instance, in Massachusetts Superior Court. Massachusetts, which is one of the smaller states geographically, has 13 counties, with a superior court in each county. Boston in Suffolk County can be as far apart as 137 miles from Pittsfield in Berkshire County. A litigant does not want to travel far to get to court. If distance makes a difference for a small state like Massachusetts, then imagine the impact on litigation when hundreds of miles must be traversed to arrive at a particular court in Texas, California, or Alaska, states considerably bigger than some countries. The plaintiff, in the first instance, must pick one of the many locales where the court has both personal and subject matter jurisdiction as the location in which to file her lawsuit. This geographic choice is called a question of "venue."

Although the general policies behind venue are fairly constant — convenience and fairness to one or more of the parties and efficiency of the court — states have chosen a wide variety of ways to deal with this requirement. For some types of actions, particularly those dealing with real estate, states have said that action must be brought in the venue, usually a county, in which the property is located. These cases are called "local actions." All other types of causes of action are typically called "transitory" and where they can be brought differs widely. States frequently give the plaintiff a choice; sometimes the choices are prescribed for particular types of cases.[57] The choices include a

---

56. Some scholars have argued for greater extension of supplementary jurisdiction beyond "factually interdependent civil claims initially presented within cases or controversies." Jeffrey A. Parness & Daniel J. Sennott, *Expanded Recognition in Written Laws of Ancillary Federal Court Power: Expanded Recognition in Written Laws of Ancillary Federal Court Powers: Supplementing the Supplemental Jurisidiction Statute*, 64 U. Pittsburg L. Rev. 303, 304 (2003).

57. In Massachusetts, for example, if the instrument of the action is a forged check or credit card, the action may be brought in the county where the instrument was presented for payment, if located in Massachusetts. M.G.L. c. 223, § 1.

combination (and we give you only examples of the many possibilities) of where the cause of action arose; where a particular fact or situation occurred; where the defendant resides or does business or has a place of business; where the plaintiff resides or does business or has a place of business; where the defendant is found or served; in any county; or where the seat of government is located.

Interestingly, these are the variables other countries consider in determining personal jurisdiction. The United States, by contrast, layers its constitutional gloss on personal jurisdiction with this statutory requirement on venue. The state legislature typically has enacted a state venue statute for the state courts; similarly, the federal Congress has promulgated a federal venue statute for the federal district courts. Lawyers apply the relevant state venue statute in state courts and the federal venue statute when bringing cases in federal courts. Venue statutes locate the litigation more specifically in a court with jurisdiction *and* with the most sensible relationship to the litigation.

In both state and federal court, there are also statutes permitting the defendant to make a motion to transfer the case to a more convenient venue within the court system. For example, a Massachusetts state court can only transfer within the Massachusetts state court system,[58] but a federal district court can transfer a case to another federal district court within the entire federal court system. The statutes tend to define both what the court should consider before allowing the motion to transfer (such as "the convenience of parties and witnesses, in the interest of justice" in the federal statute) and the venues to which the case can be transferred. A federal district court judge, for example, can transfer a federal case to a federal district court in which the case could have originally been brought,[59] which means in the federal courts that the plaintiff could have originally achieved personal jurisdiction and proper venue.[60]

Both federal courts and state trial courts can also dismiss a suit for *forum non conveniens*, if they find that there is no court within their system in which the case can be conveniently tried. For example, at the state level, if the more convenient court is in another state, the state court in which the case was originally brought does not have the power to transfer the case to another state. Unlike the situation in federal court, different state courts are totally different court systems. In that scenario, a state judge will usually have to dismiss the case on a *forum non conveniens* motion, but only if she is certain the plaintiff will have another forum in which she can refile the case. This may mean that the state judge will not permit the defendant's motion unless the defendant waives a statute of limitations defense and submits to personal jurisdiction in the new forum state.[61]

---

58. For example, see the Massachusetts change of venue provision, found at M.G.L. c. 223, § 13.

59. 28 U.S.C. § 1404(a).

60. 28 U.S.C. § 1404(a) reads: "For the convenience of parties and witnesses, in the interest of justice, a district court may transfer any civil action to any other district or division where it might have been brought." Under 28 U.S.C. § 1406(a), a federal district court can transfer a case from an improper federal venue to a proper federal court venue.

61. The idea of venue has ancient origins, dating back nearly to the dawn of the British nation-state, during the rule of William II (1087-1100). William Wirt Blume, *Place of Trial in Civil Cases: Early English and Modern Federal*, 48 Mich. L. Rev. 1, 2 (1949) (citing Thomas Maddox, History and Antiquities of the Exchequer 6 (1711)).

Because the United States is such a large country, venue has been a hotly contested topic at the federal level, as well as in the states. Congress has tinkered with federal venue statutes since 1789. But a version of the statute enacted is still in effect.

In 1990, Congress changed the venue statute so that for both diversity of citizenship and federal question cases, venue would lie in a district where any defendant resides, if all defendants reside in the same state.[62] Courts are in disagreement over the meaning of the term "residence." Some say that it is the same as citizenship, which in turn is the same as domicile (which is residence and intent to stay for the foreseeable future). Others say that citizenship (and therefore domicile) is evidence of residence, but not alone determinative. The federal venue statute also makes a corporate defendant a resident "in any judicial district in which it is subject to personal jurisdiction at the time the action is commenced."[63]

Congress also changed the venue statute language to "a judicial district in which a substantial part of the events or omissions giving rise to the claim occurred, or a substantial part of property that is the subject of the action is situated." This makes clear that there can be more than one district in which events occurred that are substantial enough to sustain venue. Although the language is now slightly different with respect to diversity of citizenship and federal question cases, it is probably true that for both types of cases, plaintiffs can also achieve venue whenever all defendants are subject to personal jurisdiction, "if there is no district in which the action may otherwise be brought."[64] Some federal substantive statutes have their own particular venue provisions within the statute for that particular kind of federal claim.

In the *Cherryum* case, you, as the plaintiffs' lawyer, would have no trouble establishing venue in Massachusetts in either federal or state court. As you have seen, the federal venue statute, 28 U.S.C. § 1391, permits federal diversity cases to be brought, among other places, in the judicial district where "a substantial part of the events or omissions giving rise to the claim occurred." The allegedly tainted Cherryum drink was bought and drunk in Massachusetts and the injuries occurred in Massachusetts.

Unlike larger states, Massachusetts has only one federal district court, so the venue of that court is proper. The same federal venue statute permits venue "where any defendant resides, if all defendants reside in the same state," and defines the residence of corporations as "any judicial district in which [the defendant corporation] is subject to personal jurisdiction at the time an action is commenced." Because the defendants, Cherryum, Inc., and Cherryum Bottling Company, are subject to personal jurisdiction in Massachusetts, appropriate federal venue is also appropriate in Massachusetts under this provision.

---

62. 28 U.S.C. § 1391 (a) and (b), as amended by the Judicial Improvements Act of 1990, Pub. L. 101-650, Tit. III, § 311, 104 Stat. 5114. Older versions permitted venue in diversity cases to where the plaintiff or defendant resided but for no logical reason, restricted venue to the defendant's residence in federal question cases.
63. 28 U.S.C. § 1391(c).
64. 28 U.S.C. § 1391 (a) and (b).

If you had chosen to bring the law suit in a Massachusetts state court, you would instead seek compliance with the state venue statute. You would find that suit could be brought, among other places, in the county of the plaintiffs' residence (in this instance, Hampden County). Suit could be brought in the Massachusetts Superior Court sitting in Hampden County.

Similar to jurisdiction, the provisions of venue statutes have their practical and political considerations. For example, when Congress in 1966 added the district "where the claim of action arose" as a venue option, it in effect permitted some plaintiffs to go to federal court (provided there is subject matter jurisdiction) who otherwise would have had only the possibility of suing in state court. The 1990 statutory language of "a substantial part of the events or omissions" together with the liberal provision of permitting wherever the defendants could be served rendered the federal court even more accessible to plaintiffs than was previously the case.

Defendants have argued that the federal venue statute is too pro-plaintiff. For instance, it permits United States agencies and officers of the federal government to be sued where they reside or where a "substantial part of the events or omissions" occurred.[65] This wording in effect permits plaintiffs in environmental cases to sue the responsible federal agencies in the Washington, D.C. District, where the agencies and also where many potential public interest plaintiffs have their offices. A series of victories by pro-environmental plaintiffs in the D.C. District Court resulted in a call for a substantial "venue-shift." Senators from the western states sought to propose a bill that would have limited all civil cases in which the federal government is a defendant to be heard in the judicial district in which "a substantial portion of the impact of injury" occurred, essentially taking cases against the federal government out of the Washington, D.C. venue.[66] The bill did not get out of the Senate Judiciary Committee. As was stated at a hearing on the venue-shift bill: "If it had been necessary to litigate about an environmental-impact statement affecting Micronesia in the far Pacific rather than in Washington, D.C., within approximately 10 blocks of the Interior Department where the decisions had all been made, [the plaintiffs] undoubtedly would not have able to do it."[67]

Venue, then, like personal and subject matter jurisdiction, can have enormous impact on the cost of the litigation, whether suits will be brought at all, and whether they are won or lost. This is why legislators, often with lobbyists for interest groups in the background, fight over the language of statutes governing jurisdiction and venue. This is also why lawyers, and their clients, often expend great resources of time and money on the four squares of personal jurisdiction, subject matter jurisdiction, venue, and notice.

---

65. 28 U.S.C. § 1391(e).

66. Paul D. Laxalt et. al.,Venue at the Crossroads 7 (Steven R. Schlesinger ed., National Center for the Public Interest 1982) (quoting Hearings on Federal Venue Statutes, § 759 and § 1472, before the Subcommittee on Improvements in the Judicial Machinery of the Senate Committee on the Judiciary, 96th Cong., 2d Sess. 22 (Feb. 20, 1980).

67. *Id.* at 68 (Remarks of Mr. Butler); Hearing, 79, David Siegel, *Changes in Federal Jurisdiction and Practice Under the New Judicial Improvements and Access to Justice Act*, 123 Fed. Rules Decisions 399, 402 (1989). Laxalt *supra* note 66, at 68 (quoting Hearings at 79 (Remarks of Mr. Butler)).

CHOICE OF LAW

We have left until the end of this chapter one other question of civil procedure that has a significant impact on choice of forum. What law will apply? This area of law is called "choice of law" and the doctrine involved is frequently called "conflicts of law." Like personal and subject matter jurisdiction, it is frequently tied to considerations of the appropriate distribution of power between the states and between the state and federal government.

Because the United States is a federal union, there are two distinct types of conflicts of law problems. When transactions involve more than one state, state courts are frequently in the position of having to decide which state law to apply in these disputes. These are called "horizontal" conflicts of law questions. The United States is also a federal system in which each state also has at least one Federal district court. As a result of diversity and supplemental jurisdiction, state law claims are frequently brought to the federal court. The issue of what law to apply — federal or state — in these cases are called "vertical" conflicts of law.

When discussing conflict of law doctrine, it is critical to keep one central fact in mind. The Supremacy Clause of the U.S. Constitution provides that when the United States Constitution, a United States Treaty, or a federal statute covers a given situation, then all American courts, state and federal, must apply the federal law. In other words, federal law, when applicable, is the supreme law of the land. When a state court hears a federal cause of action it must apply the federal substantive law to that action. It must also apply its own state law in a way that does not violate the United States Constitution or its own state constitution.

Horizontal conflict of law doctrine — the rules that help state and federal courts decide which state's law to apply when state law, rather than federal, is applicable — has become quite complicated. It was not always so complex. In the nineteenth and early twentieth century, the choice of law rules were such that in tort cases, the law of the state where the injury occurred would apply, while in contract cases, the applicable law was usually the state law where the contract was made.[68] These rules were later summarized in the Restatement, an influential treatise published by the American Law Institute.

By the time of the Restatement (Second) of Conflicts was published in 1971, the conflicts of law doctrine had dramatically changed. Even under the older conflicts of law doctrine, there were exceptions to the firm rules; for example, a court might refuse to apply the law of another state if it found that the law violated the public policy of its own law in a major way. But by the 1950s and 1960s, horizontal conflict of law doctrine had dramatically shifted to less definitive rules in many areas of law. The doctrine evolved to the point where courts began looking on a case-by-case basis to the interests of the competing states when there was a conflict and to the strength of their underlying policies. The Second Restatement "called for application of the law of the state that, with respect to the issue, had the 'the most significant relationship' to the

---

68. Silberman & Stein, *supra* note 18, at 218-221 (supplying a good summary of the evolution of horizontal conflict of law doctrine in the United States).

occurrence and the parties. [69] If there is no statutory provision applicable, then the court is to consider a multi-variable test of:

> (a) the needs of the interstate and international systems; (b) the relevant policies of the forum; (c) the relevant policies of other interested states, and the relative interests of those states in the determination of the particular issues; (d) the protection of justified expectations; (e) the basic policies underlying the particular field of law; (f) certainty, predictability and uniformity of result; and (g) ease in the determination and application of the law to be applied." [70]

Like personal jurisdiction, this move to a multi-variable, more amorphous test signaled to lawyers to take the opportunity to forum shop. [71] Plaintiffs' lawyers, loyal to the interests of their clients, hunted for venues that would give them the best opportunity for victory, by virtue of the court's procedure, jury pool, character of judges, and the substantive law to be applied Defendants countered with motions to remove, transfer, or dismiss for forum non conveniens. [72]

"Vertical" conflicts of law rules were especially susceptible to lawyer's forum shopping. Corporate defendants, especially from 1890 to 1910, were known to remove diversity cases to federal court in the search for more favorable federal common law; plaintiffs often attempted to destroy diversity by adding parties or reducing their damages to below the proscribed monetary amount. This seeking of advantage through vertical choice of law doctrine (conflicts of law doctrine applicable between state and federal courts) led to another of the most taught and analyzed cases, *Erie Railroad Co. v. Tompkins*.

The facts of *Erie Railroad Co. v. Tompkins*, [73] more commonly known as *Erie*, are fairly simple. Harry J. Tompkins, a 27-year-old factory worker, was injured by an Erie Railroad train while walking home one night along a path owned by the railroad in Pennsylvania. [74] Tompkins brought suit against Erie Railroad, a New York corporation, in New York federal court, based on diversity subject matter jurisdiction. Pennsylvania state tort law, however, would have barred Tompkins, who was technically a trespasser at the time of accident, from

---

69. *Id.* at 220.

70. Restatement (Second) of Conflicts of Law § 6 (1996).

71. In some areas of law, such as estates and property, the more settled traditional approaches continue to apply.

72. One should note, however, that in federal district court a transferred case is supposed to carry with it to the transferee court the same law that would have been applied in the transferor court. *Van Dusen v. Barrack*, 376 U.S. 612 (1964). Although the law may remain the same, its interpretation may of course be different, depending on the judges in each court, and the attitudes of the judges and juries may be substantially different. Then, too, if a *forum non conveniens* dismissal takes place, then the new court would in no way be bound by the transferor court's law.

73. 304 U.S. 64 (1938).

74. Tompkins, out of work, ate dinner at his mother-in-law's house in Hughestown, Pennsylvania, and shortly after midnight began the six-mile trip home. Friends took him part way home and then dropped him off "near a well-trod footpath that ran along the freight tracks toward his home." As he walked at about 2:00 a.m. in July 1934, a train approached. "Suddenly and too late, Tompkins looked up. Protruding from the train and coming right at him 'was a black object that looked like a door.'" He was later found unconscious, with his right arm severed between the tracks. "At a nearby hospital the remainder of the arm was amputated." The description of the underlying facts is taken from Edward A. Purcell, Jr., Brandeis and the Progressive Constitution: Erie, the Judicial Power, and the Politics of the Federal Courts in Twentieth Century America 96 (Yale U. Press 2000) (citations omitted).

recovery unless he could prove that the defendant railway had acted "willfully" in causing him injury. Horizontal conflicts of law principles in both New York and Pennsylvania would apply the law of the place of injury, in this case, Pennsylvania tort law.

But by bringing the case in a federal court, Tompkins was hoping to apply the doctrine from *Swift v. Tyson*, a prior U.S. Supreme Court case that held that federal district courts could apply and develop a federal common law in diversity cases when the applicable state substantive law was not contained in a statute.[75] The New York federal court agreed and applied federal common law, allowing the plaintiff to win by proving ordinary negligence. The jury awarded Tompkins a jury verdict of $30,000, a sizable sum at the time. The Second Circuit affirmed the judgment. Erie Railroad appealed.

The Supreme Court granted the defendant's petition for *certiorari*. Justice Louis D. Brandeis, a well-known advocate for the public at large as opposed to large national corporations, issued the monumental decision in 1938, the same year that the Federal Rules of Civil Procedure became law.[76] The decision overturned *Swift v. Tyson* and ordered the lower Federal Courts to apply the state common law, rather than relying on federal common law in diversity cases.

Law school professors and students have been trying to decide ever since what Brandeis relied on in overturning *Swift v. Tyson*. Part of the Brandeis opinion focuses on Section 34 of the Judiciary Act of 1789, called the Rules of Decision Act, which provided:

> The laws of the several States, except where the Constitution, treatises, or statutes of the United States otherwise require or provide, shall be regarded as rules of decision in trials of at common law, in the courts of the United States, in cases where they apply.[77]

In *Erie*, Justice Brandeis said that new scholarship suggested that the "laws of the several States" when it was written was meant to include both statutory and common law.[78] Therefore, in diversity cases, the federal courts did not have the authority under the Rules Decision Act to create federal common law and instead must apply the state substantive law of the state in which the federal court was located but federal procedure law.

The Brandeis opinion concentrate on forum shopping and the inequality under *Swift* between in-state and out-of-state plaintiffs. Out-of-state plaintiffs could achieve diversity of citizenship, get into federal court, and in turn, apply federal common law in situations that in-state plaintiffs could not.[79] But *Erie* replaced one type of forum shopping with another. It reduced forum shopping within the same state (intrastate) for a federal court by eliminating federal common law, but it increased inter-federal court forum shopping.

---

75. 41 U.S. 1 (1842).

76. Justice Brandeis dissented from the Supreme Court's promulgation of the Federal Rules of Civil Procedure. Order of Dec. 20, 1937, 302 U.S. 783 (1937).

77. The current provision is found in 28 U.S.C. § 1652.

78. For a discussion of the scholarship regarding the Rules of Decision Act, see Silberman & Stein, *supra* note 18, at 461-462. Some legal historians do not think Brandeis was correct in his interpretation of the history of the Rules of Decision provision.

79. Professor Purcell has demonstrated that in fact in many cases, it was the defendant who had the uneven forum choice, because of limited removal possibilities. We have relied heavily in this chapter on two books by Professor Purcell, *supra* notes 74 and 42.

Absent federal common law, there is no incentive to shop for a federal court over a state court in the same state if the cause of action is a state law cause of action. State substantive law would apply in this case whether the case was brought in federal or state court. But *Erie* allowed a plaintiff to forum shop for the application of different state law depending on where the federal court is located. Forum shopping for state law has increased dramatically given the expansion of personal jurisdiction doctrine and venue possibilities, *Erie*, and the multivariable tests in conflict of law doctrine.

The *Erie* opinion permitted Brandeis to express his strongly held opinions about federalism, separation of powers, and the nature of law itself. The states' rights focus of his philosophy dovetailed with his desire to eliminate extensive federal judicial power to replace state law with federal common law in diversity cases. He had also witnessed decades of the Supreme Court using an expansive view of due process (sometimes called "substantive due process") to whittle down both state and federal laws dealing with social welfare. In response, his *Erie* decision reined in the federal judiciary's power to create law in areas in which the U.S. Congress had not yet acted. Where the U.S. Congress did constitutionally act, as in enacting a federal statute, all courts, state and federal, were bound to apply that federal statute.

Finally, at a jurisprudential level, *Erie* incorporated a positivistic view of law that insisted that laws are to be made, not found, and made by those granted the power to make them. Federal judges, unlike state judges, according to this view, had no freewheeling power to create a common law. The Constitution gave Congress, not the federal courts, the power to make law.

Since *Erie*, in diversity of citizenship cases and with respect to state supplemental jurisdiction claims, federal judges are to apply the substantive law of the state in which they sit, but federal procedural law. In the *Cherryum* case, for instance, the federal district court of Massachusetts, whose subject matter jurisdiction is based on diversity of citizenship, would apply state law to the substance of the case but the Federal Rules of Civil Procedure,[80] so long as such rules do not exceed the rule-making power granted to the Supreme Court under the Enabling Act of 1934 (discussed in Chapter 3). The Enabling Act does not permit a Federal Rule to "abridge, enlarge or modify any substantive right."[81] It is not always easy, though, to decide what is substantive and what is procedural. Although no Federal Rule of Civil Procedure has yet been held unconstitutional or beyond the Enabling Act, at some point a case will reach the Supreme Court in which a state procedural rule, in unavoidable collision with a federal rule, is so enmeshed with the state substantive law that one cannot disentangle the substance and procedure.[82]

80. *See Hanna v. Plumer*, 380 U.S. 460 (1965).
81. 28 U.S.C. § 2072.
82. A similar situation, but in reverse, occurred in *Gasperini v. Center for Humanities, Inc.*, 518 U.S. 415 (1996), in which the Supreme Court adjusted state procedure, without voiding it, in order to meet U.S. Constitutional constraints. The case held that a state law for controlling excessive damage awards can be applied without detriment to the Seventh Amendment's reexamination clause if the review standard set out in the state statute is applied by the federal trial court judge and appellate review is limited to an "abuse of discretion" standard. One prominent American scholar, Professor Burbank, has maintained that the Enabling Act should not be construed as limitation on federal as opposed to state power, but rather as limiting the Supreme Court to make what they call procedural rules that in fact have an impact on litigants in

Do not conclude from this brief excursion through *Erie* doctrine that federal courts never make common law. There are many occasions when federal courts are forced to interpret broad congressional mandates and their interpretation looks very much like creation of substantive law. Particularly in the area of federal bonds and checks, the federal courts have created law so that there is a uniform federal common law in those areas.[83] This means that state and federal courts alike have to apply that law under the Supremacy Clause.

The choice of law questions you have been introduced to in this chapter, along with the jurisdictional and venue issues, have perplexed American law students for decades. Much of the complexity is the result of the American federal system, with the states maintaining some degree of sovereignty and the federal government having supremacy where it is permitted to constitutionally act.

Countries other than the United States are also forced to confront the same types of doctrinal problems when they join together in treaties or seek to create some kind of union with sovereignty shared by each country and by a joint body. The European Union, for instance, has been forced to confront personal jurisdiction problems when there are disputes among citizens of different countries. Yet, what jurisdictional doctrine such federal-like unions decide on may be considerably different from what has evolved in the United States. You have read in this chapter, for instance, how personal jurisdiction is treated differently in the European Union than in America.

But the three major themes of our book that we have emphasized in this chapter — power, legitimacy, and the correspondence between culture and the law — will not be avoided by other countries acting alone or in their attempts at creating federal-like solutions. To the extent a country's culture, and in turn its lawyers, are competitive and adversarial, the lawyers will try to use the procedural law to benefit their clients. There will inevitably be power clashes among the individual countries and between the countries and a central court. Will one country's law apply or a supra-national law that trumps the law of the individual countries? These questions will inevitably evoke heated disagreement.

Furthermore, procedural doctrines, such as due process, will help determine the extent to which citizens of various countries deem the legal system legitimate. If citizens are to obey, and their countries are to enforce the judicial decrees of the courts of other countries or of some supra-national court, notice and the right to be heard will likely be an integral piece of the dispute resolution process. Fairness and perceptions of fairness are the foundational steps leading to legitimacy and acceptance of any legal system.

---

a manner calling for legislative, not judicial action. Stephen B. Burbank, *The Rules Enabling Act of 1934*, 130 U. Pa. L. Rev. 1015 (May 1982).

83. *See, e.g., Clearfield Trust Co. v. United States*, 318 U.S. 363 (1943).

CHAPTER

6

Thinking Like an American Lawyer: Burdens of Proof, Pleadings, and a Lawyer's Obligation

A pleading that sets forth a claim for relief . . . shall contain . . . a short and plain statement of the claim showing that the pleader is entitled to relief . . . .
Federal Rule of Civil Procedure 8(a).

. . . I think you will see at once these pleadings follow a general philosophy which is that detail, fine detail, in statement is not required and is in general not very helpful . . . . [I]f any of you feel you need more information to develop your case, if you need more information from your opponent, we have provided for that, and I think have provided for that much more directly and simply than ever you will obtain by attempting to force the correction of the pleadings. That is in the section on Deposition and Discovery.
Charles E. Clark, October 6, 1938[1]

Almost every legal system has some initial "gate-keeping" requirements on what litigants must file at the commencement of their lawsuits. How a legal system compels the parties to reduce their dispute to manageable proportions that will permit sensible resolution is the focus of this chapter. Again, we are confronted with a tension inherent in every litigation system: that is, the tension between rule and the broader narrative. While it may be more equitable to allow parties to simply tell their story in its entirety, the legal system requires greater predictability, consistency, and efficiency than a story without parameters. The procedural rules constrain what will be entertained in a legal dispute and what will be considered extraneous, what will be confined by rule and what will break out through narrative. As we examine this tension, we will see once again how American society is reflected and in turn, constructed by the civil litigation system that has evolved.

In America, the initial articulation of the parties' positions is done through what are called "pleadings," pieces of paper filed by the parties in a court, as you have seen, initially chosen by the plaintiff. Fed. R. Civ. P. 7 defines a

---

1. Charles E. Clark, *Comments, Proceeding of the Institute at Washington, D.C. on the Federal Rules of Civil Procedure* 33-44 (American Bar Association 1938).

pleading as "a complaint and an answer, a reply to a counterclaim..., an answer to a cross-claim..., a third party complaint..., and a third party answer." The plaintiff files a "complaint" (some state courts call it a "declaration") and serves it on the defendant; the defendant must file an "answer." As we explain in Chapter 9 on the joinder of claims and parties, defendants can make multiple claims against the plaintiff and in some cases add additional parties. In each instance, plaintiffs and defendants must answer the others' complaints.

This chapter covers these initial documents, that is, the pleadings that must be filed in any civil case and the circumstances under which they can be amended. Exploration of the pleadings and amendments requirements (notably, Rules 8 and 15) helps one to understand the pragmatic nature of civil procedure reform in the United States — reform generated from a variety of interested groups — and that procedural rules affect who sues, who wins, and the cost of litigation. We will explore pleading obligations in other countries so that we have a comparative basis for considering the peculiar nature of the American experience. Finally, we will examine the obligation of lawyers, notably, under Rule 11, to investigate the facts and law of the underlying dispute before filing a complaint and other court documents. Lawyers in the American adversary system have an obligation to investigate before filing, or they can face court-imposed sanctions.

THINKING LIKE AN AMERICAN LAWYER: BURDENS OF PROOF

It is difficult to understand the pleading rules without an understanding of how American lawyers think about civil law suits. If we could get into a lawyer's head, what will we learn about her thinking process as she listens to a potential client describing a grievance? In Chapter 4, we described the *Cherryum* case. Albert Lee's grievance was that he was made violently ill after drinking a can of Cherryum soft drink. As the prospective lawyer for the plaintiffs, how would you sift through his story?

Of course you would think about the jurisdictional issues, where you would file, and how you will be paid. But there is another concept deeply embedded in the mind of American lawyers. Often it is called "cognizability," does the law recognize and provide a remedy for this particular harm? This same concept is present in some form in most legal systems; after all, the law does not recognize, or take "cognizance of," all harms that befall people. You might fall at home because of your own clumsiness or because you were daydreaming. You might feel slighted because of the way another person looked at you or uttered an unkind word. If this is all that happened, the legal system will not ordinarily permit recovery. An American lawyer might say you did not have a "cause of action."

One way to think about "a cause of action" is that it describes those variables that if true will permit an aggrieved person to go to court and ask the government to force another person to give her relief, usually in the form of a monetary award. The law says that if "A," "B," "C," and "D" are true, then a person harmed by the confluence of "A, B, C, and D," can go to court and have that court order "X" — some relief that the law says is the legal consequence of a defendant's doing "A, B, C, and D."

In the United States, there are hundreds of substantive laws that describe that if a plaintiff can prove that a defendant did certain things, then the plaintiff can get relief from the defendant. Other laws say that if you have done certain things, then the government or some other entity must do something for you (like pay you a pension or monthly income after you reach a certain age), or that the government or other entity can force you to do something (like pay taxes or stop you from trespassing on land). In each of these instances, a lawyer, by looking up the law, will try to predict for a client whether a certain set of circumstances will permit court-enforced relief. In other words, a lawyer must assess whether there is a plausible "cause of action."

The variables or events that add up to a cause of action are known as the elements of a cause of action. When law students take substantive law courses they learn, among many other things, what the elements of various causes of action are in the field of law they are studying. In a torts course, the students learn the elements of the more common torts and the elements of the common defenses asserted by defendants' lawyers. The most common tort relied upon by plaintiffs' lawyers is called "negligence." As you listen to the story of Albert Lee in the *Cherryum* case, one thing you would think about is whether the story adds up to a cause of action for negligence. A negligence cause of action includes the elements of duty of the defendant to the plaintiff to act reasonably, breach of the duty of reasonable care, in fact causing a harm (cause in fact) that was foreseeable (proximate cause), resulting in damage to the plaintiffs.

But you would not just think about Albert Lee's cause of action and its elements in an abstract way. The American lawyer, operating in an adversary system, is responsible for amassing and introducing evidence, leaving the judge or jury to decide the case on the basis of the evidence the lawyers present. Consequently, as early as the first interview with the client, you would be thinking about what you must prove in order to prevail, as well as thinking about what the defendant's lawyer will try to prove in opposition. Some lawyers have told us that from the moment that they agree to accept a case they already start thinking about what their final argument to a jury will be if the case reaches trial.

In thinking about what evidence to amass, a lawyer must bear in mind the technical issue of burden of proof. In an adversary system, because the parties, not the court, bear the responsibility of investigation and coming up with evidence, the system must also allocate the burden of proof between the parties — that is, who of the two opposing parties must gather the evidence and how much. And so, when we say that the plaintiff must prove something, we usually mean the plaintiff has the burden of proof.

The burden of proof normally has two parts: the "burden of production" and the "burden of persuasion." For a plaintiff to win on a cause of action (assuming the defendant's lawyer raises the appropriate defense), she must first convince a judge that she has produced sufficient evidence as to each element of her cause of action to permit the judge or jury to find that the element is true (production burden). She must then convince the fact finder (judge or jury) to find in her favor on each element (persuasion burden). The party with the burden of proof on a claim or defense normally also has a burden to plead the claim or defense correctly.

Consider this simple case. Robert walked down the street and fell as Sally approached him, and Robert sued Sally for negligence. It is unlikely that Robert will have any evidence that Sally acted unreasonably or that anything Sally did in fact caused the harm. An American lawyer hearing Robert's story would probably conclude that Robert could not meet the production burden — that is, Robert could not produce evidence that would permit a reasonable judge or jury to find that Sally acted unreasonably (one element) or caused the harm (another element). We will later discuss the motions that a defendant can bring, either before trial or after the plaintiff has put in her evidence at trial, which will permit the judge to dismiss the plaintiff's case because she has not met the production burden as to at least one element of her cause of action.[2]

But even if a plaintiff is able to meet her production burden for every element of a cause of action, she may not have met her entire burden of proof. The jury may not believe the evidence or it may not think that what the defendant did was "unreasonable." So, in the above case, if Robert testifies that as they were walking, Sally's arm brushed against his and caused him to fall, a judge may find this testimony sufficient evidence to permit a jury to find Sally acted unreasonably; that is, that Robert has met his production burden. But Sally may deny that she ever touched Robert in any way as they passed each other. The jury may believe Sally and not Robert, or the jurors may believe that even if Sally touched Robert, what Sally did was not unreasonable. In that instance, then, even though Robert has met his production burden, he did not meet his persuasion burden. Robert (or, in reality, his lawyer) must have enough evidence to persuade the fact finder that it is "more likely than not" that Sally did touch Robert in an unreasonable way and that her touching caused Robert to fall.

In civil litigation in the United States, the plaintiff ordinarily has the full burden of proof (both of production and persuasion) as to each element of the alleged cause of action. She must also plead her case according to the rules that describe the requirements for a complaint (her burden to plead). She must then compile sufficient evidence to permit a fact finder to find that every element of her cause of action is true (her production burden). The plaintiff must also meet her persuasion burden at trial, that is, to convince the fact finder that it is "more likely than not" that each element is true in order to win. When there is a jury, the jury is usually instructed by the judge that the defendant must win if the plaintiff has not persuaded the jury that each element is "more likely than not" to be true or if the jury cannot decide as to any one element whether to believe it.

In response, the defendant may have affirmative defenses to the plaintiff's cause of action. For instance, lawsuits ordinarily have to be brought within a certain number of years from when the cause of action arose, usually from the date when the plaintiff suffered the harm. Typically, states will have a statute of

---

2. These motions for summary judgment, directed verdict, and judgment notwithstanding the verdict are discussed in Chapters 8 and 11.

limitations that says that tort cases must be brought within three years from when the cause of action arose. If the defendant thinks that the case was not brought within the statute of limitations, or if in the case of Robert against Sally, Sally's lawyer thinks that Robert fell because of his own negligence, she can raise such an issue as an affirmative defense. Usually the defendant has the burden to plead and the entire burden to prove — both production and persuasion burdens — as to affirmative defenses.

In a legal system in which judges are vested with the responsibility to uncover the truth, such allocations of burdens between the parties may not be necessary. But in the adversary system where it is the parties who bear the responsibility for unearthing the proof, the allocation issue of who must prove which element and to what degree, is often fought over and can determine whether a case wins or loses.

So as you (the lawyer) hear Albert Lee's story in the *Cherryum* case, you will automatically start thinking to yourself about potential causes of action, how you will state your allegations, meet your production and persuasion burdens, and how to defend against the potential defenses the defendant or defendants might have. Sometimes American lawyers will say they are analyzing the "prima facie case" of the plaintiff. This might mean that they are trying to figure out if there is any possible cause of action and what its elements are or whether they have evidence for each element sufficient to meet their production burden.

If you are in private practice, you will also be thinking about the financial implications of the case. How will you be paid, how much will you be paid, is the case worth taking? As you have read, private plaintiffs' lawyers normally take tort cases in the United States on a contingent fee basis. They are paid a percentage of the plaintiff's recovery, typically one-third. If the plaintiff receives no recovery, then the plaintiff's lawyer receives no fee. In order to promote the enforcement of some federal claims, Congress on occasion has passed statutes obligating the defendant to pay the plaintiff's legal fees if the plaintiff wins. Such statutes are particularly important in attracting lawyers to represent plaintiffs in lawsuits that are difficult to win, such as civil rights and environmental cases. Congress has passed over 180 fee-shifting statutes, but none of them will cover Albert Lee's negligence and implied warranty case, which is not based on federal law.[3]

Having read a little about the *Cherryum* case, consider whether you, as an American lawyer, would agree to represent the plaintiff. Do the harm and potential damages seem substantial? Even at this early stage, can you determine whether it is likely you could meet your production burden on at least one cause of action? What about meeting the persuasion burden? Is the story credible? Without having heard anything of the defendant's side of the cause, what problems do you foresee? What possible defenses are there?

If you decide to take the case for Albert Lee, you will, of course, have to decide who will be the plaintiff or plaintiffs and defendants and what the plausible causes of action are. You will also have to decide in what court to

---

3. For a discussion of attorneys' fees, billing, and fee-shifting statutes in the United States, *see* Stephen N. Subrin, Martha L. Minow, Mark S. Brodin, & Thomas O. Main, Civil Procedure–Doctrine, Practice, and Context 118-140 (Aspen Publishers 2d Ed. 2004).

bring the lawsuit, as discussed in Chapter 5. As you recall, plaintiffs can only sue in a state court or in a federal court within the state to which the defendant has a sufficient connection. Since the sale of the Cherryum drink took place in Massachusetts, and Albert Lee suffered his harm in Massachusetts, the defendant or defendants are probably subject to suit in Massachusetts and will be bound by a judicial decision issued by a state or federal court in Massachusetts. Subject matter jurisdiction in this case can be achieved in state court or federal court on diversity of citizenship grounds, and there would be no trouble obtaining venue in either state or federal court.

COMMENCING A LAWSUIT IN THE UNITED STATES: THE COMPLAINT

Assume that based on your favorable experience with the federal court, and because the federal courthouse is close to your office, you have decided to bring the *Cherryum* case in the Federal District Court for Massachusetts. This means that the Federal Rules of Civil Procedure will apply to the case. Rule 8(a) dictates what you must put in the complaint, which is rather minimal. According to Rule 8(a), you need to state the subject matter jurisdiction that permits the case to be filed in federal court, a statement of the claim, and the relief sought. The complaint needs simply to state "a short and plain statement of the claim showing that the pleader is entitled to relief." Under Rule 8, fine details in the complaint are not required; "notice" pleading is sufficient.

The quote at the beginning of this chapter came from Charles Clark, the major draftsman of the Federal Rules. It explains why details of statement were perceived as unnecessary in a federal complaint. The concept is that a pleading is not the appropriate battleground for ferreting out the details and merits of a case. Rather, that task should be reserved for later discovery. What has been called "notice pleading" was thus premised on the philosophy that pleading requirements should simply act as guides to the litigation, and not as barriers to the court system. Pleadings are not expected to further the development of the case any more than merely giving general notice to the defendant of the nature of the suit against her and providing a basis for later discovery.

Rule 8 is based on that philosophy, and other Federal Rules and subsequent Supreme Court cases express this same thought. For example, Rule 8(e)(1) states that "[e]ach averment of a pleading shall be simple, concise, and direct. No technical forms of pleading or motions are required." Furthermore, Rule 8(f) states: "All pleadings shall be so construed as to do substantial justice."

This is a departure from the prior 1848 Field Code,[4] which, while rejecting the forms of action and single issue pleading, nevertheless preserved the common law jurisprudence of using pleadings to narrow disputes. Indeed, the Field Code continued to force plaintiffs to investigate their cause of action before filing and to provide, under oath, specific details of their case. The

---

4. The Field Code was explained in some detail in Chapter 3.

original 1848 Code obligated plaintiffs to state "facts constituting the cause of action, in ordinary and concise language without repetition, and in such manner as to enable a person of common understanding to know what is intended."[5] This was later amended to a "plain and concise statement of facts constituting a cause of action without unnecessary repetition,"[6] but nevertheless retained its requirement of specificity.

In his early drafts of the Federal Rules, Charles Clark adhered closer to the Field Code than what was ultimately adopted. His first draft initially required more specificity and a "statement of the acts and occurrences upon which the plaintiff bases his claim or claims for relief,"[7] while his second draft required all pleadings to state "facts [or as an alternative acts, omissions, and occurrences] without detail, upon which the claims of the pleader are based."[8] Ultimately, however, the drafters chose the "claim showing that the pleader is entitled to relief," language dictating a much less stringent requirement.

For years, Clark thought that arguments over the exact wording of pleadings were largely a waste of time. It was therefore not difficult to convince him to require little of pleading and to rely on the advantages of liberal discovery provisions. Clark thought that the legitimate goals for a complaint were met so long as the complaint told the court why it had subject matter jurisdiction, stated the relief sought, and gave general notice to the defendant sufficient to commence intelligent discovery, such that would later permit a subsequent court to apply *res judicata* doctrine (preclusion law)[9] to prevent needless relitigation of the same cause of action.

The proposition that pleadings should ordinarily not be the battleground for finding the details of each side's position was reaffirmed by the United States Supreme Court in 1957. In *Conley v. Gibson*, the Supreme Court not only upheld liberal pleadings, but also stated that pleadings would not ordinarily serve as a means of disposing cases:

> ... [T]he Federal Rules of Civil Procedure do not require a claimant to set out in detail the facts upon which he bases his claim. To the contrary, all the Rules require is a 'short and plain statement of the claim' that will give the defendant fair notice of what the plaintiff's claim is and the grounds upon which it rests.... Such simplified 'notice pleading' is made possible by the liberal opportunity for discovery and other pretrial procedures established by the Rules to disclose more precisely the basis of both claim and defense and to define more narrowly the disputed facts and issues.[10]

5. N.Y. Laws c. 379, § 142 (2) (1848).

6. N.Y. Law, c. 438 (1848); N.Y. Laws c. 479, § 142 (2) (1851). The plaintiff, in § 142 (3) of the 1851 Act, also had to include in the complaint a "demand of the relief, to which the plaintiff supposes himself entitled. If the recovery of money be demanded, the amount thereof shall be stated."

7. This story, and citations to where the various drafts can be found, may be found in Stephen N. Subrin, *How Equity Conquered Common Law: The Federal Rules of Civil Procedure in Historical Perspective*, 135 U. Pa. L. Rev. 909, 976 (Apr. 1987).

8. *Id.*

9. *Res judicata* and other finality doctrine are covered in Chapter 12.

10. *Conley v. Gibson*, 355 U.S. 41 (1957).

On the few occasions when the drafters thought it would help to have more specificity in the pleadings, they have so stated. For example, Rule 9(b) provides: "In all averments of fraud or mistake, the circumstances constituting fraud or mistake shall be stated with particularity..." In other words, with the exception of fraud or mistake and a few other exceptions, the norm under the federal rules is that averments do not have to be stated with particularity.

Rule 8(e)(1) further permits parties to set forth claims or defenses "alternatively or hypothetically." That is, parties may state as many separate claims or defenses as the party has "regardless of consistency and whether based on legal, equitable, or maritime grounds." The Federal Rules even provided sample forms in the Appendix of Forms to demonstrate "the simplicity and brevity of statement which the rules contemplate."

Despite the language of Rule 8, which seems to require simply a general statement of the claim, some federal judges have in recent years required more detailed allegations in certain cases.[11] This has been particularly true in lawsuits against city governments for alleged violations of plaintiffs' civil rights. Such cases prompted a unanimous United States Supreme Court in 1992 to reaffirm that portion of *Conley v. Gibson* holding that a plaintiff is not required under the Federal Rules "'to set out in detail the facts upon which he bases his claim.'" *Leatherman v. Tarrant County Narcotics Intelligence and Coordination Unit*, 507 U.S. 163 (1992). This same point was reiterated by the Supreme Court unanimously, in *Swierkiewicz v. Sorema*, 534 U.S. 500 (2002). Nevertheless, notwithstanding *Conley v. Gibson, Leatherman,* and *Swierkiewisz,* federal courts continue to impose a variety of heightened pleading standards in numerous disfavored subject matter areas outside the scope of Rule 9.[12]

While the rules do not require great specificity in pleading, they also do not prohibit a more detailed complaint if you so desire. There are a number of strategic considerations that might prompt a lawyer to draft a more elaborate complaint. In federal courts, a single judge is ordinarily assigned to the case on a random basis at the time the complaint is filed. Since the same judge will be presiding in all matters concerning the case, a lawyer may want that judge to read a very full and detailed account of why her client was aggrieved very early on. Most judges and lawyers continually return to the pleadings when they want to get reacquainted with the case.

Additionally, a complaint will also be read by the opposing lawyers and their clients. A more detailed complaint may help convince your opponents to settle on terms favorable to your client. In other instances, you may want your complaint to tell a more complete story with an eye to the press or the public at large. Finally, your client is also part of the audience who will read the complaint. It may be important to your client to see that you have taken the

---

11. One scholar of the American experience under the Federal Rules has noted that while the language of Rule 8(a) has remained constant, it has undergone different interpretations depending on what the legal culture seeks. It may require more detailed pleadings if the legal culture seeks to discourage litigation in a given area; or it may require less specific factual allegation in order to make it easier to sue. Thomas O. Main, *Procedural Uniformity and the Exaggerated Role of Rules: A Survey of Intra-State Uniformity in Three States That Have Not Adopted the Federal Rules of Civil Procedure*, 46 Vill. L. Rev. 311 (2001).

12. *See, e.g.*, the numerous examples provided in Christopher Fairman, *The Myth of Notice Pleading*, 45 Ariz. L. Rev. 987 (2003).

time to understand the case and to write up a more detailed, convincing complaint.

On the other hand, a more specific complaint will tip the defendant off on how much you already know or what your strategy may be. Or this may also be a case in which you have insufficient knowledge at the beginning of the case for a more detailed complaint. Further, you may not want your complaint to commit your client to positions at the beginning of the lawsuit that you and the client may later regret. These contrary considerations may prompt you to draft a less detailed complaint.

In practice, the typical complaint, to comply with Rule 8 (a), needs to simply state who the parties are and the provision of federal law on which subject matter jurisdiction is based. The plaintiff's lawyer then usually takes several paragraphs to generally tell the plaintiff's story and what the defendant did wrong. The complaint then usually has what are called "counts" for each specific cause of action against each named defendant. For instance, in the *Cherryum* case, you might sue the manufacturer of the Cherryum syrup and the bottler for negligence and for breach of implied warranty. After telling the story generally in paragraphs, a plaintiff's lawyer would ordinarily recite one count after another. In the *Cherryum* case, the complaint might begin with "Count One: Implied Warranty Against Cherryum Bottling Co., Inc," and then continue by incorporating the preceding paragraphs by reference and telling why the story adds up to an implied warranty claim against the bottler.

A plaintiff's lawyer will add counts for each cause of action against each defendant. This method satisfies the Rule 8(a)(2) requirement of making "a short and plain statement of the claim showing that the pleader is entitled to relief." Finally, either at the end of each "count" or at the end of the entire complaint, the plaintiff's lawyer will demand a judgment for the relief plaintiff seeks, in compliance with Rule 8(a)(3). Once again, the Federal Rules are quite liberal in what they permit. Rule 54(c) states: "... Except as to a party against whom a judgment is entered by default, every final judgment shall grant the relief to which the party in whose favor it is rendered is entitled, even if the party has not demanded such relief in the party's pleadings."

Although the Federal Rules do not require that the complaint be signed under oath, Rule 11 does require that at least "one attorney of record," if the party has an attorney, to sign "each pleading, written motion, and other paper..." The signature acts as a certification that the lawyer has done reasonable factual and legal investigation before filing the document and believes that the factual allegations and legal contentions are supportable or at least, "are likely to have evidentiary support." The certification requirement does not change the pleading requirements, but, as we will later discuss, it may influence how detailed you decide to be in your complaint.

A federal case is commenced by filing the complaint, by mail or in person, in the clerk's office in the appropriate federal court. The clerk's office then issues a summons, that is a paper notifying the defendant of the commencement of the suit and that the defendant has a certain number of days, usually 20, in which to file an answer to the complaint. It is the responsibility of the plaintiff (or, realistically, the plaintiff's attorney) to have the complaint and summons served on the defendant within what is usually 120 days from the filing of the complaint in court. Service of process meets the notice requirement, which is one of the foundational requirements in commencing a lawsuit.

The Federal Rules provide a number of different ways in which the plaintiff can have the summons and complaint served on the defendant. Service may be rendered by an adult personally handing the papers to the defendant or by mailing the papers to the defendant if the defendant consents and signs a waiver of the need for personal service or by leaving copies at the defendant's "dwelling house or usual place of abode." Under Rule 4, service is also satisfied by compliance with any method for serving the defendant permitted under state law in the state in which the federal court is sitting. Similarly, one can serve a corporation using the previously described mail and waiver method, or "by delivering a copy of the summons and complaint to an officer, a managing or general agent, or to any other agent authorized by appointment or by law to receive service of process...." Fed. R. Civ. P. 4(h). If service of the summons and complaint are not waived by the plaintiff, than whoever served the complaint "shall make proof thereof to the court." Fed. R. Civ. P. 4(l). Filing an affidavit with the court normally satisfies proof of service.

THE DEFENDANT'S RESPONSE

The defendant is ordinarily obligated to serve an answer to the complaint on the plaintiff "within 20 days after being served with the summons of the complaint." If the defendant has waived the need to be personally served, then the defendant has "60 days after the date when the request for waiver was sent" in which to answer. This extended time period is one incentive for the defendant to waive the necessity for more formal service, and to accept the more informal mail service. Fed. R. Civ. P. 12(a).

The defendant may raise certain preliminary defenses by motion prior to answering (which delays the time in which an answer must be filed) or may put those defenses in the answer. These special preliminary motions raise objections to foundational issues such as subject matter jurisdiction, personal jurisdiction, venue, service of process, or failure to join a necessary or indispensable party. Fed. R. Civ. P. 12(b). The defendant may also move to dismiss by preliminary motion on the ground that there is no cognizability for what the plaintiff has claimed or in other words, there is no legal cause of action for what happened to the plaintiff. This is the well-known 12(b)(6) motion or defense for "failure to state a claim for which relief can be granted." Fed. R. Civ. P. 12(b)(6).[13]

The defendant's answer must reply to each and every allegation individually. The answer must either deny or admit each allegation in plaintiff's complaint. If "a party is without knowledge or information sufficient to form a belief as to the truth of an averment," then the party must so state and this has the effect of a denial. Defendant must also include in her answer any and all affirmative defenses claimed by the defendant. This includes any preliminary defenses (such as objecting to venue or personal jurisdiction), unless they

13. We discuss these preliminary motions in great detail in Chapter 8.

were previously raised by a pre-answer motion. Defendant must assert any claim she may have against the plaintiff (counterclaims) that arise from the transaction or occurrence that is the subject of the plaintiff's complaint. Fed. R. Civ. P. 8(b), (c); 13(a). These are called compulsory counterclaims.[14]

Consistent with the modern day "notice pleadings" philosophy of the Federal Rules, defendants do not have to be any more factually specific in their allegations than was required of the plaintiff. Thus, "a party shall state in short and plain terms the party's defense to each claim asserted . . ." Fed. R. Civ. P. 8(b). If either the defendant or plaintiff wishes to have a jury decide the case, then she ordinarily must demand in writing her right to jury trial within ten days after the answer is filed or the right is waived. Fed. R. Civ. P. 38(b).

Unless the court so orders, there is no requirement for the plaintiff to reply to the defendant's answer, and the defendant's allegations in the answer are taken as denied by the plaintiff. Fed. R. Civ. P. 8(d). In fact, the plaintiff is not permitted to reply to an answer unless the court orders it. Fed. R. Civ. P. 7(a). This is one more indication of how little the Federal Rules drafters meant for the pleadings to supply much information or to be a means of siphoning out irrelevant issues. Pretrial discovery, pretrial conferences, and summary judgments (all topics later covered) will bear the task of focusing the litigation on its most important points.

AMENDMENTS

The drafters of the Federal Rules continued their liberal approach to pleadings in their drafting of the amendment rules. In general, a plaintiff may amend its complaint as a matter of right before an answer is filed. The defendant may amend its answer as a matter of right within 20 days after it is served on the plaintiff. Ordinarily, if evidence is admitted at trial that goes beyond the allegations of a pleading, the court will permit an amendment to the pleading or treat the relevant pleading as if it has been amended. Fed. R. Civ. P. 15(b). Motions to amend pleadings are to be freely granted, "when justice so requires." Fed. R. Civ. P. 15(a).

The most important issues with respect to amending pleadings concern whether the amendment will relate back to the date of the original pleading. This is most significant if the amended complaint is filed beyond the statute of limitations (the statutory period within which a particular claim must be filed). For example, assume that *B* allegedly intentionally hit *A* on January 1, 2003, and an applicable three-year statute of limitations for tort actions starts running the day *A* was hit. A files a complaint against *B* on April 8, 2003, well within the expiration of the three years for battery, but fails to include the cause of action of negligence. In February, 2006, 40 days beyond the statute of limitations period, A moves to amend the complaint to add a cause of action (often called a "count") for negligence based on the same incident as the initial

---

14. We discuss counterclaims and other joinder devices in more detail in Chapter 9.

complaint. Unless the amended complaint relates back to the date of the original complaint, that cause of action will be deemed beyond the statute of limitations and dismissed by the court.

Rule 15(a) rests discretion with the court in deciding whether a complaint may be amended. Rule 15(e) says that "leave shall be freely given when justice so requires." Rule 15(c) says that the amendment will relate back to the date of the original complaint if the "complaint or defense asserted in the amended pleading arose out of the conduct, transaction, or occurrence set forth or attempted to be set forth in the original pleading." Therefore, if the court thought that justice was served by granting the amendment, it is likely that the negligence claim will be treated as if it were part of the complaint filed on April 8, 2003. The plaintiff will be able to defeat the statute of limitations defense even though the amendment was filed 40 days after the statute of limitation has run.

The Rule 15 amendment rules also permit amendments to change or add to the parties. Once again, such amendments are to be freely granted, "when justice so requires." The "relation back" provisions, that is, whether the added parties will relate back to the date of the first complaint, are, however, more stringent when one is adding a new party. Fed. R. Civ. P. 15(c)(3)(A, B). Of course, if the statute of limitations has not yet run, then the amending party does not have any need for a "relation back."

The Debate in America about "Frivolous Litigation"

With such liberal pleading requirements, how are frivolous law suits to be prevented? Like the drafters of the Field Code in an earlier period, Clark in his first Federal Rule draft initially proposed a verification requirement. Lawyers were to certify in pleadings that to the best of their knowledge the matters alleged were true. But other members of the Advisory Committee who drafted the Federal Rules thought that the idea of a signature under oath by attorneys was "naïve" because neither lawyers nor their clients would know at the beginning of a case what facts would later be found to be true.[15] The verification requirement was eliminated from the 1938 Federal Rules.[16] What replaced it was a Rule 11 requirement that pleadings must at least be signed by a lawyer, when the party had a lawyer, as a certification that "he has read the pleading; that to the best of his knowledge, information, and belief there is good ground to support it; and that it is not interposed for delay." Potential penalties for violating this rule included striking the guilty pleading or "[f]or a willful violation of this rule any attorney may be subject to appropriate disciplinary action." According to critics, this version of Rule 11 was very sparingly used and was not effective in inhibiting frivolous litigation in any serious way. Today, however, Rule 11 has became the weapon and the battleground for reform efforts to curb what many alleged was widespread frivolous litigation.

15. Subrin, *supra* note 7, at 977.
16. *Id.* (citations omitted).

Starting in the mid-1970s, the intensity of criticism about civil litigation in the United States escalated markedly.[17] Much of the criticism was, and continues to be, directed at the alleged frivolousness of personal injury tort claims and the deleterious effect such claims have on the American economy. The much-publicized 1981 book, The Litigious Society, exemplified this concern: "Ours is a law-drenched age.... So widespread is the impulse to sue that 'litigation has become the nation's secular religion.'...These days one hears a crescendo of concern that America has become a litigious society, posing dangers to individuals and to the commonweal."[18] Examples of preposterous lawsuits ranged from the case of the Italian Historical Society of America suing to stop the United States Postal Service from issuing a stamp commemorating Alexander Graham Bell (the Society contended that it was an Italian who invented the telephone) to the case of football fans suing because of a disputed result in a close game.[19] The author then states:

> The plaintiffs lost most of these cases; some were blatantly frivolous. But that is not the salient point. Most — perhaps all — would have been impossible to conceive only a quarter century ago or less, and many worked their way through the court system before being dismissed. Taken together, critics charge, these lawsuits and the millions of others that are filed every year in the 17,000 courthouses that dot the landscape amount to a "legal explosion," a "society bent on waging total law," a litigious storm of hurricane proportions...[20]

By 1983, allegations of civil litigation abuse reached a high pitch. The debate focused around whether the Federal Rules of Civil Procedure and the state procedures patterned after the federal model are overly permissive to plaintiffs; whether there are too many lawyers in the United States; whether Americans are litigious by nature; and whether frequent, delayed, and costly litigation in America is both a drag on the economy and unfair to defendants. The critique is rarely based on empirical data, but instead, as pointed out by one opponent of such views, often relies on the "common sense" view:[21]

> According to this "common-sense" view, there are too many tort claims, Americans sue too readily, "at the drop of a hat"; egged on by avaricious lawyers, they overwhelm the congested courts with mounting number of suits, including many frivolous claims. Irresponsible juries, biased against deep-pocket defendants, bestow windfalls on undeserving plaintiffs, particularly arbitrary and capricious damages for pain and suffering and random outsize

17. *See, e.g., The Pound Conference: Perspectives on Justice in the Future* (A. Levin & R. Wheeler eds. 1979) (proceedings of the National Conference on the Causes of Popular Dissatisfaction with the Administration of Justice), especially speeches by Chief Justice Burger, and attorneys Kirkham and Rifkind.
18. Jethro K. Liberman, The Litigious Society xi (Basic Books, Inc. 1981) (citation omitted).
19. *Id.* at 4-5.
20. *Id.* at 5 (citations omitted). "By 1980 lawsuits were being filed in the fifty state court systems and the local courts of the District of Columbia at the rate of 5 million a year. And according to the National Center for State Courts in Williamsburg, Virginia, the number could be as high as 12 million a year. Federal courts, a much smaller, though far more noticeable, judicial operation, were receiving nearly 170,000 suits annually." (citations omitted).
21. Marc Galanter, *Real World Torts: An Antidote to Anecdote*, 55 Md. L. Rev. 1095 (1996) [hereinafter Galanter, *Real World Torts*].

awards of punitive damages. Not only are the untold billions that the system costs an alarming drain on national wealth, but the system stifles enterprise and innovation, depriving society of useful products and services and undermining the international competitiveness of American business. To avoid these effects, we need to adopt various "tort reform" proposals to inhibit claims (e.g., loser-pays) and limit awards (e.g. eliminating joint and several liability, capping damages, etc.).[22]

One respected empiricist, Marc Galanter, challenged this "common sense" view to argue that the allegations of an overly litigious America are either untrue or grossly overstated. Using the limited empirical data available, Galanter pointed out that "[l]ooking at the country as whole, filings of tort cases peaked in the late 1980's, and have been relatively flat or trending downward since.... The great bulk of the growth in state court caseloads has been and continues to be in criminal cases and in domestic relations cases."[23] Galanter recognized that there has been an increase of one type of tort claims (products liability) in federal courts in recent years,[24] but noted that mass tort cases, in which thousands of plaintiffs claim injury from the same product, represent only 2 percent of the national total of tort cases. Yet, because these mass tort cases are frequently brought in federal court, they occupy "a major place in professional discourse about torts and the media image of the civil justice system, and it animates the salience of torts as a political issue."[25]

Are Americans in fact more litigious than citizens of other countries? Are frivolous lawsuits a bigger problem in the United States than elsewhere such that a stricter pleadings regime may be required? This is not easy to document empirically for a number of reasons. For one, what would be the appropriate guidelines to decide whether citizens of a country sue too much and what would be the definition of a frivolous suit? Many lawsuits that seem frivolous to a defendant may seem appropriate to the plaintiff and the plaintiff's lawyer.

From what we can surmised, however, from 1969 to 1978, there were 44 civil filings in all American courts per 1000 citizens per year. This includes domestic (divorces) and probate (will) cases, which compose a large proportion of American civil cases. The comparable statistics on civil filings for Australia were 62 per 1000 citizens per year; for Canada, it was 46; New Zealand, 53; Denmark, 41. Some of the low figures were the Netherlands at 8, Spain at 3, and Japan at 12.[26] If true, then the United States seems hardly out of line, and as Galanter so concluded:

> ...[O]nly a small portion of troubles and injuries become disputes; only a small portion of these becomes lawsuits. Of those that do, the vast majority are abandoned, settled or routinely processed without full-blown adjudication. Comparisons of current with past litigation rates shows a recent rise, but present

22. *Id.* at 1095.
23. *Id.* at 1102-1105.
24. "Product liability filings in federal district courts rose from twenty-nine percent of all personal injury filings in 1984 to forty-three percent in 1995." *Id.* at 1105. The surge of product liability claims in federal court was first driven by a massive increase of asbestos claims in the 1970s and 1980s, and since then by other types of claims, such as those including airplanes, motor vehicles, and toxic torts.
25. *Id.* at 1109.
26. Marc Galanter, *Reading the Landscape of Disputes: What We Know and Don't Know (And Think We Know) About Our Allegedly Contentious and Litigious Society*, 31 U.C.L.A. L. Rev. 4 (Oct. 1983), at 52.

levels are not historically unprecedented. Admittedly weak comparisons with data from other jurisdictions suggest that per capita rates of litigation in United States courts fall in the same general range of those of England, Australia, Ontario (Canada) and others, but are higher than those of other industrialized countries.[27]

Even if it is fair to conclude that there is a good deal more per capita civil litigation in the United States than in most other countries, it is much more difficult to ascertain whether there is a disproportionate amount of *frivolous* litigation in the United States. A rough estimate is that of those who perceive to have an injury and blame another person for that injury (called a "grievance" by those who analyze data in this field), only 38 of 1000 (4 percent) end up with a court filing.[28] Certainly, this would not support the conclusion that Americans are quick to sue. While we still do not know what percentage of lawsuits that were brought was without merit, data does suggest that plaintiffs do win in tort cases that reach a final verdict about 50 percent of the time.[29]

One legal scholar in the United States, Professor Robert Bone, attributes frivolous law suits to the problem of asymmetric information.[30] In other words, if a frivolous lawsuit is defined as a lawsuit filed even when a plaintiff knows that there is no factual basis for the suit or does not do reasonable investigation that would have shown the absence of factual support, asymmetric information will invite plaintiffs to bring such suits. If the plaintiff's lawyer knows that the case is factually insupportable but thinks that the defendant's lawyer does not know this and cannot know this without the expenditure of money, the plaintiff may still bring suit on the game theory that the defendant will have an economic incentive to settle what is in fact a frivolous case.

However, Bone also admits that the results of his formal analysis "neither rule out nor clearly confirm a serious frivolous suit problem."[31] Nor does Bone think that stricter pleading would deter many frivolous suits. The plaintiff who knows her lawsuit lacks factual basis but brings the suit anyway would probably be willing to fabricate the necessary allegations to meet the stricter pleading requirements. The plaintiff who lacks information but knows that the pre-filing investigation is too expensive will bring suit in order to learn from the defendant or from discovery what the facts are. Thus, Bone does not think that

27. *Id.* at 5. Changes in patterns of governmental activity, in the organization of legal work, and the relation of the media to the law combine to enlarge litigation as a symbolic presence even when direct personal experience of full-blown adjudication has become relatively less frequent. It is suggested that contemporary patterns of disputing should be seen as a relatively conservative adaptation to changing conditions, including, for example, changes in the production of injuries, knowledge about them, education, and so forth. Elite perceptions of an eruption of pathological litigiousness are viewed as a symptom of the weakness of contemporary legal scholarship.

28. Galanter, *Real World Torts, supra* note 21, at 1101, adapted from Richard E. Miller & Austin Sarat, *Grievances, Claims and Disputes: Assessing the Adversary Culture*, 17 Law & Soc'y Rev. 525, 544 (1980-1981).

29. *Id.* at 1110-1113.

30. Professor Robert Bone provided this definition of a frivolous suit: "(1) when a plaintiff files knowing facts that establish complete (or virtually complete) absence of merit as an objective matter on the legal theories alleged, or (2) when a plaintiff files without conducting a reasonable investigation which, if conducted, would place the suit in prong (1)." Robert G. Bone, *Modeling Frivolous Suits*, 145 U. Pa. L. Rev. 519, 533 (Jan. 1997).

a stricter pleading requirement would do very much to solve a frivolous litigation problem, if in fact, there is such a problem.

In thinking about whether stricter pleading would deter frivolous lawsuits, consider once more the *Cherryum* case. What if Albert Lee did put the insecticides in the drink and sought to make a substantial amount of money from an ungrounded lawsuit either through settlement or by winning a case through fabrication? Lee's lawyer would have no way of knowing that the suit was frivolous when Mr. Lee came in the office and told the story. Lee did, after all, drink from a Cherryum can that apparently had poisons in it, and a fact finder may believe his version of the story. This would be a tort case that no amount of stricter pleading would have deterred.

Trying to Curb Frivolous Law Suits: Amending Rule 11 Twice

Whether or not frivolous litigation is a problem in the United States, legal reformers were nevertheless motivated to act. Although there have been periodic proposals in the United States for stricter pleading requirements, most of the reform energy has centered more in amending Rule 11 and in heightening the lawyers' responsibilities under that rule. As you recall, the 1938 version of Federal Rule 11 initially required the attorney of record to sign every pleading, and to certify "that he had read the pleading... [and] that to the best of his knowledge, information, and belief there is good ground to support it..." By 1983, the Advisory Committee (composed of judges, lawyers, and academics, appointed by the Judicial Conference)[32] in charge of drafting the Federal Rules, concluded that Rule 11 needed to be tightened. The Advisory Committee noted that between 1938 and 1976, there were only 11 reported cases resulting in a finding that Rule 11 was violated.[33] Thus, the Advisory Committee argued that Rule 11 must be expanded to cover more attorney misconduct. In 1983, the Advisory Committee argued "Greater attention by the district courts to pleading and motion abuses and imposition of sanctions when appropriate, should discourage dilatory or abusive tactics and help to streamline the litigation process by lessening frivolous claims or defenses."

The 1983 amendments to Rule 11 expanded the rule's certification requirement to cover all court filings, in addition to pleadings. Rule 11 in this incarnation required the lawyer to conduct a reasonable inquiry to ensure that each allegation is "well grounded in fact and is warranted by existing law or a good faith argument for the extension, modification, or reversal of existing law, and that it is not interposed for any improper purpose, such as to harass or to cause unnecessary delay or needless increase in the cost of litigation." Under the 1983 test, it was not enough that the filing lawyer

32. 28 U.S.C. § 2073 (appointment of Advisory Committees); 28 U.S.C. § 331 (composition of the Judicial Conference). The Judicial Conference is presided over by the Chief Justice of the United Supreme Court and composed of the chief judge and a district court judge of each judicial circuit and the chief judge of the Court of International Trade.
33. Michael Risinger, *Honesty in Pleading and its Enforcement: Some "Striking" Problems with Federal Rule of Civil Procedure Rule 11*, 61 Minn. L. Rev. 1, 34-37 (Nov. 1976).

thought in good faith that the pleading or other document was justified; there must be a "reasonable inquiry" by the lawyer. If there was not objectively a reasonable pre-filing inquiry into the facts and the law demonstrating a basis for the lawsuit, then the lawyer or the client *must* be sanctioned by the judge under Rule 11. Mandatory "appropriate" sanctions "may include an order to pay the other party or parties the amount of the reasonable expenses incurred because of the pleading, motion, or other paper, including a reasonable attorney's fee."

The Advisory Committee, in commenting on the 1983 version of Rule 11, cautioned that "the rule is not intended to chill an attorney's enthusiasm or creativity in pursuing factual or legal theories," but also noted that the new rule "seeks to dispel apprehensions that efforts to obtain enforcement will be fruitless . . ." It was thought that mandatory sanctions would encourage lawyers to seek enforcement of the rule. The encouragement worked and perhaps worked too well.

In the years following the 1983 amendments to Rule 11 there was a huge increase in utilization of Rule 11 and in the number of cases in which sanctions were being imposed. There was some evidence that Rule 11 worked as intended to force lawyers to do more rigorous investigation of the facts and the law prior to filing pleadings and other papers in court. A thorough one-year study of the operation of the new Rule 11 in one federal circuit concluded that indeed, Rule 11 "had an impact on pre-filing conduct of a kind that the rulemakers intended." Many lawyers on both sides apparently reported that they took greater care in pre-filing inquiries as a result of the amended rule. The data, however, did not permit findings as to whether frivolous claims and defenses were lessened.[34]

More problematically, this same report also spoke to the troubling aspects of Rule 11. Plaintiffs were targets of Rule 11 motions at about twice the rate as defendants. Plaintiffs were sanctioned in about 16 percent of the motions made against them, while defendants were sanctioned at a lesser rate of 9 percent. Plaintiffs were targets of about 71 percent of the Rule 11 motions in civil rights cases, and they were sanctioned in 47.1 percent of these motions, as compared to 8.45 percent for all Rule 11 motions.[35] Although this was data from only one federal circuit for one year, the results were similar to what other Rule 11 watchers were finding elsewhere. Rule 11 motions were launched against plaintiffs and their lawyers (in particular, in civil rights cases) far more frequently and more successfully than against defendants. Although Rule 11 did not change the pleading requirements of Rule 8(a), a cautious plaintiff's lawyer might well have to plead a considerably more detailed complaint in order to dissuade a Rule 11 motion for sanctions if the case was lost.

This disparity was particularly troubling to civil rights lawyers because such lawyers usually were not wealthy and penalties against them would have a definite chilling effect on what cases they bought. In some district courts in the United States, defendant lawyers who won cases, especially at the pleading or

---

34. Stephen B. Burbank, Reporter, Rule 11 in Transition — The Report of the Third Circuit Task Force on Federal Rule of Civil Procedure 76 (American Judicature Society 1989).
    35. *Id*.at xiv, 58.

summary judgment stage, would bring Rule 11 motions as a matter of course. Some federal district court judges even regularly used the sanction of awarding attorney fees to the defendant's counsel as sanctions to be paid by plaintiffs' lawyers or the clients. Rule 11 was turning into a "fee-shifting" statute, that is, shifting defendant's attorney's fees to the plaintiff. As a result, some lawyers reported that, on occasion, they did not bring cases they thought were meritorious out of fear that if they lost the case, they would be subject to Rule 11 sanctions.

It may not be surprising that Rule 11 sanctions were disproportionately sought and granted against plaintiffs, and particularly, against civil rights plaintiffs. A plaintiff is particularly vulnerable to a Rule 11 accusation, because a plaintiff, in complaining about the defendant's action or inaction, often starts the case with incomplete knowledge. This is particularly true in a civil rights case in which plaintiff must prove the defendant's intent to discriminate. Plaintiffs rarely have direct evidence of such intent and, instead, will generally have to prove intent inferentially, after painstaking discovery. The defendant, on the other hand, in its answer to the complaint must merely admit or deny facts or state that "it is without knowledge or information sufficient to form a belief as to the truth of the averment." Fed. R. Civ. P. 8(b). Clearly, the defendant has better knowledge about its own activities than the plaintiff.

The accusations that plaintiffs, and in particular civil rights plaintiffs, are disproportionately burdened by Rule 11, along with other criticisms, led to a 1993 amendment of Rule 11, this time, in the opposite direction to reduce its use. The Advisory Committee's Note to the 1993 amendments states: "This revision is intended to remedy problems that have arisen in the interpretation and application of the 1983 revision of the rule. . . . [The new Rule 11] . . . should reduce the number of motions for sanctions presented to the court."

Under the 1993 amendments to Rule 11, which are still in effect, signing, filing, submitting, or later advocating a pleading, written motion, or other paper means that one is certifying "that to the best of the person's knowledge, information, and belief, formed after an inquiry reasonable under the circumstances" that it is not being presented for an improper purpose, such as harassment or to cause delay or the needless increase of costs and:

> (2) the claims, defense, and other legal contentions therein are warranted by existing law or by a nonfrivolous argument for the extension, modification, or reversal of existing law or the establishment of new law;
> (3) the allegations and other factual contentions have evidentiary support or, if specifically so identified, are likely to have evidentiary support after a reasonable opportunity for further investigation or discovery; and
> (4) the denials of factual contentions are warranted on the evidence, or, if specifically so identified, are reasonably based on a lack of information or belief.

Yet several revisions in the rule make it less likely that Rule 11 motions will be brought or sanctions levied. The party seeking the sanctions must provide a "safe harbor" — that is, give the opponent at least 21 days to withdraw or appropriately correct "the challenged paper, claim, defense, contention, allegation, or denial" before filing a Rule 11 motion in court. Rule 11(c)(1)(A). This "safe harbor" provision gives the challenged party the opportunity to correct a mistaken filing. Further, even if a judge finds a violation of Rule 11, sanctions are now discretionary, rather than mandatory as previously under the 1983 version. Clearly rejecting the use of Rule 11 as a fee-shifting statute, the new rule now makes clear that sanctions are for deterrent purposes only and "shall be limited to what is sufficient to deter repetition of such conduct," and ordinarily to be paid into court and not to the opposing party or its lawyer. Fed. R. Civ. P. 11(c)(2).

Not all agree that Rule should be amended. Justice Scalia of the United States Supreme Court asserted: "The proposed revision would render the Rule toothless, by allowing judges to dispense with sanction, by disfavoring compensation for litigation expenses, and by providing a 21-day 'safe harbor' within which, if the party accused of a frivolous filing withdraws the filing, he is entitled to escape with no sanction at all." Noting that ordinarily monetary sanctions will not be paid to the opposing side that sought the sanction, Justice Scalia suggested that "[t]he net effect is to decrease the incentive on the part of the person best situated to alert the court to perversion of our civil justice system."[36]

WHY DOES AMERICA STAND APART IN ITS PLEADING REQUIREMENTS?

Why did the drafters of the American pleading rules adopt such a liberal pleadings regime? How do American pleading rules compare to other countries? By comparison to other countries, the United States appears to stand apart in giving party control of the pleadings with minimum requirements for specificity either from the rules or the courts.

For example, the European civil law family, more specifically, the German model which adheres closest to the United States model, has historically moved away from such complete party autonomy. While the German system theoretically emphasizes party responsibility, and adheres to the maxim "*ne eat iudex ultra petita partium*," (the parties control the subject matter) in civil proceedings,[37] a plaintiff must nevertheless state specific relief based on particular facts and must disclose relevant facts. Furthermore, simple written pleadings are merely preparatory to a later hearing in open court at which the attorneys orally present their client's allegations, arguments, and prayer for relief. In German law, there is no direct equivalent to the Federal Rule motion for failure to state a claim for which relief can be granted. Rather, at the later preparatory hearing, it is the court, and not necessarily the defendant, has the

---

36. Dissent of Justice Scalia, joined by Justice Thomas, accompanying Letter from William H. Rehnquist, Chief Justice of the United States Supreme Court to Thomas S. Foley, Speaker of the House of Representatives (April 22, 1993), reprinted in 146 F.R.D. 401, at 403.
37. Sec. 308 CCP.

obligation to review the complaint. In Germany, as in the United States, ever-increasing caseloads and delays have led to increased judicial management. Hence, recent reform discussions in Germany call for increasing a party's duty to provide even more information rather than less.

In Japan, the latest civil procedure code in 1998 added stricter pleadings requirements as well as an improved full hearing (called "plenary") held after the complaint to identify the real issues as early as possible. Japanese reformers attempted to maintain respect for the parties' intentions while expanding the court's powers. Thus, under the 1998 Japanese civil procedure code, the complaint must specify the full name and addresses of the parties, "the object of the claim," (meaning the content of judgment that the plaintiff seeks), and the "cause for the claim" (which must be specific in identifying which rights or legal relations are asserted). In addition to specification and particularization of the claim itself, the new code requires that the "operative fact-basis of the claim" be specified and if such facts are disputed in the answer, the plaintiff may be required to submit "indirect facts." The reform also requires that evidence be itemized and written out according to each point to be proved. The role of the complaint is to disclose all of the important facts and evidence at an early stage, as well as to identify the nature of the claim.[38] Only if the court finds the complaint satisfactory will it be served on the opposing party.

Likewise, in China, a separate filing department has been established in which complaints are reviewed for conformity before the case can proceed. Chapter XII, Section 1, Article 110 of the Civil Procedure Law of the People's Republic of China states: "A statement of complaint shall clearly set forth the following: . . . (2) the claim or claims of the suit, the facts and grounds on which the suit is based; and (3) the evidence and its source, as well as the names and home addresses of the witnesses." Not only must a complaint state the claim and facts and grounds on which it is based, it must also include attachments concerning the evidence and its sources and the names and addresses of witnesses. The complaint can be quite general, but the court will assess the complaint's attachments to ensure that there is evidentiary support for each claim.

An American Law Institute project, in conjunction with Unidroit,[39] to adopt a transnational set of procedure recognizes the United States as the renegade with respect to pleading requirements and seeks to harmonize its requirements with rules that harken back to fact pleading and specificity. The American Law Institute (the ALI) is a prestigious organization of elected scholars, lawyers, and judges, changed with the drafting of model codes that governments of different states or countries might wish to adopt. Most recently they have engaged scholars to draft model procedural rules for international disputes, primarily meant to apply to "business disputes" and not tort actions.[40] The ALI "Transnational Rules of Civil Procedure," adopted in 2005, contain a pleading

---

38. Takeshi Kojima, *Symposium Honoring Professor Robert C. Casad: Japanese Civil Procedure in Comparative Law Perspective*, 46 Kansas L. Rev. 687, 699 (May, 1998).

39. Unidroit is the International Institute for the Unification of Private Law, an organization with some 50 member countries, with a central office in Rome, Italy.

40. The American Law Institute, Transnational Rules of Civil Procedure (Proposed Final Draft, March 9, 2004), adopted 2005.

rule that adheres closer to the language and spirit of the Field Code and civil law countries pleading provisions, than to those of the Federal Rules:

> 12.1 The plaintiff must state the facts on which the claim is based, describe the evidence to support those statements, and refer to the legal grounds that support the claim, including foreign, law, if applicable.
> 12.3 The statement of facts must, so far as reasonably practicable, set forth detail as to time, place, participants, and events....[41]

If most countries around the world require more than a "simple pleading," what can account for the American difference? One answer is procedural history. The differences in pleading rules can in part be traced to the distinct ways procedures have developed through the years in particular countries. For example, the move to liberal complaints in the United States were a reaction to the rigid, technical code pleading that dominated civil procedure in the preceding century. The Advisory Committee was reacting to the interpretive problems posed by the 1848 Field Code in distinguishing what was a "fact" from what was "evidence," and how much specificity was required. They also wanted to avoid any temptation by courts to require litigants to conform and revert back to ancient forms of action. The Federal Rule phrase "claim upon which relief can be granted" assiduously avoided the terms "fact," "law," or "cause of action."

But broader political and historical context is at work as well. As we saw in Chapter 3, the liberal pleading system that became law in 1938 also fit the political and professional agendas of politicians, lawyers, judges, and law professors. Each of these groups had an interest in having flexible pleading rules that readily permitted the growth of the law and also permitted the legal profession to more easily join in the experimentation of President Roosevelt's New Deal. Most of those involved thought the pre-trial discovery would provide the specificity and focus lacking in the federal pleading rules.

At the time Charles Clark was drafting the 1938 Federal Rules, it was a combination of powerful social, economic, political, and jurisprudential currents that pushed in the direction of a less constraining procedural system. As a result, Clark eschewed a more rule-bound common law system and instead looked to equity with its more free-wheeling narrative style that had been used in equitable bills. The belief was in creative lawyers who would bring to the courts complex cases that would challenge the judges to create new rights to meet new needs. Liberal pleading, along with liberal joinder rules and liberal discovery, helped facilitate expansive roles for lawyers and judges. This in turn led to more lawyers and larger law firms. More lawyers and larger law firms in turn pushed the boundaries of permissible discovery and judicial rights-creation that in turn invited more lawyers and more lawsuits. And the cycle continued until the backlash: the move toward constraints on lawyers and lawsuits, as characterized by the 1983 amendments to Rule 11.

---

41. Id. at 12.2, 12.3.

Liberal pleadings may also reflect underlying goals of the American legal system. The goals of any legal system are multiple. They span from merely resolving individual private disputes peacefully to the use of civil litigation for the creation of societal norms. In bringing conflicts to the courts, parties have turned to and substituted public office and law for settling differences on their own. When a judge applies general preexisting law in the settlement of disputes, that law becomes an element of social control.[42] As we discussed in Chapter 2, civil litigation in the United States has evolved to enable citizens to act as "private attorney generals" to enforce social norms. In this sense, then, the United States may have greater tolerance for allowing broad pleadings and in waiting for later supporting evidence. It may be said that the American legal system would prefer to open the doors to civil litigation with liberal pleadings and to utilize lay juries because ordinary people, and not only the government, should participate in the development of social norms. Here again we see the American distrust of government and public officials at work.

Other countries may also carry the view that adjudication of civil cases is not purely the private business of the disputing parties, but the social duty of the state.[43] But this social duty of the state is often defined as a duty to resolve the individual disputes, rather than to establish broader social norms through litigation in the courts. With such a different emphasis for the role of the courts, countries other than the United States may hold a general sense that a plaintiff should not bring a claim until she is able to prove her case. Other legal systems with their emphasis on resolving the individual dispute and not necessarily on making common law or expanding legal rights may have led to the belief that the judicial system should not be called upon until the evidence is clear. Furthermore, this sense of social duty in other countries to resolve disputes, leads to this reliance on the professional judge rather than the parties (and their lawyers) in shaping complaints. By contrast, in the United States, the historic mistrust of the judiciary has led to reliance on lawyer rather than judicial discretion to shape the disputes that are taken to the courts — disputes that after an adversary contest could establish new social norms. Liberal pleadings give lawyers this discretion. Pleading requirements, then, not only reflect the doctrinal and broader historical currents, but also the differences in the goals of the legal systems and the role of the courts.

On a practical level, differences in pleading requirements may simply be traced to the availability of legal professionals in the society, as well as to the development of a legal culture. As we saw in the beginning chapters of this book, the United States has a large body of lawyers and a tradition of heavy reliance on law and litigation. When plaintiffs do not have access to the lawyers or are not expected to have lawyers, as a cultural matter, the judges cannot rely on outside professionals to screen out frivolous or unwise litigation before it reaches the courts. Consequently, plaintiffs may be required to show more in

---

42. Martin Shapiro, Courts: A Comparative and Political Analysis 25-26 (University of Chicago Press 1983).
43. Peter Gottwald, Civil Justice Reform: Access, Cost, and Expedition. The German Perspective, in Civil Justice in Crisis: Comparative Perspectives of Civil Procedure 207 (Adrian A.S. Zuckerman, ed. Oxford University Press 1999).

order to gain access to the judicial system, and judges may need to scrutinize complaints early on for legal sufficiency.

Ultimately, there is one more important aspect of the American experience in determining how and why ease of pleading developed in the United States. The reliance on lawyers and litigation to shape social norms in America was taking place, and still takes place, in a country that holds great distrust of an enlarged role for the government to regulate safety and health standards or to police the operations of commerce. Although citizens in the United States have come to expect more health and safety and more opportunity for the good and protected life, Congress — like the rest of the nation — is split on basic value-laden questions relating to such issues as wealth distribution, race, medical care, and the role of government. What this means is that American courts will remain a battleground for important socio-economic issues. These issues find temporary resolution, at least for the parties, through individua-lized litigation rather than through grand policy-implementation fostered by the other two branches of government. Such lawsuits often do not easily lend themselves to rigid pleading before there has been an opportunity for discovery.

Professor Galanter aptly describes Americans' dilemma of wanting protec-tion from the harshness of life but not wanting huge government programs:

> We want our legal institutions to yield both comprehensive policy embodying shared public values and facilities for the relentless pursuit of individual interests. But we are suspicious of the concentrated authority required for the former and reluctant to support the elaborated public machinery required to provide the latter routinely to ordinary citizens. We prefer fragmented government and reactive legal institutions with limited resources, so that in large measure both the making of public policy and the vindication of individual claims are delegated to the parties themselves who are left to fend according to their own resources. In such a complex system, lawyers form a major component of these resources....[44]

However, Galanter believes that although other countries retain "the distinctive structure and flavor" of their own legal cultures, the United States is by no means alone in its evolution to "soft, pluralized, participative and expansive law, with more lawyers who play a more central and expansive role."[45]

Other countries may confront the same diverging desires that we have described in this chapter. Like the United States, these countries may want a civil justice system that is open to new and diverse claims, but at the same time, a system that is neither swamped with frivolous claims nor stifling of business and commerce. Given such competing values, it is perhaps not surprising that the United States federal courts have liberal pleading rules that are accompanied by less liberal rules requiring reasonable pretrial factual and legal investigation, with potential sanctions for noncompliance. Nor is it

---

44. Marc Galanter, *Predators and Parasites: Lawyer-Bashing and Civil Justice*, 28 Ga. L. Rev. 633, 679 (Spring, 1994).
    45. *Id.* at 680.

surprising that rules relating to the pre-filing obligation of lawyers were amended in opposite directions twice in the last ten years.

LESSONS LEARNED FROM THE U.S. PLEADING REFORM

If legal systems are converging (or at least confronting similar diverging desires), as some scholars have predicted, then what lessons can we share from the course of U.S. pleading reforms? First, it does not make sense to consider one set of rules without reference to the others — in this instance, revision of the pleading rules cannot be done without reference to other procedural rules such as Rule 11 or discovery rules. The liberal pleading regime in the federal courts was initially promulgated in conjunction with greater opportunities for discovery and exchange of evidence prior to trial. In the United States, liberal pleading requirements were drafted because of a belief in a procedural system in which "the preferred disposition is on the merits, by jury trial, after full disclosure through discovery."[46] Pleadings and discovery cannot be treated as two distinct, isolated phases; they are co-dependent aspects of pretrial procedure.

And so, one could only have a strict pleading regime, such as the obligation to state facts more specifically underlying the cause of action and still not impact plaintiffs too negatively if: 1) the defendant cannot effectively challenge the motion until after extended discovery; and 2) amendments to pleadings are freely granted. Liberal discovery and amendment would allow a plaintiff to rectify its mistake of pleading too generally. One set of reforms must necessarily generate another, and procedural rules must be understood in context with other rules.

Pleading requirements must also be understood in relation to substantive law. As we have seen, in the United States legal system, the plaintiff normally has the burden of proof as to her claim, and the side with the burden of proof on an issue normally also has the pleading burden with respect to that issue. If the elements to that issue were reduced by substantive law and placed as an element of the defendant's affirmative defense, then the plaintiff has to plead and prove fewer elements of her case. If the case is litigated more through affirmative defenses as defined by substantive law, than even under a strict pleading regime, the plaintiff will be less prejudiced. One can affect substantive rights through procedural changes and vice versa.

This was the tack taken by the U.S. Congress in 1995 when it passed the Private Securities Litigation Reform Act to alter some of the procedures for securities cases in which private plaintiffs sue a company for wrongdoing in the issuance of stocks. The Act was in response to allegations that plaintiffs' lawyers were bringing class action suits too quickly after a company's stock price dropped, even if they had no evidence of fraud or wrongdoing by the defendant company or its management, for the sole purpose of inducing

46. Charles Clark, *The Handmaid of Justice*, 23 Wash. U. L. Q. 297, 318-319 (April, 1939).

defendants to settle, even if the case lacked merit, to avoid the high costs and risks of defending the litigation. The 1995 Private Securities Litigation Reform Act in response both required considerably more factual allegation in the complaint *and* prohibited any discovery, unless the court orders otherwise, pending any motion to dismiss, which includes motions to dismiss for failing to plead specifically. Although there is disagreement about the effect of this statute,[47] at least one law professor has found that this prohibition of discovery along with the stricter pleading standard has in fact dramatically forestalled both legitimate as well as frivolous litigation. "Accordingly, the Reform Act's pleading standard, if strictly applied and interpreted, will eliminate most private securities-fraud lawsuits and be over inclusive in its impact."[48] Procedure has in turn limited substantive rights.

In sum, it is important not to think about pleading requirements as disconnected from the legal culture in which they operate or from other procedural rules and substantive law. Information about a procedural regime must go beyond selected anecdotes retold by commentators who have a limited a view or a bias for or against certain types of litigants. Gaining empirical information is time consuming and expensive, but it helps one to modify distortions caused by ignorance or bias. Regardless of what the rules say, one should examine how lawyers actually use them and how judges interpret them. As Senator Thomas Walsh, in arguing against the Enabling Act, suggested, the subdued habits of the English bench and bar were more critical to what happened in civil litigation than the procedural rules.[49] It is only through an understanding of the historical and sociological context of these pleading rules that one can truly understand their development, rationale, and role.

47. One commentator concludes that "[t]he picture that emerges from studying . . . [the] data is that the PSLRA did not work as intended." He demonstrates, along with others, that different circuits have interpreted the act differently, and he shows that there is some evidence pointing in the direction that the heightened pleading requirements have not caused attorneys to wait longer before filing claims nor has the act diminished class action filings; some of the evidence may show an increase in class filings subsequent to the act. Michael A. Perino, *Did the Private Securities Litigation Reform Act Work?*, 2003 U. Ill. L. Rev. 913 (2003).

48. Hillary A. Sale, *Heightened Pleading and Discovery Stays: An Analysis of the Effect of the PSLRA's Internal-Information Standard on '33 and '34 Act*, 76 Wash. U. L. Q. 537, 579 (Summer, 1998) (citation omitted).

49. Subrin, *supra* note 7, at 997, 998.

CHAPTER
7

Discovery and Judicial Case Management

[T]he deposition-discovery rules are to be accorded a broad and liberal treatment. No longer can the time-honored cry of "fishing expedition" serve to preclude a party from inquiring into the facts underlying the opponent's case. Mutual knowledge of all the relevant facts gathered by both parties is essential to proper litigation.

Justice Murphy, *Hickman v. Taylor* (1947)[1]

There has been almost universal agreement that discovery has become a nightmare. . . . The current discovery practice is a monster out of control. . . . [D]iscovery devours millions of dollars and countless hours of a lawyer's time in cases that would be better settled or tried with far less ado.

Loren Kieve, *Discovery Reform* (1991)[2]

Discovery in the United States is the step in the litigation process during which parties formally obtain information relevant to the case. This can take the form of written or oral questions that must be answered under oath, requests for written or electronic documents that must be met, and even physical examinations of places, persons, and things relevant to the dispute.

It is difficult to sufficiently convey to one unfamiliar with American civil litigation how truly central and controversial the "pretrial discovery" has become. The editors of *Litigation*, the magazine published by the Litigation Section of the American Bar Association, devoted an entire issue to discovery and captured the role that discovery plays in American civil litigation:

. . . Most cases settle, and victory is not in the scathing cross[-examination], but in the tedious review of documents. Success is in the details, the expertly drafted interrogatories or request for records, and the ingenious strategy to obtain the statement allegedly protected by privilege. This is numbing, ditch digging work that determines the winner. . . . [W]e know without devoting our time and sweat to discovery, the thought of a favorable jury verdict is a mere dream.[3]

---

1. *Hickman v. Taylor*, 329 U.S. 495, 507 (U.S. 1947) (footnote omitted).
2. Kieve, *Discovery Reform*, 77 A.B.A.J. 79, 79-80 (Dec. 1991).
3. American Bar Association, *Discovery*, 23 Litigation 5 (Winter 1997) (cited in Stephen N. Subrin, Martha L. Minow, Mark S. Brodin, & Thomas O. Main, *Civil Procedure – Doctrine, Practice, and Context* 338-339 (Aspen Publishers 2000)).

This reliance on intense and extensive pretrial discovery conducted by the lawyers is one of the distinguishing features of the American legal system. In most of the rest of the world, it is government financed rather than privately financed, judge led rather than lawyer led factual inquiry. Even then, these intrusions into the documents and minds of the opposing sides are relatively circumscribed and limited when compared to the broad, wide-open discovery that is available to, and conducted by, American lawyers. By contrast, in civil law countries, as explained by Professor Hazard, "recognizing in a party a *right* to require production of evidence, as distinct from a party's right to ask the *court* to require production of evidence violates a constitutional principle of adjudication in the civil law system."[4]

What can account for this attorney controlled, entrepreneurial model rather than judge controlled model of obtaining information relevant to litigation? As we have discussed throughout this book, the cultural distrust of official power that infuses the United States may be one answer. And nowhere are the burdens and benefits of this individualism, distrust of government, and belief in private litigation more evident than in civil pretrial discovery.

Discovery in America can and often does add dramatically to the time and expense of litigation. It can also lead to questionable, if not immoral, practices by lawyers who not infrequently go out of their way to hide relevant information or to seek largely extraneous material to harass the opposition. Yet, private civil litigation has also been an important force in trying, however imperfectly, to keep the securities industry honest, protect against impure foods, enforce environmental laws, ferret out discriminatory practices, and uncover the deceit of rapacious corporations. It is through massive discovery done by dogged and persistent plaintiffs' lawyers that hidden information is revealed to the public eye and civil cases are turned into what are usually justified settlements, and with less frequency, trials.

All four of the issues that we emphasize: culture, power, rule/narrative tension, and legitimacy — underlie the course of discovery and discovery reform. So much a part of the American lore, discovery expands and contracts with every cultural turn. The liberalism and pro-plaintiff sentiments of the New Deal and the 1960s and early 1970s was replaced by a more conservative, pro-defendant mood. As some of the burdens of discovery unfolded, waves of amendments to the Federal Rules of Civil Procedure (in 1980, 1983, 1993, 2000) were enacted specifically to control alleged and real discovery abuse. Throughout the battles to reform the discovery process are a myriad of power struggles, between lawyers and the judiciary, corporations and individuals, and plaintiffs and defendants. Underlying it all is the ongoing tension between the goal of the original equity-based federal rules to provide a broad narrative with multiple parties, multiple claims, and broad discovery and a more constrained, rule-bound system that contracts the story, limits discovery, and seeks efficiencies of time and expense. For some, permissive American discovery, conducted by adversarial lawyers rather than the state, lends legitimacy to the system. Discovery permits the parties to control the process

---

4. Geoffrey C. Hazard, Jr., *Discovery and the Role of the Judge in Civil Law Jurisdictions,* 73 Notre Dame L. Rev. 1017, 1024 (May 1998).

of uncovering the relevant facts so that the law can be applied to what actu happened in a dispute. In this sense, discovery permits the participation of parties in the consistent, predictable application of law to govern our society. To others, however, the expense of discovery in time, money, and loss of privacy with party controlled discovery is contrary to the lofty ideals of an enlightened dispute resolution process.

Pretrial discovery is such a large part of civil litigation that many law schools devote an entire upper class course to the topic. Although we necessarily must omit some of the detail you would learn in such a course, we will provide you with a sense of the doctrine, dimensions, and impact of pretrial practice. We will discuss the history and the heart of the discovery rules and then look at the 25-year debate about it and the consequent amendments. We then consider the part played by pretrial conferences in attempting to rein in what is perceived as a run-away civil litigation system and marvel at how it seems to converge with the role of judges in civil law systems. We end with a discussion of the many ways discovery has intensely shaped, and will continue to shape, the American civil litigation experience.

DISCOVERY AND ITS EARLY HISTORY

What is discovery? In general, discovery is the right of civil litigants to acquire, under the auspices of the judicial system, information bearing on disputes to which they are parties. Discovery helps to preserve evidence, ascertain issues that are in true controversy, locate information that can lead to admissible evidence, and educate litigants to the point they can settle intelligently or try the case in a prepared manner. Consequently, discovery is viewed by litigators in conjunction with the applicable rules of evidence, although evidence is a separate body of law and a separate law school course in America.

Party-initiated discovery is in stark contrast to civil law countries where (although changing) it is the civilian law judge who decides what evidence is needed and proceeds to request documents and interrogate witnesses in person, summarizing the testimony in writing. In the United States, it is the lawyers who conduct pretrial discovery, albeit supervised in a general way by judges when there is active case management. It is also the lawyer who shapes the theory of the case and decides what evidence is needed to support her theory.

Towards that end, the American lawyer has a broad array of permissible formal discovery mechanisms to select from to get information from the opposing party and witnesses. Of course, apart from the formal discovery conducted under the auspice of court supervision, each side can engage in informal discovery through informal investigation techniques, such as searching official records, telephone books, and prior publications and examining the scene of accidents. The hiring of private detectives to seek information surreptitiously is not uncommon. The cost of informal discovery is usually considerably less than formal discovery.

Formal discovery devices include written questions, called *interrogatories*, sent to the opposing side and requiring answers under oath; *oral depositions* in which parties and other witnesses are orally questioned under oath and the answers precisely recorded; *written depositions* of a similar nature; *requests for documents* that must be obeyed; examinations of relevant land, machinery, vehicles, and the like; and even *mental and physical examinations* of opposing parties. In addition, the rules permit each side to demand that the opposing side *admit or deny facts*; the failure to admit the truth is subject to penalty. In addition to all of this are rules requiring the disclosure of some information to the opposing side, without request, at various stages of the litigation, called *mandatory disclosure*.

This broad panoply of formal discovery devices again marks the United States legal system as unique even from its common law counterparts. In most other countries, for example, in civil law Japan, only document exchange and interrogatories are allowed between the parties and only with judicial permission. Yet, broad discovery was not always an integral part of the American common law system. Prior to the 1938 federal rules, discovery in civil cases in the federal court was also severely limited.[5] While some forms of pretrial discovery existed in equity cases, such as interrogatories or requests for production of documents, very little was allowed at common law. The reasons are historical and cultural.

For one, at early common law, the litigation process was looked at not as a rational quest for truth, but rather as a method by which society could determine which side God took to be truthful or just. In a world of ordeal, battle, and oath takers, discovery had no role nor did it make sense. Furthermore, when the jury was initially utilized, jurors were people in the community who already had knowledge of the facts, and discovery was not needed to add more information to the case. As for the need to simplify the case, it was the pleadings (rather than discovery) in early English law that assumed a critical role in reducing the case to a single legal issue to be decided by a judge or to a limited question of fact for the jury.

While parties have traditionally assumed the responsibility for assembling the evidence, the idea of exchanging evidence with the opposing side seemed contrary to the belief, in both England and the United States, in the independence and self-sufficiency of each citizen. That one should cooperate with opponents in preparation of their case was distasteful and contrary to this idea of individualism and self-reliance. Further, the persistent fear of government intrusion accompanied the feeling that individuals should be left alone and that the privacy of citizens should be protected from an expansive role of the judiciary and government in overseeing and managing discovery.

There was also a long standing and widely held belief that if either side could discover the factual position of the opponent, the discovering side would perjure testimony. Although there was recognition that a system of secrecy in the preliminary stages of litigation could lead to surprise and confusion at trial, the widespread fear of "fishing expeditions" before trial remained for a long time a traditional and powerful taboo against liberalizing discovery. In

---

5. For a more detailed discussion of the historical development of discovery rules, *see* Stephen N. Subrin, *Fishing Expeditions Allowed: The Historical Background of the 1938 Federal Discovery Rules*, 39 B.C. L. Rev. 691 (May 1998).

the adversary system, one was expected to do one's own investigation and not rely on "fishing" from an opponent's minds and files and certainly not under the auspices of the judiciary and state.

By 1938, however, sentiment against expanded discovery had for many shifted to support. Experimentation with discovery practices had already taken place in some state courts. There was widespread dissatisfaction with specific fact requirements of code pleading. Litigation under the prevailing code pleading method had become stilted and overly technical, with parties wrangling over whether their opponents had alleged sufficient facts in the pleadings. Reformers urged for simpler pleading and proposed expanded discovery as the method for narrowing issues for trial.

The change in sentiment is also consistent with the legal realism prevailing in American jurisprudence at the time. Legal realism stressed the importance of amassing facts and the application of rationality and scientific methods before deciding social policy or a case. In his now famous, but infrequently read, 1906 speech entitled "The Causes of Popular Dissatisfaction with the Administration of Justice," Roscoe Pound urged society and lawyers to give up their "sporting theory of justice" and to turn to scientific legal experts to help solve the complicated problems of the new century.[6] For this to happen in litigation, it was necessary to create more expansive methods for discovering a wide range of adjudication facts.

Consistent with the legal realist line of argument, George Ragland, Jr.'s influential book, Discovery Before Trial (1932) continued the campaign for broad discovery by pointing out that discovery would focus controversies on the real and disputed issues and would make trials and settlements more rational.[7] But what probably guaranteed the inclusion of broad discovery rules in the drafting of uniform federal rules in 1935 was the appointment of Edson Sunderland to the Advisory Committee, who saw discovery as serving "much the same function in the field of law as the x-ray in the field of medicine and surgery; and if its use can be sufficiently extended and its methods simplified, litigation will largely cease to be a game of chance."[8]

Consequently, when the discovery portion of the Federal Rules was drafted, it included every discovery device known in the United States at the time, but few of the limitations that some states had imposed to curtail the scope and breadth of its use. Virtually unlimited discovery complemented the procedural jurisprudence adopted at the time, which urged flexibility and simplicity in the system. Broad discovery was a necessary companion to simplified pleading. Expansive discovery, it was thought, would fill in the dearth of information provided by simple complaints and answers. The new discovery rules were dependent on the past experiments in states, but at the same time they were thought to be liberal, modern, and simple.

It is discovery, along with simplified pleading and broad joinder of parties and claims (Chapter 9), that has moved American procedure towards an extremely broad, all-encompassing narrative in civil litigation. As you will see,

6. Rosco Pound, *The Causes of Popular Dissatisfaction with the Administration of Justice*, 29 A.B.A. Rep. 395, 404-405 (1906); *see also,* Subrin, *supra* note 3.

7. George Ragland, Discovery Before Trial 266 (Callaghan and Company 1932).

8. Edson R. Sunderland, *Improving the Administration of Civil Justice*, 167 Annals of the American Academy of Political and Social Science 60, 75-76 (May 1933).

however, recent amendments of the discovery rules have repeatedly tried to restore a more constrained system — through a blend of numeric limits, certification requirements, mandatory disclosure, a reduced scope of permitted discovery, and judicial case-management.

THE GENERAL SCOPE AND CONTOURS OF FEDERAL DISCOVERY: RULE 26

Federal Rule of Civil Procedure 26 is the umbrella rule that articulates the scope of permissible discovery. It sets the broad scope of discovery but also some limits, reflecting the persistent ambivalence Americans have about discovery. Recognizing that broad discovery is critical to the system, but with the potential for abuse, these rules sought to balance the need to eliminate surprises at trial with the assurance that adversary lawyers should not be required to prepare the opponent's case; to balance the knowledge that lawyers are paid to vigorously represent their clients with the need to cooperate with their adversaries in working out discovery plans, dates, and disposition.

In an attempt to balance adversariness with cooperation, Rule 26 begins with the requirement of "mandatory disclosure." Added in 1993, mandatory initial disclosure imposes on parties a duty to disclose basic information without awaiting formal discovery requests from the opposing party.[9] In response to protest from the bar, the 2000 amendments to Fed. R. Civ. P. 26(a) limited the scope of mandatory initial disclosure to a more narrow criteria of information the party "may use to support its claims or defenses," rather than the prior language that broadly required disclosure of information "relevant to disputed facts," even information relevant to the opposing party's claims or defenses.

Mandatory disclosure includes basic information such as the names and identifying information of individuals with discoverable information to support the disclosing party's claims or defenses, copies or descriptions of documents or tangible things in the possession or control of the disclosing party (again, in support of that party's claims and defenses), damage computations and copies of backup materials, and access to relevant insurance agreements. Mandatory disclosure also includes identification of any expert witnesses and, if the expert is expected to testify at trial, a detailed report of the opinion to be expressed. Finally, closer to the trial dates, parties are also expected to identify the particular evidence that may be offered and witnesses who may be called at trial.

9. The 1993 amendment provided for an "opt out" provision to Fed. R. Civ. P. 26(a), which allowed district or individual judges to "opt out" in part or in whole from the initial disclosure requirement. This resulted in a balkanization of the federal discovery rules with one-third of the districts choosing to adopt initial disclosure, one-third staying with the pre-1993 rules, and one-third adopting local rules. The 2000 amendment put an end to this by eliminating the "opt out" provision for individual courts. The amendment, however, continued to permit the parties to stipulate out of mandatory disclosure and for the trial judge, by court order, to eliminate mandatory disclosure in a particular case.

Ordinarily, only after mandatory disclosure can a lawyer commence formal discovery. In formal discovery, a lawyer must consider Rule 26(b), which states in relevant part:

> Parties may obtain discovery regarding any matter, not privileged, that is relevant to the claim or defense of any party.... Relevant information sought need not be admissible at trial if the discovery sought appears reasonably calculated to lead to the discovery of admissible evidence.

In other words, Rule 26(b) provides within the scope of discovery matters that are not "privileged" and are "relevant to the *claim or defense* of any party." Prior to this language, Rule 26 afforded even broader discovery of matters "relevant to the *subject matter* involved in the pending action." Responding to the argument that such a scope of formal discovery was overly broad, the 2000 amendment to Rule 26(b) tied the scope of discovery more closely to the specific "claims or defenses alleged in the pleadings," and allows the court to order broader "subject matter" discovery only if "good cause" is shown.

The last sentence of Rule 26(b)(1), allowing for discovery of information that "appears reasonably calculated to lead to the discovery of admissible evidence" is significant. Because discovery is intended to discover and clarify matters prior to trial, discovery is not limited to evidence that will itself be admissible evidence, but also includes matters "reasonably calculated" to lead to admissible evidence. This broad nature of discoverable information under Rule 26 has been blamed for many of the perceived abuses in civil discovery – that is, overwhelming the other side with unnecessary requests and engaging in "fishing" expeditions.

As it reads today, Rule 26 further empowers the federal judge to supervise this process, keeping two interests in mind: the importance of discovering relevant information and the burden to the opponent of providing discovery. Through protective orders, the court can limit the frequency or extent of the use of the discovery methods. If a discovery request is deemed unduly burdensome or expensive or if a party has had ample opportunity to obtain the information sought less expensively, a party can request a protective order from the court to limit the terms and conditions of the discovery, mandate that certain information not be revealed or be revealed only in a designated way, and even order that certain discoverable information be placed under seal.

Even though a party can seek discovery of even nonadmissible evidence, American discovery rules nevertheless operate within the constraint of evidentiary rules. A party or witness need not answer questions seeking information deemed "privileged" under the rules of evidence, even if the information sought to be discovered is relevant or might lead to admissible evidence. Under rules of evidence, certain relationships and communications are legally protected from public exposure whether in the discovery process or at trial. Although various states and the federal courts differ as to which relationships and communications merit protection, these privileges often include communications between husband and wife, attorney and client, priest and parishioner, and doctors and mental health professionals and their patients.

Consider the *Cherryum* case in which Albert Lee and his wife, Mabel, sue the manufacturer and bottler for damages resulting from Albert's allegedly drinking a poisonous beverage. The Federal Rule discovery provisions, along with American evidence law, would forbid Cherryum from inquiring into what Albert told Mabel about the incident. This communication would be protected by the marital privilege and remains so during discovery and at trial. In effect, society, acting through the courts or the legislature, has deemed marriage and other relationships (such as priest-penitent), and the communication between such people, more important than the search for truth in litigation.

There are also additional "softer" protections – that is, protections that can, under some circumstances be overcome, making discoverable otherwise nondiscoverable matter. The "work product" protection shields materials prepared by lawyers and their experts in anticipation of litigation or for trial from discovery by the opponent.[10] Work product information is only discoverable upon a showing by the party seeking discovery of substantial need and undue hardship and an inability to obtain equivalent information by any other means than discovery. This work product protection, developed through case law, has been codified as "trial preparation materials" under Rule 26(b)(3).

The policy underlying the work product protection lies within the adversary process itself, which anticipates that each side should do her own work to prepare her case and not piggyback on the work of opposing counsel. The idea is to enhance the vitality of an adversary system by insulating an attorney's work from intrusion or borrowing by the other party. Lawyers should be able to entertain various paths and options in their own research and to prepare without fear that the other side will see, benefit from, and undermine their handiwork.

Thus, an attorney's mental impressions and conclusions are always protected under the work product rule, even though other information gathered by the lawyer may at times be discoverable upon a showing of substantial need and undue hardship. Purely factual information underlying the lawyer's conclusions can be discoverable if there is demonstrated need, but the thoughts, ideas, and theories of the lawyers or their helpers who gather information in preparation for trial are protected. In the *Cherryum* case, if Albert Lee's lawyer interviewed Albert's employee, who is now deceased, and the lawyer took notes of what the employee said, and if the defendants never had access to that witness while she was alive, then a court could order the lawyer to reveal what the deceased witness had said, based on the substantial need and undue hardship standard.

A final wrinkle of the work product rule is that any witness may obtain a copy of her own statement, even though that statement otherwise would be considered work product. Fed. R. Civ. P. 26(b)(3). This is in anticipation that a single, continuous trial is the final phase of litigation in the American legal system. Because a witness' statement is likely to have substantial impact on a trier of fact, it would be unfair to preclude one who made it from examining it prior to the all-important trial. Common decency would seem to permit one to

10. Parties can also seek judicial protection of other matters, such as trade secrets or other confidential research. Fed. R. Civ. P. 26(c)(7).

ascertain what she has said or written prior to being questioned about it in open court; and examination of such statements would be essential to her attorney's case preparation and consideration of settlement.

While in other legal systems, such as in civil law countries, experts are appointed by the court as needed and their opinions accepted, it is the parties in the American legal system who solicit expert witnesses to support their positions. As a result, the same balancing of the adversarial process with eliminating surprises at trial also applies to the discovery rules concerning expert witnesses. Expert witnesses, in contrast to fact witnesses, have added protection under the discovery rules. Fed. R. Civ. P. 26(b)(4).

Experts retained by the opposing side "in anticipation of litigation" are discoverable by other parties under defined limited circumstances. An initial threshold to overcome is whether a witness is a fact witness or an expert witness. A fact witness is a person who has knowledge of a relevant fact or event, such as a doctor who just happened to witness a car accident. Experts are defined by their broad knowledge, experience, training, or education and are retained by a party for their expertise to render an opinion about the litigation, not because they have first hand knowledge of a relevant fact.

Discovery is permitted of fact witnesses even if they have expertise. In the Cherryum case, for example, the doctors at the hospital who examined Albert Lee immediately after he was admitted for poisoning could be deposed about what they witnessed in their examination of him. This is true even if the plaintiffs were not going to use the doctors as their experts and even if they had no intention of ever calling them for testimony at trial. Those doctors witnessed relevant facts, and they are therefore a fact witness and fair target for discovery.[11]

But discovery of expert witnesses, particularly nontestifying experts, is more limited and the same work product theory underlies such limitations. While discovery is allowed as of right for testifying experts, it is more restricted for nontestifying experts. Thus, as to testifying experts, a party must voluntarily disclose her own testifying expert and has discovery as of right from an opposing party's testifying expert as to information concerning the identification, subject matter, and the substance of opinions. By contrast, discovery of nontestifying experts is never as of right, except in the case of physical or mental examinations pursuant to Rule 35(b). Discovery of nontestifying experts can take place only by leave of court on a showing of "exceptional circumstances" by the party seeking discovery.

It is not difficult to understand why there should be a delineation between nontestifying and testifying experts. Discovery is necessary in the case of testifying experts so that the opposing party has the time and opportunity to understand, prepare, and intelligently cross-examine (that is, question at trial) complicated testimony. As for nontestifying experts, the adversary system deems that it is more important that each party get her own witnesses and her own expert assessment, if she thinks that desirable, and not piggyback on the opposing counsel's nontestifying expert, unless "exceptional circumstances" dictate otherwise.

11. The doctor-patient privilege would not apply because there is an exception when a party injects his or her physical or mental condition into a law suit. In fact, even what Albert Lee said to the doctors would probably be admissible because it would be non-hearsay under the Federal Rules of Evidence or an exception to the hearsay rule. But it is hard enough to learn civil procedure; evidence can await another book or another course.

TYPES OF DISCOVERY METHODS

In a market, entrepreneurial legal system such as the United States, cost is a big factor. Before serving formal discovery requests, lawyers normally assess the cost and delay to the clients that may result. Much information can be obtained without formal discovery through an attorney's own clients, witness interviews, and other sources. For the lawyer proceeding with formal discovery, she has a wide variety of methods at her disposal: written interrogatories, oral and written depositions, requests for admissions, requests for documents, requests to examine places and things, and physical and mental examinations.

Parties often begin their formal discovery by sending each other written questions known as interrogatories. Fed. R. Civ. P. 33. These interrogatories are to be answered by the other side under oath. The number of questions can range from 25, which is the normal limit, to 400 or 500 questions, by stipulation or leave of court, in more complex cases. It is relatively inexpensive to draft interrogatories, but because there is no immediate follow up to the answers, their use may be limited to getting certain basic information such as names of persons with information and relevant documents. Written interrogatories should be carefully framed in an attempt to avoid evasive answers and, in some instances, to avoid the possibility of alerting opposing counsel to one's theory of the case. Since the opposing lawyer usually helps the client to carefully draft answers, interrogatory answers tend not to reveal as much as more spontaneous depositions. In the *Cherryum* case, we would expect the Lees' lawyer to ask the defendant beverage manufacturer Cherryum whether it had previously been notified of any instance in which a consumer of Cherryum had become sick as a result of an impure Cherryum drink and what the notification said. The lawyers might then argue about the extent to which that question might (or might not) lead to admissible evidence.

Another common discovery tool is the oral deposition, which permits the oral questioning of witnesses and parties under oath, but outside the courthouse. Fed. R. Civ. P. 27. The side desiring the deposition must give notice of the time and place of the deposition. Opposing parties to the litigation must show up for depositions without being subpoenaed. For other witnesses, however, a subpoena is sent, along with notice to the opposing party that the deposition is taking place. Depositions generally take place in an attorney's office, usually resulting in the presence of a lawyer or lawyers taking the deposition, a lawyer or lawyers defending the deponent (the person being questioned), and an official stenographer who records the actual questioning and answers.

Depositions can be quite expensive. Not only must you factor in the preparation time and time spent at the deposition for yourself, the client or employees of the client, and any accompanying help (other lawyers, experts, paralegals, etc.), but the stenographic cost as well. Stenographers often charge $4 per page or more. Apart from the attorney's fees, an average oral deposition in a simple case costs between $500 and $1000 in Massachusetts while the same deposition could cost as much as $1200 or more in California.

A transcript of the testimony will ordinarily be submitted to the deposed witness for inspection and signing. Although the testimony itself may not be admissible at trial (under the evidentiary rules, a witness must usually provide testimony while physically present at trial), nevertheless, it can be used to cross-examine the witness who later changes her testimony at trial. The deposition of a party opponent, however, is usually admissible at trial.

Oral depositions have several advantages over interrogatories. Although deponents are usually coached by the opposing side prior to the deposition, the answers are still more spontaneous than those provided in response to interrogatories. In a deposition, you can alter your questions in response to the previous answers of the deponent. If the deponent provides new and surprising information, you can follow that path instead of what you had prepared in advance. The deposition permits you to gage how the deponent will react upon questioning; it gives you an opportunity to assess the witness's credibility in ways that interrogatory answers do not permit. At the deposition, usually attorneys for all parties, and sometimes the parties themselves, are present. This then also provides a natural opportunity for settlement talk.

It used to be common attorney lore not to cross-examine witnesses at a deposition, but instead to use a nonadversarial, open manner. Lawyers were reluctant to ever question their own client or a friendly witness at the deposition. "Why show your cards in advance of trial?" was the traditional dictate. But with so few cases now being tried, some lawyers now feel that the deposition is a perfect opportunity not only to show their opponents the weaknesses in their witnesses through at least some cross-examination, but the strengths of their own case.

In the *Cherryum* case, defendants' counsel, suspecting that Albert Lee poisoned himself in order to achieve a big insurance settlement, might decide to use the deposition as an opportunity to cross-examine him about his need for money. Some lawyers on occasion now depose their own client, even if the opponent has not asked for the deposition. The defendants in *Cherryum* might depose their own plant managers in order to show the plaintiffs and their counsel how totally unlikely it would be for poisons to find their way into a Cherryum bottle prior to sale to the consumer because of multiple precautions taken by Cherryum. This would lead to the inescapable inference, defendants would suggest, that Albert Lee put poison in the can. With settlement as the main goal, it may make sense to make the deposition more trial-like. By showing the opposing client and her lawyer what they are up against early in the litigation, a lawyer can improve the odds of advantageous settlement.

Despite the many advantages of the oral deposition, at least one survey challenged its utility. In a 1979 study, litigation attorneys in big cases (involving $1,000,000 or more) stated that in 60 percent or so of their cases, the depositions taken resulted in witnesses not revealing arguably significant information.[12] Nevertheless, most lawyers use oral depositions as a routine way of preparing their cases for settlement or trial.

Interrogatories and deposition requests are often accompanied by a request for production of documents. Fed. R. Civ. P. 34. The request can be done independently, whether or not the other discovery methods are used. A witness or party receiving this request must bring forward the requested

---

12. Wayne D. Brazil, *Civil Discovery: Lawyers' Views of Its Effectiveness, Its Principal Problems and Abuses*, 1980 Am. B. Found. Res. J. 789, 819 [hereinafter Brazil, *Civil Discovery: Lawyers' Views*].

documents. When framed carefully, documents requested can reveal information critical to the case. The documents can include contracts, leases, bank records, invoices, letters, documents in other cases, internal memoranda, and any other relevant documents. These documents, when properly authenticated, may be admissible at trial.

"Document" under the Federal Rules has a very broad meaning (Fed. R. Civ. P. 34(a)), and can include electronic communications and storage, such as e-mails and data in the hard drives of computers. It is frequently asserted that "over ninety percent of the 'information' developed by corporations and governmental agencies is presently electronic and never put into hard copy form."[13] What is called "e-discovery" has created countless problems. How deeply into the computer must a party search for information? When there are billions of bytes of information in electronic files, how will one know if all relevant information has been unearthed? Who should bear the cost of searching? Does turning over portions of the hard drive to an opponent amount to waiving a trade secret, if confidential information is buried in the drive? The 2005 Advisory Committee on Federal Rules of Civil Procedure has proposed amendments in five general subject areas relating to e-discovery. For instance, "proposed amendments to Rules 16 and 26 would require parties to address, during their preliminary conferences, procedures for preserving electronically stored information, and avoiding inadvertent privilege waivers, and to determine the form in which electronic information will be produced."[14] Other proposals deal with electronically stored information that is not reasonably accessible and with the problem of information lost during the routine operation of a party's computer system.[15]

Document requests can necessitate the production of thousands and even millions of pieces of paper or billions of bytes of computer-stored information. Many defense lawyers believe that this is the most onerous, wasteful, and unjustifiably burdensome type of discovery, the expense of which (ordinarily borne by the responding party) acts like blackmail in precipitating settlement even in cases lacking merit. And yet, in complex litigation, it is hard to see how lawyers can do their job well absent their requesting and examining relevant documentation and electronic files the discovery of which "appears reasonably calculated to lead to the discovery of admissible evidence." Fed. R. Civ. P. 26(b)(1).

Fed. R. Civ. P. 34, which allows for requests for permission to produce and permit copying of documents, also provides for requests to enter land and to inspect and test other property, such as machinery. If you represented Albert Lee, you might well request the opportunity to enter and inspect the manufacturing and bottling plants and their relevant machinery. Additionally, a party may also request the mental and physical examinations of a party. Fed. R. Civ. P. 35. In the Albert Lee litigation, Cherryum would rightly request the physical examination of Albert Lee to assess the extent of his injuries.

---

13. Richard Marcus, *Only Yesterday: Reflections on Rulemaking Responses to E-Discovery*, 73 Fordham L. Rev. 1, 10 (Oct. 2004) (citation omitted).

14. Henry R. *Chalmers, Proposed Electronic Discovery Rules Prompt Comments from Section Leaders*, 30 Litigation News 1 (May 2005). The proposals, even if ultimately adopted, would not become law any earlier than December 2006.

15. *Id.* at 6.

However, requests for mental and physical examinations of a party will not be granted lightly. Concerned for the protection of the integrity of the body, a court will not easily order a party, or a person in her custody or under her legal control, to submit to physical or mental examination. The requesting party must demonstrate to the court that the physical or mental condition is "in controversy" and that "good cause" is shown for the examination.

Finally, a party may request admissions of certain matters from another party. Fed. R. Civ. P. 36. There are penalties for not admitting uncontested facts. Any matter admitted is conclusively established unless the court on motion permits the withdrawal or amendment of the admission. Admissions are most often used to facilitate proof with respect to certain issues that may be expensive or unnecessary to prove (such as authenticating a document or proving that a signatory had authority to sign) and to narrow the focus of the case by eliminating facts known to be true. Lawyers can try to achieve the same goals through stipulation.

JUDICIAL CASE MANAGEMENT: THE PRETRIAL CONFERENCE AND RELATED SANCTIONS

In some respects, the American legal system has "converged" somewhat with our civil law counterparts. This is most evident in the amendments to increase judicial intervention and control of litigation in the federal courts. Despite its historical distrust of bureaucracies, the American legal system has opted for inclusion of the judiciary in an attempt to control and ensure that discovery is proportionate only to the needs of the case. This has led some scholars such as Judith Resnik to label the activity of federal judges as "managerial judging."

To carry out their new responsibilities, federal judges call on the assistance of the pretrial conference and sanctions. Scheduling conferences and pretrial conferences with judges were made mandatory, and the purposes of pretrial conferences were expanded to "establish early and continuing control," to discourage "wasteful pretrial activities," and to facilitate "the settlement of the case."[16] The tremendous role that pretrial conferences and orders now play in American litigation is in stark contrast to how the pretrial conference was perceived in its last minute inclusion in the early 1938 drafting of the federal rules.[17]

Originally designed as a meeting between judges and lawyers to prepare for trial, the pretrial conference was later expanded to include judicial case management and settlement discussions. Thus, at any pretrial conference, there are two focuses to keep in mind — to settle and to prepare for the extremely unlikely event of trial. Proponents of intensive judicial management believe that judicial involvement at this early stage can help all participants in the process to more quickly understand the dispute and what is needed to resolve it.[18]

16. *See* Advisory Committee's Notes to 1983 Amendments to Fed. R. Civ. P. 16.
17. Judith Resnik, *Trial as Error, Jurisdiction as Inquiry: Transforming the Meaning of Article III*, 113 Harv. L. Rev. 924, 935-936 (Feb. 2000).
18. *See* Advisory Committee's Notes to 1983 Amendments to Fed. R. Civ. P. 16.

Unless altered by court rule or judicial order, Federal Rule 16 requires parties and lawyers to meet with the judge at least 120 days after service of a complaint. There could be several pretrial conferences throughout the life of a civil litigation, depending on the complexity of the case. Ultimately, if the case does not settle, there will be a final pretrial conference, at which parties will formulate a plan for trial, including a program for facilitating the admission of evidence. These pretrial conferences are reminiscent of the discontinuous hearings conducted in civil law countries, but while the civil law judge is in charge of compiling the evidence, the American judge typically only manages the process.

Reflecting that responsibility for discovery rests with the parties, lawyers and/or unrepresented parties are required to have an initial outside-the-courthouse meeting with each other to come to an agreement as to a plan for discovery, which will be presented to the judge at the initial pretrial conference. If adopted, this plan will serve as a scheduling order that will control the subsequent course of the action. The scheduling order normally includes a timetable within which to file motions, to amend pleadings, to join other parties, and to complete discovery and a date for trial. It is thought that the fixing of time limits will stimulate litigants to narrow the areas of inquiry, to prioritize discovery priorities, and to reduce the amount of resources expended in any given litigation. Once a scheduling order is entered, a court may only modify the schedule upon a showing of good cause.

The other important issue to be discussed at a pretrial conference is settlement. Rule 16 authorizes the judge to explore settlement but does not expound on the standard for, and limits of, that role. This raises the issue of a judge's role in settlement discussions and how much should the presiding judge push for settlement of cases without infringing or undermining the adversary process.

Recent studies suggest that while federal judges encourage settlements, most stop short of suggesting a numeric figure as being appropriate for settlement. Some empirical evidence suggests that judges with the highest rates of settlement are those who simply move cases quickly towards trial by setting a firm trial date rather than actively engaging in settlement negotiations or other forms of case management.[19] Other studies suggest that in addition to a firm trial date, courts should also set firm cut-offs for discovery in order to insure prompt resolution of cases.[20]

Last but not least, formal discovery can be judicially enforced and sanctioned, in cases of noncompliance. Litigants are specifically prohibited from filing papers or taking positions that are for an improper purpose, such as harassment, or causing an unnecessary delay in the proceedings or increase the cost of litigation. When a litigant does that, the judge has the authority to

19. *See* Marc Galanter & Mia Cahill, *"Most Cases Settle": Judicial Promotion and Regulation of Settlements*, 46 Stan. L. Rev. 1339 (July 1994).

20. James S. Kakalik, Terence Dunsworth, Laural A. Hill, Daniel McCaffrey, Marian Oshiro, Nicholas M. Pace, Mary E. Vaiana, *Just, Speedy and Inexpensive? An Evaluation of Judicial Case Management Under the Civil Justice Reform Act*, 14-16 (RAND Institute for Civil Justice 1996); James S. Kakalik, Deborah R. Hensler, Daniel McCaffrey, Marian Oshiro, Nicholas M. Pace, Mary E. Vaiana, *Discovery Management: Further Analysis of the Civil Justice Reform Act Evaluation Data* 55-56 (RAND Institute for Civil Justice 1998).

impose sanctions, most commonly by ordering that litigant to pay the expense of the other side in having to respond to the improper action.

If the discovery process becomes overly burdensome or oppressive, the court pursuant to Rule 26(c) can enter a protective order that discovery not be had or only be had on specified terms and conditions. The court can also order that the discovery be by a method other than that selected by the party seeking discovery, be limited to certain matters, or that confidential information be sealed or revealed only in a designated way.

The federal civil procedure rules also empower judges to sanction parties who do not make the required mandatory disclosures or parties and other witnesses who do not comply with a judicial order to engage in a type of discovery. Motions to compel discovery must be accompanied by a certification that the movant has in good faith conferred or attempted to confer with the opposing party to resolve the discovery dispute. If granted, the rules further provide for sanctions at a party's request for failure of the opposition to comply with a discovery order. The sanction can include a refusal to allow the disobedient party to support or oppose designated claims or defenses, to strike pleadings or parts thereof, and even an order that the matters regarding which the order was made be taken as established.

Notwithstanding all of this power in the judiciary to supervise and control discovery, it is a common complaint by lawyers that judges choose not to intervene in discovery disputes. Some lawyers think that judges and magistrates should be much less tolerant of discovery abuse and much more willing to guide and control the discovery process.

THE CURRENT DEBATE

Discovery has and will continue to dominate American debate on civil litigation; it is probably fair to say that in large-scale litigation, and probably even cases with mid-range stakes (say over $50,000) discovery is the most important stage in the lawsuit in terms of cost, time, and influence on ultimate result. In one sense, American discovery gains its legitimacy by its reliance on the individual rights concept – that is, it is the responsibility of private litigants rather than the court to unearth information relevant to a dispute. Historically speaking, in other industrial countries (e.g., Germany), it was the government and a judicial bureaucracy who fulfilled this task with an inquisitorial style of litigation and a reliance on substantiated statements about the facts of the case, rather than a required exchange of information between the parties. A general obligation on the parties to give or to disclose to each other information had been rejected on the grounds of protection of the private sphere and business secrets.[21]

Americans resisted this inquisitorial model and hold a general skepticism about the ability of bureaucratic government to protect the interests of either

---

21. In the German context, substantive law contains duties to provide information, but such substantive claims for information must be made in a separate action, especially if against a "third party." Peter Gottwald, *Civil Procedure Reform in Germany,* 45 Am. J. Comp. L. 753, 760 (Fall 1997).

ordinary citizens or businesses. Further, recognizing that an entrepreneurial model of litigation may perpetuate inherent disparities, discovery rules also are said to assist in leveling the playing field. By providing for mandatory disclosure as well as court sanctioned exchanges of evidence, discovery helps to ensure that even less powerful litigants lacking initial information can commence suit and obtain the necessary proof in support of their case. This is especially necessary in cases in which it is an impoverished individual litigant who is suing a corporate defendant that controls much of the relevant information.

The discovery rules frown on "trial by ambush," but seek to maintain individual initiative and competition in the litigation process. Discovery seeks to adjust imbalances in economic power and knowledge of important information between the parties, but avoids the specter of government intrusion, by giving the right to seek the information to the parties. With good lawyering, no longer can the party with the greater resources lay sole claim to relevant evidence. However, with equally astute and aggressive lawyering, discovery can also work to the detriment of the party with lesser economic power; that party is more apt to buckle under burdensome discovery demands.

As has been noted already, liberal discovery has been blamed for excessive expense and delay in civil litigation. Many of the objections posed against liberal discovery at the time of the drafting of the discovery rules have resurfaced. These include fears of overreaching by zealous lawyers, time-consuming discovery disputes, and excessive costs of discovery forcing settlement unrelated to the merits of the case. Most detrimentally, some argue that it was expansive discovery that has made civil litigation expensive beyond what most Americans can afford and has limited access to civil justice except when there are damages so extensive (and hence, greater attorneys fees) that lawyers will take the case.

Although some current complaints about discovery were predicted and its potential short-comings even known, the drafters of the rules probably could not have anticipated the immense size of today's cases nor how prominent a role discovery plays in that process. Nor could they have anticipated the impact of technology on litigation with the introduction of copier machines, faxes, and computers. The technology has assisted in the growth of law firms and litigation departments, the development of class actions, and the gigantic awards and legal fees in some cases. The drafters could not have predicted what some have called a literal "discovery explosion."

Then, too, there may have been an important conceptual flaw in the discovery drafters' assumption that facts were static and knowable. They probably did not fully realize just how creative lawyers would be in finding increasing numbers of witnesses who might have relevant information and increasing numbers of documents, e-mails, and electronically stored information that just might reveal something ultimately admissible. The cut-offs for legitimate discovery have not proven easy to ascertain. Where many of the current questions of law and fact are pliable and open-ended, it is unclear how many years backward one should be permitted to discover evidence or what witnesses or how many documents should be included in justifiable discovery.

It is probably difficult for those from other countries, undergraduates studying law, or new American law students, who have not worked in large firms as paralegals, to truly comprehend what a staggering amount of discovery can take place in large cases that justify large fees by defendant lawyers (paid by the hour) or huge fees for plaintiffs' lawyers (contingent fees taken as a percentage of settlements). Nor is it easy for those unfamiliar with American legal practice to realize how the adversary system causes some lawyers to engage in overly aggressive behavior in either engaging in excessive discovery (always justified because one more deposition or one more document request just might yield new information or important cumulative evidence) or in unsavory attempts to conceal or muddle clearly relevant evidence legitimately sought by the opposition (because "my job is not to make it easy for the other side; I have a client to represent.").

Here is how one American civil procedure casebook tried to convey the sense of "the elephantine mass of discovery" in some contemporary American civil litigation:

> ...In the *Exxon Valdez* oil spill cases, for example, 'discovery took almost five years; the defendants were required to produce millions of pages of materials; the plaintiff took over one thousand depositions; Exxon deposed thousands of individuals and required them to produce tax records and other business records; and Exxon employed hundreds of expert witnesses, most of whom produced expert reports and most of whom were deposed by the plaintiffs.' Keith E. Sealing, *Civil Procedure in Substantive Context: The Exxon-Valdez Cases*, 47 St. Louis U. L.J. 63, 77 (2003). *See also In re Brand Names Prescription Drugs Antitrust Litigation*, 123 F.3d 599, 614 (7th Cir. 1997) ("Pretrial discovery included the taking of a thousand depositions and the production of *fifty million* pages of documents.").

> Extensive discovery can also be a problem in more traditional and simple litigation. In an action by a construction worker against his employer and the companies that designed the equipment and materials involved in his injury, the plaintiff's attorney invested over 5100 attorney hours in two-and-a-half years of discovery, taking 19 depositions, accumulating 52 expandable files of documents that are over 22 feet, arguing nearly 20 oral and written motions, reviewing hundreds of thousands of records and consulting more than 10 experts. *See Mitzel v. Westinghouse Elec. Corp.*, 72 F.3d 414 (3d Cir. 1995).

> In each of these cases, of course, the lawyers for both sides must review — perhaps even scrutinize – every piece of paper. Indeed, in an article recounting her role in the tobacco litigation, Martha Wivell, a partner in the law firm of Robbins, Kaplan, Miller & Ciresi, L.L.P., answered the question how her firm reviewed the 30 million documents that were produced in her case. Her answer: "One at a time." *See* Martha Wivell, *Key to the Tobacco Fortress*, 38 Trial 45, 45 (Dec. 2002).[22]

It is not just the mass of discovery that has taken place in some cases that has attracted the ire of discovery critics, but also its ability to incubate unprofessional behavior. In an article with the evocative title *Stupid Lawyer Tricks: An Essay on Discovery Abuse*, Professor Charles Yablon describes several

22. Stephen N. Subrin, Martha L. Minow, Mark S. Brodin, Thomas O. Main, *Civil Procedure – Doctrine, Practice, and Context* 302-303 (2d ed., Aspen Publishers 2004).

different instances of disturbing discovery misconduct, sometimes conducted even by otherwise well-regarded and competent lawyers. The misconduct ranged from the thoughtless use of burdensome boilerplate interrogatories, false and misleading statements made by lawyers to the other side, and even stealing documents from an opposing party's trash dumpster. Here is Yablon's most pungent example:

> In a defamation action brought by Philip Morris Company against the American Broadcasting Company, lawyers for ABC alleged Philip Morris had produced twenty-five boxes containing approximately one million documents.... The documents had been transferred onto a special dark red paper with squiggly lines, which made them hard to read and impossible to photocopy. ABC's lawyers alleged that the paper gave off noxious fumes that made it "difficult to work with the altered copies for extended periods of time." The smelly paper was reported to have nauseated one partner and given someone else a headache.[23]

Probably the most well-known chronicler of discovery abuse is Wayne D. Brazil, who authored a series of widely cited articles about untoward discovery practices among lawyers in Chicago, Illinois.[24] His thesis, which is difficult to judiciously controvert, is that the adversary system and the economic incentive structure for lawyers make it inevitable that there will be a substantial amount of discovery abuse, "[T]here is generally no ethical pressure or financial incentive for attorneys voluntarily to disclose the fruits of their investigations or in any way make ascertainment of the truth easier for opposing counsel or the trier of fact."[25] As a result, lawyers over-supply documents in answer to the requests by the opposing party with the hope that the most damaging relevant information will be lost or obscured in the avalanche of what has been supplied. At the other extreme, they narrowly read legitimate discovery requests and produce minimally in the attempt to conceal information detrimental to their client's position. "Indeed," Brazil writes, that not "to resort to at least some of these devices may be construed as a breach of an attorney's obligation 'to represent his client zealously within the bounds of the law.'"[26]

However, the massiveness of discovery in some cases and the ubiquitous nature of discovery abuse must be balanced with consideration of empirical studies that concluded that there is very little discovery or no discovery at all, and not disproportionate discovery costs, in the vast majority of cases. In a 1997 survey of civil cases likely to have discovery, the Federal Judicial Center still found that 15 percent of them had no discovery.[27] An earlier study by the

---

23. Charles Yablon, *Stupid Lawyer Tricks: An Essay on Discovery Abuse*, 96 Colum. L. Rev. 1618 (Oct. 1996) (footnotes omitted).

24. Wayne D. Brazil, *The Adversary Character of Civil Discovery: A Critique and Proposals for Change*, 31 Vand. L. Rev. 1295 (1978) [hereinafter Brazil, *Adversary Character*]; Brazil, *Civil Discovery: Lawyers' Views, supra* n. 12; Wayne D. Brazil, *Views from the Front Lines: Observations by Chicago Lawyers About the System of Civil Discovery*, 1980 Am. B. Found. Res. J. 217.

25. Brazil, *Adversary Character, supra* note 24, at 1304.

26. *Id.* at 1313. The "zealously" quote is taken from Canon 7 of the American Bar Association Code of Professional Responsibility.

27. Thomas E. Willging et al., *An Empirical Study of Discovery and Disclosure: Practice Under the 1993 Federal Rule Amendments*, 39 B.C. L. Rev. 525, 544 (May 1998).

Federal Judicial Center looking at six metropolitan districts found that 52 percent of the cases had no discovery at all, and 72 percent of the cases had no more than a total of two discovery events.[28] The RAND Institute for Civil Justice conducted a study of over 5,000 federal cases filed in 1992-1993 (excluding from its sample those cases that usually had little or no discovery). In the cases that closed after issue was joined in 270 days or less, which was 55 percent of the total cases, there was either no discovery or (about half of those) a median of only three hours spent on discovery – and this, remember, is after RAND excluded cases apt to have no discovery.[29]

This paucity of discovery in most civil cases may also true for state courts. In a study of five state trial courts, the National Center for State Courts found that 42 percent of general civil litigation cases did not have recorded discovery.[30] As to discovery costs, the later Federal Judicial Center study concluded that for cases in which discovery was conducted, the median expenditure per side for discovery, as a percentage of the stakes in the litigation was a mere 3 percent. At the 95th percentile, however, the expenditures were 32 percent of the amount at stake.[31] Thus, only in the small percentage of high cost cases was discovery expenditure high.[32] This has led the Federal Judicial Center to conclude: "[T]he typical case has relatively little discovery conducted at costs that are proportionate to the stakes of the litigation, and . . . discovery generally – but with notable exceptions – yields information that aids in the just disposition of cases."[33]

Despite this data, popular American beliefs lie in the opposite direction. One explanation may be that litigation horror stories are more compelling and gripping. They attract the attention of judges, who are oppressed by the time consumed in protracted cases and who witness the abusive conduct of lawyers in exorbitant fee litigation; lawyers in the large firms that litigate high stakes cases and can afford massive discovery; the press, looking for attention-grabbing stories; and the public, who read and remember the unusual and are not typically told about the mundane. Moreover, it is in the interest of insurance companies and other corporate defendants in defense of potentially large liabilities to advertise and lobby against discovery – discovery that is needed to uncover corporate misconduct.

As far as we can ascertain, the true discovery picture is as stated by the former Director of the American Bar Foundation: "[A] rather small number of cases thus generated a very large amount of discovery."[34] A former Chair of the

28. *See generally* Paul R. Connolly et al., Judicial Controls and the Civil Litigative Process: Discovery (Federal Judicial Center 1978).

29. For a good review of the RAND and other studies, *see* Elizabeth G. Thornburg, *Giving the "Haves" a Little More: Considering the 1998 Discovery Proposals,* 52 S.M.U. L. Rev. 229, 246-249 (Winter 1999).

30. Susan Keilitz et al., *Is Civil Discovery in the State Trial Courts Out of Control?,* 17 St. Ct. J. 8, 9 (Spring 1993).

31. *Id. See also,* Thomas E. Willging, *Discovery and Disclosure Practice, Problems, and Proposals for Change: A Case-Based National Survey of Counsel in Closed Federal Civil Cases* 17, table 6; 18, table 8; 38, table 29 (Government Printing Office 1997).

32. This has also been argued elsewhere. Marc S. Galanter, *Reading the Landscape of Disputes: What We Know and Don't Know (and Think We Know) About Our Allegedly Contentious and Litigious Society,* 31 UCLA L. Rev. 4 (Oct. 1983).

33. Willging, *supra* note 27, at 527 (cited in Thornburg, *supra* note 29, at 246).

34. Bryant G. Garth, *Two Worlds of Civil Discovery From Studies of Cost and Delay to the Markets in Legal Services and Legal Reform,* 39 B.C. L. Rev. 597, 600 (May 1998).

Federal Civil Rules Advisory Committee presided over a major conference with participants with a wide variety of perspectives. He concluded that "discovery is now working effectively and efficiently in a majority of the cases, which represent routine cases . . . and that in cases where discovery is actively used, it was thought to be unnecessarily expensive and burdensome. . . ."[35]

AMENDMENTS TO CONTAIN DISCOVERY

There are problems with the attempt to rein in discovery in the fewer than 5 percent or 10 percent of the cases in which there is discovery abuse. As we have seen, the Federal Rules of Civil Procedure, and for that matter, most state procedural rules, are "trans-substantive rules" – that is, the same rules apply to all case-types, regardless of the substantive law involved.[36] This means that the discovery problems of a distinct minority of cases have driven solutions that must apply to all cases. Let us trace the course of those amendments and see what lessons can be drawn.

In 1980, judicial case management was the dominant approach adopted to curb discovery abuses. Amendments were enacted that invited parties to ask for a discovery conference with the judge and to seek a judicial order for discovery limitations and a discovery schedule. Fed. R. Civ. P. 26(f). The amended rule obligated parties to confer in advance and to use reasonable efforts to frame a discovery plan in advance if any side asked for a discovery conference. Sanctions were added under Rule 37(b)(2) for failure to "participate in good faith in the framing of a discovery plan by agreement" or for failure to comply with a discovery order issued after the discovery conference with the judge.

The year 1983 gave even more authority to judges to act on motion or their own initiative to insure that discovery did not exceed what was proportionate for the case. Except if exempted by district court rule, scheduling conferences and pretrial conferences were now made mandatory, and the purposes of pretrial conferences were expanded. Also in 1983, attorneys were required to certify that they had conducted a reasonable inquiry as to the law and facts underlying any filings with the court. This certification requirement was extended to discovery papers, under which an attorney must verify that she has read the documents and that the discovery sought was "not unreasonable or unduly burdensome or expensive, given the needs of the case, the discovery already had in the case, the amount in controversy, and the importance of the issues at stake in the litigation." Sanctions for the 26(g)

35. Paul V. Niemeyer, *Here We Go Again: Are the Federal Discovery Rules Really in Need of Amendment?*, 39 B.C. L. Rev. 517, 523 (May 1998).

36. As we will discuss in the Epilogue, the trans-substantive nature of procedural rules makes them look apolitical, although even general procedural rules clearly have substantive results favoring some litigants to the disadvantage of others. But once the judiciary starts making procedural rules for particular case-types, the political nature of the enterprise becomes obvious and points to the legislature as the appropriate rule-maker. But the legislature may not be a particularly attentive or sound procedural rule promulgator.

violations, and the Rule 11 violations with respect to discovery motions, were mandatory.

Congress, meanwhile, entered the fray more directly with the Civil Justice Reform Act of 1990.[37] Undercutting the uniformity sought by the Federal Rules of Civil Procedure in 1938, Congress, citing discovery problems among other concerns, mandated that every federal district court experiment on its own with plans to reduce judicial delay and costs in the civil justice system. The 1993 amendments drew on experiments in federal local rules and in the state courts and established limits on the number of depositions and interrogatories and bolstered the obligation to supplement discovery. In addition, they required attorney-drafted discovery plans and instituted an initial disclosure requirement (described earlier), over the protests of much of the bar.

The "mandatory disclosure" requirement proved to be most controversial because it fundamentally contradicts the assumptions of the adversary process. Opponents pointed out that mandatory disclosure forced lawyers to reveal facts they had discovered on their own to the opposing side, in violation of the concepts that each side should prepare its own case and that lawyers represented their own clients, not the opposition. On a practical level, opponents also argued that mandatory disclosure was of quite rudimentary information and did nothing to dispense with the other formal discovery.

The next set of discovery amendments, in 2000, refined the attempts to limit wide open, liberal discovery. The 2000 amendments narrowed the scope of discovery to any matter, not privileged, that is relevant "to the claim or defense of any party," rather than "to the subject matter involved in the pending action." Only in cases of "good cause," can the court order broader discovery into "any matter, not privileged, which is relevant to the subject matter involved in the pending action." Depositions were curtailed to "one day of seven hours." Recognizing the argument that mandatory disclosure could be a derogation of the adversary system that underlies American civil adjudication, the new rule tempered mandatory disclosure to disclosure of names and addresses of witnesses and descriptions of documents "that the disclosing party may use to support its claims or defenses. . . . " Fed. R. Civ. P. 26(a)(1)(A). In other words, one does not have to reveal information through mandatory disclosure that helps the opponent prove its case.

The 2000 amendments were preceded by intense lobbying against the change by plaintiffs' lawyers, particularly those engaged in products liability suits, and intense lobbying for the change, by defense lawyers and their corporate clients. With such intense lobbying, it is difficult to see the decision as apolitical,[38] but far easier to see how procedural rules add or detract power from particular types of litigants. In general, it is the plaintiff asserting rights who wants, and often needs, expansive discovery in order to prove her case.

You should be aware that many of the states have gone considerably further than the federal courts in trying to contain discovery and to provide more guidance for lawyers and their clients about the parameters of discovery for their type of case. Many states have tracking systems, with different discovery

---

37. Pub. L. No. 101-650, §§ 101-106, 104 Stat. 5089 (1990). This statute had a "sunset" provision and has expired; but many courts still have local rules passed pursuant to it.

38. *See, e.g.*, Jeffrey W. Stempel, *Politics and Sociology in Federal Civil Rulemaking: Errors of Scope*, 52 Ala. L. Rev. 529 (Winter 2001).

limitations and cut-off dates of when discovery must be completed for different categories of cases. Some states have different discovery limitations for large, medium-sized, and small cases, depending on the amount of recovery sought. Other states have two or four categories. In general, the larger the stakes, the more discovery and time permitted.

Some states require a good deal more divulgence of information to the opposition through mandatory disclosure than under the Federal Rules, but then forbid or curtail further discovery. It is probably fair to say that many states rely more on precise limits on time and number and less on ad hoc judicial case management than their federal counterparts. With considerably fewer judges per number of cases and much less judicial backup (magistrates, judicial clerks, secretaries) than federal judges have, state courts view intensive ad hoc case management as a less possible and less attractive alternative.

In summary, the year 1980 brought the advent of discovery conferences at the instance of any of the parties; the 1983 amendments further expanded the purposes and the frequency of pretrial conferences. The 1993 amendments brought mandatory disclosure, and obligated lawyers, when possible, to bring their own agreed upon discovery plans to the now mandated scheduling conference. The 2000 amendments further curbed the scope of discovery and disclosures. All of these amendments were adopted in reaction to intense lobbying and political debate that expanded from the merits of discovery to the fundamental goal of civil litigation in America.

THE PERVASIVE INFLUENCE OF DISCOVERY

Discovery and other pretrial activity are now the "tail that wags the dog" of American civil litigation. Particularly in federal court, litigators are not experts at pleading as at common law or trial experts as under the Field Code. Rather, they are discovery experts, experts at planning sessions with opposing counsel, experts at discussing and advocating before judges at conferences, and experts in negotiations. Added to these roles, you will see in a later chapter, is their role as consumers of Alternative Dispute Resolution (ADR) and most particularly as advocates at arbitrations and negotiators in the presence of, and with the help of, mediators. Many litigators are themselves now arbitrators and mediators.

A spectator of the American civil litigation process cannot help but be astonished at the changes wrought by the federal discovery rules and by state discovery that followed in their path. The change is not limited to the attorney's altered role from trial lawyer to litigator, but also includes the role that broad discovery has played in unearthing hidden information necessary for the public good and safety. It is difficult to imagine the enforcement of legal rules relating to the environment, discrimination, securities, safe products, and a myriad of other areas absent discovery in civil law suits. For example, it is unlikely that the asbestos and tobacco manufacturers would have divulged their long time knowledge of the dangers in their products without the determined discovery by plaintiffs' lawyers, often against stubborn and unsavory opposition, in civil cases lasting over several decades.

The former Chair of the Federal Advisory Committee on Civil Rules emphasized the symbiotic relationship of discovery to the ability to enforce legal norms as such:

> Congress has elected to use the private suit, private attorneys-general as an enforcement mechanism for the anti-trust laws, the securities laws, environmental laws, civil rights and more. In the main, the plaintiff in these suits must discover his evidence from the defendant. Calibration of discovery is calibration of the level of enforcement of the social policy set by Congress.[39]

There are other results attributable to the discovery revolution. Perhaps discovery encouraged, as part of discovery abuse, lawyer incivility. The increase of lawyers in America and the sensational increase in the size of trial departments certainly coincided with more lawyers spending more time on discovery, with the consequent growth in the size of large firms. Two scholars tie the growth of hourly billing directly to the advent of broad discovery,[40] which in turn would link discovery to the evolution of lawyer time records.

In the absence of liberal discovery, it is also unlikely that trial would be perceived by some to have become a "pathological event,"[41] and unlikely that judges would have said:

> I believe that the time I spend in trial is wasted effort.

> ...My goal is to settle all my cases.... Most of the time when I try a case I consider that I have somehow failed the lawyers and the litigants.[42]

Perhaps the increased civil caseload as a result of the rights revolution would have led to judicial management in civil cases even absent the discovery revolution. Or the number and complexity of transactions in the modern world, combined with broad joinder of parties and claims, would have made civil litigation sufficiently unwieldy that case management would have still emerged. All of this is possible. And yet, when one reads the literature about discovery abuse, true or false, one has the distinct impression that it was broad discovery that turned trial lawyers into litigators and trial judges into case managers and settlement provokers.

Further, one also wonders whether members of Congress would have taken such an interest in procedural rulemaking, as evidenced by their entrance into the procedures for securities cases and by their passage of the Civil Justice Reform Act, but for the alleged abuses of discovery practice. Last but not least, one wonders about the impact of discovery, and the case management reaction to it, on the growth of ADR (Alternative Dispute Resolution). The fact is,

39. Patrick Higginbotham, *Foreward*, 49 Ala. L. Rev. 1, 4-5 (Fall 997), cited in Marcus, *supra* note 13, at 3, footnote note 12.

40. George B. Shepherd & Morgan Cloud, *Time and Money: Discovery Leads to Hourly Billing*, 1999 U. Ill. L. Rev. 91.

41. *See* Judith Resnik, *Many Doors, Closing Doors? Alternative Dispute Resolution and Adjudication*, 10 Ohio St. J. on Disp. Resol. 211, 261 (1995) (referring to the incidence of trial as a "pathological event," saying that the description came from minutes of a meeting of the Federal Advisory Committee on the Rules of Civil Procedure).

42. These quotes from judges are found in David Neubauer, *Judicial Role and Case Management*, 4 Just. Sys. J. 223, 228 (1978).

-yer-dominated discovery in America is a natural part of a
ides itself in citizen autonomy and distrusts governmental
ctivity. It is the result of a culture that has competing needs,
government but more protection, castigating lawyers but seeking
ication of grievances.

quite well the dangers of generalization and that what actually
a litigation is often a faint distorted shadow of what appears in the
the academic literature, it is nevertheless useful to refer to a general
outline of the civil law countries. As we have stated earlier, other legal systems,
even many common law ones, have chosen to rely on government financed
and controlled, rather than on private initiative in unearthing information
relevant to litigation. As a general matter, lawyers do not conduct pretrial
depositions nor do they conduct any pretrial document production. A party
can request the court to require the opposing party to produce a document,
but in some civil law systems, the opposing party cannot be compelled to
produce a document that will establish liability against him. In others, "a party
may be compelled to produce a document [only] when the judge concludes
that the document is the only evidence concerning the point of issue."[43]
Judicial responsibility for fact gathering is less to unearth the truth but more to
assist the parties to resolve their individual disputes.

American discovery is so related to other aspects of civil procedure in the
United States and so reflective of American culture that one would probably
conclude that American discovery provisions could never be lifted out of the
unique American context. Yet, as of this writing, some convergence is afoot as
civil law countries such as China and Japan have reformed their systems to
adopt evidentiary exchanges somewhat closer to American discovery. Thus,
for example, in Japan "each party [since 1998] may, during the course of
litigation, submit a written inquiry to the other party, asking for answers to
questions that are necessary to prepare the inquiring party's case."[44] France
and Swiss law already introduced a general duty of disclosure to their litigation
system, and such duty is under discussion in Germany.[45]

Should or could discovery be transplanted to other legal systems? There are a
number of considerations as to whether American discovery can be or should
be transplanted to other legal systems. For one, the discovery regime a country
adopts is related to the functions of civil litigation in that country. If civil
litigation serves an expansive public function in regulating the social and
economic fabric of the country, rather than relying on direct intrusions by the
government, than the nature of civil disputes will be more complicated and
discovery will be needed in order to obtain relevant information. Legal
systems that serve mainly to resolve individual disputes may not require a
complex discovery system geared towards lawsuits with multiple parties and
issues.

Private discovery also needs a large body of lawyers to effectuate. Bear in
mind that the United States, with just over 290,000,000 people has over a

---

43. Geoffrey C. Hazard Jr., *From Whom No Secrets Are Hid,* 176 Tex. L. Rev. 1665, 1682 (June 1998).
44. Takeshi Kojima, *Japanese Civil Procedure in Comparative Law Perspective,* 46 U. Kan. L. Rev. 687, 701 (May 1998) (citation omitted).
45. Gottwald, *supra* note 21.

million lawyers or about one lawyer for every 290 residents.[46] By contrast, some countries, — China, for instance — has only about 110,000 lawyers for 1.26 billion citizens, a ratio of about one lawyer per 11,450.[47] Unless the legal system has a core body of legal professionals, the adversary process and with it, discovery, would not be the most equitable or most efficient method to unearth facts about a dispute. Those who could afford the rare lawyer in those countries would have an added advantage over those without the assistance of a lawyer. And so, civil law countries such as France, Italy, Japan, and China may well choose to adhere closer to their tradition of judges being responsible for the investigation of the case with the added advantage that it can alleviate the disparity of resources between the parties.

Interestingly, even as we are pondering the comparative advantages of different legal systems, we are also seeing convergence on the part of the United States to move closer to civil law systems with more case management, mandatory disclosure, and judicially imposed stringent requirements for pleadings. We cannot predict the future course of discovery as it remains unclear what the effects of the latest discovery reforms will be. The advent of ADR, and particularly the growth of mediation, may naturally lead to a reduction of discovery. The increased monitoring of businesses over the costs of litigation could also lead to a reduction. But the complexity of some types of cases, particularly those reliant on scientific evidence, and the increased availability of computer data could lead in the opposite direction.

The transnational economy will likely bring us closer to international norms. The American Law Institute's project on drafting transnational civil procedure rules included a section on discovery blending civil and common law features. Then again, the fractured composition of the American bar and the divergent interests of plaintiff and defendant lawyers, accompanying the increased impact of politics on the rulemaking process, may make it unlikely that there will ever be dramatic reform. Perhaps most importantly, American lawyers assume, accept, and are unlikely to veer from the belief that broad discovery is integral to our litigation process.

There are still additional considerations that may predict the future course of American pretrial practices. Perhaps judges will begin to believe the data that case management only requires firm trial dates and discovery cut-off dates. Will the judges themselves decide that they want to return to their traditional roles and require less case management paperwork from lawyers, making trials more likely? On the other hand, perhaps the United States government in the future will take an increased role in regulating society,

46. According to the U.S. Census Bureau, the total population estimate for 2003 was 290,809,777. U.S. Census Bureau, *USA Quick Facts from the U.S. Census Bureau*, http://quickfacts.census.gov/gfd/states/00000.htm/ (accessed Sept. 15, 2005). According to the A.B.A., the total number of active attorneys in the U.S. in 2003 was 1,058,662. Memorandum from A.B.A., Market Research Dept., *National Lawyer Population Trends* (June 16, 2005) *available at* http://www.abanet.org/barserv/lawyerpopulation98-03.pdf (accessed Sept. 15, 2005).

47. China's total population figure comes from Bingham Kennedy, Jr., *Dissecting China's 2000 Census*, http://www.prb.org/Template.cfm?Section=PRB&template=/ContentManagement/ContentDisplay.cfm&ContentID=3024 (accessed Sept. 10, 2004). China's number of lawyers figure is from Legal500.com's *General Notes on China*, http://www.icclaw.com/as500/edit/ ch1.htm (accessed Sept. 24, 2004).

making civil litigation, and in turn discovery and case management, less necessary.

Discovery, then, will continue to evolve in ways that reflect overall changes in American culture. Discovery will remain a battlefield, infused with issues of power, between those who want to expand the individual rights of plaintiffs and those who want to protect the privacy and purse of defendants, most frequently corporations and the government. In large stakes cases, it will be the plaintiffs' lawyers who usually seek to expand their clients' stories, their narrative, and the defendants' lawyers and their clients who seek to limit that story, by reducing the scope of the litigation, including the amount of permitted discovery. And the legitimacy of the discovery system and by extension, the entire legal system will be viewed, and in fact turn, on how the system balances the vindication of rights with curbs on excesses of expense, time, and intrusions on privacy.

Procedure is a tricky business. Discovery can protect the innocent plaintiff, but also make it prohibitively expensive to sue or be sued. Discovery, resulting in liability, can ultimately enhance the safety of the public at large, but it can also reduce the incentive for defendants to create new products or provide new services. Discovery can help unearth and punish illegal conduct, but it can also thwart the creativity, privacy, peace of mind, and profit of innocent defendants – those who are sued and those who, although innocent, fear suit. Ultimately, we believe that so long as the adversary system remains, with its reliance on private initiative, and the idea that civil litigation can serve to enforce public norms, the discovery process in America will remain robust.

CHAPTER

8

Adjudication Without Trial: Dispositive Motions

The very mission of the summary judgment procedure is to pierce the pleadings and to assess the proof in order to see whether there is a genuine need for trial.

1963 Advisory Committee Notes to Rule 56[1]

[S]ummary judgment has assumed a much larger role in civil case dispositions than its traditional image portrays or even than the text of Rule 56 would indicate, to the point where fundamental judgments about the value of trials and especially trials by jury may be at stake.

Patricia Wald, *Summary Judgment at Sixty*, 1998[2]

The celebrated image of the American lawyer is one of a relentless advocate presenting a dramatic closing statement to a jury on behalf of her client at trial. This image suggests not only that many civil cases culminate in a trial but that an attorney's most exercised skills lie with oral advocacy. On the contrary, much of what happens in American civil litigation happens in the pretrial stage. The trial itself is an increasingly rare occurrence for all cases filed. Settlement and ADR account for many of the cases that do not reach trial, but part of this reduction in trials is probably attributable to the granting of what are called "dispositive motions" — motions that tend to end litigation.[3] We say "probably," because accurate statistics about how civil cases are actually terminated are difficult to come by. In placing higher thresholds for getting to trial in the form of dispositive motions, procedural rules are shifting the balance of power from plaintiffs to defendants, from parties to judges.

Much of what happens in American civil litigation happens in the pretrial stage, largely through documents and what is called "motions." The word "motion" bespeaks movement, going from one place to another. In civil

---

1. Advisory Committee's Notes to 1963 Amendments to Fed. R. Civ. P. 56.Federal Rules of Civil Procedure Advisory Committee, *Advisory Committee Notes to Rule 56*, Federal Rules of Civil Procedure (Foundation Press 2000).

2. Patricia Wald, *Summary Judgment at Sixty*, 76 Tex. L. Rev. 1897, 1898 (June 1998).

3. *See* Stephen C. Yeazell, *The Misunderstood Consequences of Modern Civil Process*, 1994 Wis. L. Rev. 631, 632; Stephen B. Burbank, *Vanishing Trials and Summary Judgment in Federal Civil Cases: Drifting Toward Bethlehem or Gomorrah?*, 1 J. of Empirical Legal Stud. 591 (Nov. 2004).

litigation, a "motion" is the request of one party, frequently in writing, to the judge trying to "move" the judge to do something in favor of the party bringing the motion. In the courtroom, in the rare instance that a civil case is now tried, you will hear a lawyer say "I move for a directed verdict." As "trial practice" in American civil litigation is gradually overtaken by "motion practice," a lawyer's indispensable skill is not her ability to tell a compelling story at trial; rather, her best asset may lie in written advocacy and her ability to convince the judge to rule in her favor on a motion and in particular, a dispositive one that will decide the underlying issues without going to full trial.

This chapter explains the principle kinds of pretrial motions that are employed in civil litigation to terminate a case without going to or completing a full trial. These motions, addressed to judges, are the motion to dismiss for failure to state a claim (which you have already read some about in the chapter on pleading), the motion for judgment on the pleadings, the motion for summary judgment, and the motion for directed verdict. The chapter will also talk about two other important post-trial motions: the motion for judgment notwithstanding the verdict and the motion for a new trial. These motions are permitted after a jury has rendered its verdict. The first, if granted, takes the jury verdict away by substituting the judge's decision for the verdict. The second, when granted, results in a new trial, or, as often happens, precipitates a settlement.

As you read this chapter, bear in mind three of the four prominent themes recurrent in our account of American civil procedure. The first theme highlights the complicated interplay between a formal system of rules and culture. On the one hand, formal rules can change litigation conduct, as revealed by recent federal rule amendments to the discovery process requiring mandatory disclosure of relevant information on the part of opposing parties. These changes in rules do not take place in a vacuum, but rather are influenced in both promulgation and application by the legal culture and the culture at large. Sometimes rule amendments track conduct by judges or lawyers that has already occurred.[4] Other times, courts implement their own policies, notwithstanding, or perhaps more accurately, in addition to or in reaction to, the formal rules in place. For example, in the summary judgment context, judges have, in effect, frequently shifted the burden of convincing the court to the nonmoving party, usually the plaintiff.[5]

Building from the first theme, the second theme reveals how cultural changes in the rules or in the judicial policy enforcing these rules have a profoundly political dimension; that is, these rules and their application provide an advantage for some litigants and types of lawsuits and a disadvantage for others. As political tides ebb and flow in the legal profession and at large, the vision of a proper system of formal procedure also fluctuates. For instance, many scholars correlate the conservative makeup of the federal bench with procedural requirements that tend to restrict litigation, such as

---

4. *See, e.g.*, David L. Shapiro, *Federal Rule 16: A Look at the Theory and Practice of Rulemaking*, 137 U. Pa. L. Rev. 1969, 1992 (June 1989) (increased case management by many judges had already taken place prior to a federal rule amendment encouraging this phenomenon).

5. *See, e.g.*, Wald, *supra note 2, at* 1930-1931 (noting that the district courts in the District of Columbia use Rule 12 motions to dismiss as "informal" summary judgments); Richard L. Marcus, *Slouching Towards Discretion*, 78 Notre Dame L. Rev. 1561, 1572-1573 August (2003).

heightened pleadings for civil rights claims and the liberal exercise of summary judgment, both of which in the main have had a detrimental effect on the claims of plaintiffs.[6]

A final theme emerges from the impact that the "vanishing trial" phenomenon has had on an attorney's ability to convey orally a compelling narrative to the court. Trial lawyers know that the art of persuasion was in large measure the art of creating and telling stories. As adjudication by trial becomes more infrequent, it is critical that litigators perfect the art of conveying on paper what traditionally would have been told through live testimony and opening and closing arguments at trial. This growing reliance on paper as a result of motion practice tracks the importance of paper (interrogatories and answers, transcripts of depositions, and documents produced upon request) spawned through liberal discovery. Motion practice thus reshapes the narrative telling of the case from the oral trials to the more narrow parameters of the written page.

We start our survey of dispositive motions (motions designed to dispose of cases without trials) with some general introductory thoughts on litigation strategy, as well as on the function and reality of motions in civil practice. The aim of the plaintiff and plaintiff's lawyer is to move the case along to advantageous settlement or, in rare instances, a victory at trial, while the aim of the defendant and defendant's lawyer is to have the case dismissed before trial or to achieve a "cheap" settlement.

The way American lawyers seek the aid of judges in the processing of civil litigation is through the use of motions. A motion is an application to the court to issue an order. Fed. R. Civ. P. 7. At any stage in the litigation, any party may "make a motion" or in other words, request the court for an order on a wide variety of matters. This can range from motions for an extension of time, court ordered sanctions, or interim emergency relief to the more critical dispositive motions that ask the court to decide cases without trial.

While motions are customarily written, motions can be made orally if they are made during a hearing or trial and in the presence of opposing party. Otherwise, motions must be made in writing with a copy mailed to the opposing party to provide notice and an opportunity to respond. The motion should state the relief or order sought and the grounds supporting it. Motions are often accompanied with a written memorandum consisting of a narrative giving that side's view of the facts, supporting arguments, and legal authority.

Depending on the complexity of the motion, the written memorandum can range from a few paragraphs to more than a hundred pages. Permissible lengths for memoranda (frequently called "briefs," especially on appeal) are often found in the local rules of a court. Motions are sometimes accompanied

6. *See, e.g.,* Orley Ashenfelter, Theodore Eisenberg, and Stewart J. Schwab, *Politics and the Judiciary: The Influence of Judicial Background on Case Outcomes,* 24 J. Legal Stud. 257, 261 (June 1995) (noting the correlations between the appointing president and the liberalism or conservatism of the judge in civil rights cases); Roy L. Brooks, *Critical Race Theory: A Proposed Structure and Application to Federal Pleading,* 11 Harv. BlackLetter J. 85, 107-108 (1994) (arguing that the heightened pleading standard is race-specific); Eric K. Yamamoto, *Efficiency's Threat to the Value of Accessible Courts for Minorities,* 25 Harv. C.R.-C.L. L. Rev. 341, 421-422, n. 358 (1990) (noting that the courts are narrowing substantive rights through procedural practice due to the conservatism on the bench); Timothy B. Tomasi and Jess A. Velona, Note, *All the President's Men? A Study of Ronald Reagan's Appointments to the U.S. Courts of Appeals,* 87 Colum. L. Rev. 766, 782-783 (May 1987) (articulating that Reagan's appointments to the U.S. Courts of Appeals are more conservative when it came to discrimination suits).

by affidavits, verifying the facts upon which the request is made, and signed by the lawyer in accordance with Rule 11 requirements. The attorney signature verifies, under threat of sanctions, that the motion was not filed for improper basis and that a "reasonable inquiry" was made into the factual and legal basis for the motion.

All written motions are filed with the court, with a copy mailed to the nonmoving party, who then has opportunity to respond. In most courts, a party now has to ask for the right to argue to the court orally, but oral argument is usually permitted on dispositive motions. In such cases, there is typically a hearing before the presiding judge during which both parties will present oral arguments and be subject to questioning from the judge. In sum, no decision on a case can be rendered without an opportunity for the affected parties to be "heard" on the matter, either in writing or orally.

Many courts have "motions sessions," that is, a portion of the day reserved for hearing oral arguments on these motions. In federal court, the judge assigned to the case usually hears any dispositive motions concerning the case. In most federal districts, judges are assisted in their pretrial matters by magistrate judges. A magistrate judge in the federal court system is appointed with a set term of eight years and is generally delegated with the authority to handle nondispositive pretrial matters, such as discovery motions.[7] In some state courts, judges rotate through "motions sessions," during which they hear motions even on cases that will not be assigned to them for trial.[8] A judge or magistrate hearing a pretrial motion will either grant or deny the motion (in whole or in part), either immediately at the hearing or sometime later by issuing a written order, often with an explanation of the reasons for the order.

As late as 30 years ago, virtually every motion in state or federal court was heard by a judge with lawyers having the opportunity to argue orally and answer questions. Novice trial lawyers typically learned how to handle themselves in a courtroom and how to explain and argue cases at motions sessions in which they would try to compel answers to interrogatories, resolve questions about depositions, win motions to dismiss for jurisdictional reasons, or ask for a continuance for discovery responses or for a later trial date. Young lawyers would learn a good deal about trial practice by watching more experienced lawyers at motions sessions and by generally being in the courthouse where they could also witness trials.

Today, motions, except for dispositive ones, are most frequently decided on written papers, with the lawyers given no opportunity to make oral arguments. This is especially true in the state courts. Many lawyers and commentators have attributed the decline of the trial lawyer, in part, to the failure to permit young lawyers the opportunity at motions sessions to cut their teeth in oral advocacy and courtroom behavior.[9] The reduction of oral advocacy at motion sessions highlights the increasing importance to litigators of written advocacy and of developing the skill to write persuasive narratives about one's case.

---

7. 28 U.S.C. §§ 631 *et. seq.*
8. For instance, judges in the Massachusetts courts system rotate through motion sessions.
9. *See* Roger J. Miner, *Confronting the Communication Crisis in the Legal Profession*, 34 N.Y.L. Sch. L. Rev. 1, 7-8 (1989).

The concept of burdens of proof underlies the workings of these pre-trial motions. As we discussed in Chapter 6, in any civil case, it is the parties, and not the court, that bear the burden of proof. Ordinarily, a plaintiff has the burden of proof on all elements of her claims. This means that she has the burden to plead her claim properly, to produce sufficient evidence to permit a fact finder to find that every element of the claim is true, and to persuade the fact finder that "it is more likely than not" that each element is true. A defendant, meanwhile, bears the burden of pleading, production, and persuasion as to most of her affirmative defenses. At various times in a given litigation, the case may be dismissed against the plaintiff if she fails to meet her burdens. This is true even if the defendant fails to meet her burdens on an affirmative defense. A plaintiff can ultimately only win if she meets her burden of proof, including the collective burden of production and persuasion, *and* the defendant fails to meet her burden as to any affirmative defenses. Historically, whoever makes a motion (called "the moving party") was thought to have the burden of convincing the judge that the motion should be granted. For example, even though the plaintiff has the burden to plead correctly, it was the defendant who moved to dismiss because the pleading was improper who must convince the judge that the motion should be granted. As you will see, now it is often the plaintiff who must demonstrate why the defendant's motion's dispositive motion should be denied.

The percentage of civil cases terminated by trial in the United States District Courts dropped from 15.2 percent in 1940,.[10] to 11.5 percent in 1962,[11] to 1.7 percent by 2003.[12] This gradual decline and shift of focus in American civil litigation away from the trial and toward the pretrial process is troubling to many lawyers and scholars. Critics have pointed out that while aiding judicial economy, the granting of these pretrial dispositive motions can infringe on a plaintiff's right to "her day in court." This is particularly troubling if her right was guaranteed a trial by jury, as the U.S. Constitution specifically preserved for most civil cases in federal court.[13]

THE PRE-ANSWER MOTION TO DISMISS

In the Anglo-American legal system, a court usually accepts all filed complaints initially without question. This means that the court will not ordinarily review the complaint for sufficiency *sua sponte*, or in other words, "on its own initiative." Under the adversary system, it is the defendant's responsibility to

10. *See* Marc Galanter, *Reading the Landscape of Disputes: What We Know and Don't Know (and What We Think We Know) About our Allegedly Contentious and Litigious Society*, 31 UCLA L. Rev. 4, 44 (Oct. 1983).

11. Adam Liptak, *U.S. Suits Multiply, But Fewer Ever Get to Trial, Study Says*, N.Y. Times, Dec. 14, 2003, at 1, col. 1.

12. Administrative Office of the United States Courts, 2003 *Annual Report of the Director: Judicial Business of the United States Courts* 150, table. C-4. U.S. District Courts — Civil Cases Terminated, by Nature of Suit and Action Taken, During the 12-Month Period Ending September 30, 2003 (Washington: USGPO, 2004).

13. Wald, *supra* note 2, at 1897.

challenge any infirmities in the plaintiff's complaint. In the federal courts, Fed. R. Civ. P. 12 provides the first opportunity for a defendant to challenge the validity of a lawsuit. Under Rule 12(a), the defendant has 20 days from the day of service to respond to the complaint. Failure to respond within the 20-day time period, unless extended, could subject the defendant to a default judgment entered against her. A default judgment is a final judgment on the merits and may be set aside only on a showing of excusable neglect or if the judgment was obtained through fraud, misrepresentation, or other miscon-duct. Fed. R.Civ. P. 60.

Rule 12 further provides that the defendant can respond to the complaint in two ways – either by filing an answer to the complaint (in which case Rule 8 gives the ground rules) or a pre-answer motion raising certain defenses. Rule 12(b) sets out the defenses a defendant can raise, as an initial matter, in response to plaintiff's complaint. These defenses contest preliminary matters such as that the complaint is filed in the wrong court, that a necessary party has not been joined, or that the complaint lacks merit. These defenses can be raised in the defendant's answer or serve as a basis for the defendant's pre-answer motion to dismiss plaintiff's complaint.

The majority of these so-called Rule 12(b) defenses have roots in common law practice. In the common law courts of England, the defendant could file a challenge to the plaintiff's complaint in several ways. Some of this you have already read about in Chapter 5, on jurisdiction, and in Chapter 6, where we covered pleadings. He could *challenge the jurisdiction of the court*, file a *plea in suspension* to challenge the plaintiff's right to bring the action until some problem was resolved, or file a *plea in abatement* to argue that there was some defect in the complaint itself.[14] Alternatively, the defendant could file a *demurrer* challenging the legal sufficiency of the claim. He could also *traverse* to deny the factual allegation of the complaint, or file a *plea of confession and avoidance* to concede the legal sufficiency and factual truth of the complaint but allege a defense.

These common law methods were carried over to the Anglo-American courts, and with the adoption of the 1938 Federal Rules, are now conveniently codified in Rule 12(b) of the Federal Rules. (The common law confession and avoidance, however, known today as an affirmative defense, is found in Fed. R. Civ. P. 8(c).) It is important to note that some state court jurisdictions, such as California, have not adopted rules analogous to the Federal Rules. In these jurisdictions, these historical terms and the accompanying common law practice are preserved and still in use, rather than the Rule 12(b) pre-answer motions.

Under Rule 12(b), defendants are given the opportunity to challenge plaintiff's complaint early on, by filing a pre-answer motion to dismiss the complaint based on the above defenses. And so, a defendant can move for dismissal on the grounds that the suit was filed in a court without subject matter jurisdiction of the case, that it was filed in the wrong geographic location due to

14. We have used "she" throughout most of this book out of a habit fostered by our teaching at a law school with more women students than men and in deference to the attempt to counterbalance centuries of the opposite usage. When writing here about common law defenses in England we use "he" because in common law England the parties and their lawyers were usually men.

lack of personal jurisdiction, or that it was filed in an improper venue. Fed. R. Civ. P. 12(b)(1)-(3). The defendant can also seek to dismiss the complaint if service of the complaint was improper or if there was some crucial defect in the summons papers themselves. Fed. R. Civ. P. 12(b)(4)-(5). The defendant can challenge the suit on the grounds that a necessary and indispensable party has not been joined. Fed. R. Civ. P. 12(b)(7). Most importantly, for purposes of this chapter, the defendant can attack the merits of the lawsuit by arguing that the complaint should be dismissed because it fails to state a claim for which relief can be granted. Fed. R. Civ. P. 12(b)(6). A motion to dismiss for failure to state a claim was known as a demurrer under common law, and today the terms are sometimes used interchangeably.

Many of these Rule 12(b) defenses can be devastating to the plaintiff's case. If the court lacks subject matter jurisdiction over the claim or personal jurisdiction over the defendant, the case cannot be heard in that court, no matter how meritorious that claim is. If the court agrees with the defendant's defense on either ground, the judge will grant the defendant's motion, and the case will be dismissed. While the case will generally be dismissed without prejudice so that the plaintiff can re-file the case in the proper court, re-filing is not always possible; for example, the case may now be beyond the applicable statute of limitations — that is, beyond the statutorily prescribed time period within which the particular action must be filed. Therefore, a defendant who moves to dismiss a complaint, even on a technical issue that it was filed in the wrong court, can score a win for her client if it is now too late for the plaintiff to re-file in a proper court. A defendant can also use such a dismissal to force the plaintiff into a court more to the liking of the defendant.

Similarly, under Rule 12(b)(7), a defendant can seek to have the lawsuit dismissed because a necessary party to the litigation has not been joined by plaintiff in the lawsuit.[15] For example, a court would likely find an indispensable party problem where two parties, *A* and *B*, jointly owned a piece of property but only one owner was sued as to that property. In that instance, if the second party *B* cannot be joined because the court does not have personal jurisdiction over *B*, then the defendant can sometimes force the dismissal of the complaint. Again, the dismissal will generally be without prejudice so that the plaintiff can re-file the complaint in the proper court with the proper parties. Nevertheless, through this defense, the defendant can again sometimes force the plaintiff to litigate in a forum not of her choosing and one that may be less convenient to her.

There is no pre-answer motion more dispositive than the 12(b)(6) motion to dismiss plaintiff's complaint for failure to state a claim. Under Rule 12(b)(6), a court may dismiss a plaintiff's case on the ground that her complaint failed to state a cause of action. In ruling on this motion, the court will assume plaintiff's factual allegations true as stated for the purpose of this motion and assess whether such factual allegations, even if true, would give rise to any claim for which there is legal relief. In some circumstances, the complaint's failure to set out a cause of action could be due to careless drafting that could be remedied

---

15. The topic of "necessary" and "indispensable" parties is covered in more detail in Chapter 9 on joinder.

by its redrafting and re-filing. In other instances, there are no further facts to support a claim and in those instances, the case ends by virtue of the dismissal.

When the failure of the complaint is not based on poor drafting, the court in deciding the defendant's motion must make a judgment as to whether the law provides for legal relief for the scenario stated by plaintiff. The rationale for dismissal is that because the judgment is a legal one rather than one based on factual proof, a trial is deemed unnecessary. A factual judgment requires a finding as to the truth or falsity of the facts in the plaintiff's complaint, which is a task befitted to trial with its examinations and cross-examination of witnesses. By contrast, a legal judgment such as a motion to dismiss for failure to state a claim, requires no proving of facts. Thus, if the court agrees with the defendant that the plaintiff's allegations do not make out a proper cause of action, then it will summarily dismiss plaintiff's complaint. The dismissal is a final judgment, and plaintiff will usually be prohibited from re-filing another complaint based on those same facts.[16] Often, the plaintiff is given a certain amount of time — typically 30 days — to amend the complaint in an attempt to cure the defect.

In a case like *Cherryum*, it is unlikely that a manufacturer or bottler of a soft drink could ever win a 12(b)(6) motion. If Albert Lee, the plaintiff purchaser of the drink, merely alleges that he bought a can of Cherryum and it had poison in it when he opened it, causing him harm, he has stated a claim for breach of the warranty of merchantability. And if he alleges negligence, because either the manufacturer or bottler acted unreasonably in permitting poison to get into the drink in the can, American courts are likely to permit discovery on the negligence issue and allow Lee the opportunity to unearth evidence to prove the facts as he stated them.

In other types of cases that are not as straightforward as *Cherryum*, there has been much controversy, as you have read in Chapter 6, around the issue of how much specificity should be required in the complaint. Traditionally, a Rule 12(b)(6) motion to dismiss for failure to state a claim was decided with reference to the pleading requirement of Rule 8. With the liberal pleading regime anticipated under the Federal Rules, one would assume that complaints rarely got dismissed for failure to state a claim. Indeed, Rule 8 simply requires "a short and plain statement of the claim" for a complaint. However, federal courts have applied with increasing frequency a stricter pleading requirement that defendants have utilized in conjunction with Rule 12 to seek dismissals of cases at an early stage of the litigation. This is particularly true for certain "disfavored cases," such as civil rights actions against the government, with the result that many civil rights plaintiffs now find the courthouse door not as open to their claims.

The stricter pleading requirement, often known as "heightened pleading," places a particularly heavy burden on plaintiffs. Undeniably, the burden to plead should rest initially with the plaintiff, but in many cases, the evidence and factual details lies with the defendant in the initial stages of the litigation.

---

16. It can be a close question of the effect of a prior 12(b)(6) motion granted when the plaintiff in a subsequent suit adds large numbers of facts to what is much the same story that was in the previous complaint and then argues that she is now bringing a new claim and not one barred by the prior final judgment.

It is frequently only through the discovery process by a diligent plaintiff that such facts are uncovered. To require such specific pleadings at the complaint stage with such a substantial risk of dismissal can chill many creative or social reform claims at the outset. This concern was not lost on the Supreme Court when it reaffirmed in 1992 that a plaintiff is not required under the Federal Rules "to set out in detail the facts upon which he bases his claim." *Leatherman v. Tarrant County Narcotics Intelligence and Coordination Unit*, 507 U.S. 163, 168 (1992).

Yet, here again, the legal culture and the political climate of the times seem to overshadow the formal rule. While the Supreme Court's declaration reaffirmed a "notice pleading" regime and a close adherence to the language of Rule 8, the effectiveness of its condemnation on the actual conduct of judges is questionable. Professor Christopher Fairman articulates the sentiment of many skeptical scholars: "[H]eightened pleading requirements have risen like the phoenix from the ashes of *Leatherman*."[17] Despite the Supreme Court's decision, many federal courts continue to require heightened pleadings and to dismiss cases under Rule 12(b)(6) in numerous contexts, often civil rights cases.[18]

These courts appear to be responding to the public outcry against the so-called litigation explosion and the judgment that certain litigation — civil rights and securities fraud cases especially — are frivolous and unfairly damaging to a defendant's reputation. Yet in civil rights litigation, discriminatory intent is frequently an element of the plaintiff's claim, and heightened pleading requirements in civil rights litigation can mean an overwhelming burden on plaintiffs, as the information of a defendant's subjective intent may be impossible to determine without discovery.[19] According to Professor Fairman, this procedure contravenes the mission of civil rights legislation, a system grounded on merits determination, and clouds the vision of a simple, uniform, and trans-substantive procedure that led to the adoption of the Federal Rules in the first place.[20] This is an example of legal culture trumping rules through on-the-ground judicial practice, with a heavy dose of politics in the mix.

Heightened pleading requirements have also been implanted in statutes. By enacting the Private Securities Litigation Reform Act of 1995 and the Y2K Act of 1999, Congress, as is its right, eschewed the conventional rule-making process in the securities fraud and Y2K litigation context by enacting stricter threshold requirements.[21] Given the heightened pleadings legacy that followed *Leatherman*, many scholars are pessimistic that neither courts nor Congress will abandon these particularized pleadings policies, notwithstanding the Court's most recent affirmation of its pro-notice pleading message in *Swierkiewicz v. Sorema, N.A.*, 534 U.S. 506 (2002).[22]

The requirement of heightened pleadings standards, backed by defendant's aggressive use of the 12(b)(6) pre-answer motion to dismiss for failure to state a

---

17. Christopher M. Fairman, *Heightened Pleading*, 81 Tex. L. Rev. 551, 572 (Dec. 2002).
18. *Id.* at 596.
19. *Id.* at 576.
20. *Id.* at 554.
21. *Id.* at 552-553.
22. *Id.*

claim, not only undermines the procedural model fueling the current Federal Rules; it also reveals how substance and procedure can intersect. Seemingly neutral procedures can profoundly affect substantive law. Obviously, lawsuits can be limited through changes in substantive rights, for instance by eliminating certain legal remedies or by adding elements to a cause of action. The same end may be accomplished procedurally by requiring stricter pleadings under threat of dismissal. A strict procedure can inhibit the litigation of cases that otherwise would have promoted substantive law. The requirement of more particularized pleadings in civil rights litigation especially underscores the interdependence of substantive and procedural law.[23]

Given such importance, defendants will spend substantial time and effort on their preliminary defenses, whether they chose to raise them by pre-answer motion or place them in their answer. If a defendant wins at this initial stage, she will have saved the expense of protracted litigation, with its potentially extensive discovery and the threat of trial and ultimate loss.

If defendant does raise a pre-answer motion to dismiss, the defendant must consolidate many of her 12(b) defenses in one motion. A defendant will have only one shot at a pre-answer motion as to four of the seven Rule 12(b) defenses — personal jurisdiction, insufficiency of process, insufficiency of service, and improper venue. Any of these four defenses, if omitted, are deemed waived by the defendant and cannot be raised at a later stage in the litigation. The remaining Rule 12(b) defenses are preserved, even if they are omitted in either the pre-answer motion or, if the defendant files no pre-answer motion, from the answer. The three preserved defenses are a failure to state a claim, failure to join a party, and lack of subject matter jurisdiction.

The delineation of which defenses are preserved and which ones are waived makes sense pragmatically and as a policy matter. The defenses of personal jurisdiction, insufficiency of process, insufficiency of service, and improper venue are defenses for the protection of the defendant, and hence, can be deemed waived by the defendant if not raised. Efficiency is also a consideration; defendant should not be able to strategically and successively raise these foundational defenses one at a time and thereby drag out the litigation to the plaintiff's disadvantage and wasting court time and resources.

As for the other Rule 12(b) defenses, they are sensibly preserved. Naturally, the federal courts reserve the authority to dismiss for lack of subject matter jurisdiction at any point in the litigation. Private parties cannot agree simply by a defendant's waiver of the defense to give the court subject matter jurisdiction in an area not granted by Congress or that may be beyond what the Constitution permits. As to failure to state a claim, it makes no sense to continue the case if the law does not permit recovery, even if this is not discovered until later in the litigation. How can a judge or jury find for a plaintiff who does not rely on any claim that permits relief? Finally, due process considerations for the protection of parties who will be bound by a decision in their absence render it logical to keep the defense of failure to join a necessary party alive, even if the case is quite far along.

---

23.   For a examination of the interdependence of substantive and procedural law in the civil rights litigation context, see Phyllis Tropper Baumann, Judith Olans Brown, and Stephen N. Subrin, *Substance in the Shadow of Procedure: The Integration of Substantive and Procedural Law in Title VII Cases*, 33 B.C. L. Rev. 211 (March 1992).

JUDGMENT ON THE PLEADINGS

After the answer is filed and the pleadings are closed, either party will have another chance to ask the court to decide the case without trial. Any party may move for a judgment based on the pleadings — the complaint and answer — alone. At common law, this was known as a demurrer. It is now codified in the Federal Rules as a "judgment on the pleadings." Fed. R. Civ. P. 12(c).

Federal Rule 12(c) provides that a party may move for judgment on the pleadings, "after the pleadings are closed, but within such time as not to delay the trial." Fed. R. Civ. P. 12(c). While a 12(b) motion to dismiss for failure to state a claim considers only the complaint, a motion for judgment on the pleadings asks the court to consider both the complaint and answer. Thus, if the defendant did not sufficiently answer the complaint to deny the allegations, plaintiff may move for a judgment on the pleadings and win without trial. If the defendant pleads an affirmative defense that has no legal basis, and does not deny plaintiff's allegations, the plaintiff may move for a judgment on the pleadings and win at this stage. Similarly, if the defendant raises an affirmative defense for which there is no possible legitimate response, and it must be taken as true, the defendant would prevail on such a motion.

In sum, a judgment on the pleadings is similar to a motion to dismiss for failure to state a claim. The court will look at the face of the complaint and the answer as alleged to determine whether the complaint is sufficient and whether the answer stated facts, which as stated, constitute an absolute bar to the plaintiff's claim. If the case survives the initial challenges to dismiss the case, it will proceed to the next stage of the litigation — that of discovery. After discovery, there frequently is yet another device — arguably one of the most important and controversial pretrial devices — to end cases summarily.

MOTION FOR SUMMARY JUDGMENT

At any time during the discovery process, or even before it is under way, either party may file a motion for summary judgment, supported by evidentiary materials showing that she should be entitled to judgment without the need for trial. Fed. R. Civ. P. 56. Rule 56(c) authorizes the entry of a summary judgment when: "the pleadings, depositions, answers to interrogatories and admissions on file, together with the affidavits, if any, show that there is no genuine issue as to any material fact and that the moving party is entitled to a judgment as a matter of law." In other words, if there has been an opportunity for discovery, and the record of the case indicates no genuine issue of material fact, then there is no need for a trial. A motion for summary judgment enables a court to render a judgment on either the entire case or merely a portion without going forward with a trial.

A party moving for summary judgment is in essence arguing to the court that the pretrial discovery (if any), admitted facts, and affidavits point to undisputed facts or a failure of proof of facts — and that these undisputed facts or the failure to come up with potential evidence leads to only one conclusion in the movant's favor. If the court agrees, then judgment is entered, and the case does not go to trial on that claim. A total summary judgment, if granted, is a final judgment on the merits of the case and can be appealed by the losing party. If the motion is denied, the case goes to trial, and the parties can raise again any of the issues dealt with on the motion. A denial of summary judgment is not a final decision on the merits, as it reflects a decision of the court that there remains at least one material factual issue to be tried. Because a denial of summary judgment is not a final judgment, it may not be appealed until the case is concluded.

The American summary judgment rule finds its origin in the English Bill of Exchange Act of 1855.[24] This bill originally provided for a resolution without trial in a narrow category of contract cases involving liquidated claims, where defendants had only spurious defenses. When carried over to the American courts, summary judgment was used to strike "any frivolous defenses and to defeat attempts to use formal pleadings to delay the recovery of just demands."[25] Until the promulgation of the Federal Rules in 1938, summary judgment remained an exceptional practice in state courts.[26] However, the drafters of the Federal Rules chose to include the summary judgment device, and in its inclusion, made it available to all parties and for all cases, including cases in equity.

The policy underlying Rule 56 and summary judgment is to provide for the early termination of claims that have no legitimate factual basis or are so strong that they must be won in order to save the court, taxpayers, and litigants time and money. It is a judge who decides summary judgment. A motion for summary judgment is a "trial on the papers," without juries or the live testimony of witnesses. As such, summary judgment, while time-efficient and cost-effective, can frustrate a party's right (usually the plaintiff) to experience a full trial on her case. For cases for which a jury trial is preserved, summary judgment collides with the Seventh Amendment right to have a jury hear and decide her claim.

The Federal Rules have such liberal pleading requirements that it is easy to see why the drafters would value summary judgment as a purifying device to filter out unmeritorious claims. Discovery might demonstrate that the plaintiff lacks any evidence of one element or that the plaintiff must win because every element is clearly true. Until recently, most cases survived a Rule 12(b)(6) motion to dismiss challenge, so some cases lacking merit could reach trial except for the possibility of termination by summary judgment.

Procedurally, a motion for summary judgment can be made at any time after pleadings are filed. In fact, a court may even treat a Rule 12(b)(6) motion to dismiss or a motion for judgment on the pleadings as a motion for summary judgment if matters outside of the pleadings are considered. While motions for summary judgment are normally made after a period of time for discovery,

---

24. Samuel Issacharoff and George Lowenstein, *Second Thoughts About Summary Judgment*, 100 Yale L.J. 73, 76 (Oct. 1990), citing to *The Summary Procedure on Bills of Exchange Act*, 1855, 18 & 19 Vict. c. 67; see also, Charles E. Clark and Charles U. Samenow, *The Summary Judgment*, 38 Yale L.J. 423, 423 (1929) 424, and Martin B. Louis, *Federal Summary Judgment Doctrine: A Critical Analysis*, 83 Yale L.J. 745, 745 (1974).
25. Clark and Samenow, *supra* note 24, at 423.
26. *Id.* at 440-470.

the rule does not prohibit a party from moving for summary judgment even before the discovery process begins. However, summary judgment should not be granted if there was insufficient time for discovery, because the information derived from the discovery process is typically critical to summary judgment motion practice and to the litigation as a whole.

Either party, the plaintiff or the defendant, can raise a motion for summary judgment. Often, cross motions are filed with each side claiming summary judgment in its favor. The motion can be directed toward an entire case or toward part or all of a single claim or defense. The court can enter partial summary judgment on some issues, thereby narrowing issues for trial so that the trial judge or jury can focus only on those factual disputes requiring a trier of fact to decide.

In deciding a motion for summary judgment, the court will consider the "pleadings, depositions, answers to interrogatories and admissions on file, together with the affidavits, if any," in determining whether summary judgment is appropriate. Fed. R. Civ. P. 56(c). The materials submitted in support of summary judgment must point to evidence admissible under the Federal Rules of Evidence. The admissible evidence, like the scope of discovery, is defined not only by the evidentiary rules but also by the parameters of the pleadings. An astute plaintiff's attorney must therefore frame her pleadings properly and conduct discovery appropriately, all while bearing in mind the admissibility of the evidence and its possible use in the initiation or contest of a motion for summary judgment down the road.

In deciding whether to grant summary judgment, the court will assess whether there is a genuine issue as to any material fact, such that a trial is necessary. In some jurisdictions, local rules require the moving party to submit statements of material facts not in dispute, with notations to the record identifying the evidence supporting these statements.[27] If there is a genuine issue as to any material fact, summary judgment cannot be granted. Thus, the task of the nonmoving party (the party opposing the motion) is to identify material issues of disputed facts that must be weighed by the trier of fact in a full trial.

The facts in dispute must be material to the legal controversy. If the disputed facts are not material to the controversy, then they are irrelevant to the consideration of whether summary judgment can be granted. The judge will decide whether there exists a body of evidence that points to undisputed facts, whether these facts are material to the claim, and whether the law governing the case mandates only one conclusion — a judgment for the moving party. This normally means considering the sufficiency of the party's evidence with respect to each element of the *prima facie* case. Some issues, such as the reasonableness of defendant's conduct in a negligence claim, are generally questions of fact for the jury to decide. Other issues, such as interpretations of contracts, are questions of law for the judge to decide. These latter issues may be most appropriate for summary judgment.

In deciding a motion for summary judgment, the court will construe the evidence in the light most favorable to the nonmoving party. Theoretically, the

---

27. The Eastern District of New York is one jurisdiction that requires parties to submit statements of material facts not in dispute. Peter J. Ausili, *Summary Judgment in Employment Discrimination Cases in the Eastern District of New York*, 16 Touro L. Rev. 1403, 1419-1422 (Summer 2000).

court should not weigh the evidence, a task reserved for trial. Summary judgment is not to be used a substitute for a trial on disputed facts. However, the device does permit a court to resolve cases without trial, if there are no issues of fact requiring resolution by a trier of fact. In essence, under Rule 56, a court should strictly determine whether there are factual issues to be tried without weighing the relative credibility of supporting evidence.

Summary judgment is efficient in allowing judges to decide cases that need not be subject to the time and cost of trial. In the past, judges tended to use summary judgment rather sparingly, cautioning that "[t]rial by affidavit is no substitute for trial by jury which so long has been the hallmark of 'even handed justice.'"[28] Judges were particularly hesitant to grant it in complex cases and cases involving public policy. Civil rights, antitrust, and patent cases especially were deemed to be resistant to summary judgment because they involve questions of credibility, intent, and motive; such issues are typically deemed more appropriate for trial, as they more acutely require the weighing of evidence.[29] The prevailing wisdom was that summary judgment was the exception and courts were expected to be tough on the moving party. As Professor Wright concluded: "Judges will be quite demanding in their examination of the moving party's papers, but will treat the papers of the party opposing the motion indulgently."[30] Summary judgment was so frowned upon that in the District Court of New Orleans there was even a sign explicitly stating "No Spitting, No Summary Judgment."[31]

In light of this cautious approach to summary judgment, the burden traditionally was on the moving party seeking a summary judgment — either the moving plaintiff or defendant — to positively show the absence of genuine issues of material fact in the record such that summary judgment was warranted. In the early days of the summary judgment rule, even a simple denial by the opposing party would have been sufficient to defeat summary judgment. Some courts would deny summary judgment if there was even "the slightest doubt" as to whether a nonmovant might persuade a jury of the merits of her claim.[32]

The Supreme Court's decision in *Adickes v. S.H. Kress &Co.* epitomized this cautious approach to Rule 56.[33] The plaintiff in the case, Sandra Adickes, a white school teacher, brought a suit alleging civil rights violations against the Kress restaurant and local police. Ms. Adickes and her six black students sought food service at Kress' lunch counter. Kress begrudgingly served the schoolteacher's six black students out of forced compliance with government-issued desegregation orders, yet refused to serve Ms. Adickes as a punishment for her association, as a white woman, with black youth. She was arrested by the local police for vagrancy when she left the store.[34] Ms. Adickes sued the state government and the restaurant for violation of her civil rights.

---

28. *Poller v. Columbia Broadcasting Sys., Inc.*, 368 U.S. 464, 473 (U.S. 1962).

29. For an excellent account of the history of the summary judgment rule, *see* 10A Charles A. Wright, Arthur Miller and Mary K. Kane, Federal Practice and Procedure 187-295 (3d ed. West, 1998).

30. *Id.*, at 484.

31. *Id.*

32. The Second Circuit used the "slightest doubt" standard. *See, e.g., Arnstein v. Porter*, 154 F.2d 464, 468 (2d Cir. 1946); *Doehler Metal Furniture Co. v. United States*, 149 F.2d 130, 135 (2d Cir. 1945).

33. 398 U.S. 144 (U.S. 1970).

34. *Id.* at 149.

In order for Ms. Adickes to win under the civil rights statute, she had to prove what is called "state action," that is, the state government or a subdivision thereof, such as a municipality, participated in the discrimination against her. She had to show that a police officer (the government) was in the store when she was denied service, and that therefore there was an inference that the police and the store were acting in concert, thus permitting a finding of state action.

Summary judgment was granted for the defendants in the trial court and the Circuit Court, but the Supreme Court unanimously reversed, heralding a period of strict summary judgment standard for moving parties. Summary judgment was not denied on the basis of any direct admissible evidence submitted by the nonmoving party, Ms. Adickes, but rather because the moving party (here the defendant) had "failed to show the absence of any disputed material fact."[35] In other words, the burden is on the moving party, here the defendants, to come forward with evidence to demonstrate a lack of disputed material facts and that summary judgment is warranted.[36]

Professor David Shapiro poignantly articulates the role the civil rights movement played in the Supreme Court's interpretation of Rule 56:

> Doubtless, the nature of the underlying controversy in *Adickes*, a controversy that was a significant part of the ongoing struggle of black citizens to obtain equal treatment in places of public accommodation and in society generally, influenced the outcome in that case. Moreover, summary judgment was far from a dead letter in federal practice, and Judge Frank's strong opposition to granting the motion when there was even the faintest possibility that the burden of proof might be met at trial was not slavishly observed. But in at least some courts, and perhaps in many, summary judgment was frowned upon.[37]

Adickes represents the Supreme Court's reprimand to judges hostile to civil rights litigation by delineating a summary judgment standard that substantially restricted their pretrial authority. The *Adickes* decision also conveys a liberal Supreme Court's endorsement of progressive legal claims, especially those involving civil rights, and its deep distrust of less progressive trial judges.

A swing of the political pendulum in the United States mirrored a shift in the substantive and procedural policy of the Supreme Court. By the mid-1980s, concerns about the "litigation explosion" led to an overhaul of civil procedure rules, which in turn granted district courts unprecedented powers in the management of cases. As we have discussed in earlier chapters, this was seen in changes in Rule 11, pleadings, and discovery. By the time the Supreme Court revisited the summary judgment rule in a series of three decisions known as the Trilogy Cases,[38] the Court's message on pretrial dispositive motions had

35. *Id.* at 158. There are footnotes in the opinion that indicate that in a previous case there was some testimony that the policeman was seen in the store at a relevant time, but this testimony was apparently neither in proper affidavit form nor in discovery that revealed admissible evidence.

36. *Id.* at 159.

37. David L. Shapiro, *The Story of Celotex: The Role of Summary Judgment in the Administration of Civil Justice*, Civil Procedure Stories 346-347 (Kevin M. Clermont ed., Foundation Press 2004).

38. The trilogy of cases is: *Celotex Corp. v. Catrett*, 477 U.S. 317 (U.S. 1986), *Anderson v. Liberty Lobby Inc.*, 477 U.S. 242 (U.S. 1986) and *Matsushita Elec. Indus. Corp. v. Zenith Radio*, 475 U.S. 574 (U.S. 1986).

changed just as its political demographics changed. In the Trilogy Cases, the Court, in effect, encouraged the greater use of summary judgment as a screening device and eased the standard for summary judgment.[39] Underlying this view, as we will explore in some detail in Chapter 11, is skepticism, if not a downright distrust, of juries.

The more well known of the Trilogy Cases, all decided in 1986, was *Celotex v. Catrett*, a wrongful death suit brought by the widow of a laborer who allegedly died from exposure to the defendants' asbestos products.[40] The suit was part of a considerable campaign to recover for the widespread injury and death caused by the American asbestos industry.[41] In its decision, the Supreme Court overturned the appellate court's decision, which had applied the standard delineated in *Adickes*, to hold that summary judgment on the issue of causation had been improvidently granted by the trial court. In contrast to the appellate court and the holding in *Adickes*, the majority in *Celatex* signaled that summary judgment should no longer be regarded as a "disfavored procedural shortcut." Instead, the Supreme Court encouraged litigants to embrace the device as "an integral part of the Federal Rules as a whole, which are designed 'to secure the just, speedy and inexpensive determination of every action.'"[42]

While the tone of *Celotex* stands in stark contrast to *Adickes*, the Court's standard functioned more as an announcement of the standard that had been in increasing use by trial courts, rather than a revelation of a novel rule. In this instance, the Supreme Court merely mirrored what had already been in practice in lower courts.[43] Nonetheless, as Professor Shapiro observes, the trilogy unmistakably casts aside key "shibboleths that had long affected summary judgment practice," such as the beliefs that summary judgment should be avoided in complex litigation or that subjective matters, such as good faith, are always inappropriate for pretrial adjudication.[44]

More dramatically, the Supreme Court tied summary judgment considerations more closely to who has the underlying burdens of proof at trial. In *Celotex*, the Court held that while the burden remains on the moving party, summary judgment might nevertheless be properly granted when the moving party simply pointed out that the nonmoving party lacks a sufficiency of evidence as to one element of her claim, if the nonmoving party has the underlying burden of proof at trial on that issue or claim.[45] In other words, if the moving party does not have the underlying burden of proof at trial as to that claim or issue, the moving party in seeking summary judgment is under no obligation to come forth and support its motion with evidence negating the nonmoving party's claim.

Summary judgment now forces the party with the underlying burden of proof (generally the plaintiff) to come forward with her proof earlier in the

39. *Id.*
40. *Celotex Corp. v. Catrett*, 477 U.S. at 317 (citing Fed. R. Civ. P. 1).
41. Shapiro, *supra* note 37, at 347.
42. *Id.* at 327.
43. Burbank, *supra* note 3, at 620.
44. Shapiro, *supra* note 37, at 362-363.
45. *Celotex Corp. v. Catrett*, 477 U.S. at 323.

litigation and often long before a scheduled trial. Under the *Celotex* standard, in determining whether there are triable issues, the court must assess the evidence in accordance with the underlying burden of proof at trial and who has that burden. The effect of the current standard is that the plaintiffs, who normally have the burden of proof at trial, must come up with evidence earlier on, simply to defeat defendant's motion for summary judgment. Strategically, a defendant can force a plaintiff to show her hand before trial, because to defeat the defendant's motion for summary judgment against her, the plaintiff must demonstrate to the court that she has sufficient evidence to meet her burden of production and that there are triable issues as to her claims.

Even more difficult, to win her own summary judgment motion, a plaintiff must demonstrate that she has sufficient evidence such that not only *may* a jury find for her, but that they *must* find for her. If the plaintiff is the moving party seeking summary judgment, the plaintiff must show there can only be but one reasonable conclusion from the evidence produced – that is, a judgment in her favor. The "only one reasonable conclusion" standard is an overwhelmingly difficult one for plaintiffs to meet by contrast to defendant's lesser burden in seeking summary judgment.

Under the *Celotex* standard, the defendant now has an easier time in getting a summary judgment because defendants normally do not have the underlying burden of proof as to the claims asserted (the exception being that defendants bear the burden of proof on affirmative defenses). Even as the moving party, a defendant can win summary judgment by simply pointing out the failure of plaintiff to come forward with evidence to establish existence of any single essential element for which she bears the burden of proof at trial. For example, in the *Cherryum* case, if after discovery Mr. Lee does not have a sufficiency of potential evidence as to one element of his claim, that the drink caused his injuries, then he will lose on summary judgment even if there are many factual disputes as to the other elements of his claim. Once it is clear that Mr. Lee cannot meet his production burden as to one element of his claim, all other disputes of fact are immaterial, and Cherryum will win the case.

There is a good deal of logic in the Trilogy Cases view that summary judgment should be a prediction of what will happen at the trial. If the plaintiff lacks evidence as to an element of her *prima facie* case, why waste time with a trial? What this hides, though, is that in many cases the question of what is a sufficiency of evidence to permit a jury to decide the issue forces the judge to weigh what is enough, and in so doing, renders the judge perilously close to replacing the jury, which contravenes the Seventh Amendment right to jury trial when that right is justifiably claimed.

There are, of course, many cases that even under the *Celotex* shift in favor of summary judgment are not susceptible to having the motion granted. For example, in the *Cherryum* case, if the plaintiff had potential evidence, through discovery or by affidavit, that there was poison in the can when he opened it and that he was made ill by drinking it, he will so testify at trial. If the can had poison in it, it probably got there either at the manufacturing or bottling stage and this would be a breach of warranty of merchantability. So even if the defendants have persuasive evidence that they had been careful in every respect, that it is almost impossible for poison to evade their careful barriers to pollution, and that the plaintiff was in financial difficulty and despondent and probably poisoned himself seeking a fraudulent recovery, the jury issue remains: Was the poison in the can when he opened it, as he will testify?

As we have already indicated, the shift in the summary judgment standard from *Adickes* to *Celotex* generally means that a heavy burden now falls disproportionately on plaintiffs, because plaintiffs are forced to come up with evidence earlier on.[46] Since the Trilogy Cases were handed down, some studies have attempted to document the suspicion that the change in the summary judgment standard also meant the increased use of summary judgment to dispose of disfavored cases.

There are, though, but a handful of studies conducted on the effects of the changing summary judgment standard. In her study of the District Court of the District of Columbia, Judge Patricia Wald found that for the calendar year 1996, 42 percent of civil cases in the District Court were dismissed, 19 percent were settled before trial, 3 percent were terminated by trial, 22 percent were terminated by summary judgment, and 7 percent were transferred to other courts.[47] These statistics led her to conclude that summary judgment is the more commonly used mode of disposition on the merits, outnumbering cases disposed of by settlement.

Judge Wald also found that summary judgment in her district was applied in a wide variety of cases and was no longer limited to simple cases with limited policy implications. Even more distressing, she confirmed that pretrial motions to dismiss and motions for summary judgment were being used to dismiss cases disfavored by some judges, such as discrimination cases or cases against the government.[48] Summary judgment was often based on what she viewed as a "gestalt verdict based on an early snapshot of the case."[49] As more cases are resolved by summary judgment, more law is created without the benefit of a full trial record that could have better represented the complexity of the litigation.[50] As such, Judge Wald cautioned that summary judgment was being stretched beyond its proper or intended limits.

Other judges, such as Richard Posner, also voiced concerns about the growing trend of "summary judgment as a substitute for trial, and judgment on the pleadings a substitute for summary judgment."[51] Judges facing disfavored claims may limit the time or scope of discovery and then render summary judgment for the defendant on the basis of lack of evidence. This all works to

46. The majority in *Celotex* claim that they are not changing the summary judgment standard. They insist that *Adickes* and *Celotex* are reconcilable because there was potential evidence in *Adickes* that a policeman was in the store at the relevant time, and the defendant in that case could not point to an absence of any admissible evidence on the point and was therefore not entitled to summary judgment. But the tone and language of *Celotex* are clearly different and more pro-summary judgment than in *Adickes*, particularly when read with the other two cases comprising the "trilogy." Many judges and lawyers certainly saw *Celotex* as an invitation for summary judgment to be granted in cases in which it previously would have been denied.
47. Wald, *supra* note 2, at 1915.
48. *Id.* at 1930-1931.
49. *Id.* at 1917.
50. *Id.* at 1941.
51. Richard A. Posner, The Federal Courts: Challenge and Reform 180 (Harvard Univ. Press 1996).

the disadvantage of plaintiffs who are less likely than defendants to be able to make a credible motion for summary judgment or for judgment on the pleadings. Scholars fear that liberal use of summary judgment also skirts the Seventh Amendment, which entitles civil litigants in federal courts to trial by jury of contestable issues of factual nature.[52] Ultimately, summary judgment could also have the effect of depriving the legal system of the effective check of juries on the broad discretion of judges.

In a meticulous assessment of the empirical studies in this area, Professor Stephen Burbank examined perhaps the most reliable statistics to date on the summary judgment activity in the Federal courts.[53] Professor Burbank concludes that the case termination rate due to summary judgment rose dramatically from approximately 1.8 percent in 1960 to roughly 7.7 percent in 2000.[54] His analysis also offers an essential framework to interpret the findings of Judge Wald, among others. While he found the District of Columbia study compelling, its conclusions about summary judgment may not readily apply to all jurisdictions. Professor Burbank found that summary judgment has not contributed to the vanishing federal civil trial phenomenon in every jurisdiction or in every area of law.

> Summary judgment may be an "industry" in Chicago, but it does not appear to be that in Philadelphia. Certainly, juxtaposing the 1996-97 District of Columbia and the 2000-2003 Eastern District of Pennsylvania data suggests the possibility that summary judgment plays a very different role in those courts.[55]

Summary judgment may be a major force behind the vanishing trial in some jurisdictions and in some litigation areas, but its impact is not universal. This paints a credible picture, especially given the overhaul of civil procedure in so many areas since the 1980s, as well as other variables, such as the increased amount of civil litigation, extensive use of discovery, and the growth of ADR. Motion practice alone is unlikely to account for the vanishing trial. Rather, as several chapters of this book reveal, a complex combination of forces are at play, and motion practice is but one contributing factor.

The question of how far judges should go in controlling the litigation process, as we have seen in the dismissal of cases before trial, carries over into the trial itself. We could leave the jury-control mechanisms at trial totally to our subsequent chapter on juries and the trial, but it makes sense to also write about them here. After all, summary judgment is a prediction of directed verdict; at trial, it is usually a defendant's motion asserting that the plaintiff lacks evidence as to at least one element. The same tensions between jury

52. *See, e.g.,* Paul W. Mollica, *Federal Summary Judgment at High Tide,* 84 Marq. L. Rev. 141, 181-205 (Fall 2000) (noting that "the prevalence of summary judgment in federal court today abrades our Fifth and Seventh Amendments' guarantees to a trial to decide contested issues of fact," at 142); JoEllen Lind, *The End of Trial on Damages? Intangible Losses and Comparability Review,* 51 Buff. L. Rev. 251, 259-260 (Spring 2003) (finding that the court's "commitment to jury trial is more doubtful, due to its decisions in critical cases involving summary judgment, judgments as a matter of law, and punitive damages").
53. Burbank, *supra* note 3.
54. *Id.* at 617-618.
55. *Id.*

freedom and judicial control that we have seen in discussing summary judgment underlie several additional important motions that a party can make at trial or even after the jury verdict has been rendered. They are the motions for directed verdict, judgment notwithstanding verdict (also known as judgment as a matter of law), and a new trial.

JUDGMENT AS A MATTER OF LAW:
DIRECTED VERDICT

If both parties survive summary judgment and the case does not settle, the lawsuit proceeds to trial. The judge will set up a final pretrial conference, during which the parties will formulate a plan for trial, including "a program for facilitating the admission of evidence." Fed. R. Civ. P. 16. The trial normally begins with the plaintiff presenting her case. If the plaintiff presents sufficient evidence to meet her burden of production, then the case will usually proceed with the defendant submitting her evidence.

At trial, there are opportunities for a party to move the court for a judgment as a matter of law. In a trial by jury, Rule 50(a) provides for an entry of a judgment as a matter of law against a party if "a party has been fully heard on an issue and there is no legally sufficient evidentiary basis for a reasonable jury to find for that party on that issue." Fed. R. Civ. P. 50(a). If the party with the burden of production on a claim or defense did not meet that burden, Rule 50(a) provides for a judgment to be entered as a matter of law without submitting the case, or a portion of the case, to the jury.

Earlier in America this was known as a *directed verdict* or "direction of verdict," as in, the court should direct the entry of a verdict. The 1991 amendment to the federal rules changed the familiar terminology from motion for directed verdict to motion for "judgment as a matter of law," and tightened the relationship between the Rule 50 trial motion and the Rule 56 pretrial summary judgment motion. Both now seek judgment as a matter of law and apply the same "no legally sufficient evidentiary basis" standard. It also, according to the Advisory Committee, eliminates the "anachronism" that the judge is somehow interfering with the Seventh Amendment right to jury trial because the judge is just fulfilling her due process duty of "fidelity of the judgment to the controlling law."[56] This, of course, begs the perplexing question of whether the judge in deciding whether a party has "enough evidence" is in fact jury-intrusive in a manner that improvidently or unconstitutionally steps on the toes of the jury.[57]

The Rule 50 motion for judgment as a matter of law may be made at any time before submission of the case to the trier of fact, but as soon as it is apparent that a party is unable to carry her burden of production on an issue essential to the case. Fed. R. Civ. P. 50(a)(2). In practice, however, the motion is usually not made until the plaintiff has presented whatever evidence she has and "rested." Often, a defendant's lawyer will stand up and move for a Rule 50(a) judgment as a matter of law after the plaintiff's presentation of her case. Similarly, after

---

56. Advisory Committee's Notes to 1991 Amendments to Fed. R. Civ. P. 50(a).
57. This and other matters concerning jury trial are the topic of Chapter 11.

the presentation of the defendant's case, the plaintiff's lawyer and the defendant's lawyer can each stand up and move for judgment as a matter of law in their favor.

The moving party must articulate the basis on which judgment as a matter of law may be rendered. The defendant usually argues that the plaintiff lacks evidence as to at least one element of her cause of action or that the defense of the defendant is so strong that it must be believed. The plaintiff can argue, after the defendant has put in her case, that the evidence of each element is so strong that it must be believed. If the court agrees with one of the moving parties then it will enter the judgment against the nonmoving party, and the case ends without a jury decision. A directed verdict is a final judgment and if not reversed on appeal operates to bar a second action by the same party on the same claim.

In a jury-tried case, the standard under Rule 50(a)(1) is that judgment as a matter of law should be granted when "there is no legally sufficient evidentiary basis for a reasonable jury to find for that party," on an issue essential to any "claim or defense that cannot under the controlling law be maintained or defeated without a favorable finding on that issue." Fed. R. Civ. P. 50(a). If this were the case, it would save time and money to have the judge announce a decision that a reasonable jury would reach anyway. If a plaintiff is relying on several causes of action, a judge can grant a directed verdict on one and still let others go to a jury.

This Rule 50(a) "sufficient evidentiary basis" standard is different from the "scintilla rule" observed in some state courts. In these state jurisdictions, a motion for directed verdict would be denied if there was even a scintilla of evidence on which the jury could find in favor of the nonmoving party. The "scintilla rule" is more forgiving to the party with the burden of proof, usually the plaintiff, than the federal rule. Obviously, it is also more trusting of juries.

In a judge-tried case, a court may enter a judgment as a matter of law under Federal Rule 52(c). Rule 52(c) in some ways parallels Rule 50(a), but is applicable to nonjury trials. Under Rule 52(c), once a party has been fully heard on an issue in a nonjury trial, the judge "may enter judgment as a matter of law against that party with respect to a claim or defense that cannot under controlling law be maintained or defeated without a favorable finding on that issue." Fed. R. Civ. P. 52(c).

Since the judge is the trier of fact in a judge-tried case, she can enter judgment as a matter of law if she does not believe the evidence of the party with the burden of production. Since there is no jury, and the judge is the fact finder, she can decide credibility issues. In the *Cherryum* case, for instance, if the case were tried without a jury, the judge could grant judgment as a matter of law for the defendant after Albert Lee's testimony if the judge did not believe that the can had poison in it before it was opened and if the plaintiff's lawyer says that Albert Lee's testimony is the only testimony relating to whether poison was in the sealed can.

In a Rule 52(c) ruling, the judge's findings of fact and conclusions of law must be recorded in written form. Fed. R. Civ. P. 52(a). These findings of fact are not reversible on appeal unless they are "clearly erroneous." This is a high standard of appellate review, because unlike summary judgments, which are rulings on law based on the absence of contrary evidence, Rule 52 findings of fact are made after the trial judge has heard and weighed all the evidence and decided credibility issues.

You might wonder how a case that survived the summary judgment stage can be won or lost at the directed verdict stage. First of all, parties do not always ask for a summary judgment. Defendant's lawyer might prefer to wait for trial in order to bring a directed verdict motion, when it is too late for the plaintiff to cure a lacuna in the evidence. Moreover, even when a summary judgment motion is brought and heard, there are judges who are reluctant to grant the motion if there is any chance that a trial might improve the evidence for the nonmoving party. Some judges may not grant summary judgment but may be less protective after the nonmoving party has had every opportunity to prove her case at trial, including the opportunity of cross-examining opposing witnesses. Also, potential evidence in an affidavit or discovery response in opposition to summary judgment can turn out to be less expansive and more measured when the testimony is actually orally given in court before a judge. Consequently, there can be a summary judgment motion rationally denied, but a directed verdict motion later allowed on the same issue in the same case.

JUDGMENT AS A MATTER OF LAW: JUDGMENT NOTWITHSTANDING THE VERDICT

In a jury-tried case, a losing party may renew her motion for judgment as a matter of law even after a jury verdict is rendered. Under common law, this was known as judgment notwithstanding the verdict or judgment *non obstante verdicte* (judgment n.o.v.). The Federal Rules renamed the motion as a Rule 50(b) motion for judgment as a matter of law. If it is granted, the court essentially enters its judgment in lieu of the jury verdict.

In order to move for a Rule 50(b) judgment as a matter of law (j.n.o.v.), the party must have previously made a Rule 50(a) motion for judgment as a matter of law (directed verdict) prior to the close of trial. A court will deny a post-trial motion for judgment as a matter of law (j.n.o.v.) if no prejury motion for judgment as a matter of law was previously made. The standard for the post-trial motion is the same as the prejury motion for judgment as a matter of law (directed verdict).

It may seem mysterious how a court will deny a motion for judgment as a matter of law before the jury deliberates, but then later take away the jury verdict by granting a motion for judgment as a matter of law. However, courts sometimes reserve decision until after the jury verdict because a jury may decide for the moving party anyway. This eliminates the opportunity to appeal the question of whether there was enough evidence to permit the jury to make a finding; there is nothing to appeal on this point because the jury did not believe the evidence even if the sufficiency of evidence standard was met for directed verdict purposes. Additionally, if the case is appealed, a reversal of a post-jury verdict judgment as a matter of law will simply mean a reinstatement of the original jury verdict. By contrast, reversal of a pre-jury verdict judgment as a matter of law (directed verdict) would mean the more cumbersome process of convening a new trial.

MOTION FOR A NEW TRIAL

One final avenue for a losing party to contest the court's judgment prior to a formal appeal is the Rule 59 motion for a new trial. Fed. R. Civ. P. 59(a). A losing party may petition for a new trial no later than ten days after the entry of judgment. Fed. R. Civ. P. 59(b). The losing party may also file a motion to alter or amend a judgment. Fed. R. Civ. P. 59(e). The court may also order a new trial *sua sponte*. While not a dispositive motion per se, Rule 59 grants the court an opportunity to revisit decisions made in the heat of trial and marks a departure from the adversary system of party controlled procedures.

Under Rule 59, there are two general grounds for granting a new trial. The first ground is an error in the procedure leading up to the verdict. This could entail, for example, the erroneous admission of nonadmissible evidence or improper jury instructions. The second ground involves a verdict that was "against the weight of the evidence" even though the procedure was correct. This second ground gives the court discretion. By comparison to the standard for granting a directed verdict or a judgment notwithstanding the verdict, the standard for granting a motion for a new trial is less stringent, in part because the grant of this motion results in a new trial and not the entry of a judgment.

In ordering a new trial, the trial judge is deciding that the ends of justice will be properly served by another jury hearing the case. This may occur when the jury verdict seems excessive and appears to be influenced by passion or emotions rather than the evidence presented. However, the trial judge cannot displace the jury verdict simply because the judge disagrees with the jury. The discretionary new trial motion is often sought by the losing party in jury trials but infrequently granted.

On appeal, the standard of appellate review of a decision on a motion for a new trial varies depending on whether the decision was based on a legal error or on "verdict against the weigh of the evidence." If the decision was based on the latter, then the grant of a new trial is reversible only for an abuse of discretion. The rationale is that the decision was made based on the trial judge's balancing of the evidence and assessment of live testimony that only the trial judge had the opportunity to hear. It is therefore rare for an appellate court to second guess the trial court's decision. On the other hand, if the new trial motion was granted based on a legal error, the appellate court will fully review the issue of an alleged legal error.

DISPOSITIVE MOTIONS AND THE AMERICAN JURY

As we will discuss more fully in Chapter 11, motions such as those for summary judgment, directed verdict, and judgment notwithstanding the verdict display the ambivalence in the American civil process towards juries. The American adversary system has long placed its faith in trials and trials by jury and, indeed, the federal and state constitutions protect them as of right. Yet, judges still very much want to control them and even alter their results. Congested dockets, perceptions of a litigious society, and the feeling in some quarters that defendants have been unfairly treated in civil litigation, further add to the impetus to use procedural tools to eliminate trials, streamline cases, and reduce delays. This has resulted in the resurgence of a panoply of procedural mechanisms that enhance judges' authority to take cases away from the jury.

The fear that dispositive motions may be a "stealth weapon" depriving plaintiffs of their day in court and the right to a jury trial is not a new one.[58] The present debate is but a revival of the historical debate between Charles Clark, the Reporter to the Advisory Committee of the 1938 Federal Rules of Civil Procedure, and Judge Jerome Frank on the proper use of the summary judgment.[59] During their debates with each other as judges of the Second Circuit federal court, Judge Frank set aside his deep and well-known personal doubts about the American jury to argue for the limited use of summary judgment to cases for which there was not the "slightest doubt" about the relevant facts. Taking the pro-jury position, Judge Frank insisted that judges should not trust their instincts in making inferences from undisputed facts because their instincts were less trustworthy than those of laypersons.[60] He thought that even if at the summary judgment stage the plaintiffs lack evidence, they might later uncover facts unknown to them through cross-examination at trial. In his position on this issue, Judge Frank (atypically for him) represents tremendous faith in the adversary system and the jury's ability to unearth the truth.

The opposing position, represented by Judge Clark, focused on the risk of surrendering too much power to unsophisticated lay jurors. In a more elitist tone, perhaps, Charles Clark argued that as a result of experience and ability judges could discern facts and apply law better than lay people; this equipped them to summarily decide cases.[61] Judge Clark probably would have approved of the present expanded use of summary judgment.

It should be clear by now that the rules governing the dispositive motions we have discussed, in much the same way as other procedures, such as pleading, the lawyer's signature on pleadings, oath, and discovery, are not neutral on their effect on the parties. They affect some of the parties and some types of cases more than others. Making it easier to win a 12(b)(6) motion for failure to state a claim for which relief can be granted or making it easier to win at summary judgment will usually have more of a negative impact on plaintiffs than defendants, because it is plaintiffs who normally have the burdens of pleading and proof.

As such, changes in how the rules are applied have differential impact on different parties and different kinds of cases. In some types of claims, for example discrimination cases, circumstantial evidence and the use of inferences are more critical than in others. Whether there is a sufficiency of evidence to permit a jury to find discriminatory intent often has a highly discretionary aspect to it. The encouraged use of summary judgment to dispose of cases will result in judges more likely to take away the power of

---

58. Wald, *supra* note 3, at 1898.
59. *Id.* at 1898-1904.
60. *Id.* at 1903.
61. *Id.*

jurors to draw inferences about discriminatory intent, which a trial would allow. This in turn has a chilling effect on what cases are actually brought to court by plaintiffs, and even when cases are brought, their settlement value is lowered. Procedure rules are clearly not divorced from substance law. And procedure rules, in distributing power, do not stray far from political and cultural forces.

Finally, the pretrial motions have changed the nature of legal practice, which has become largely based on the written word: pleadings, discovery documents, affidavits, and memoranda. The trend to utilize these dispositive motions in greater numbers means that it is especially important for today's litigator to learn the skills of written advocacy. Increasingly, the opportunities for oral advocacy at motions sessions and at trial have decreased, and the oral tradition of legal practice has substantially diminished. It is as yet unclear what this change in practice means or how our legal education system should change to accommodate this trend.

But this trend may be bringing us closer to the civil law tradition that relies more heavily on written advocacy and the greater authority of judges to manage and decide cases. If the future will bring a "convergence" of legal systems, as some scholars have predicted, then the present course in America is unsurprising.[62] There may be no reason for the technical and often time-consuming adversarial system of gearing the entire litigation process towards a formal jury trial when that trial occurs in less than 2 percent of the cases. Yet, there is no other country that utilizes civil litigation to implement social policy and change to the extent that the United States has. If we have made the commitment to put important issues before the courts, then the jury, in our view, should be maintained and improved to avoid judicial fiat. Motion practice should not displace an indispensable voice that has long sustained the democratic process and added to the legitimacy of our civil dispute resolution system.

62. *See* John Henry Merryman, *On the Convergence (and Divergence) of the Civil Law and the Common Law*, 17 Stan. J. Int'l L. 357 (1981) (suggesting that the civil law and common law are converging in different ways and diverging in others).

CHAPTER
9

Joinder and Class Actions

...[T] here are several instances where the codes or governing rules themselves should be amended to permit of desirable changes.... These include such matters as freer joinder of parties, plaintiff and defendant, and of causes of action and counterclaims, including freer privileges of bringing in new parties and of intervention....
    Charles E. Clark (1928)[1]

At common law the rules on joinder of actions were governed chiefly by the forms of action and not by principles of trial convenience.... On the other hand, in equity the test was largely one of trial convenience with a view to settling the entire controversy in one suit.
    Charles E. Clark & James Wm. Moore (1935)[2]

No set of rules, perhaps, exemplifies more vividly the convergence of social and historical forces in American civil procedure than the rules on joinder of claims and parties. In the mid-twentieth century, civil rights activists, discouraged with the slow pace of legislative reforms, turned to the courts and found that with liberal joinder of parties and claims rules, they could craft lawsuits that reach far beyond the named individual litigants before the court. It is through expansive joinder rules, combined with flexible pleading and broad discovery, that American civil litigation evolved into its modern-day role as a forum for dramatic social change.

The story of joinder of claims and parties in the United States follows an historical trajectory that should now be familiar. At common law, such joinder was limited. While mid-nineteenth century code reforms broadened joinder rules somewhat, it was the drafters of the 1938 Federal Rules who adopted every type of procedural joinder known at the time, and in 1966, went even further to enact a more permissive and flexible class action rule.[3] Concerns about the permissiveness of joinder abound in recent years, just as they did

---

1. Charles E. Clark, Handbook of the Law of Code Pleading 35 (1928).
2. Charles E. Clark & James Wm. Moore, *A New Federal Civil Procedure II. Pleadings and Parties*, 44 Yale L. J. 1291, 1319 (1935).
3. In addition, in 1968, Congress passed a multidistrict transfer statute, authorizing the temporary transfer of two or more civil actions "involving one or more common questions of fact" to a single district "for coordinated or consolidated pretrial proceedings." Act of April 29, 1968, 82 Stat. 109. The multidistrict transfer provision is now found in 28 USC § 1407.

with pleading and discovery. Today, commentators, judges, and legislators are taking an increasingly dim view of liberal joinder, and focusing specifically on class actions, argue for greater limitations.

By now, our recurrent themes for civil procedure should not be surprising. The down-side risks of an all-equity procedural system with the resultant permissiveness in pleading, discovery, and joinder have brought a counter-revolution. The competing tensions between wide-open, all-encompassing narratives with the desire for more manageability and confinement by rule have led to procedural pendulum swings. In discussions of procedural reforms, power and politics will once again take center stage. It is difficult to disentangle the problems of a permissive procedural system from the concerns of American business leaders and conservative politicians who perceive a litigation system run amuck. The combustibility of this mix has prompted the movement toward restriction and management (more detailed pleading requirements, Rule 11 certification, discovery amendments, judicial case management, more utilization of summary judgment, and restrictions on class actions). Yet, in spite of these restrictions, present day American joinder provisions, along with liberal pleading and discovery, still render the American procedural system unique when compared to other legal systems in the world.

In this chapter, we briefly look at the pre-Federal Rule history to explain how and why the Federal Rule drafters went so far with joinder rules. We examine the current joinder rules in some detail, with a closer look at class actions. We assess the pros and cons of the class action when compared with systems in other countries and follow with an explanation of the roller coaster history of American class actions and current developments and arguments. We end with some of the surprising consequences and procedural dilemmas of liberal joinder provisions.

LEADING UP TO THE 1938 FEDERAL RULES

After the Revolution, American courts adopted much of English practice with respect to pleading and joinder rules. The subsequent 1848 Field Code opened up joinder possibilities somewhat, by providing that "plaintiffs could be joined only if they had 'an interest in the subject of the action, and in obtaining the relief demanded,' and defendants if they had 'an interest in the controversy, adverse to the plaintiff.'" It was not, however, until 1851 that equitable joinder procedures such as counterclaims, class action, interpleader, and intervention, were added in a limited fashion;[4] and they all faced strict interpretations by the courts at the time.

Present day federal joinder rules were in large part the work of Charles Clark, the major academic on the Advisory Committee that drafted the 1938 Federal Rules of Civil Procedure. As you recall from earlier chapters, Clark

---

4. Stephen N. Subrin, *David Dudley Field and the Field Code: A Historical Analysis of an Earlier Procedural Vision*, 6 L. & Hist. Rev. 311, 332 (1988) (citations omitted).

bemoaned the fact that the Field Code had not carried procedural reform to its logical end, which according to Clark, should have included some of the most salient features of procedure from the equity courts, including broad joinder of parties and claims.

By the beginning of 1935, the Supreme Court, having sought the advice of federal judges around the country, was leaning in the direction of keeping the rules for law and equity cases separate, for fear that merging the rules would trigger the requirement that Congress review the newly drafted rules and reopen the controversial issue of resting the promulgation of procedural rules with the court. But Charles Clark, with his co-author James William Moore, lobbied vigorously to have a unified system, including writing two articles urging merger of law and equity, with full reform of pleading and joinder requirements.[5] Simplified pleading and broad joinder, they insisted, required that a plaintiff be able to bring both legal and equitable claims in the same lawsuit and that all claims be subject to the same procedural rules. In arguing the advantages of equity over common law in matters relating to the joinder of parties and issues, they stressed convenience and efficiency in settling the entire controversy in one suit.[6]

Of course, none of this happened in a political or jurisprudential vacuum. As you have read in Chapter 3, the agendas of conservatives, liberals, and the legal profession, along with currents of legal realist thought, all moved in the direction of a more permissive legal system that empowered lawyers and judges, eased the development of new substantive rights, and paved the way for liberal joinder of parties and claims. Clark and Moore succeeded with the assistance of this political climate, and the present day Federal Rules now include such joinder mechanisms from equity as representative suits (class actions), intervention, and third-party procedure.

JOINDER PROVISIONS IN THE FEDERAL RULES

A number of broad joinder provisions can be found in the Federal Rules, most of which have several features in common. With a few exceptions, they *permit* the parties to join additional parties or claims, but do not *compel* joinder. These provisions frequently draw on two concepts in defining what is permissible and what is mandatory — that is, some variation of whether the claims arose from "the same conduct, transaction, or occurrence," and whether there are "questions of law or fact common" to the joined claims or parties.

5. His co-author, James William Moore, was a graduate student at Yale Law School and later authored one of the two leading multivolume treatises on United States civil procedure. Charles E. Clark & James Wm. Moore, *A New Federal Civil Procedure I: The Background*, 44 Yale L.J. 387, 434-435 (1935) [hereinafter Clark & Moore I]; Charles E. Clark & James Wm. Moore, *A New Federal Civil Procedure II: Pleadings and Parties*, 44 Yale L.J. 1291, 1310 (1935).

6. "... [I]n equity the test was largely one of trial convenience with a view of settling the entire controversy in one suit.... [T]he concept of an equitable cause of action was in general sufficiently broad to embrace all operative facts dealing with a transaction." Charles E. Clark & James Wm. Moore, *A New Federal Civil Procedure II. Pleadings and Parties*, 44 Yale L.J. 1291, 1319 (1935) (citations omitted).

While power rests with the parties to join claims and parties of their choice, judges are given broad discretion to sever portions of joined claims or joined parties for separate trials.

The most practical and easiest way to explain current American joinder practice may be to describe the most important Federal Rules that relate to joinder. Even those states that have not explicitly adopted the Federal Rules will usually have similar state rules to govern suits in their state courts.

Permissive Joinder of Claims and Remedies

Fed. R. Civ. P. 18 provides that a party asserting a claim may join "either as independent or as alternate claims, as many claims, legal, equitable, or maritime, as the party has against the opposing party." Under Rule 18, when a plaintiff sues a defendant, she may, but is not compelled to, include any (related or unrelated) causes of action for any permissible remedies that she has against the same defendant.

For example, in the *Cherryum* case, Albert Lee may sue a defendant for any cause of action he has, whether the causes of action arise from the same conduct, transaction, or occurrence. Under this joinder of claims rule, Lee may sue Cherryum, Inc., the manufacturer of the drink, for both negligence and breach of implied warranty. And if Cherryum, Inc., owed Lee for gardening work he had done, the pleading rules permit Lee to join that contract claim, even though unrelated to his claim for being poisoned by a drink produced by Cherryum, Inc.

Moreover, Lee may claim both equitable relief and money damages in the same case if such relief is warranted. For instance, if Mr. Lee had brought his lawsuit as a class action alleging that there had been widespread contamination by the Cherryum drink, Mr. Lee could seek an injunction against Cherryum preventing the sale of the drink until selected bottles are tested for contamination, as well as monetary compensation. This would be an example of joining what was historically a claim for equitable relief (an injunction) with a claim for relief at law (monetary damages).

Why did the drafters of the Federal Rules think it was a good idea to permit a claimant to join unrelated claims and remedies against the same defendant? The rationale was that once two parties are adverse to each other, it is efficient and less costly to permit them to resolve all of their disputes, if they choose to do so. Litigation is an expensive, time-consuming, and often painful process. Once the parties are in court for one grievance, why not let them get rid of all their disputes with each other at once? Since most cases settle anyway, it also makes sense for a more comprehensive peace to have parties resolve every complaint they have against each other. Settlement of all claims is more likely if they are all in the same lawsuit.

But there are three *caveats* to demonstrate that Rule 18 on joinder of claims is not as user-friendly as it first appears. Although Rule 18 provides that a plaintiff may, *at her discretion*, join any claims of any kind that she has against the opposing party, other fields of procedural law may compel joinder or limit a plaintiff's ability to join claims. These are the law on preclusion, statute of limitation, and jurisdiction.

The law on preclusion will be discussed in greater detail in Chapter 12, but preclusion, or *res judicata,* in general, means that a claimant in the United States must bring all of her theories or causes of action and all of her remedies that arise from the same transaction or occurrence at the same time or forever be barred from bringing them in the future. These causes of action will be deemed as the "same claim," and under preclusion doctrine, once a case reaches final judgment, the claimant cannot sue again on the same claim against the same party. For *res judicata* or preclusion purposes, the second lawsuit will be deemed as the same claim as the first if the subsequent lawsuit is based on the same conduct, transaction, or occurrence as the previous litigation.

For example, in our *Cherryum* case, if Albert Lee sues Cherryum, Inc., for breach of warranty arising out of his drinking of the Cherryum in question, and if that case reaches final judgment (it doesn't matter whether Lee wins or loses), he cannot sue Cherryum, Inc., later for the same harm even though based on a different theory — for example, a negligence cause of action. Moreover, once the case reaches final judgment, Lee cannot sue Cherryum, Inc., again for a new injury he has arising from the same incident of drinking the contaminated Cherryum. Even if he later develops an unforeseen disease as a result of drinking the Cherryum, once the first case against Cherryum, Inc., reaches final judgment, Lee cannot sue again for any cause of action or remedy arising from the same occurrence. So, although Rule 18 permits but does not compel a plaintiff to join many causes of action or theories, *res judicata* principles will, in effect, provide a penalty if the plaintiff does not join all of her transactionally related causes of action, theories, and remedies in her first action.

Second, statutes of limitations also serve to compel joinder of claims. Aggrieved parties have statutorily prescribed periods of time within which to sue, dating from when their cause of action accrued, often defined as the time they were injured. A tort action typically can only be brought within three years from the date the action accrued; a contract cause of action may have six years. Statutes of limitations can force the joinder of claims, or the bringing of an independent action, in order to be within this statutory period. Claims brought beyond the statute of limitation face dismissal. To be safe, then, most claimants join all possible claims to avoid facing a statute of limitations bar later.

Finally, especially in federal court, there is the problem of subject matter jurisdiction. If the plaintiff in federal court also wants to join an unrelated state law claim to her original federal claim, she may do so pursuant to the joinder of claims rule, but the federal court may not have subject matter jurisdiction over the unrelated state cause of action. Unless "supplemental jurisdiction" of the federal court (discussed in Chapter 5) applies to allow the federal court to take jurisdiction of the state claim, the state claim, though properly joined pursuant to Rule 18, cannot be sustained in federal court. The important point to keep in mind is that claims joined in one lawsuit must meet the joinder of claims rule as well as jurisdictional requirements. In sum, although Fed. R. Civ. P. 18 may permit broad joinder of claims by a plaintiff against the defendant, there are other legal restrictions to consider — *res judicata*, statute of limitations, subject matter jurisdiction.

As discussed above, the joinder provisions under the Federal Rules are quite broad. To avoid prejudice or confusion at trial, however, a trial judge has a good deal of discretion to separate out claims, issues, or parties, in furtherance of convenience or prejudice. Fed. R. Civ. P. 42(b).

Consider again Albert Lee's lawsuit against Cherryum, Inc., for producing the contaminated Cherryum. Lee could have put in the same complaint, as he is allowed by Rule 18, a claim for unpaid bills for gardening services. A trial judge might well decide that it would complicate the *Cherryum* case, and might be prejudicial to Cherryum Inc., to try the dispute over the alleged contaminated drink at the same time and before the same jury as the claim for money owed for gardening services. The judge under Rule 42(b) could "sever" the cases for purposes of trial.

Permissive Joinder of Parties

Fed. R. Civ. P. 20 permits additional persons to join as plaintiffs and be joined as multiple defendants in the same litigation so long as the persons seeking the relief are asserting rights that 1) arise "out of the same transaction, occurrence or series of transactions or occurrences" and 2) at least one question of law or fact common to all these persons will arise in the action. Consider again the *Cherryum* case. Albert Lee could join in one action as multiple defendants the following persons: the manufacturer of the compound for Cherryum; the bottling company of the Cherryum in question; and the store that sold him the can of Cherryum. He could sue these defendants in the same litigation because 1) the occurrence related to all three is the same — his drinking from the allegedly contaminated Cherryum; and 2) there are common questions of fact related to all three potential defendants. Some common questions of fact are whether the Cherryum was contaminated and the amount of harm to Lee as a result of drinking the Cherryum in question.

In the United States, Lee's wife would also have causes of action against the multiple defendants for her harm as result of her husband's drinking the allegedly contaminated Cherryum. A spouse can sue for what is called "loss of consortium," that is, the loss to her of her husband's company as a result of the accident. Under Rule 20, Mr. and Mrs. Lee could choose to join together as co-plaintiffs, because her harm arose from the same occurrence (the drinking of the Cherryum by her husband) and there is a common question of fact in Mr. Lee's case and his wife's (whether the Cherryum was contaminated when Lee bought the can). As long as the "same transaction, occurrence or series of transactions or occurrences," and the "common question of law or fact" requirements are satisfied, multiple plaintiffs and defendants may be joined together in the same litigation.

Again, Rule 20 was drafted in permissive rather than compulsory language. Rule 20 does not mandate or require joinder of parties, but rather permits it if the plaintiff so chooses. In other words, Rule 20 does not *require* Albert Lee to sue all potential defendants at the same time nor to join his wife in the same lawsuit. The drafters of the Federal Rules were reluctant to force parties to be adverse to one another if they did not want to be. Under the adversary system, each party is in control of her litigation. Each has a right to decide to sue or not to sue.

Similar to permissive joinder of claims, permissive joinder of parties must also consider basic jurisdictional requirements. Even though Rule 20 might permit the joinder of parties, there is still the question of whether a court has personal jurisdiction over each defendant. Moreover, if the case is in federal court based on diversity of citizenship, joinder of additional parties may destroy the diversity and in turn eliminate subject matter jurisdiction. Even though Rule 20 requirements are met, the case must be brought in a court that has both personal and subject matter jurisdiction.

Finally, Rule 20 has a provision very similar to Rule 42(b), giving judges the discretion to separate out the trials of joint plaintiffs or defendants: Rule 20(b) provides that a court may "make such orders . . . and may order separate trials or make other orders to prevent delay or prejudice." And so, if the court finds that the joinder of Mr. and Mrs. Lee as co-plaintiffs is unduly prejudicial to the defendant, the court may, in relying on Rule 20(b), separate the parties and order separate trials.

Joinder of Persons Needed for Just Adjudication

Fed. R. Civ. P. 20, as you have seen, permits, but does not mandate, the joinder of multiple plaintiffs and defendants when there is both a transactional overlap and at least one common question of law or fact. But there are occasions when the Rules will force parties to be joined if the joinder is possible, essentially taking the decision out of the plaintiff's hands and putting it into the hands of the defendant and the court.

Rule 19 prescribes the conditions requiring that some parties must be joined, provided that basic requirements of subject matter jurisdiction, personal jurisdiction, and venue requirements are also met. The three situations calling for mandatory joinder are defined in Fed. R. Civ. P. 19 (often called a rule relating to "necessary and indispensable parties"). Each of these situations is based on common sense reasons. Let us take each one in turn.

Rule 19(a) provides that a party must be joined if subject to service of process and whose joinder will not deprive the court of jurisdiction if "in the person's absence complete relief cannot be accorded among those already parties." For example, assume *A* and *B* jointly have a deed to a piece of real estate called Blackacre. *C* says that *A* and *B*'s deed was fraudulently procured, and that she, *C*, owns Blackacre. *C* sues only *A*, choosing not to sue *B*, seeking to have *C* declared the owner of Blackacre. Rule 19(a) would mandate that *C* join B as a co-defendant if jurisdictionally feasible. The court would not have the power to give the property allegedly jointly owned by *A* and *B* to *C*, without *B* being a party to the lawsuit and having her day in court to contest *C*'s allegations. If *C* sues only *A*, it would be a waste of time, because "complete relief cannot be accorded among those already parties," namely *C* and *A*, in *B*'s absence.

Rule 19(a)(2) says that a party should be joined if "the person claims an interest relating to the subject of the action and is so situated that the disposition of the action in the person's absence may . . . as a practical matter impair or impede the person's ability to protect that interest. . . ." Assume Cherryum, Inc., the holder of the secret formula for Cherryum, gave *Y* Bottling Company the exclusive right to bottle and sell Cherryum in the state of Ohio. Afterwards, *Z* Bottling Company claims a contractual exclusive right to sell Cherryum in Ohio, and sues Cherryum to enforce that contract. *Y* Bottling Company would be a necessary party under this portion of Rule 19, because if *Z* were given an exclusive right to bottle and sell Cherryum in Ohio, *Y* would end up with no such right, or, in any event, without an exclusive right. As a practical matter, *Y*'s right would be impaired or impeded, even though *Y* was absent from the litigation. To protect *Y* and the integrity of judgments, Rule 19(a)(2) dictates that *Y* should be joined as a party if possible, so that *Y*'s interests will be heard. Underlying this portion of Rule 19 (a) are the values of the due process clause of the Fourteenth Amendment to the United States Constitution, which provides the state cannot deprive persons of property without due process of law. Having the litigation proceed absent the necessary party may result, as a practical matter, in depriving the absent person of property without due process of law.

Rule 19(a)(3) also seems fair and makes common sense. A person is deemed a necessary party if in its absence the litigation would "leave any of the persons already parties subject to a substantial risk of incurring double, multiple, or otherwise inconsistent obligations by reason of the claimed interest." Assume there was a life insurance policy covering James Smith's life and listing Albert Lee as the sole beneficiary. Upon James Smith's death, three different persons named Albert Lee wrote the life insurance company (the Company) claiming the proceeds of the policy. Only one Albert Lee has sued the Company. The other two Albert Lees would be necessary parties under this provision, because if the Company is told by a court to pay one Albert Lee, other courts may find in favor of the other Albert Lees, and the Company may have to pay on the same policy multiple times.[7] Joining the other Albert Lees to the litigation would better protect the interests of the Company as well as those of the other Albert Lees.

It is the defendant who is most likely to use Rule 19 to call the presence of absent but necessary parties to the attention of the court. After all, a plaintiff is the master of her litigation and can use Rules 20 and 18 to join any party or claim to the extent those rules permit. If a party is deemed necessary and if jurisdictional and venue requirements are met, the court would order joinder of that party to the litigation. But what if, for example, the court does not have

7. On the facts of this insurance case, the Rule 22 "interpleader" provision may also be applicable. Under the interpleader provision, the Company may bring a lawsuit on its own against all of the Albert Lees in question in order to have one court decide which Albert Lee it should pay. The Company does not want to have to pay more than once or be subjected to inconsistent orders from different courts. Once again, similar to most of the other federal joinder rules, the interpleader mechanism has antecedents in historic equity practice.

personal jurisdiction over the absent party? Rule 19(b) permits the court to dismiss the litigation "for failure to join a necessary party," when an absent party is deemed necessary but joinder of such party is impossible. Before dismissal, however, Rule 19(b) lists the factors the court must consider. Fundamentally, the court should try to make sure that the plaintiff has some other court in which she can bring the case against all necessary parties if the instant suit is dismissed. If the case is not dismissed, if this is the only court where the plaintiff can proceed, then the court should find ways to lessen any potential prejudice against the absent party.

In sum, if a party is a necessary Rule 19(a) party, that party should be brought in if possible. If joinder is not possible because of a lack of personal jurisdiction, subject matter jurisdiction, or venue, the judge must then turn to Rule 19(b) and decide whether the case can proceed without the necessary party. If, after considering the Rule 19(b) factors, the judge decides that the case cannot proceed, she must dismiss the case. At that point, we know that the absent party has been deemed indispensable, in the sense that the case cannot proceed without her presence.

Intervention

By "intervention," the Rules mean that an outside party may, usually by motion, be permitted to become a party in an already existing lawsuit. Fed. R. Civ. P. 24 describes when parties have the right to intervene (intervention as of right), Rule 24(a), or may, in the discretion of the court, be permitted to intervene (permissive intervention), Rule 24(b).

Two circumstances define Rule 20(a) intervention as of right. Some federal statutes specify who has a right to intervene for a substantive cause of action, and Rule 24(a) also allows such persons the right to intervene. Rule 24(a) also says that a person can intervene as a matter of right if such applicant, "claims an interest relating to the property or transaction which is the subject of an action and the applicant is so situated that the disposition of the action may as a practical manner impair or impede the applicant's ability to protect that interest, unless the applicant's interest is adequately represented by existing parties." This language is similar to Rule 19 language and the same "due process" concerns underlie this rule. If an outsider's interest will be impaired or impeded by an existing litigation, she should be able as a matter of right to join the suit in order to protect that interest. However, if one already a party to the litigation adequately represents the interest, then intervention is not as of right. This concept of "adequate representation" is a fundamental one to which we will return later when we address representative suits or class actions.

Under Rule 24(b), a person may be permitted, with the court's discretion, to intervene "when an applicant's claim or defense and the main action have a question of law or fact in common." The test of commonality of question of law or fact is the same as part of the test for permissible joinder of parties under Rule 20. By contrast to intervention as of right, a person in permissive intervention may be permitted to apply for intervention, but the court in exercising its discretion may deny intervention if it deems the intervention will unduly delay or prejudice the rights of original parties.

By now, you have seen that "the commonality of law or fact" language underlies many of the joinder rules, including Rules 19, 20, and 24.[8] That language makes sense if we recall that one major reason for the joinder rules, borrowed from equity practice, was efficiency in trying to resolve entire disputes once and for all. The commonality of law or fact language or test also appears in Rule 42(a) *consolidation*. Fed. R. Civ. P. 42(a), the companion to Rule 42(b) concerning separate trials, provides that a court may order actions involving common questions of law or fact consolidated "to avoid unnecessary costs or delay." Consolidation is applicable when there are independent lawsuits filed in the same court with such commonality that it is sensible, from a management point of view, for the court to join them for trial purposes or for other hearings. Both plaintiffs and defendants can make motions to consolidate pending cases.

Three other joinder of claims and parties devices form the primary procedural methods used by defendants to enlarge the scope of the action in which they are sued.

Compulsory Counterclaims

Fed. R. Civ. P. 13 divides counterclaims into two types. Rule 13(a) is the *compulsory counterclaim* rule and obligates a defendant to bring certain claims against the plaintiff as a counterclaim or forever be barred from raising this claim. With certain exceptions, such as if the counterclaim is already part of another pending suit, Rule 13 (a) provides that a defendant must raise a counterclaim

> if it arises out of the transaction or occurrence that is the subject matter of the opposing party's claim and does not require for its adjudication the presence of third parties of whom the court cannot acquire jurisdiction.

For example, what if Albert Lee, after bringing his lawsuit against Cherryum, Inc., appeared on a television program and announced to the viewing audience that Cherryum, Inc., carelessly puts poison into its drinks and that all people who drink Cherryum are putting their health in jeopardy? Cherryum, Inc., may well have a libel or slander cause of action against Albert Lee for intentionally or negligently publicizing a false statement about its company and its product in a way that has caused them harm. This may be a compulsory counterclaim — that is, one that the defendant Cherryum, Inc., must allege in its answer to the complaint or lose the opportunity forever.

In sum, a compulsory counterclaim is one that arises out of the transaction or occurrence that is the subject of the initial case. One of two tests most often used to assess whether a counterclaim "arose out of the same transaction or occurrence" that is the subject of the initial case is whether there is factual, legal, or evidentiary overlap between the initial claim and the counterclaim.

---

8. 28 USC § 1407 also uses similar language. This multidistrict panel legislation authorizes the temporary transfer of civil actions "involving one or more common questions of fact" that are pending in different federal district courts to a single district "for coordinated or consolidated pretrial proceedings."

A more liberal test requires simply that the counterclaim be "logically connected" to the initial claim.

Under either the "evidentiary overlap" or the "logically connected" test, Cherryum, Inc.'s libel or slander claim would probably be deemed a compulsory counterclaim, which must be alleged in the answer or Cherryum, Inc., will be forever barred from raising the claim in a separate litigation. Whether insecticides or other contamination were in the Cherryum soda that Lee purchased is central to Lee's case for negligence against Cherryum, Inc., and is also central to Cherryum, Inc.'s counterclaim against Lee for libel. Each claim would involve much of the same evidence about contamination. Under the more liberal "logically connected" test, one would need to consider whether Lee's alleged libelous television statement appears logically connected with his purchase and drinking of the Cherryum, the topic of the initial law suit. Mr. Lee would probably not have allegedly libeled Cherryum, Inc., but for his drinking from the fateful can. If the libel or slander claim is deemed compulsory, Cherryum, Inc., must allege the claim in its answer to the Lee's complaint or forever lose the opportunity.

The logic behind compulsory counterclaim rules relates to efficiency once again. If the court is adjudicating a certain transaction or occurrence between parties, the thought is that it should adjudicate all claims arising out of that transaction at one time so that the legal system does not have to hear the same evidence many times. Separate litigation of the same transaction would also be inefficient for the parties. Apart from efficiency, the legitimacy of a legal system also demands uniformity. When feasible, there should not be multiple cases involving the same facts and the same parties but resulting in different outcomes.

Permissive Counterclaims

Covered in Fed. R. Civ. P. 13(b), are claims by an opposing party that "do not arise out of the transaction or occurrence that is the subject matter of the opposing party's claim." A defendant may join a permissive counterclaim, or alternatively, she may bring it as a separate action in a later lawsuit. Unlike the compulsory counterclaim, if a defendant does not bring a permissive counterclaim, the opportunity is not lost forever. For instance, if Albert Lee, while gardening for Cherryum, Inc., had allegedly negligently ruined the lawn in front of the factory, Cherryum, Inc., as the defendant, would have a counterclaim to Lee's own lawsuit against it for selling him an impure drink. However, Cherryum, Inc.'s counterclaim for Lee's negligent gardening would be permissive and not compulsory. It arose out of an entirely different transaction or occurrence, with no apparent factual or legal connection to the claim arising out of the Cherryum drink.

In practice, most defendants will bring available counterclaims whether compulsory or permissive, fearful that a later court may deem the claim compulsory and bar the defendant from bringing it as a separate litigation. Defendants also bring counterclaims for strategic advantage during settlement negotiations. Counterclaims, if at all meritorious, will alter the dynamics and change the bargaining power of settlement discussions.

Cross-claims

Co-defendants, such as those in the *Cherryum* case, are also permitted to bring *cross-claims* against each other if they have a claim "against a co-party arising out of the transaction or occurrence that is the subject matter either of the original action or of a counterclaim therein or relating to any property that is the subject matter...of the original action." Fed. R. Civ. P. 13(g). In the *Cherryum* case, the co-defendants, the manufacturer Cherryum, Inc., and the bottler Cherryum Bottling Co. may blame each other. The manufacturer, Cherryum, Inc., may even have made actual warranties or implied warranties to the bottler. Consequently, the bottling company would have potential cross-claims against Cherryum, Inc., arising from the occurrence of the initial law suit (Lee's drinking the allegedly impure Cherryum).

Cross-claims between co-defendants, unlike counterclaims, are not compulsory, meaning they may be brought in a separate action. Drafters of the Federal Rules did not want to force parties who are not already adverse to each other into an adverse position. In the compulsory counterclaim situation, the plaintiff and defendant are already adverse to each other. Co-defendants, though, are not in an adverse position to each other, at least not until one brings a cross-claim against the other. Once a co-defendant asserts a cross-claim against another, the defendants are then deemed adverse to each other, and the compulsory counterclaim rule is triggered. At that point, any counterclaims that that defendant has against the co-defendant's cross-claim, if compulsory, must be brought or be lost forever.

Third-Party Impleader

The final method defendants often use to expand the scope of a lawsuit is called "third-party practice" or "impleader." The core of Rule 14 is that a defendant may bring into the litigation "a person not a party to the action who is or may be liable to the third-party plaintiff for all or part of the plaintiff's claim against the third-party plaintiff." In other words, if *A* sues *B* and *B* thinks that *C* will have to pay *B* all or part of what *B* is liable to pay *A*, than *B* can implead *C*.

Assume that Albert Lee sues Cherryum, Inc., and that Cherryum, Inc., believes it has an insurance policy requiring the insurer to indemnify it for any losses it suffers as a result of being sued because of a defective product. If the insurer refuses to defend Cherryum, Inc., in the lawsuit or to reimburse Cherryum (as for example, by claiming that the insurance policy had lapsed), then the defendant, Cherryum, Inc., can become a third-party plaintiff and "implead" — that is, bring into the lawsuit through a third-party complaint — the insurer, on the grounds that it has agreed to indemnify Cherryum, Inc., in this situation. The insurer would then be the third-party defendant, and would have to answer Cherryum, Inc.'s third-party complaint against it.

Rule 14(a) says that a defendant/third-party plaintiff may serve a third-party claim against a third-party defendant as a matter of right if it is done within ten days after serving its answer to the original complaint. Otherwise, the impleader can only be done with permission of the court. Once again, the reason for this "impleader" joinder provision is efficiency. If A sues B, but C ultimately will have to pay B all or part of what B must pay A, then it may make sense to decide all of this in one lawsuit, rather than requiring the expense of two separate lawsuits.

CLASS ACTIONS: BEFORE THE FEDERAL RULES

The most controversial and yet probably the most powerful joinder device in the United States is the class action or what is sometimes called a "representative suit." The class action allows thousands of plaintiffs or defendants to be joined under one or more named "representative" plaintiffs or defendants.[9] As such, class actions are a departure from the traditional individual litigation model. Precisely because of the flexibility beyond what individual litigation can offer, class actions in America have enabled mass litigation dealing with important social policies and provided compensation for individual harms suffered by groups of people from the same unlawful action.

To plaintiffs, the class action lawsuit is an effective vehicle to force public policy changes, to enforce collective rights, and to adopt new legal norms against governments and corporate defendants. In contrast, defendants often view the class action lawsuit as nothing more than legal blackmail, forcing otherwise innocent defendants to settle or else bear the incredible cost of defending a massive lawsuit. No other country has utilized this kind of joinder provision to the same extent or in the same manner as the United States. And no other procedural instrument has had such impact in crafting social policy — from bringing down asbestos companies to reorganization of schools and changing police policies. Although other countries do provide for some form of group litigation (e.g., China, Canada, Germany, Sweden), they are primarily mass joinder of individual lawsuits or "representative" action under very limited circumstances. The expansiveness of the American class action lawsuit and the idea of a "representative" plaintiff have fascinated people both within and without the borders of the United States.

The lynchpin to understanding the American class action is the due process clause of the Fifth and Fourteenth Amendments to the United States Constitution. As discussed in Chapter 5, both these clauses provide that no person can be deprived by the federal (Fifth Amendment) or state (the Fourteenth Amendment) government of life, liberty, or property without due process of law. The due process clauses have been interpreted to mean that a court, with personal jurisdiction over a person, cannot bind a person to a judicial decree unless that person has been notified of the pending lawsuit and given an opportunity to present her case. This includes the right to choose one's own lawyer, put in evidence at a trial, and cross-examine the opposing side's witnesses. That is, if A files a complaint against B, and B is not served with the complaint in a constitutional manner (that may include service in hand or

---

9. Defendant class actions are very infrequent, however.

some kind of mail notice, accompanied by the complaint) than the court cannot render a valid judgment against *B*, consistent with the Constitution.

There are situations, though, when it has historically been constitutional for a court to bind (that is, to obligate by a court judgment) a defendant even though he or she has not been made a party. For instance, a trustee of a trust can be sued, and the beneficiaries of the trust will ordinarily be bound by the judgment. Or a corporation can be sued, and the shareholders will ordinarily be bound by the judgment. These are representative lawsuits in a very real sense. The trustee must represent the interests of the beneficiaries; the substantive law of trusts and estates requires this. So, too, the corporation's management must act in the best interests of the shareholders. The law permits the beneficiaries and the shareholders to be bound even though they are not in the lawsuit because there is a party in the lawsuit who represents and is obligated to act in their interest. With appropriate representation, the due process right of the beneficiaries and shareholders has not been violated because they have had their day in court, in effect, by virtue of their being represented by others; in this case, by the trustee and the corporation's management. This concept of "adequate representation" has been extended to and now serves as the backbone of class actions; in other words, a class action is only constitutional (does not violate due process) if the named plaintiff (or group of named plaintiffs) is an adequate representative of the class interest as a whole.

The antecedents to the procedural mechanism of the class action in the United States can be traced to two different sources – the bill of peace and contemporary notions of party joinder. The bill of peace, developed by the English Chancery or Equity Court, allowed a number of individuals, who could, by virtue of their membership in a preexisting group such as a guild or church, have their individual rights established to a pro-rata share of a fund held for their joint benefit. Two other notions of party joinder also found their way into contemporary practice. One is the idea that there were necessary parties to a litigation when such parties, if absent, would have their rights impeded by that litigation. The other is the concept of permissive joinder when persons, even if previously unrelated, had common questions of law or fact that could be conveniently adjudicated in one lawsuit.

It is not difficult to see how the requirement of joining necessary parties can evolve to the recognized need for something like "representative lawsuits." What if there are multiple parties whose rights will in practice be affected by adjudication and bound by a judgment but that it is virtually impossible to know all of their identities?

In the mid-nineteenth century and pre-Federal Rules twentieth century, the Supreme Court of the United States was confronted with such cases, forcing the Justices to decide whether named representatives in lawsuits could bind hundreds and thousands of absent parties whose interests were identical to the named parties. In *Smith v. Swormstedt*, 57 U.S. (16 How.) 288 (1853), the Supreme Court bound both plaintiff (numbered at 1500) and defendant (numbered at 3800) classes of people by a judgment that divided the property of a church whose preachers had split over the slavery issue. In *Supreme Tribe of Ben-Hur v. Cauble*, 255 U.S. 356 (1921), the Court ruled that over 70,000 certificate holders of a fraternal benefit association were bound by a prior suit that upheld the reclassification of their certificates.

In both the *Swormstedt* and *Supreme Tribe of Ben-Hur* cases, each member of the class to be bound had a joint prior association (with a church or fraternal benefit association); and therefore, it made sense to treat all members of the class equally. Later formulations of class actions expanded representative lawsuits beyond this scenario to bind those even without a prior joint association.

THE 1938 FEDERAL CLASS ACTION RULE

The drafters of the 1938 Federal Rules set up a tripartite classification for class actions. The first category — which became known as a "true" class suit — encompassed cases described above and reflective of the guild and society bill of peace cases recognized by the Chancery Court in England. The second category, known as "hybrid" class actions, involved classes of people who had individual rights, the adjudication of which did or "may affect specific property involved in the action." The third, called "spurious" class actions, applied when "there is a common question of law or fact affecting the several rights and a common relief is sought."

According to the 1966 Notes of the Advisory Committee, the original 1938 class action rule was problematic. Under the original rule, the terms *joint* and *common* and *the abstract nature of the rights involved*, the basis for the Rule 23 classification, proved obscure and uncertain. The original class action rule did not "provide for an adequate guide to the proper extent of the judgments in class actions," and it was unclear who would be bound by the judgment. Moreover the original rule did not squarely address itself to the question of "the measures that might be taken during the course of the action to assure procedural fairness . . ." In 1966, the class action rule was substantially amended.

CLASS ACTIONS: THE CURRENT FEDERAL RULE

The 1966 Committee was determined to describe, in more practical terms, the occasions for maintaining a class action and be more precise about who would be bound and take measures to assure the fair conduct of these actions. Despite numerous efforts to change it through the years, the core of the 1966 federal class action rule, Fed. R. Civ. P. 23, remains substantially the same to this day.

Rule 23 lists four prerequisites for all class actions, be they plaintiff or defendant class actions, and then requires that the case be identified as one or more of four types of class action. (In actuality, there are very few defendant class actions.) The four prerequisites, found in Rule 23(a), are loosely referred to as "numerosity," "commonality," "typicality" and "representativeness."

Rule 23(a)(1) says that one "or more members of a class may sue or be sued as representative parties on behalf of all only if (1) the class is so numerous that joinder of all members is impracticable...". How many are sufficiently numerous is decided on a case-by-case basis. Groups of as many as 350 have been held as too small for a class action, while groups of 25 have been held sufficient.[10] Fed. R. Civ. P. 23(a)(2) requires "questions of law or fact common to the class," and invites analysis similar to what we discussed under permissive joinder of parties (Rule 20). Rule 23(a)(3) requires that "the claims and defenses of the representative parties are typical of the claims and defenses of the class," in an attempt to insure that the interests of the class as a whole are being protected. The 23(a)(4) requirement also mandates that the named representatives in the class action "fairly and adequately protect the interest of the class." This obligates the judge to determine that the named representatives and their counsel have the expertise, resources, and interests at stake to fairly represent the whole class. These four requirements overlap to some extent, but the goal is obvious: to give due process protection to the non-named class members by making sure that their representatives have the same interests as they have and will diligently represent those interests throughout the suit.

After meeting the four pre-requisites of "numerosity," "commonality," "typicality," and "representativeness," the litigation must fall within one of four categories of class actions. The first two types of class action, delineated in Rule 23(b)(1)(A) and 23(b)(1)(B), are grounded in considerations and language similar to what we encountered in the Rule 19 necessary party doctrines. Rule 23(b)(1)(A) covers cases in which the prosecution of separate actions creates a risk of establishing "incompatible standards of conduct for the party opposing the class." Rule 23(b)(1)(B) covers cases in which the adjudication would "as a practical matter be dispositive of the interests" of absent members of the class who are not parties "or substantially impair or impede their ability to protect their interests." As you can see, these two types of cases are reminiscent of the situations covered by the historic equitable bills of peace in England (the pre-Federal Rule representative suits in which nonparties have been bound) and the "true" class action category under the 1938 Federal Rule.

But Rule 23(b)(2) and (b)(3) also permit class actions less grounded in previous English or American precedents. Each of these categories of class actions reflects important currents in the social-political milieu of 1966 America, the year Rule 23 was amended. Fed. R. Civ. P. 23(b)(2) covers cases in which:

> the party opposing the class has acted or refused to act on grounds generally applicable to the class, thereby making the final injunctive relief or corresponding declaratory relief with respect to the class as a whole;...

The year 1966 was the height of the civil rights movement and its struggle for racial equality in the United States. Recognizing the need for legal vehicles to remedy civil rights violations, the 1966 Advisory Committee's Notes

---

10. Charles Wright, Law of Federal Courts § 72 (West Pub. Co. 5th ed. 1994).

specifically stated, as illustrative of an appropriate Rule 23(b)(2) class action, "various actions in the civil-rights field where a party is charged with discriminating unlawfully against a class, usually one whose members are incapable of specific enumeration." Since 1966, civil rights plaintiffs have often used Rule 23(b)(2) class actions seeking injunctive relief to affect change on a structural level rather than on an individual basis. This has meant class actions brought to change the functioning or even the structure of private and public institutions, as in the restructuring of prisons or the desegregation of schools, and in obtaining new regulations over companies relating to financial and commercial practices.

The last category, 23(b)(3), has proven the most controversial. It covers cases in which "the court finds that the questions of law or fact common to the members of the class predominate over any questions affecting only individual members, and that a class action is superior to other available methods for the fair and efficient adjudication of the controversy." The rule then lists matters pertinent to these issues of "predominance" of common questions and "superiority" over other adjudicatory methods. These include such matters as the interests of individual members of the class in controlling their own separate actions, what litigation has already been commenced, and "the difficulties likely to be encountered in the management of a class action." Unlike the other three categories, the 23(b)(3) class action has a "notification" and an "opt-out" requirement – that is, each member of the class must be notified of the pendency of the class action and each member must be afforded the opportunity to be excluded from the class and not be bound by the litigation.

Rule 23(b)(3) is often called the "consumer" class action, because it has been most frequently used by consumers, who may have lost only a small amount of money and might not have brought suit absent the class action vehicle. Another use of this type of class action is the "mass tort" situation, in which hundreds or thousands of people who suffered harm from the same illegal conduct can join in one single action under the banner of a "representative" plaintiff. While drafters of the rule could not possibly have anticipated all the effects of such a rule, they were drafting at a time in American history when new types of litigants were asserting their rights, including those seeking consumer protection.

Yet, the 1966 Advisory Committee's Notes to 23(b)(3) cautioned against mass tort cases as not ordinarily appropriate for class action because:

> of the likelihood that significant questions, not only of damages but of liability and defenses to liability, would be present, affecting the individuals in different ways. In these circumstances an action conducted nominally as a class action would degenerate in practice into multiple lawsuits separately tried.

Notwithstanding this caution, the plaintiffs' tort bar has been successful in having class actions certified not only for some "mass accident" cases, such as airplane accidents and collapsed buildings, but also, with some success, for mass tort cases involving toxic substances. Much of the current debate about class actions in America concerns massive tort class actions involving tens of thousands of people.

Rule 23 specifies that the court must determine whether to certify the litigation as a class action at "an early practicable time." The party seeking certification as a class action (almost always the plaintiff) is normally required to define the scope of the class for the court. The language "at an early practicable time" is an amendment from the prior "as soon as practicable" language, a change which the Advisory Committee hoped would give the court more flexibility in deciding when a class should be certified. This amendment recognizes the enormous impact of class certification on the parties and the need for quick action, but also responds to the critique that the original "as soon as practicable" language led to undue haste in class certification.

The class can be further subdivided into "subclasses," each with their named representative or representatives, necessary to protect the differing interests of the subclasses. Fed. R. Civ. P. 23(c)(4). Except where members of a 23(b)(3) class opt out, all members of all four types of federal class actions are normally bound by the judgment given for or against the named parties. A 2003 amendment added a second opt-out opportunity, at the time of settlement in addition to the time of certification, for members of a class, in recognition that the ramifications of being a member of a class are often not evident until a settlement is reached. Fed. R. Civ. P. 23(e)(3)

Class actions (along with discovery and summary judgment) have drawn the attention of reformers seeking to rein in a litigation system perceived to have run amuck. Ten years' worth of intensive consideration and review resulted in a new set of amendments to Rule 23 adopted in 2003. As a whole, these changes are reported to be uncontroversial, at least insofar as they fail to dramatically modify class action practice. They are, however, consistent with the overall trend to impose greater restrictions on and judicial oversight over civil litigation in America. As the 2003 Advisory Committee Notes explained, "the overall goal of the advisory committee has been to develop rule amendments that provide the district courts with the tools, authority, and discretion to closely supervise class-action litigation." And so, we see amendments providing for greater judicial control over when a class may be certified, when and who may be appointed as the attorney for the class, and the amount of attorney's fees. This is in addition to the requirement of judicial monitoring and approval of class action settlements.

CLASS ACTIONS: PROS AND CONS

The debates surrounding the merits of class actions in the United States are highly charged and ideological. Professor Geoffrey C. Hazard, Jr., one of the most respected procedural scholars in the country, summarized the dispute this way:

> The contending sides often seem to be talking about very different transactions. On behalf of votaries for claimants, it is asserted that wholesale rip-offs are involved, in which the defendants have unjustly enriched

themselves at the expense of unprotected ordinary citizens. On behalf of defendants, it is alleged that the class suit itself is blackmail. . . . [11]

With such disagreement, one might hope to get some distance, detachment, and enlightenment by comparing the American class action to representative suits used in other countries. The fact is, though, that a host of factors make the American class action experience almost incomparable to other systems. For one, there is the unusually deep reliance by Americans on the private law suit to vindicate rights, as well as the historic American distrust of government. The lack of a national health system or generous safety net for the disadvantaged or unlucky propelled the greater use of the American class action as a viable vehicle for redistribution. The utilization of the jury (perhaps in some cases sympathetic to plaintiff's claims) combined with the potential awards of punitive damages reinforced the class action's potential as a powerful weapon. Finally, the American system of the contingent fee to finance litigation and the American rule of not normally shifting legal fees to the losing party provided economic incentives for lawyers to bring class actions.

In writing about the American class action "with a comparative eye," Professor Linda Silberman of the New York University School of Law noted that:

> . . . [T] he American class action has been molded in a system that (1) relies on a strong adversary tradition, (2) is powered by entrepreneurial lawyering, (3) is comfortable with a culture of robust judicial lawmaking, and (4) is complicated by the intricacies of an expansive dual system of courts [i.e. federalism] .[12]

By contrast, other countries, while recognizing the need for group litigation, have not conceived of group litigation with such liberality. Rather, group litigations, if provided for at all, are only utilized in particular instances of collective interests, such as a specific consumer interest and environmental protection. For example, the European Directive on Injunctions for the Protection of Consumer Interests (2000) assigns rights of action to "qualified entities," which are either organizations or independent public bodies. It is normally the duty of the state and government, not private individuals, to represent such collective interests. Group litigation is conducted in only a few areas of supra-individual goals, such as environmental and consumer protection, and is generally conducted under strict bureaucratic governmental control.[13]

There may be changes in the air, however, as some European countries (Netherlands (1994); Portugal (1995); England and Wales (2000); Spain (2001); and Sweden (2002)), have recently introduced general group litigation

---

11. Geoffrey C. Hazard, Jr., *Class Certification Based on Merits of the Claims*, 69 Tenn. L. Rev. 1, 2 (2001).

12. Linda Silberman, *The Vicissitudes of the American Class Action — With a Comparative Eye*, 7 Tul. J. Int'l & Comp. L. 201, 201 (1999).

13. Some European countries have enacted national laws that allow consumer organizations to take legal action on behalf of consumers. Italy and Germany for example. Michele Taruffo, *Some Remarks on Group Litigation in Comparative Perspective*, 11 Duke J. Comp. & Int'l L. 405, 419 (2001).

rules.[14] In Germany, there is a procedure allowing a "community" of litigants to file a joint action if the central claim is based on similar factual and legal grounds. In Sweden, the Group Proceedings Act of 2002 allows private persons to take collective legal action on behalf of other persons, who are identified by name and address in the summons and individually registered with the court. In both countries, only those who have expressly joined the action are bound by its outcome.[15]

But the use of group litigation is usually not permitted for the compensation of individual harm, as in the American rule 23(b)(3) class action. This is, according to Professor Michele Taruffo, Professor of Law at University of Pavia in Italy, because class actions contradict traditional notions of standing in civil law countries — that is, only individuals are vested with a right of action for the protection of their own individual substantive rights.[16] In civil law countries, generally speaking, the idea that an association or an individual can represent broad collective or diffuse interests, rather than their own institutional rights or individual interest, does not fit well with traditional ideas of how civil litigation is pursued.

Thus, European group actions are brought primarily for declaratory and injunctive relief, and in the infrequent case for damages, the damages are paid to the body that represents the interest. Where group litigation is allowed, such legislation originated not to compensate for harms or injuries individually suffered by members of a class.[17] Rather, the goal for the limited European legislation in this area is to provide for new or changed legal norms in specific and relatively narrow areas of the legal system. The mass tort kind of American class action, applicable to any areas of misconduct and pursued to compensate thousands, is unheard of in these countries.

It is therefore unclear whether group litigation will have such dramatic impact in Europe as it has in the United States. There are a number of disincentives to using group litigation in Europe ranging from high court fees to the lack of contingency fee arrangements and lack of punitive damages (except France and Greece) to such procedural differences as limited discovery and no jury trials. In the end, European lawyers have less economic incentive to pursue such claims.

These differences have led to positive and negative class action characteristics that are perhaps distinctively American. Proponents of the class action argue that it is efficient for the legal system to allow group litigation rather than the expense of numerous individual lawsuits. Class action ensures greater uniformity in treatment of like cases by pooling cases under one result. Uniformity of results in turn adds to the legitimacy of a legal system. Further, allowing individual claims to be grouped together means that claims that cannot be litigated individually either because of cost or inconvenience will be

14. Linda A. Willett, *U.S.-Style Class Actions in Europe: A Growing Threat?* Vol. 9, No. 6 National Legal Center for the Public Interest, June 2005, at 8.
15. OECD Workshop on Consumer Dispute Resolution & Redress in the Global Market Place (April 19-20, 2005) at 29 <http://www.oecd.org/dataoecd/59/21/34699496.pdf> (accessed on September 21, 2005).
16. Michele Taruffo, *Some Remarks on Group Litigation in Comparative Perspective*, 11 Duke J. Comp. & Int'l L. 405, 416 (2001).
17. Harald Koch, *Non-Class Group Litigation Under EU and German Law*, 11 Duke J. Comp. & Int'l L 355, 359 (Summer 2001).

brought. It provides access to courts to hundreds or thousands of people who could not afford to adjudicate alone (or may not even know of their rights) by allowing their common grievance to be combined, heard, and perhaps vindicated.

For class members and their lawyers, there are multiple strategic advantages in bringing a class action in America. In a class action, the defendant cannot eliminate the case by settling with the named plaintiff alone; the class action will continue with new class representatives appointed. In other words, plaintiffs' interests as a whole can be continued beyond the demised or dismissed individual plaintiffs. Additionally, in a contingency fee system such as the United States (where the lawyers lay out the expenses initially and will be paid only out of the client's winning recovery), a class action may be the only way to make a case sufficiently economically profitable or politically visible to entice talented lawyers to commence suit. As a proportion of the damages sustained by the entire class rather than as a portion of damages to one individual, the successful plaintiff class action attorney's fees can be in the hundreds of thousands of dollars.

Class actions in America have also been a way to gain publicity for groups of people who lack political clout. As a case affecting thousands of people, class actions are followed and reported with great interest in the press. The publicity from a class action litigation sometimes alone can assist in reaching favorable settlements, whether monetary or injunctive relief, or achieving legislative initiatives. In sum, successful class action settlements (and almost all class actions that remain certified do settle) not only benefit all members of the class, but they can also serve as a superb method of enforcing laws that would otherwise lack enforcement. Chastened by seeing the drastic financial losses and bad publicity that can result in class actions, defendants facing class actions will likely be deterred from future illegal behavior.

A RAND Institute for Civil Justice study of ten settled damage class actions found that in all six of the ten consumer cases they studied "the litigation was associated with changes in the defendants' business practices . . . In four of the six cases the evidence strongly suggests that the litigation directly or indirectly produced the changes in practice."[18] But interestingly, in three of the four mass tort cases studied, the class action followed, rather than preceded, the "removal of the product from the market or change in the product."[19]

Filing a class action is not without risks for both the plaintiff's attorney and her client. Although the threat of a class action may improve the settlement for a client, once the case is certified as a class, the named representatives normally must be treated the same as all other class members. Settlement cannot be achieved without notice to all of the class members and approval of the court. Fed. R. Civ. P. 23(e). Once a class is certified, the lawyer's loyalty is to the more amorphous interest of the entire class and not to her original individual client. Lawyers for class action plaintiffs must bear in mind that if they lose the case, the loss is borne not only by the individual named plaintiff, but the entire class.

18. Deborah R. Hensler, Bonnie Dombey-Moore, Beth Goldens, Jennifer Gross, Erik K. Moller & Nicholas M. Pace, Class Action Dilemmas, Pursuing Public Goals for Private Gain, Executive Summary 20 (RAND Institute for Justice 1999).

19. *Id.*

In large class actions, in which the stakes are high, there is often fierce competition to determine who the lead lawyers will be, and ultimately, the amount of their fees. A lawyer commencing a class action can find herself totally excluded from later control of the case if the court decides that other counsel is more appropriate. More problematically, in a class action with tens of thousands of members in a class, it is the appointed lawyer's fees, rather than the diffused interest of the plaintiffs, that can dominate, posing a real conflict of interest between the plaintiff and her lawyer. It is this concern with protecting the plaintiffs' interests that led to the 2003 amendment of Rule 23, which includes provisions on who can be appointed class counsel (by giving discretion to the court to determine which lawyer has sufficient experience and expertise to act as class counsel) as well as detailed rules on appointment procedure and attorney fees determination.

The expense and time in litigating a class action can be enormous, making it impossible for an attorney to attend to her other clients and work. Since the stakes can be so high in a class action, defendants will often pour great resources of people and money in the fight against the plaintiff class. This means that one cannot lightly commence a class action, and it requires the conscientious attorney to explain carefully to the client the risks, as well as the benefits, of undertaking a class action.

Just as the class action can empower a whole class of plaintiffs and their lawyers, it can have the opposite effect for defendants. The 23(b)(3) damages class action, in particular, has been vigorously attacked with the result that plaintiffs that seek monetary relief frequently seek to have their class certified under other types of class action as well, by characterizing the case as one of limited funds or by tacking on damages to injunctive relief.[20] But regardless how a class action is structured, class actions against corporations have many untoward results for the defendant companies. Company management is often tied up in litigation for years. The uncertainty of outcome can force down a company's stock price and make it more difficult for the company to borrow money at reasonable interest rates or to merge with or buy other companies. Most obviously, an award against the company in a mass tort class action can be so high as to put the company out of business. Indeed, litigation resulting from asbestos claims, as well as mass tort claims in other fields, has made bankruptcy an appealing and realistic option for some corporate defendants.

According to class action detractors, even the threat of a class action, let alone its commencement or certification, has a grossly unfair blackmail effect on innocent defendants because of the devastating risk of loss and the enormous resources in time, money, and company personnel to defend the lawsuit. Often, class action plaintiffs' lawyers piggyback on the success of government lawyers who have already, through research and public litigation, exposed the defendants to liability through government civil prosecutions.[21] Riding on the

---

20. *See, e.g.,* Linda S. Mullenix, *No Exit: Mandatory Class Actions in the New Millenium and the Blurring of Categorical Imperatives,* 2003 U. Chi. Legal F. 177, 208-239.

21. *See, e.g.,* Howard M. Erichson, *Coattail Class Actions: Reflections of Microsoft, Tobacco, and the Mixing of Public and Private Lawyering in Mass Litigation,* 34 U.C. Davis L. Rev. 1 (2000).

coattails of government victories reduces the argument that the private plaintiff class action lawyers are responsible for improving public safety or that the lawyers need huge fees because in this case they are not at great risk of losing. Opponents of the class action point out that in the mass tort context in which a plaintiff has been badly injured or sustained large losses, there is no need for the class action. Such injured parties are already able to find capable lawyers, and the lawyers will be handsomely paid through the normal contingent fee structure.

Class action detractors point out that damage class actions benefit the lawyers rather than the plaintiff class members. In a class action, the plaintiff lawyer fees as a percentage of settlement or as based on their amount of work almost always exceed what any one member of the plaintiff class receives and sometimes even exceed the aggregate of the benefits to all class members.[22] In some class action settlements, the plaintiffs' lawyer's fee is based on a percentage of the total value of coupons or other benefits that the plaintiff class may ultimately receive; in reality, though, the actual amount collected by members of the plaintiff class is often far less because large numbers of coupons or other future benefits go unused.

The economics involved in class actions also seem to bring out the worse of the adversary system. Class action plaintiffs' lawyers are accused of unprofessional conduct, seeking out representative plaintiffs, in effect stirring up litigation for their own benefit. All members of the plaintiff class are, by rule, supposed to be treated equally. But there are accusations (which are denied) that some plaintiffs' lawyers, including very prestigious ones, make large illegal "kickbacks" to individuals who become the lead, named plaintiffs in dozens of class actions against corporations.[23]

The attack against class action has not been limited to the Rule 23(b)(3) damage class action. Opponents of the class action have argued that the 23(b)(2) institutional reform cases improperly stretch the traditional concept of judicial role. In proscribing future relief, as in the reformation of prisons or the desegregation of schools, the judge in institutional reform cases sets herself the task not only of policymaking but also of rule implementation. Rather than ordering relief to compensate for past injuries in "a dispute retrospectively oriented towards the consequences of a close set of events," the judge in institutional reform cases orders specific relief, in the form of changing defendant's conduct, in a "controversy about future probabilities."[24] If the defendant is the government or governmental agency, the judge, as part of her inherent authority to order and enforce remedies, finds herself overseeing public institutional reforms and in the controversial position of supervising government programs on a long-term basis. For example, a wave of cases in the mid-1990s resulted in judicial supervision of some of the largest public housing authorities in the country. Judges became embroiled in specified methods of tenant selection, determining the sites of new units,

---

22. *Id.* at 21.

23. See, e.g., Timothy L. O'Brien & Jonathan D. Glater, *Robin Hoods or Legal Hoods? The Government Takes Aim at a Class-Action Powerhouse*, N.Y. Times, July 17, 2005, at Sect. 3, pp. 1, 4.

24. Abram Chayes, *The Role of the Judge in Public Law Litigation*, 89 Harv. L. Rev. 1281, 1292 (1976).

demolishing old ones, and even overseeing the hiring of "mobility counselors" who urge tenants to move to different parts of town.[25]

Some scholars question the legitimacy and ability of the judiciary to take on such activities so different from the normal process of adjudication. They argue that institutional reform litigation vests judges with powers that are "inconsistent with the text, structure and original understanding of the Constitution." It is the executive office, not the judiciary, who is charged with implementation of governmental programs.[26] As such, critics claim these cases are not only unconstitutional but also anti-majoritarian and undemocratic in having a single judge formulate policy rather than through the democratic legislative process. Others, meanwhile, recognize the polycentric nature of institutional reform lawsuits — that is, involving multiple interests requiring institutional reform remedies that are negotiated between various stakeholders, but urge limits and judicial self-restraint in this "democracy by [judicial] decree."[27] While recognizing such negotiations can be subject to the "rent seeking" problems found in government actions,[28] defenders of institutional reform class actions argue that such localized participation of stakeholders through litigation "may be more democratic than rulemaking by national bureaucrats and agencies who are only loosely supervised by Congress."[29]

With such divergent views of the class action, it is difficult to achieve a balanced view of the overall efficaciousness of the device. Surely, some form of the damage class action is needed to enforce laws, deter illegal conduct, and allow class members to achieve recoveries that could not be achieved if left to traditional individual lawsuits. Damage class actions are also needed in some mass tort cases to avoid swamping an already overburdened court system. But it is equally true that in some class actions, plaintiffs' lawyers are receiving unjustifiably large fees and some innocent corporations are paying huge settlements merely to avoid the risks and costs of class action litigation. Although institutional reform class actions can serve to vindicate civil and constitutional rights, they also put an enormous strain on the judiciary in terms of time and resources. In addition, they raise the legitimate question of how much power should be afforded to nonelected officials in a democracy.

---

25. *See, e.g., Davis v. N.Y. Housing Auth.*, 278 F.3d 64 (2d Cir. 2002).

26. William A. Fletcher, The *Discretionary Constitution: Institutional Remedies and Judicial Legitimacy*, 91 Yale L. J. 635 (1982); John Choon Yoo, *Who Measures the Chancellor's Foot? The Inherent Remedial Authority of the Federal Courts*, 84 Cal. L. Rev. 1121 (1996).

27. *See* The new principles for framing, managing, and ending judicial decrees, in Ross Sandler & David Schoenbrod, Democracy By Decree: What Happens When Courts Run Government, Table 9.1 at 189 (Yale University Press 2003); *See also* Malcolm M. Feeley & Edward L. Rubin, Judicial Policy Making and the Modern State: How the Courts Reform America's Prisons (Cambridge University Press 1998).

28. Richard Posner, Economic Analysis of Law 36 n.3 (6th ed., Aspen Publishers, Inc. 2003), (citing to essays collected in Toward a Theory of the Rent-Seeking Society (James M. Buchanan, Robert D. Tollison & Gordon Tullock, eds. 1980)).

29. David Zaring, *National Rulemaking Through Trial Courts: The Big Case and Institutional Reform*, 51 UCLA L. Rev. 1015, 1028 (2004); *see also* Susan P. Sturm, *A Normative Theory of Public Law Remedies*, 79 Geo. L.J. 1355, 1382 (1991).

CLASS ACTIONS: UPS AND DOWNS

Given the strong feelings about class actions, it is probably not surprising that the representative suit in America has experienced a roller-coaster history. To paint with a very broad brush, the American class action has traversed at least four distinct, although sometimes overlapping, periods. Prior to 1966, the class action was primarily used in circumstances in which plaintiffs and/or defendants had a preexisting community of interest, by virtue of membership in a church, society, guild, or the like.

In the decade following the 1966 amendments, class action suits proliferated. There was much enthusiasm for the class action as a device that could be "instrumental in providing access to justice for economically disadvantaged groups, and the new rule was being construed in liberal fashion leading to an abundance of class certifications."[30] Beginning in the early 1970s, a third period started evolving in reaction to rising criticism that class actions contribute to the overall litigiousness in American society. The Supreme Court responded with a restrictive view of class actions, especially in diversity of citizenship cases (for example, requiring that each plaintiff meet the requisite amount in controversy),[31] and in consumer protection (b)(3) actions (requiring that individual notice be given to each identifiable member of the class).[32] The notice requirement made it prohibitively expensive for most such class actions to be financed. An increasingly conservative Supreme Court, and in turn lower federal courts, also found many ways, both through substantive and procedural law, to make it considerably more difficult for civil rights plaintiffs to obtain either injunctions or damages in federal class actions.[33] By the end of the 1970s, the use of class actions had substantially decreased in the federal courts, and this trend continued through the 1980s.

But the 1990s brought a fourth development. There was a remarkable revival in the 23(b)(3) damages class action, with its previous detractors (defendants and the defense bar) reversing to become its staunchest advocates. Defendants saw the potential of class action to limit their liability. With the proliferation of mass torts lawsuits, often involving thousands and even hundreds of thousands of people allegedly harmed by the same wrongful act, substantive law responded by developing such concepts as market share liability, permitting recovery even when it can't be determined which particular manufacturer produced the product that caused the harm. Asbestos litigation brought by thousands injured by exposure to the chemical is perhaps the most obvious example of the proliferation of mass tort cases brought as class actions. This "asbestos-litigation crisis" added to the already overburdened legal system such that

---

30. Silberman, *supra* note 12, at 205.

31. *See Snyder v. Harris*, 394 U.S. 332 (1969); *Zahn v. International Paper Co.*, 414 U.S. 291 (1973).

32. *See Eisen v. Carlisle & Jacquelin*, 417 U.S. 156 (1974).

33. *See, e.g.*, Phyllis Tropper Baumann, Judith Olans Brown & Stephen N. Subrin, *Substance in the Shadow of Procedure: The Integration of Substantive and Procedural Law in Title VII Cases*, 33 B. C. L. Rev. 211 (1992); Myriam Gilles, *Reinventing Structural Reform Litigation: Deputizing Private Citizens in the Enforcement of Civil Rights*, 100 Col. L. Rev. 1384, 1391-1399 (2000).

dockets in both federal and state courts continue to grow; long delays are routine; trials are too long; the same issues are litigated over and over; transaction costs exceed the victims' recovery by nearly two to one; exhaustion of assets threatens and distorts the process; and future claimants may lose altogether.[34]

In the midst of this "litigation crisis," some of those who have been antagonistic to the class action in the past, including members of the judiciary, the defense bar, and corporate executives in companies faced with such suits, have in recent years embraced rather than rejected the class action. If large numbers of potential plaintiffs can gain from a class action, why couldn't large numbers of potential plaintiffs also be barred by a class action settlement? In other words, if the defendant can buy, as it has been called, "global peace" with class actions, then the class action has become a friend rather than an enemy for defendants. In some instances, settlements are first negotiated, and then class actions are subsequently brought in order to bind current and potential litigants in the future. This kind of a "settlement class action" proved controversial because it is brought for the sole purpose of having a judge certify the class or classes and approve the settlement in a way that binds all class members, past and future plaintiffs. In such a way, the defendant has limited its liability dramatically.

CURRENT CLASS ACTION DEVELOPMENTS AND ARGUMENTS

The settlement class action is one of the most controversial issues in American civil procedure. It forces those interested in civil procedure to reconsider the goals of civil litigation — to settle individual disputes or to enforce legal norms on an institutional scale. The issue of "representativeness" is also very much called into question. When can a class bind present as well as future potential plaintiffs? As we have noted, whenever there is a class action, the judge must decide whether the representatives of the class are truly representing the interests of all of the class members who will be bound. Even in a class action brought to remedy alleged discrimination by a school system, usually brought as a 23(b)(2) institutional reform class action, the plaintiff members may have competing, if not conflicting, goals, rendering it difficult to define the parameters of the class. Thus, in a class of African Americans seeking to desegregate public schools, the class may not be representative because some African Americans may believe that their children would be better off in segregated but well-financed schools. Binding future potential class members brings the difficulty of defining the class interest even more sharply into focus.

34. Report of The Judicial Conference Ad Hoc Committee on Asbestos Litigation 2-3 (Mar. 1991), cited in *Amchem Products, Inc.*, 521 U.S. at 598.

Some of these considerations caused the Supreme Court in *Amchem Products, Inc. v. Windsor*, 521 U.S. 591 (1997) to affirm the Circuit Court's vacating of the certification of an asbestos class action brought after settlement was reached in an attempt to bar future plaintiffs. The Supreme Court was not convinced of the adequacy of representation for those absent class members, some of whom could not even be notified because they could not be identified and therefore could not voice their concerns. The Supreme Court also thought the potential was particularly high for conflicts of interest on the part of lawyers *vis a vis* their clients.

Indeed, the settlement class action also brings to front and center an issue that lurks in all litigation: Is the lawyer truly representing the interests of her client? In a simple litigation, the attorney has a known client with whom she should consult regularly and whose desires must ordinarily be followed. In the class action, "the client" has become a much more diffuse entity. In consumer class actions, in which frequently no single plaintiff has sustained sufficient damages to bring individual suit (for example, those contesting an over-charging of interest, the sale of defective toasters, or fraudulent information about securities), there may be a settlement in which the attorneys receive thousands or millions of dollars, but no one class member receives more than a few hundred dollars. The motivations of the plaintiffs' lawyers who join with the defendants' lawyers and their clients in settlement class actions are suspect in these circumstances. Plaintiffs' lawyers may have entered into settlements for the attorney's fees rather than in the public interest or their client's interest.

Class actions also raise the issue of what law to apply. Tort laws, upon which mass tort class actions are usually based, often vary from state to state. In a common law system such as the United States, mass class actions have the potential of setting law on a national level with one lawsuit. The Supreme Court has not been willing to let the trial courts, through the class action vehicle, create national substantive law applicable to all states given that state laws are materially different and that creation of national substantive law is within the purview of Congress[35] The conflicts of interest, lack of adequate representation for all types of injured parties, and conflict of law problems were some of the reasons that the Supreme Court gave for not permitting *Amchem* to proceed as a class action.

Congress has not been absent from the fray. In the securities litigation area, the securities industry, joined by their defense bar, lobbied Congress vigorously to place restrictions on securities class actions, pointing to anecdotes that plaintiffs' lawyers were bringing frivolous securities fraud class actions for quick settlements and large attorneys fees.[36] Their efforts succeeded in the promulgation of the same Private Securities Litigation Reform Act of 1995 that required heightened pleadings in securities cases (discussed in Chapter 6). Congress's attempt to inhibit litigation in a given substantive area through procedure suggests once again the political nature of procedural rules. Such congressional action certainly contravenes the trans-substantive nature of the Federal Rules of Civil Procedure, which,

---

35. *See, e.g., Phillips Petroleum Co. v. Shutts*, 472 U.S. 797, 811 (1985).
36. Private Securities Litigation Reform Act, Pub. L. No. 104-67, 109 Stat. 737 (1995).

for the most part, apply to all civil cases, regardless of the applicable substantive law.

The latest reform to class action is a 2005 federal statute that permits the removal of some state class actions to federal court.[37] The defense bar and the business community thought that class actions had become too easily certified in what were thought to be pro-plaintiff state courts, such as Alabama, Louisiana, and Mississippi. The statute permits removal from state to federal court, with only minimal diversity (any one plaintiff and any one defendant from different states), if the aggregate amount of the controversy is more than five million dollars and if the plaintiff class has more than one hundred members. Ironically, this measure to take class actions out of the state courts may well be unnecessary. By the time the statute was passed, the courts in many of those pro-plaintiff states had already headed in the opposite direction and clamped down on class actions.[38] President George W. Bush, nevertheless, heralded this new legislation as "a strong step forward in our efforts to reform the litigation system and keep America the best place in the world to do business."[39]

If mass tort cases cannot proceed as a class action, what might result? When the costs of individual suits often far exceed the amount that a winning individual plaintiff could recover, a class action may be the only viable procedural vehicle to protect such plaintiffs. There is also a certain "crap shoot" or chance phenomenon with individual litigation of mass torts, where plaintiffs with seemingly identical injuries experience drastically different results, depending on the particular judge, jury, and state substantive law that is applied. When early litigants can gain recoveries so vast that no funds are left for equally injured subsequent plaintiffs, class action may be the most equitable way to ensure compensation. Repeat individual litigation could also hamper business and courts.

One respected American scholar, Professor David Shapiro, has suggested that it may make more sense to conceptualize class actions as "an entity in itself for the critical purposes of determining the nature of the lawsuit, the role of the lawyer and the judge, and the significance of the disposition."[40] When multiple small claims are involved, the purpose of private litigation is less in compensating those harmed or in providing a sense of personal vindication, but more and perhaps entirely, in allowing a private attorney general (in the form of private plaintiffs in a class action) to contribute to social welfare by bringing an action whose purpose is to force the wrongdoer to internalize the cost of the wrong. In other words, deterrence and changing wrongful conduct, rather than compensation, is really the main goal of such litigation.[41] If this is true, then class actions are necessary and should continue without requiring individual notice and the right to opt-out to individual class members.

---

37. 28 U.S.C. § 1453.

38. *See, e.g.*, Linda S. Mullenix, *Abandoning the Federal Class Action Ship: Is There Smoother Sailing for Class Actions in Gulf Waters?*, 74 Tul. L. Rev. 1709, 1779 (2000).

39. Stephen Labaton, *Senate Approves Measure to Curb Big Class Actions*, N.Y. Times, Feb. 11, 2005, at A1.

40. David L. Shapiro, *Class Actions: The Class as Party and Client*, 73 Notre Dame L. Rev. 913, 917 (1998).

41. *Id.* at 924.

Even when the individual claimants in mass torts have a larger stake, Shapiro thinks that the uncertainty of outcomes and the expense and delay of the traditional individual model, among other reasons, make it more desirable to view the class as an entity.[42] Judges could make certain that the representation of the class is truly adequate rather than trying to ensure that through individual notice (although there should be sufficient notice "to make a *representative* group aware of the action") and the right to opt-out. Due process should be shaped to practical needs and "to the costs and benefits involved and to the substantive interests at stake."[43] In societies in which the sense of community is weighed more than individual autonomy, Professor Shapiro's conceptualization of the class action as an "entity" model may be particularly acceptable.

As we are putting final touches on this book, recent developments may have already placed the United States class action in yet another, and potentially final, stage of development. In our terms, this would be a fifth historic phase. Myriam Gilles has pointed out that the 1980s and 1990s have already brought numerous decertifications of previously accepted class actions in such fields as asbestos, tobacco, and products liability.[44] Moreover, corporations are increasingly forcing contractual class action waiver provisions on the consumer. Most courts have enforced these provisions and in so doing forbid class actions and enforced binding arbitration clauses. The courts, using a number of devices such as restrictive standing requirements, had already stomped out most public law class action litigations that rely on structural reform injunctions.[45] If Gilles is right, then we have already entered the fifth class action historical period, which regrettably (both from her and our points of view) could be the final one for class action.

On the other hand, dire predictions of the demise of the class action may be premature. Most litigation in America ends in settlement and often is not appealed. Where much of the clout in class actions can come from the threat rather than the actual commencement of a class action, the effect and the importance of class actions may not show up in any formal records. There may be developments more supportive of class actions that we are unaware of. It may be that in some regions of the country, states are developing more plaintiff-friendly class action jurisprudence than in the federal courts. Finally, and most importantly, the creativity, resilience, and profit motive of the American plaintiff's bar and the ultimate good sense of American judges and legislators should not be underestimated. The class action is perhaps the strongest example of American dependence on private litigation to enforce public norms and to challenge governmental authorities. We are placing our bets on a sixth class action phase, or on other methods in which private parties can, in a representative capacity, vindicate public policy and private rights.[46]

---

42. *Id.* at 934.

43. *Id.* at 937.

44. Myriam Gilles, *Opting Out of Liability: The Forthcoming Near-Total Demise of the Modern Class Action*, forthcoming in the Michigan Law Review.

45. *Id.*

46. In fact, Professor Gilles in her previous article has already suggested a method by which private individuals could join with public officials to aid in the enforcement of civil rights law. *Id.*

ISSUES AND PROBLEMS WITH JOINDER GENERALLY

The problems inherent in class actions, and particularly settlement class actions, may just be an exaggerated example of issues and problems raised by the liberal joinder of parties and claims generally. At the beginning of this chapter, we saw that efficiency considerations repeatedly lay behind the evolution of joinder mechanisms, whether Rule 18 joinder of claims, Rule 20 joinder of parties, Rule 13(a) compulsory counterclaims, Rule 13(b) permissive counterclaims, Rule 42(a) consolidations, Rule 24 intervention, or Rule 14 impleader. Yet, one may question whether such joinder rules truly add to efficiency. For instance, doesn't the compulsory counterclaim, in some instances, force the defendant to bring a claim she might otherwise delay or never bring? Doesn't the joinder of multiple plaintiffs and defendants in some instances complicate issues and extend the litigation? Doesn't a case with every conceivable cause of action joined render the litigation so unwieldy that, in some instances, a judge is tempted to encourage settlement because of the difficulty of disentangling the complications? Doesn't the availability of the class action device provide incentives to litigation and lead to inefficiency, rather than the opposite?

More broadly still, massive joinder of parties and claims may encourage, if not force, judges into a managerial role that has become the hallmark of federal court litigation in the late twentieth and early twenty-first century. To some, this has resulted in a concomitant loss of neutrality on the part of the judiciary and a failure to have law actually applied to facts in open court. Judges, both federal and state, now feel that they have failed if they do not help precipitate a settlement. In cases that do not settle, the complexity of cases with extensive joinder prompts judges into trial techniques that, as we will discuss in Chapter 11, may materially change the experience of the jury and, in some cases, the ultimate outcome. For example, complicated cases as a result of joinder will be "bifurcated" or "trifurcated" by separating out a factual issue for determination by the fact finder before going on to other issues. This can make the trial a more disconnected and antiseptic experience for a juror than it would otherwise be.

Finally, joinder of claims and parties, and particularly the settlement class action, force us to confront once again what the goals of a civil dispute resolution system should be and what the role of lawyers and judges should be. Maybe our view of the simple two-party litigation in which lawyers are obligated to serve the needs of clients, in which the dignity and autonomy of clients are fostered, and in which the judge is merely a neutral referee is empirically inaccurate and normatively undesirable. If, as Deborah Hensler has pointed out, American lawyers are lax about keeping their clients informed and it is the lawyer and not the client who makes most decisions,[47] then the romantic view of litigation with its all-important attorney-client relationship, with the client telling her story with the aid of her attorney is just simply an unrealistic view. Even when clients are permitted to testify in open

---

47. *See* Deborah R. Hensler, *Resolving Mass Toxic Torts: Myths and Realities*, 1989 U. Ill. L. Rev. 89.

court — in the fewer than 2 percent of the cases that are tried — their stories are so circumscribed by evidence law and coaching by lawyers that it may be pure fantasy to think that they have truly been heard.

If the above is accurate, then class actions and other group litigation may deprive the individual litigant of very little but give more in return. In this increasingly global world, problems are no longer isolated individual problems. Environmental pollution crosses borders nationally and inter- nationally, as do economic and trade disputes. So, it may be that the traditional notion of individual-based litigation is frequently no longer applicable and that liberal joinder of parties and claims are inevitable. Ultimately, then, we are back to where we started in this book. What should a society want from its civil litigation process, from the lawyers who participate in it, and the judges who preside over it? To resolve individual disputes? To change social norms? To effectuate governmental policies? What is the place of broad narrative, as in the historic equity case, as opposed to stories confined by stricter rules, as in the historic common law case? How should a civil litigation system allocate power to lawyers, litigants, judges, juries, states, the federal government, corporations, and individuals? Seriously considering the effects of joinder provisions raises normative questions that confront all civil litigation systems wherever and whenever they evolve.

CHAPTER

10

Public Adjudication, Private Resolution, and the Alternative Dispute Resolution Movement

> Persuade your neighbors to compromise whenever you can. Point out to them how the nominal winner is often a real loser – in fees, expenses and waste of time. As a peacemaker, the lawyer has a superior opportunity of being a good man. There will still be business enough.
> Abraham Lincoln, Notes for a Law Lecture, 1850[1]

> Settlement is a capitulation to the conditions of mass society and should be neither encouraged nor praised . . . Civil litigation is an institutional arrangement for using state power to bring a recalcitrant reality closer to our chosen ideals.
> Owen M. Fiss, *"Against Settlement,"* 1984[2]

In 1976, America celebrated the 200th anniversary of the Declaration of Independence. That same year, leaders of the American bar commemorated Roscoe Pound's famous speech, "The Causes of Popular Dissatisfaction with the Administration of Justice,"[3] with a large conference.[4] The tenor of the conference was reminiscent of Pound's 1906 speech in which he asserted that the American "sporting theory" of justice was outdated and that we needed less technical and more scientific procedures. Like the Pound speech, this conference signaled the beginning of a new period of retrenchment for American civil litigation.

The 1938 Federal Rules of Civil Procedure were in many ways the child of Pound's impulse, as rules that would reform the American civil litigation system by allowing judges to dispense justice with minimal procedural interference and broad discretion. At the 1976 Pound Conference, the theme was again that the

---

1. Abraham Lincoln, Notes for a Law Lecture (July 1, 1850), *in* 2 Collected Works of Abraham Lincoln 81 (Roy P. Basler ed., Rutgers U. Press 1953).
2. Owen M. Fiss, *Against Settlement*, 93 Yale L. J. 1073, 1075, 1089 (1984)
3. Roscoe Pound, *The Causes of Popular Dissatisfaction with the Administration of Justice*, 29 A.B.A. Rep. 395, 409-413 (1906).
4. *See* The Pound Conference: Perspectives on Justice in the Future (A. Levin & R. Wheeler eds., West Pub. Co. 1979) (proceedings of the National Conference on the Causes of Popular Dissatisfaction with the Administration of Justice).

civil justice system was askew, that cases took too long and cost too much, and that the system, most particularly discovery, was out of control. Prominent lawyers and judges excoriated what they claimed was the sorry plight of the American civil litigation system; the time had come to reign in this tragically flawed process. You have read some of the results of that impulse: heightened pleading standards, more demanding requirements for lawyer's oaths in filing papers (amended Rule 11), enlarged case management (amended Rule 16), constraints on discovery (amendments to Rule 26 and other discovery rules), less restraint on the use of summary judgment (*Celotex*[5]), and controls on class actions (amendments to Rule 23 and 2005 removal legislation).

Speakers at the Pound conference not only decried the alleged sorry plight of American civil litigation; they also proposed solutions.[6] One of those proposing solutions was Harvard law professor Frank Sander, whose speech, "Varieties of Dispute Processing,"[7] has perhaps become as representative of the times and as widely cited as Pound's speech was 70 years earlier. Sander proposed a "multidoor" courthouse in which litigants would have a choice of not only formal dispute resolution leading to trial, but also a range of other less formal possibilities, such as arbitration and mediation. Although there were precursors to these "alternate" methods of dispute resolution, Sander captured the beginnings of a more intense and sustained movement away from traditional civil litigation and toward a wide range of alternatives. These alternatives to traditional civil litigation and trial, packaged together, became what is now a full-blown movement called Alternative Dispute Resolution or ADR. While informal methods of settling disputes are certainly not unique to any society, the variety of ADR methods, the force of these alternatives as part of a blossoming movement, and the pervasive underlying strain of individual choice have distinct American roots and permutations.

To start, it is not always easy to define exactly what ADR in America means or what it encompasses. One could simply say that alternative dispute resolution is any method of disposing of disputes without trial or without final disposition by a judge through a motion. But this definition would include negotiated settlement as part of ADR, even though lawyers in the formal litigation system had been settling their disputes through negotiation for decades, if not centuries, before ADR became a movement. Another common definition is: "any process or procedure, other than an adjudication by a presiding judge, in which a neutral third party participates to assist in the resolution of issues in controversy . . ."[8] Here, the emphasis is on the use of "a neutral third party" to "assist in the resolution," omitting unaided lawyer negotiation leading to a settlement. For purposes of this chapter, we include judges who attempt to promote settlements as part of ADR; they are third-party neutrals and not

---

5. *Celotex Corp. v. Catrett*, 477 U.S. 317 (1986).

6. We say "alleged" because, as you have read throughout this book and will again read in the next chapter, the empirical data shows that the critiques have been overstated and that in most cases the system is not out of control.

7. Frank E. A. Sander, Varieties of Dispute Processing, in The Pound Conference, *supra* note 4, at 65.

8. 28 U.S.C. § 651(a). Another working definition is "the use of one or more formal processes by the parties to a dispute, other than civil litigation and associated settlement negotiations, to resolve that dispute." Terry L. Trantina, *An Attorney's Guide to Alternative Dispute Resolution* (ADR): ADR 1.01, 1102 PLI Corp. L. & Prac. 29, 37 (1999).

engaged in presiding over trials at the time they are conducting settlement discussions. But we exclude unassisted lawyer negotiation because no third-party neutral is involved

Alternative dispute resolution encompasses traditional and commonly used methods, such as mediation and arbitration, as well as a wide range of more recent experimental methods. In mediation, a third-party neutral helps the parties and their lawyers in the negotiation, with settlement as the usual goal. In arbitration, a third-party neutral hears evidence and renders a decision. Traditionally, arbitrations are thought to be less formal (i.e., evidence rules are relaxed or eliminated), less expensive, and less time consuming than formal trials.

Three conceptual categories capture the wide variety of ADR methods (new and old). One category offers litigants an early, nonbinding case evaluation by experts. Such options include mini-trials or summary jury trials and other neutral evaluations. This category could also include when a judge, prior to trial, tells the parties her assessment of the case, as well as nonbinding arbitration. Such early case assessment helps the litigants and lawyers determine whether the ultimate recovery is worth the expense of continuing with the litigation.

The second category of alternative dispute resolution methods offers litigants a range of resources, other than their own lawyers or other representatives, whose goal is to help reach resolution. The methods in this category include mediation, conciliation (the two are very hard to distinguish), and judicial settlement conferences in which the judge merely facilitates discussions but does not say what she thinks the case is worth. The assumption underlying this second category of alternative dispute resolution methods is that disputes are often unresolved because the parties do not trust each other or communication has broken down between them or they want outside help for other reasons. This category addresses the problem by injecting a third person to facilitate communication and conversation. The line between these first two categories of ADR methods slips easily back and forth, depending on how far a mediating judge or other third-party neutral goes in evaluating the case.

The third category of alternative dispute resolution includes methods that provide a substituted decision maker. Instead of the judge assigned to the case or the jury selected to hear the case, parties in the litigation agree to present their case before a substituted decision maker and abide by the decision reached by that decision maker. Often, this substituted decision maker is an expert in the subject matter of the dispute. These methods include experimental methods such as "rent-a-judge" as well as traditional binding arbitration.

ADR calls to mind all of our major themes for this book: the relationship of the culture at large to the method we choose to resolve disputes, the tension between broader narrative and restriction by rule, the manner in which civil dispute resolution allocates power, and the extent to which the system is deemed legitimate by the society in which it operates. But the dimension that settlement and ADR makes us think about most, and which we hope will also engage your interest, is the question of legitimacy. Will the current trend in privatizing so much of civil litigation, with its movement away from public trials towards private negotiated outcomes, render the outcomes less legitimate? Can private negotiated outcomes have the same ability as formal trial judgments in enforcing public norms and establishing a rule of law applicable to society as a whole? Will individual satisfaction overtake unearthing truth and setting predictable legal rules as the prominent goals for a legal system? At what point will the United States cease to operate under the rule of law, when ordinary citizens cannot afford to go to court and instead, opt for private settlement? Or when these same citizens purchase a service or product with nonnegotiable contracts that forbid them to use the state-sponsored court system? All of these questions force us to revisit what our goals should be for our formal legal system, and with it, for our procedural rules.

HISTORICAL BACKGROUND

Informal methods of civil dispute resolution, including mediation and arbitration, have long existed in American society, starting with the colonies in the early seventeenth century. In his seminal book, Justice Without Law? Resolving Disputes Without Lawyers, Jerold S. Auerbach traced the many ways that members of defined communities (whether by geography, ethnicity, religion, or profession) resolved their disputes in the American colonies and even to this day, without the use of lawyers, government-provided judges, or civil courts.[9] These communities were as varied as the founders of Dedham (a seventeenth-century Christian utopian community in Massachusetts), Quaker elders in Philadelphia, followers of John Humphrey Noyes at Oneida (a nineteenth-century utopian commune), Scandinavians in Minnesota, and even Chamber of Commerce members. One can still find communities in today's America with a strong preference for informal dispute resolution methods. From the Chinese family associations in San Francisco to Hasidic Jews in Williamsburg, Brooklyn, these communities, "[s]hare a suspicion of law and lawyers, [and] developed patterns of conflict resolution that reflected their common striving for social harmony beyond individual conflict, for justice without law."[10]

Yet, the current ADR movement also has more mid-twentieth-century roots. In addition to the earlier communitarian strains, the "community justice movement," which arose in the late 1960s and early 1970s, added to the momentum of ADR.[11] As part of the community empowerment movement, community justice advocates viewed black and poor neighborhoods as alienated from, and disenfranchised by, the surrounding more powerful, richer, and whiter neighborhoods. For them, neighborhood justice centers, controlled by members of local communities were "a means of self-empowerment and building community cohesion and trust."[12] This strand

9. Jerold S. Auerbach, Justice Without Law? 4 (Oxford Univ. Press 1983).
10. *Id.* at 4-5.
11. Deborah R. Hensler, *Our Courts, Ourselves: How the Alternative Dispute Resolution Movement is Re-Shaping Our Legal System,* 108 Penn. St. L. Rev. 165, 170 (2003).
12. *Id.* at 171.

of the ADR movement shared some elements with the informal dispute resolution devices utilized in the earlier homogenous communities described by Auerbach. In emphasizing the transformative power of mediation by allowing participants to hear each other and share in their common destiny of solving disputes, the current ADR movement is akin to some of the seventeenth-century communitarian values of compassion and interconnectedness to one another.[13]

There are, though, considerably less gentle and idealistic and considerably more pragmatic and self-serving strands that also underlie the burgeoning of ADR in America. Economy and efficiency concerns were ever present and played a prominent role, as rising caseloads and decreased public funding added to the clamor for more businesslike management techniques in court administration. According to Deborah Hensler, a well-known and respected empiricist:

> After World War II, [the] laissez-faire judicial system came increasingly under attack. Critics argued that courts needed to adopt a more business-like approach to utilizing public resources, including judge time. A new field of court administration emerged that produced professional 'court administrators' to assist judges in managing their calendars. Courts also began to experiment with different approaches to preparing cases for trial and expediting resolution.[14]

At both the state and federal level, judges were encouraged to engage in settlement conferences with the attorneys, with the hope that this would reduce the need for time-consuming trials. Some municipalities and state courts experimented with conciliation sessions, at which volunteer, unpaid lawyers gave the contesting parties and their lawyers a neutral view of the value of the case; still other courts experimented with mandatory nonbinding arbitration. Ironically, even though later empirical analysis showed that "judicial settlement conference had no effect on trial rates,"[15] these court-management, mediation, and arbitration experiments continued to draw their strength from considerations of efficiency, rather than a search for more communal, gentle, or creative dispute resolution.

Those who condemned the alleged sorry state of civil adjudication at the Pound Conference did not all subscribe to the gentler, more communal ADR strain. Speeches by lawyers and judges talked about efficiency, delay, and expense. They accurately pointed out that the current civil litigation system made it difficult for ordinary citizens with smaller, less profitable cases to find lawyers to take their cases. In a more self-interested vein, some even feared that clients would cease using lawyers in potential litigation matters if the professional bar did not address the problem. As you must know by now, abusive discovery in litigation was frequently listed as the main culprit. This tenor persists today as industries across many sectors place binding arbitration agreements into their form contracts and tickets. Their motivation includes

---

13. *See, e.g.,* Robert A. Baruch Bush & Joseph P. Folger, The Promise of Mediation: Responding to Conflict Through Empowerment and Recognition (Jossey-Bass 1994).
14. Hensler, *supra* note 11, at 174 (citations omitted).
15. *Id.* at 175-176.

promotion of efficiency and a desire for a more favorable forum than traditional litigation, but most probably not a desire for a more cooperative society.

It is the coalescence of these many variables, then, that has propelled ADR. Modern procedure in combination with adversarial lawyers and complicated lawsuits has led to great expense and delay. The burgeoning criminal caseload, in part due to the criminalization of the use of drugs, has left less room for civil trials. Critics of civil litigation wanted a less cumbersome, expensive, time-consuming, abrasive system; while others simply wanted a less intrusive state. Free market choice became the dominant political force, making contract based arbitration and mediation more appealing than litigation before perceived activist judges and plaintiff-friendly juries. And of course, with multiple parties and issues and liberal discovery rules rendering billions of bytes of computer stored information available for public discovery, shortcuts in lieu of full litigation, such as arbitration, mediation, and other ADR devices, are very attractive.

In the federal district courts, mediation and arbitration programs have the longest history dating from the 1970s. The summary jury trial and early neutral evaluation came as innovative methods in the 1980s. A major expansion of ADR in the federal courts occurred in 1988 when Congress authorized ten district courts to implement mandatory arbitration programs and an additional ten districts to establish voluntary arbitration programs. This step was followed by the passage of The Civil Justice Reform Act of 1990 (CJRA), requiring all district courts to develop a district-specific plan to reduce cost and delay. One of the six cornerstone principles of the CJRA was the call to expand and enhance the use of ADR. Five years into the CJRA experiment, most district courts had authorized or established some form of ADR.[16]

With the expiration of the CJRA, court-annexed ADR programs received their next impetus when Congress passed the Alternative Dispute Resolution Act of 1998 (ADRA). The ADRA not only requires courts "to devise and implement" ADR programs, but also authorizes courts to order mandatory mediation or early neutral evaluations and to ensure that already existing ADR programs conform to the ADRA's requirements. The Act represents acceptance and recognition that ADR, when properly supported and administered, "has the potential to provide a variety of benefits, including greater satisfaction of the parties, innovative methods of resolving disputes and greater efficiency in achieving settlements."[17]

Finally, a wide variety of federal and state statutes have now been enacted to authorize ADR.[18] Some of these statutes apply to a specific form of ADR, such

---

16. The Judicial Improvements and Access to Justice Act sets out the basic structure of federal court annexed alternative dispute resolution programs. While each district is also authorized to adopt local rules and variations, the Act generally provides that suits between $50,000 to $150,000 and not involving constitutional claims or conspiracies to interfere with civil rights, be first subjected to nonbinding arbitration. In some districts, parties may make a motion to exempt the case because it involves complex and novel issues or because legal issues predominate over factual issues or because of other good cause. Hearings take place before a single arbitrator or a panel of three and take place 80 to 180 days after filing an answer. After the arbitrator renders a reward, the parties have 30 days to request trial.

17. Alternative Dispute Resolution Act of 1998, Pub. L. No. 105-315, § 2(1), 112 Stat. 2993.

18. *See, e.g.*, New Jersey Alternative Procedure for Dispute Resolution, N.J. Stat. Ann. § 2A: 23A-1 to 23A-19, and the Alternative Dispute Resolution Act of 1998, Pub. L. No. 105-315, 112 Stat. 2993.

as state arbitration acts or the Federal Arbitration Act, or to particular type of disputes, as for example, consumer protection statutes called "lemon laws" that involve automobiles and specifically require ADR prior to litigation. There are also rules for court-annexed ADR for all cases as established by the state and federal civil trial and appellate courts.[19] These rules call for either compulsory or voluntary mediation or arbitration in accordance with rules of court and set out the criteria for the referral, selection of the neutral, and conduct of the court annexed proceedings.

Today, each of the 94 federal district courts has some form of ADR program in place. Most of the federal courts offer at least two ADR procedures, with at least six courts offering a fully array of options.[20] In some courts (close to a dozen in 1995), a full time ADR Coordinator assists the court and attorneys in exploring the various ADR options available to litigants (sometimes called "multidoor dispute resolution," harkening back to Sander's 1976 speech).

Apart from court-sponsored ADR, there is also a wide selection of independent ADR entities outside the court system; they usually charge a fee for their services. Private ADR entities in the United States include the CPR Institute for Dispute Resolution (created by an alliance of major U.S. corporations and some of the nation's leading law firms) that simply assists with the selection of a neutral from their panel, the American Arbitration Association (an international nonprofit entity with regional offices in most states), the National Arbitration Forum, and JAMS/Endispute (a nonprofit organization operating in most of the United States).

As we have already noted, the breadth of ADR methods in the American legal system is astonishing. Some are more formal than others, some more closely tied to the judicial process than others, some more voluntary than others. ADR methods are also sometimes delineated as to whether they are "administered" ADR (that is, under the auspices of a court) or "nonadministered" ADR (through an independent ADR entity, such as the American Arbitration Association, or a local bar association). Nonadministered or part-administered ADR is ADR under the terms of a private agreement that normally pre-selects a neutral third party or provides the basis for selecting a neutral third party. The parties may agree to rules that define their own ADR process or incorporate a standard set of procedural rules created by an ADR entity. We will describe in greater detail each of the ADR methods in turn, as well as the nonassisted settlement of cases.

19. *See, e.g.,* L. Civ. R. 201.1 (Arbitration) and L. Civ. R. 301.1 (Mediation) (D.N.J. 2003), *available at* U.S. Dist. Ct. for Dist. of N.J. Home Page, <http://pacer.njd.uscourts.gov/> (accessed Oct. 8, 2004), local rules for the Federal District Court of New Jersey, establishing the criteria for compulsory ADR, referrals, and rules of conduct for court annexed ADR proceedings.

20. Statistics about ADR programs in the federal courts are from Elizabeth Plapinger & Donna Stienstra, ADR and Settlement in the Federal District Courts: A Sourcebook for Judges and Lawyers (Federal Judicial Center, 1996) (a joint project of the Federal Judicial Center and the CPR Institute for Dispute Resolution).

SETTLEMENT AND THE PRETRIAL CONFERENCE

Most lawsuits in the United States settle. Surprisingly, there is sparse data on exactly how many cases are terminated through settlements, and available data probably differs depending on the court and the type of case. So far as we can tell, approximately two-thirds to 70 percent of civil cases settle.[21] But we do not know whether a higher proportion of cases settle today than 25 or 50 years ago.

From the limited data available, we do know that a much smaller percentage of cases are tried than previously, down to fewer than 2 percent, and that the percentage of summary judgments has increased. There is also reason to believe, given the increase of judges who require heightened pleadings in some types of cases, that there are concomitant increasing numbers of motions granted for failure to state a claim for which relief can be granted. It is possible, then, that the settlement rate has remained fairly constant, with the reduction in trials replaced by granted motions for summary judgment and failure to state a claim or even by dismissals for failure to prosecute the claims, rather than by an increase in settlements.

It is worth asking why parties want to settle.[22] The most important motivation for settlement is, perhaps, uncertainty. There is uncertainty on how general, vaguely worded substantive and procedural rules will be applied. Many of the most important elements in cases — unreasonable care, unfair competition, intentional discrimination, material breach — are difficult to define or determine with certainty. Even more uncertain are how judges or the jury will view the facts. With fewer cases being tried, fewer lawyers have experience with trials, adding another reason to settle.

Ironically, if both sides think they can predict the result of a particular case, this certainty (like uncertainty) also points to settlement. If the outcome were certain, then settlement would be far less time consuming, less expensive, and less intrusive than a public trial. Plaintiffs have learned that trial verdicts, even when they win, are considerably smaller than they had hoped and often difficult to fully collect. Defendants have also learned that plaintiffs' lawyers are quite sophisticated, often have enough capital to sustain massive discovery, and occasionally, win huge verdicts. Most civil cases, then, will inevitably proceed to some settlement discussions, that is, meeting and conversations between party representatives familiar with the case and with the authority to negotiate a settlement to end pending or future litigation.

To further encourage settlement, Fed. R. Civ. P. 68 and similar state rules shift subsequent costs of the litigation (as a sanction of sorts) to a party who wins, but has previously rejected a more favorable offer of settlement. Fed. R. Civ. P. 16 also requires all parties to attend a pretrial conference, listing facilitation of settlement as one of the objectives of the pretrial conference, and authorizing courts to take appropriate action with respect to settlement.

21. Stephen N. Subrin & Thomas O. Main, *The Integration of Law and Fact in an Uncharted Parallel Procedural Universe*, 79 Notre Dame L. Rev. 1981, 2002 n. 95 (2004)[hereinafter Subrin & Main, *Integration*].

22. The reasons behind settlement are discussed in more detail in Stephen N. Subrin, A *Traditionalist Looks at Mediation: Its Here to Stay and Much Better Than I Thought*, 3 Nev. L.J. 196, 202-207 (Winter, 2002/2003).

In a Rule 16 conference, federal judges can require parties or representatives with settlement authority to be present or reasonably available by telephone to consider possible settlement of the dispute. Rule 16 pretrial conferences are sometimes before the judge assigned to the case, but may also be held before a settlement judge or magistrate not assigned to the case. When judges or magistrates conduct a settlement conference, they will often have the lawyers provide an oral summary of each side's case and why each lawyer thinks she should win. The judge or magistrate may engage in one of two roles or both. They might just try to encourage the parties to see the weaknesses in their own case and the strengths in the other side, thus facilitating the parties' meeting somewhere in the middle for a settlement. Or judges and magistrates might go further and tell the parties what they think a fair outcome would be. In other words, if damages are involved, a judge or magistrate might actually tell the parties what she thinks the case is worth. But in either role, the judge functions simply as a facilitator to help disputants communicate and reach an agreement. If the parties do not settle, then the case goes to trial. This is perhaps in contradistinction from civil law countries where failed court assisted settlement may be backed by court-imposed solutions.

Although there is little statistical information for Rule 16 judge-hosted settlement conferences, it is generally accepted that the most common form of settlement assistance used in the federal courts is such conferences. Almost all 94 district courts use judicial settlement conferences, with a third designating magistrate judges as the court's primary settlement officers.[23]

EARLY NEUTRAL CASE EVALUATION

Other ADR methods have been developed to provide the parties with an early neutral evaluation of the case — some quite innovative, but all hand in hand with the formal legal system. Conciliation sessions are mandated in some state courts in which a neutral attorney or group of attorneys, after hearing presentations from each side, tell the litigants and their lawyers how they value the case. The neutral evaluator's determination and assessment is not binding on the parties. The benefits of this process are that it gives parties an opportunity to hear how the opposing party sees her case and how at least one neutral third party would resolve the dispute. The idea is that more information encourages settlement.

Summary jury trial is a method that provides litigants an opportunity to present a shortened version of the case to a sample jury. Live testimony is not normally permitted in a summary jury trial. The sample jury, after hearing the expected evidence through presentations by the lawyers, will render an advisory decision. The jury may also remain for a question and answer period. The parties will then discuss settlement options using the nonbinding advisory decision as a guide. Similar to hearing from judges, magistrates, or neutral lawyers, this neutral evaluation method provides the parties, the lawyers,

---

23. Plapinger & Stienstra, *supra* note 20 at 6.

and the judge an opportunity to know early on how a jury might decide the case and armed with such information, to reach a quicker settlement. Similar to mediation, the process is confidential and closed to third parties. If the process fails, the case goes back on the court calendar.[24]

A final evaluative method is called a mini-trial, at which attorneys present evidence, sometimes with live witnesses, and arguments in a summary presentation of their side's "best case" before party representatives, usually corporate executives with full settlement authority. A neutral advisor presides over these presentations and may ask questions of witnesses or counsel, comment on the arguments, and remark on the importance or admissibility of evidence. After the mini-trial, the party representatives will then meet to discuss settlement possibilities, now with a better understanding of the issues and the strengths and weaknesses of the positions. Often, if the parties still cannot reach settlement, the neutral will serve as a mediator or will render an advisory opinion based on the presentation.

ARBITRATION AND SUBSTITUTED
DECISION MAKERS

Some ADR methods provide final solutions to the case, rather than merely make suggestions. Arbitration is one such long-established method of dispute resolution. Until recent times, it was used primarily in disputes between unionized employees and their employers as mandated in collective bargaining agreements or in disputes between those engaged in commercial transactions.

Arbitration is a consensual process by which parties present positions to a neutral third party or a panel of neutrals with decision-making authority. A neutral arbitration panel, agreed upon by the parties, will normally consist of either one or three neutrals, generally experts in the subject matter of the dispute. Typically, the parties will have agreed to arbitrate even before a dispute arises by the inclusion of an arbitration clause in a contract. Of course, parties who have not previously agreed to arbitrate may still do so.

Arbitration closely resembles the adjudication process, but often in a more summary fashion. In recent years, some arbitrations increasingly resemble formal civil litigation, including a discovery phase, with its concomitant rise in time and costs. In binding arbitration, the decision of the arbitrator is final; in nonbinding arbitration, the decision is merely suggestive.

The arbitration agreement will specify whether an arbitration award is final and binding. Most court-annexed arbitration (that is when a court requires parties to submit to arbitration) is nonbinding with a *de novo* right to trial exercised by either party. However, some jurisdictions discourage demands for trials *de novo* by imposing a financial disincentive (such as costs of the

---

24. The summary jury trial was invented in 1984 by federal court judge Thomas Lambros. Lucille M. Ponte, *Putting Mandatory Summary Jury Trial Back on the Docket: Recommendations on the Exercise of Judicial Authority*, 63 Fordham L. Rev. 1069, 1072 (1995). For criticism of the system, *see id.* at 1078-1084.

arbitration, opponent's trial costs, attorney's fees, expert's fees) if the requesting party at trial does not improve upon the arbitration award.

An arbitration award, unless voluntarily complied with, must be "confirmed" by a court in order to enforce it — that is, enter the award as a court judgment. An arbitration award may not be appealed, but a party may ask the court to vacate an award on very limited grounds. The Federal Arbitration Act only allows a court to vacate an award upon a showing that either "the award was procured by corruption, fraud, or undue means," or the arbitrator misbehaved in some way that caused harm to a party.[25]

Although arbitration has long existed, it was not until 1925 that the Federal Arbitration Act (FAA) established arbitration as a legitimate, significant form of resolving legal disputes.[26] The Supreme Court interpreted the FAA, and the federal policy underlying the Act, as favoring arbitration over litigation.[27] While there are various pros and cons of the different ADR techniques (discussed later), one clear advantage of arbitration is that it relieves the court dockets of a huge volume of cases. At least 48 states, the District of Columbia, and Puerto Rico now have modern statutes governing arbitration.[28] In fact, many states now have mandatory arbitration programs, which require certain categories of cases to be sent through arbitration prior to trial.

Not only are some courts requiring arbitration, but entire industries now require individual employees to forfeit their right to litigate future claims against their employer as a condition of employment. In *Gilmer v. Interstate/ Johnson Lane Corp.*, the Supreme Court held that employers could require new employees to agree to arbitrate any potential claims arising under the Age Discrimination in Employment Act as a condition of employment.[29] As a result of the Court's opinion in *Gilmer*, lower courts have required arbitration in a significant number of employment claims. Such boilerplate, nonnegotiated binding arbitrary clauses have some benefits: They reduce costs for the corporations, and some of that savings may get passed on to the consumer. Moreover, they reduce caseloads for the courts. But there are substantial detriments to employees and consumers resulting from industry-wide mandated binding arbitration clauses, as we will discuss later in this chapter.

Arbitration is the second most frequently authorized ADR program, lagging behind mediation at the federal level. The major group providing arbitrators in the United States is the American Arbitration Association (AAA). One measure of the growth of arbitration in the country is provided by AAA statistics. The AAA reports having administered more than 200,000 arbitration proceedings in 2002. From 1990 to 2002, the AAA's caseload increased 379 percent, as calculated from data provided by the AAA. Businesses increasingly include arbitration clauses in their consumer sales. One recent article suggests that approximately 35 percent of 161 sampled businesses in Los Angeles, California include arbitration clauses in their consumer contracts;

25. 9 U.S.C. § 10(a) (1).

26. Jean R. Sternlight, *Rethinking the Constitutionality of the Supreme Court's Preference for Binding Arbitration: A Fresh Assessment of Jury Trial, Separation of Powers, and Due Process Concerns*, 72 Tul. L. Rev. 1, 9 n.24 (1997).

27. *Moses H. Cone Mem'l Hosp. v. Mercury Constr. Corp.*, 460 U.S. 1, 24-25 (1983).

28. American Arbitration Association, Citations to State Arbitration Statutes, <http:// www.adr.org> (accessed Oct. 7, 2004).

29. 500 U.S. 20, 26 (1991).

the financial, transportation, health care, and retail service industries each had 30 percent or more of their sampled members in this category.[30] Problematically, binding arbitration clauses in consumer tickets and contracts and in employment contracts are usually in small print, not negotiated, and given to consumers and employees at the commencement of the relationship.

Another interesting, more recent form of binding ADR that provides final solutions to the case is the "rent-a-judge" program. In this ADR method, the parties and their attorneys present their case before a private judge selected and employed by the parties. These rent-a-judges can be "temporary judges" or simply referees. In California, there are private trials conducted by referees — both "special" reference proceedings ordered by the court with the findings advisory only and "general" reference proceedings, which are consensual and hence, binding on the parties.[31]

Similar to binding arbitration, the decision reached by the private judge, if the judge is a temporary judge and not a referee, is a final and binding determination. Unlike arbitration, however, the proceeding is nearly identical to formal civil litigation (e.g., the judge wears a black robe; the jury, if any, sits in a jury box; the rules of civil procedure and evidence apply). The benefit of a private judge or private jury is that the litigants take the case out of a congested court docket and are able to have a trial and decision on an expedited schedule. The parties also have control over the selection of the judge. In rarer cases, they also agree among themselves on the selection of a jury. Furthermore, unlike arbitration, these decisions can be appealed, thereby providing the parties the speed of arbitration without the risks.

The rent-a-judge business is growing as the number of retired judges for hire has increased exponentially. In the early 1990s, the Judicial Arbitration & Mediation Services (JAMS), founded in 1979, employed 230 retired judges working out of 14 offices in three states, handling about 13,000 cases a year.[32] But the number of private trials nationwide is still probably small. An 1991 estimate by the Institute for Social Analysis placed private trials at only between 200 and 300 statewide in California. Two problems with rent-a-judge are the potential for "brain-drain" — that is, judges retiring earlier in order to make more money in the private sector, and the issue of judging for profit – whether this results in greater or lesser justice. Both problems have the potential of diluting the legitimacy of our formal, public legal system.

MEDIATION

Mediation is a private, voluntary, and informal process in which the parties select a neutral third party to assist the disputants in reaching a mutually acceptable agreement. The job of the neutral third party is to listen to both

30. Linda Demaine & Deborah Hensler, *"Volunteering" to Arbitrate Through Predispute Arbitration Clauses: The Average Consumer's Experience,* 67 Law & Contemp. Probs. 55, 62, 63 tbl.2 (Winter/Spring 2004).
31. Anne S. Kim, *Rent-a-Judges and the Cost of Selling Justice,* 44 Duke L. J. 166, 169 (1994).
32. *Id.* at 175.

sides (either together or separately) and to facilitate settlement by identifying the specific issues of the dispute, the respective positions and demands, and the relative strengths and weaknesses of their positions.

To encourage frankness in the mediation, this process is generally confidential, which means that what is disclosed in mediation sessions may not be used in subsequent arbitration or court proceedings. Federal Rule of Evidence 408 makes evidence of settlement offers and conduct or statements made in settlement negotiations inadmissible at trial. State laws, however, vary widely in their degrees of confidentiality protection, absent agreement by the parties.[33]

After listening to the opposing sides, the mediator will try to assist the parties in developing a mutually satisfactory resolution of the dispute. Often, the mediator will place the parties in different rooms and go back and forth between them engaging in a form of shuttle diplomacy. The mediator will attempt to show each side the weaknesses in her case and the strength of the opponent's case. However, the mediator lacks authority to decide the dispute and her suggestions are nonbinding. It is up to the parties to actually reach a settlement agreement. A large percentage of the cases that reach a mediator results in settlement, approximately 70 percent is the figure used by many mediators.[34] The mediated settlement is usually reduced to a written contract, with the help of the mediator, signed by the parties, and then, if there is an ongoing case, made part of a formal judgment.

We have previously explained in this chapter why most cases settle. In fact it is difficult to ascertain how any ADR methods have added to the settlement rate, because most civil law suits have settled in the past without any intervention by judges, mediators, or other neutrals. A time-honored adage of trial lawyers is that civil lawsuits will settle "on the court house steps." In other words, the threat of an imminent trial, with all of its costs and risks, will itself precipitate a settlement negotiated by the lawyers.

This then presents us with a mystery. Why are lawyers increasingly turning to mediators, who can charge each party at least $1000 a day and sometimes considerably more, for assistance, when in the past lawyers negotiated settlement on their own?[35] We can only speculate, but changes in the profession that we described in Chapter 2 may play a significant role. There are now so many lawyers, over a million in the United States, from so many different backgrounds, that lawyers cannot know each other nor trust each other as they did in the past. With the increase in incivility, lawyers may need neutrals to help overcome their suspicion, hostility, and adversariness.

33. The drafters of the Uniform Mediation Act last counted some 2,500 statutes around the country that deal with confidentiality in mediations. The Uniform Mediation Act was approved by the American Association on February 4, 2002, and can be found at <http://www.law.u-penn.edu/bll/ulc/mediat/UMA2001.htm> (accessed Oct. 1, 2004). Section 4 includes a provision that says, "a mediation communication is privileged . . . and is not subject to discovery or admissible in evidence in a proceeding unless waived or precluded . . . ." Other sections of the Act provide exceptions to the privilege, including mediations that are open to the public under law and communications related to criminal acts or threats of violence. A court may also override the privilege for information relating to malpractice actions and claims of fraud, duress, or incapacity.

34. *See* Bernard Mayer, Beyond Neutrality: Confronting the Crisis In Conflict Resolution 55-59 (Jossey-Bass 2004).

35. *See* Subrin, *Mediation, supra* note 22, at 207-211, for a more extensive discussion of why lawyers turn to mediation.

Further, with the drop in cases going to trial, litigators may have little or no trial experience and may be less sure of their own abilities to evaluate cases. With increased competition, litigators may also have over sold their clients on the value of their cases (or lack of value if they are representing defendants) in order to get business and need a neutral outsider to help rebalance their client's expectations. Clients may also be more prone to lawyer-shop these days and consequently may not know or trust their lawyers as much as they did in the past.

The costs of preparing for trial and long delays before reaching a trial date in some jurisdictions may cause some litigants to seek resolution at very early stages of the process rather than settle "at the courthouse steps." And the increasing complexity of lawsuits, aided by liberal joinder rules, complicated substantive law, and the increased volume of facts elicited through discovery, make it more difficult for lawyers to untangle the multi-strands of cases. Mediators can help the parties to focus their attention on the most important facts and the most relevant law and then help them assess how a trial might turn out.

All of these factors, and probably many more that we do not yet appreciate, are likely to have joined in varying combinations to make many clients and their lawyers want to engage mediators. But the most important factor may be that lawyers who have engaged in mediations, as well as their clients, seem to like the process. Trials can be anxiety provoking for all involved. In mediation, everyone can be more relaxed and comfortable. We have been at mediations where the mediator provides coffee, tea, cookies, cheese, and crackers. It is not surprising that this experience, for many, is more attractive than waiting for hours in a crowded, often dingy, courthouse and feeling abused, on occasion, by over-burdened judges and clerks.

Further, there is the beauty of choice. Lawyers and their clients usually pick the mediator, rather than having a judge thrust upon them. If the mediation is not proceeding in an acceptable manner, one can just leave. Mediators would argue that it is because of their ability to help forge creative solutions and to lessen animosity among the parties that litigants are increasingly turning to them. This may well be true, but we think that the overall pleasantness of the experience, as compared to trial, and the ability to choose the mediator and to take or leave the process are important parts of the attraction.

A word should be said about the types of mediators. Some mediators, often because of their past experience with their own cases as lawyers, are experts in given fields. This makes them attractive to lawyers with a case in a particular field that calls for some degree of special expertise. The differing personalities and approaches of mediators draw some lawyers to them and not to others. Although most mediators may share characteristics of various types of mediating, three general attitudes are worth noting.

There are some mediators who think their role is limited to facilitating the negotiation by exploring the strengths and weaknesses with the parties and their lawyers. They do not like to, and in some instances refuse to, give their opinion about how the case should settle. Other mediators, and often judges acting as mediators, think they can help achieve settlement best by giving their neutral evaluation of the case. Some lawyers actually turn to judges as mediators so that the judge can tell them and their clients what they think the case is worth.

Still other mediators are at an opposite poll. They believe their role is to improve the ability of the parties to communicate with one another, to hear each other, and to learn how to resolve disputes in a peaceable manner on their own. They think that mediation can be "transformative" in the sense that the participants can be transformed and become more thoughtful, sensitive, accommodating, self-sufficient human beings. Moreover, they believe that, over time, by changing people as well as the situation, the effects of this type of mediation will trickle through society, making it kinder and gentler. However, many facilitating and evaluating mediators think that it is hubris to think that mediation actually transforms participants, let alone society. They think that litigants and their lawyers pay them to help settle cases and that if they can do this with openness, fairness, intelligence, knowledge, and creativity that is quite enough to justify their existence as mediators.

Whatever the style, mediation has spread to virtually every field of law. Traditionally, mediation was thought to be most appropriate in domestic disputes, including divorce and custody battles, in which it was important that the disputants remain cordial so that future friendly communication and accommodation would be possible. Today, it is difficult to name any type of litigation that has not been successfully mediated to settlement. Some industries, such as construction, even use mediation as a matter of course. Mediation is used in employment, tort, contract, commercial, discrimination, patent, trademark, real estate, and neighborhood disputes. Some lawyers and clients are finding that when there are particularly complicated and multi-interest cases, including the importance of meeting public needs, that mediation is especially useful. Environmental protection suits are a prime example.

It is perhaps unsurprisingly then, that the most widely used court-based program in the federal courts is mediation. The same is probably true in state courts.[36] Forty-four states have mediation programs in one or more of their state courts. Regrettably, though, there are no comprehensive statistics revealing how much mediation, or for that matter, any other ADR device, is being used in the aggregate in the United States. This is probably because so much mediation, arbitration, and neutral evaluation either take place in private or in courts without formal documentation. Nonetheless, some data suggests widespread use of mediation.[37] For example, one survey shows that 89 percent of American corporations have utilized mediation to resolve their disputes.[38] In one year, 1997, approximately 125,000 cases were diverted to mediation from the Florida court system.[39]

Mediation has grown so popular that it is rapidly advancing into new and perhaps controversial venues. Criminal mediation, Victim-Offender Media-

36. Deborah R. Hensler, *ADR Research at the Crossroads,* 2000 J. Disp. Resol. 71, 77.

37. For details on the extensive use of mediation in both state and federal courts, *see* Subrin, *supra* note 22, at 229-231.

38. Subrin, *Mediation supra* note 22, at 201, n. 31.

39. The Florida Bar, Bar-Related Issues Background Papers/Alternative Dispute Resolution (ADR), http://www.floridabar.org/DIVCOM/PI/BIPS2001.NSF/1119bd38ae090a748525676f0053b606/bb1f878a7d942a618525669e004d2735?OpenDocument, (accessed Oct. 8, 2004).

tion (VOM), is an early attempt to extend mediation into the criminal realm. In 1993, 16,500 cases were mediated by VOM. There were almost 125 such programs in the United States in 1994.[40] Mediation is also branching onto the Internet: ODR, On-Line Dispute Resolution, is beginning to occur more frequently.[41] The Securities Exchange Commission has approved a plan that would provide for on-line ADR.[42]

A new form of ADR is a mediation/arbitration hybrid wherein a neutral third party will initially act as a mediator attempting to assist the parties in resolving the dispute and then as an arbitrator if the parties are still unable to reach a settlement compromise. A variation of this technique is that the neutral third party will reach a sealed arbitration decision while the parties attempt to settle their dispute. This variation hopes to encourage settlement by the parties themselves by employing a threat of a decision if they are unable to reach a mutually acceptable compromise.[43] ADR has also infiltrated the appeals process. Both state and federal appellate courts have established programs calling for referral of certain civil appeals to compulsory mediation.[44]

In short, mediation seems to be the fastest growing segment of ADR. The freedom of choice in picking the mediator, the ability to leave the mediation whenever one wants, the freedom of deciding whether to accept a settlement, and the other attractions we have described have apparently now won the day for mediation. In many instances, litigators do their most important advocacy and negotiation in front of mediators.

THE PROS AND CONS OF ALTERNATIVE DISPUTE RESOLUTION

The embrace of settlement and ADR in the United States is by no means universal. In one of the most articulate defenses of adjudication and trial, Professor Owen Fiss in his article "Against Settlement"[45] set off a series of debates on the pros and cons of the formal adjudicatory process *vis a vis* settlement and ADR. The debate necessarily revolves around differing assumptions about the appropriate role for our formal court system, and hence, its underlying legitimacy.

Specifically, according to Fiss, settlement is a "capitulation to the conditions of mass society and should be neither encouraged nor praised."[46] Settlement is

40. Terenia Urban Guill, A *Framework for Understanding and Using ADR*, 71 Tul. L. Rev. 1313, 1327 (1997).

41. See Beatrice Baumann, *Electronic Dispute Resolution (EDR) and the Development of Internet Activities*, 52 Syracuse L. Rev. 1227 (2002).

42. ADR World.com, SEC Approves NASD Plan to Implement Internet-Based Arbitration Filing System, <www.adrworld.com/sp.asp?id=27245> (accessed Oct. 7, 2004).

43. Elizabeth Hunt, *ARB-MED: ADR in the New Millennium*, 42 Orange County Law 29 (January 2000).

44. For results of the Massachusetts experience with mediation of appellate cases, *see* Mass. Supreme Judicial Court, Annual Report on the State of Mass. Court System for FY 1999, at 42 (Mass. 2000).

45. Owen M. Fiss, *Against Settlement*, 93 Yale L.J. 1073 (1984).

46. *Id.* at 1075.

problematic because consent is often coerced due to imbalance of power, judicial enforcement is limited, and justice may not be done. Fiss argues that although both settlement and formal adjudication can be subject to the inequalities of resources and the imbalance of power that can distort results, formal adjudication "knowingly struggles against these inequalities" and at the very least aspires to "an autonomy from distributional inequalities, and it gathers much of its appeal from this aspiration."[47] Fiss sees judges as the bulkhead against such inequalities who can lessen such inequalities by testing the actions of the "representatives" against independent procedural and substantive legal standards. With ADR, held only "in the shadow of the law," parties are deprived of whatever formal protection is given them by the legal system, such as full discovery or the right to a jury.

For example, mediation, required by many state courts for divorce and other domestic cases, can be especially detrimental to women who are often economically less powerful than the men they are divorcing. Mediation with its focus less on the assertion of right and justice, but more on reaching agreement, may make it difficult to assert rights, even those legally guaranteed for women, the poor, and minorities.[48] Admittedly, these criticisms have considerably less bite when the litigants engaged in mediation have lawyers and a realistic opportunity to withdraw from the mediation and return, with representation, to a courtroom.

Fiss also argues that many cases require judicial involvement not only in their adjudication, but also, in their enforcement — for example, school desegregation, antitrust and reorganization of industry, and even divorce cases with resultant custody decrees. Settlement may impede vigorous enforcement of norms by rendering it under the guise of private agreement rather than a legal judgment. Absent judicial involvement, settlement precludes the role of courts to protect the rights of nonparties who may be affected by the private resolution of the dispute. Fiss points to such litigation mechanisms as class actions and mandatory joinder of parties and their procedural safeguards (Rule 23 and Rule 19, for example) as evidence of the ability of courts to protect absent interests in a formal litigation absent interests that would otherwise not be heard in private settlement negotiations.

Fundamentally, Fiss also argues that ADR proponents trivialize the role of lawsuits to simply resolving private disputes. In perhaps his most passionate argument, Fiss reminds us that the purpose of adjudication is broader than settling a private dispute between individuals. Rather, the role of adjudication is a forum for the articulation of public values embedded in our laws and in the Constitution. The resolution of a civil litigation gives force to public values. Civil litigation is not simply to maximize the ends of private parties or to secure peace between disputing parties. Rather, "[c]ivil litigation is an institutional arrangement for using state power to bring a recalcitrant reality closer to our chosen ideal."[49] By contrast, settlements deprive courts of the opportunity to render legal interpretations and to make pronouncements of public norms.

47. *Id.* at 1078.
48. Trina Grillo, *The Mediation Alternative: Process Dangers for Women*, 100 Yale L.J. 1545, 1564-1565 (1991).
49. Fiss, *supra* note 45 at 1089.

Fiss views ADR as an attack on the activist state and criticizes ADR for its lack of procedural protections for those less powerful. Settlement, he writes, "permits private actors with powerful economic interests to pursue self-interest free of community norms."[50] Fiss outlines the universe of cases that should be adjudicated rather than settled. These include

> cases in which there are significant distributional inequalities; those in which it is difficult to generate authoritative consent because organizations or social groups are parties or because the power to settle is vested in autonomous agents; those in which the court must continue to supervise the parties after judgment; and those in which justice needs to be done or...where there is a genuine social need for authoritative interpretation of law.[51]

Indeed, the most forceful argument against ADR is that ADR solutions might stifle the development of law in particular areas and discourage the assertion of rights. ADR detractors point out that one public function of law and legislators in democratic societies is to reflect the public resolution of irreconcilable differences; an example is the civil rights case. Private ADR resolutions are usually confidential, and therefore society is deprived of the public lessons that might be drawn from a public trial and the courts are deprived of the opportunity to craft and adjust legal norms for future application. Courts serve a public role that private resolution cannot replace.

More pragmatic objections to ADR include the argument that mediation is often misused as simply a delaying tactic or as an opportunity to obtain free discovery. Others criticize arbitration for the arbitrator's often seemingly willingness to split the difference and to allow random and unselective presentation of issues, evidence, and witnesses. There is the legitimate concern that sometimes substantial costs are forced on consumers and employees who agree to arbitration through an arbitration clause in a form contract and that the business organizations imposing the arbitration clauses are repeat players and may have an advantage before arbitrators whom they hire frequently. These criticisms go less to the philosophical underpinnings of ADR and can be perhaps addressed through the use of more competent and experienced neutrals and by courts refusing to enforce binding arbitration clauses forced on unwary consumers. So far, however, the courts have not been very protective of consumers and employees in this regard.

A final critique of ADR points to the failure of empirical evidence to demonstrate that ADR-resolved cases would not have otherwise settled or that there are savings of time and money when ADR methods are used. By contrast, when mediation, nonbinding arbitration, or other neutral evaluation methods are used, they cost time and money, and are in addition to, not in place of, the formal litigation process. Consequently, critics argue, there is often additional expense and time, not less. One logical answer to this critique is that when ADR is utilized at earlier points in the litigation, prior to a protracted discovery process, for instance, it will inevitably save time and money.

---

50. Owen M. Fiss, *Out of Eden*, 94 Yale L.J. 1669, 1672 (1985) (quoting Milner Ball, The Promise of American Law: A Theological, Humanistic View of Legal Process (U. Ga. Press 1981)).
51. Fiss, *supra* note 45, at 1087.

Proponents of ADR both directly refute the Fiss positions and add considerations that he ignores or, in their view, undervalues. At an initial level, they argue that Professor Fiss unrealistically places too much value on the ability of courts and judge to protect against inequalities of power. Proponents of ADR point out that judges and juries are likely to have the same prejudices against the poor and minority groups as mediators or arbitrators and the rest of society. Elected judges are not apt to go out of their way to protect noncontributors to their campaigns and infrequent voters. It may be that Fiss had liberal activist judges in mind when he lauded formal adjudication, not the current federal judiciary who, for the most part, has embraced the proclaimed view of judicial restraint.

Proponents of ADR also chide Fiss for equating justice with law, arguing instead that "[j]ustice is not usually something people get from the government. And courts...are not the only or even the most important places that dispense justice."[52] Rather, justice is something people give to one another. ADR helps vindicate community values and the attack on ADR is viewed as an attack on community, religious, or other norms and values.

Proponents further argue that the assertion of rights and the one side-take-all results of traditional litigation do not necessarily lead to balanced, fair solutions. Rather, proponents of ADR argue that ADR can lead to better solutions. By avoiding the zero-sum game of litigation, ADR can reach creative and novel solutions that are unbounded by legal rules and remedies. Matters and issues can be considered that are deemed "irrelevant" under the traditional litigation rules. Solutions need not be clouded by "issue obscuring procedural rules," but rather, can be better fitted to the dispute, because they are negotiated by parties who are familiar with the underlying dispute.

For example, in mediation, parties often have the benefit of directly presenting a case or defense to the opposing party rather than through a lawyer. In a business dispute, the business executive may be able to respond quicker and better to proposed solutions than the lawyer for the case. In some modes of ADR, such as arbitration or mediation, the solution is better fitted because the case is argued or negotiated before neutrals with expertise in the particular area of the dispute selected by the parties.

In the kind of public lawsuits that Fiss advocates, ADR proponents further suggest the "polycentric" nature of these problems renders the all or nothing result of the formal court process inappropriate.[53] These complex disputes may be best resolved through mediated solutions that can take account of multiple variables and interests and not be encumbered by the formalities of court procedure and evidence. At the other extreme, there are smaller cases, the resolution of which involves the application of well-established legal principle. In these kinds of cases, the argument is that something more efficient than a full-blown litigation is more appropriate for their resolution.[54] The focus is on resolution rather than proclamation of rights.

Pragmatic concerns also underlie ADR proponents. Adversarial fact finding, it is asserted, is expensive and unpredictable. The assumption is that more

52. Andrew W. McThenia & Thomas L. Schaffer, *For Reconciliation*, 94 Yale L.J. 1660, 1664-1665 (1985).
53. Lon L. Fuller, *The Forms and Limits of Adjudication*, 92 Harv. L. Rev. 353, 394-397 (1978).
54. Sander, *supra* note 7, at 65-86.

process adds to the costs, and formality adds to more process. ADR methods take the case in some measure out of the traditional civil litigation process and because of their relatively abbreviated and informal procedure, save time and expense. The statistics seem to support this: The U.S. Department of Justice reported that in 2003, litigants and the government saved an average of $10,000 per case that went to mediation. In addition, 89 hours of labor per case were avoided along with 6 months of litigation.[55] The costs of litigation without mediation, by contrast, are high and more difficult for the poor to absorb than the corporations and others who most frequently oppose them in litigation.

Instead of adversarial fact finding, ADR proponents make the "broken-telephone" theory of dispute resolution, suggesting that many disputes are simply failures to communicate. Unlike the adversarial system, ADR can provide the "repair" to this broken line of communication in the form of an expert facilitator.[56] In restoring and building trust, ADR overcomes the hostility fostered by the adversary system and can lead the parties to settle their differences.

The direct involvement by clients in some ADR mechanisms further minimizes problems arising from the self-interest of the lawyer. With the help of a third-party neutral, solutions are reached that are less tied to the motivations and agendas of the lawyers involved. ADR can reach solutions without the distortions rendered by the sharp tactics and bluffs of traditional unaided lawyer settlement negotiations. Properly designed ADR, proponents continue, will make it more likely that settlement is based on merits rather than on procedural technicalities or tactical maneuverings and more likely to be enforced as well. Because the parties have agreed to the solution, they will be more likely to abide by it voluntarily than if the solution were imposed by a court. Indeed, party participation in decision making will render the parties more vested in the outcome of the case than would simply presentation to a neutral decision maker.

Finally, proponents of ADR find two critiques to be particularly misplaced.[57] The first is that litigants who partake of an ADR process are deprived of their opportunity to be heard in open court. Without ADR, proponents point out, most cases settle and in the normal non-ADR settlement, the lawyers do the negotiating and parties are not heard from at all, nor do they even hear their own lawyer present their case. In mediation, on the other hand, the clients are frequently present. They sometimes speak in their own behalf, and they almost always have the opportunity of hearing their lawyer advocate to the neutral mediator and of hearing directly the arguments of the opposing side. Although this is not in open court, it does provide considerably more participation in the process than clients normally receive in the cases that settle without a mediator.

55. Jeffrey Senger, Federal Dispute Resolution: Using ADR with the United States Government 3-4 (Jossey-Bass 2004). There is, though, evidence that ADR is not usually cost effective, because it is frequently in addition to, rather than in place of, formal litigation.

56. Jethro K. Lieberman & James F. Henry, *Lessons from the Alternative Dispute Resolution Movement*, 53 U. Chi. L. Rev. 424 (1986).

57. These and other arguments for and against mediation are spelled out in more detail in Subrin, *supra* note 22, at 215-225.

The second critique, which is part of the Fiss position, is that ADR participants are denied the benefits of having the law applied to the facts of their case or, in other words, of having their rights vindicated. ADR proponents argue that it is untrue that mediations (let alone arbitration or neutral evaluation) are lawless enterprises. Lawyers' presentations to mediators concentrate on the facts of the case and the applicable law. The mediator's questions to both sides will be about the facts and the law, in addition to other considerations. In fact, most ADR mechanisms overtly concentrate on the application of law to facts in fuller ways then do non-ADR negotiations in which the lawyers quickly get to dollar figures without necessarily talking about the law and facts in the case.

As we will elaborate further at the end of this chapter, ADR proponents and detractors both tend to overlook the weaknesses and overstate the strengths in their positions; they also tend not to appreciate the commonalities and symbiotic relationship of traditional litigation and ADR methods. Where one stands in this debate may depend on how one views the priorities of our legal system – to resolve private disputes or to establish public norms. But at some level, perhaps the abstract pros and cons of ADR are less important than what is actually taking place. While binding arbitration clauses inserted in form contracts may not speak to the value of arbitration (except from the business point of view of the industry mandating these clauses), the voluntary use of mediation by opposing sides, at their own cost, speaks volumes. The rising use of ADR, especially now that more consumers are using mediation without the mandate of courts, must mean that lawyers believe they and their clients are receiving something valuable. Perhaps they are voting for ADR through their pocketbooks. Perhaps they are also revealing a changing culture in the legal profession and changing attitudes of the profession and society at large towards litigation and dispute resolution.

A DIFFERENT KIND OF LAWYERING?

The growth of ADR coincides with the general dissatisfaction that American society has with lawyers and adversarial lawyering. This invites several questions. Did the ADR movement herald a new kind of lawyer or a more civil lawyer? What is the role of lawyers in ADR? What new skills does ADR demand from a lawyer? What new ethical dilemmas are lawyers facing in ADR?

First, let us examine what roles lawyers play in ADR. There are multiple functions that lawyers can render in ADR — as legal advisors to the parties, as the dispute resolver, or as legal advisor to the dispute resolver.[58] In the pre-ADR phase, the lawyer can help parties identify appropriate ADR alternatives. In the ADR proceeding itself, a lawyer can participate as an advocate if the proceeding is one in arbitration, mini-trial, summary jury trial, or private judging. Lawyers also act as advocates at mediation sessions, while at the same

58. Frank E. A. Sander & Beth A. Paulson, Alternative Dispute Resolution: An ADR Primer 5 (3d ed., American Bar Association Standing Committee on Dispute Resolution 1989).

time they act as negotiators. During the review phase, the lawyer can be the educator, investigator, drafter, or reviewer of the draft agreement. And in many courts, lawyers have taken on the role of the neutral dispute resolver. Lawyers, usually after some type of brief training leading to certification, are frequently the mediator or arbitrator in both state and federal courts.

As an indication of greater recognition of ADR and of the new skills that might be required, law schools have added ADR and negotiation and mediation to their curricula. Generally speaking, teachers of negotiation and mediation argue that they are engaged in an effort to condition law students away from destructive hostility and away from the lawyer's "philosophical map" with its assumption of adversarial parties and rule-bound solutions.[59] The argument is that litigation and "litigators" assume that the matters they handle are adversarial — that is, if one wins, the other must lose and that the dispute is resolvable through application of some general rule of law. By contrast, mediation and mediators assume that frequently all parties can benefit through an agreed-upon, creative solution and that the situation is unique and therefore not to be governed by any general principle except to the extent the parties accept it.[60]

As a result, the skills of mediators are arguably different from those of litigators, with sensitivity occupying a prominent place on a mediator's list of skills. Mediators must be aware of interconnections between the parties and the qualities of these connections. They must be sensitive to emotional needs and recognize the importance of goals other than what law can provide, such as mutual respect, equality, and security.

While mediators share some common skills, they do vary in their approach. Some mediators merely act as a go-between; others give suggestions. Some mediators separate parties, others insist on keeping them together. Some urge parties to come up with their own proposal and some apply economic, social, or moral pressure. However, all mediators must manage communication and intervene when necessary. Mediators must perceive the underlying emotional, psychological, and value orientations of the parties and the dispute.

As we pointed out in the previous chapter on motions, written advocacy has taken on new importance in recent years. ADR has also followed this trend. Mediators, for example, frequently request that the lawyers for the parties provide brief memoranda explaining their view of the case, based on the relevant facts and the applicable law.[61] This exercise forces lawyers to focus the case on their strongest facts, causes of action, defenses, and legal theories; at the same time, they must at least give the appearance of listening to the other side, paying attention to the suggestions of the mediator, and engaging in the process of creative problem solving. The integration of law and fact took place more naturally under common law writ and code pleading; codes required the plaintiff to state the facts constituting her cause of action. By contrast, modern Federal Rule pleading requires little definition and structure. There is therefore a certain irony that mediation,

59. Leonard L. Riskin, *Mediation and Lawyers*, 43 Ohio St. L.J. 29, 43-44 (1982).
60. *Id.*
61. This topic is spelled out in more detail in Subrin & Main, *supra* note 21.

thought to be an alternative to traditional litigation, so frequently demands a fact-law integration, in writing.

What new ethical conduct is required of lawyers as a result of ADR? Courts today expect lawyers to be knowledgeable about ADR in general and about each court's ADR programs. A number of state bar associations have either amended or are considering amending ethical codes that impose a mandatory ethical duty on lawyers to discuss ADR with clients. Many courts' local rules also now require attorneys to discuss ADR with their clients,[62] to address in their case management plan the appropriateness of ADR, and be ready for a Rule 16-type settlement meeting. In many courts, case management conferences are the critical event in determining how and when ADR will be used in the case.

There are further ethical issues for lawyers serving as neutrals in ADR. For example, what is the neutral attorney's role as a mediator when the settlement agreement is patently unfair? Is her responsibility simply to help parties reach agreement or must she ensure that parties reach fair agreements? And what is the responsibility of the neutral attorney if detrimental information comes out during mediation? What if the information relates to domestic abuse or potential domestic abuse? And fundamentally, what training is sufficient before a lawyer can competently serve as a neutral? Other ethics issues can arise in ADR proceedings, such as advocates' puffery or "strategic use of the truth." There is also the question of what subsequent use can be made of confidential information gained in mediation sessions.

Increasingly, courts have attempted to address some of these questions by developing ethical guidelines or standards of practice for ADR neutrals. Mediators, meanwhile, are guided by the Model Standards of Conduct for Mediators promulgated in 1994 by the ABA Dispute Resolution Section, the American Arbitration Association, and the Society for Professionals in Dispute Resolution.[63] The standards include principles of party self-determination and mediator competence and impartiality. The American Arbitration Association has declared similar ethic codes for arbitrators in commercial cases and labor-management cases.

SHIPS PASSING IN THE NIGHT

The debate between ADR proponents and litigation advocates sometimes delineates ADR as a preference for private ordering and litigation as one for public resolution, ADR as protective of community values and civil litigation of individual rights. Yet, by comparison to legal systems in other countries, both litigation and ADR in the American adversary system represent more a preference for private ordering over public control and preservation of individual choice over community interests.

---

62. But note that the ABA Commission on the Evaluation of the Rules of Professional Conduct, known as Ethics 2000 Commission, has declined to include an express requirement in its review of the Model Rules that lawyers tell clients of alternatives to litigation.

63. The Model Standards of Conduct for Mediators are *available at* <http://www.abanet.org/dispute/modelstandardardsofconduct.doc> (accessed Oct. 1, 2004).

In the American system, even in the "public" sphere of civil litigation, it is still the private, individual parties who shape and control the public litigation. Much of newsworthy American civil litigation is a result of the "private attorney general" concept — that is, the enforcement of public norms in the form of a civil case brought by private individuals. Similarly, by comparison to other more state-dominated countries, even mediation enthusiasts in the United States are enthusiasts of private ordering and individual choice. American support for mediation relies heavily on notions of individual choice and consent, enhancing party control and furthering the policy of minimum state intervention. In the American legal system, whether in litigation or mediation or other ADR methods, it is the individual party who has the primary responsibility in amassing evidence, presentation of the case, and reaching resolution.

Furthermore, one cannot assume a strict dichotomy between litigation and ADR. In the adversarial system context, ADR works in conjunction with and in the shadow of litigation. Trial results are used as guidelines for ADR resolution, and private bargaining often takes place in the shadow of threat of litigation and trials. It may be that the proponents and opponents of ADR are in some respects like "ships passing in the night." Their arguments often do not really engage each other, and some of their positions, in the heat of argument, may be overstated.

For example, ADR enthusiasts do not like to talk about the binding arbitrations that arise from nonnegotiated contracts and tickets; but if one cares about the interests of employees and consumers, these binding clauses are not easy to defend. Then, too, ADR proponents act as if the clients are in fact listened to in mediations. However, we are aware of judges who when mediating, talk infrequently to the clients; they usually meet only with the lawyers and quickly get to the bottom line of what it will take to settle the case. There are undoubtedly non-judge mediators of much the same ilk. Such mediations are not the friendly, cooperative, issue-expanding, creative enterprises that ADR proponents like to talk about.

Similarly, litigation enthusiasts tend to forget that most cases settle; that trial results can be highly unpredictable; that judges can be ornery and outright biased; that juries can be extremely unpredictable; and that the formal system, particularly in federal court, has frequently become so inundated with discovery and so full of conferences and mandated preconference and pretrial memoranda that lawyers are fleeing from the courthouse and seeking other forums. Admittedly, one cannot ignore Fiss's argument that the judiciary has roles to play in setting public norms; roles that mediators and arbitrators cannot fulfill. But he tends to undervalue, if not ignore, the bulk of litigation that deals with such mundane matters, but important to litigants, of torts and breaches of contract that ADR serves.

At a structural level, the asserted delineation between courts and private alternative methods are surely overblown. Wayne McIntosh has pointed out that the state is and always will be present in the market place of dispute resolution institutions.[64] Since the 1960s and 1970s, courts have increasingly

64. *See* Wayne McIntosh, The Appeal of Civil Law: A Political-Economic Analysis of Litigation (U. Ill. Press, 1990).

annexed ADR, and in so doing, transformed ADR methods into a more legalistic and formal process, with many of the same problems of congestion and bias formerly lodged against the courts. Scholars, such as Sally Merry, argue that court-sponsored ADR is presenting a less distinctive alternative to court litigation.[65] For example, a comparison of the way interpersonal cases are handled in court-annexed mediation and the process they receive in court suggest that both involve similar processes and outcomes, with similar problems of routinization and mediator burnouts as the problems plaguing the courts. For some, the most important question is not how, but whether the formal legal process should so dominate all disputes.

Ultimately, the fact is that ADR needs the formal courts. There must be a formal dispute resolver of last resort; otherwise most litigants, especially defendants, would frequently not show up at all. And so, the real question for us is not whether ADR or formal adjudication is better, but rather, when one method or the other works better, how to improve both formal adjudication and alternatives, and how ADR and formal adjudication can best complement each other.

To the extent that dispute resolution methods reflect societal values and priorities, each society's choice of one method over another, how to integrate formal and less formal systems, and how to deal with the ambiguities within these methods may be specific to that society. As we have stressed, though, for reasons of elemental fairness and social harmony, those who are engaged in litigation, and the rest of society as well, must consider the system legitimate. The choices in constructing a litigation system in any country should be conscious ones that weigh the priority and proper balance between conflicting goals — resolving private disputes or setting public normative standards, formal procedural justice or consensual private accommodations, and efficiency or fairness. At a minimum, those interested in improving dispute resolution in society must recognize and understand how any chosen method of dispute resolution can affect, inhibit, or promote these goals and many others.

There are four major issues that ADR has caused us to ponder. We suspect that it would be useful for observers of civil litigation in other countries to think about them as well. First, it would be enormously helpful to have a good deal more hard data. We do not really know how many cases settle. We do not know if neutral interventions provided by ADR mechanisms in fact increase the number of settlements. We do not know the extent to which lawyers, absent mandates from the courts, are choosing some form of ADR on their own or whether, in the main, ADR is cost effective. In this chapter, as in others, we wish we had more extensive, concrete, reliable, sophisticated data of both a quantitative and qualitative nature. With more and better empirical work, normative decisions by policy makers and strategic choices by lawyers could be made with less ignorance.

The other three issues relate to direct challenges of ADR to the formality of the civil litigation system.[66] First, formal systems presuppose substantive and

65. Sally Merry, *Book Review: Disputing Without Culture,* 100 Harv. L. Rev. 2057, 2070 (1987).
66. *See, e.g.,* Paul D. Carrington, *Civil Procedure and Alternative Dispute Resolution,* 34 J. Leg. Ed. 298 (1984).

procedural law that will provide an acceptable degree of predictability and hence, legitimacy. Clients should know what to expect from the law in their daily behavior and lawyers should be able to predict results. The flight away from trial, and in some instances the flight to ADR, may signal that there can be so much law that lawyers and clients do not know what to expect from the courts, that the law does not provide fixed standards that they can apply with any degree of certainty. To put it another way, a lot of law and a lot of procedural steps may not serve a major goal of formalism: predictability and lack of arbitrariness.

A second and related challenge of ADR to court adjudication is the question of what the system should demand of its participants. Consider the litigation steps that are now integral to the federal system: pleadings; motions; mandatory disclosure in three stages — initial, experts, pretrial; memoranda for discovery conference; discovery; memoranda for each subsequent pretrial conference; lists of witnesses and contested evidence issues; and briefs. Perhaps lawyers in seeking arbitration, rented judges, or mediation are telling the formal system that in most cases too many steps are being asked of litigants. Turning every case "into a federal case" with all of the available litigation steps may not make a lot of sense. ADR should force reconsideration of not how much, but how little process we should require of the normal case.

And third, there is the issue of adversariness and the lawyers' roles. Much of the litigating lawyer's work is in the nature of getting the case ready to settle, with or without a mediator. It is rarely a matter of going to trial. Rather, it is the pretrial steps such as incisive and focused discovery, written advocacy in the nature of demand letters and written statements for mediators, advocacy at pre-trial conferences, writing summary judgment memoranda, advocacy before mediators, and negotiation, that are increasingly becoming the critical skills. This does not mean that being competitive and adversarial are no longer desirable traits for American lawyers. It does mean that cooperation, written communication, and collaboration skills have become more critical.

In short, ADR has made us think long and hard about whether aspects of the American litigation system with their attending procedures, which we have taken for granted and applauded, are as necessary, realistic, and salutary as we thought. At the same time, ADR has also forced us to revisit the considerable values of formalism, particularly for the weak in society, and the critical need for traditional courts to provide judges who judge and who make law more predictive and just. In the present day mantra of "rule of law," these questions help us to be ever more thoughtful in any reform or construction of legitimate legal systems.

CHAPTER
11

Trials and Juries

The jury is pre-eminently a political institution; it must be regarded as one form of the sovereignty of people;... The jury, and more especially the civil jury, serves to communicate the spirit of the judges to the minds of all the citizens; and this spirit, with the habits that attend it, is the soundest preparation for free institutions.[1]

   Alexis de Tocqueville, Democracy in America, Pt. I, 283, 284 (Alfred A. Knopf, Inc. 1999)

[F]or many of the millions of Americans who have exercised the power and experienced the responsibility, jury service turns out to be an unforgettable and even transforming experience.... Nearly every juror interviewed for this book is proud of the job he or she did, proud of the seriousness of deliberations. More than when they vote, or pay taxes, or attend a parade, they are realizing the democratic vision that still sustains our nation: They are governing themselves.

   Stephen J. Adler, The Jury: Trial and Error in the American Courtroom 242 (Times Books 1994)

The jury system puts a ban upon intelligence and honesty, and a premium upon ignorance, stupidity, and perjury. It is a shame that we must continue to use a worthless system because it was good a thousand years ago.

   Mark Twain, Roughing It 309 (1872)

Even in the best of cases trial by jury is the apotheosis of amateurs. How can anyone think that 12 people selected at random in twelve different ways with the only criterion being a complete lack of general qualification, would have special ability to decide on disputes between people?

   Erwin N. Griswold, Harvard Law School, Dean's Report 5-6 (1962-1963)

WHY DO WE HAVE THIS CHAPTER?

Ironically, it is not obvious why a book on American civil process and procedure should have a chapter on trials and juries. Two professors at the

---

1. The four quotes at the beginning of this chapter have been taken from Stephen N. Subrin, Martha L. Minow, Mark S. Brodin, & Thomas O. Main, Civil Procedure: Doctrine, Practice, and Context, 421-422, 427-428, 429 (Aspen Law & Business 2000).

University of Michigan Law School put it this way: "If it is true, as we often hear, that we are one of the most litigious societies on earth, it is because of our propensity to sue, not our affinity for trials."[2]

As we have already mentioned in earlier chapters, the percentage of civil cases in the United States going to trial has dramatically declined. In 1940, 15.2 percent of civil cases in federal court terminated at or after trial. This number fell to 5 percent in 1984, or "approximately one-third of the percentage of cases that got to trial at the time the Federal Rules were adopted."[3] In the 1990s, of all the civil cases filed nationally in both state and federal courts, only 2.9 percent went to trial and approximately half of those were tried to a judge sitting without a jury.[4] By 2003, less than 1.8 percent of civil cases terminated in federal court resulted in trials (judge or jury).[5] Trials are indeed few in the United States and the pressure to settle or otherwise dispose of cases intense.

Yet, even though less than 1.8 percent of terminated civil cases in the United States federal courts are tried and even less, to a jury, over 80 percent of jury trials in the world are conducted in the United States. Members of the Advisory Committee on the Federal Rules of Civil Procedure continue to reiterate that "it was a mistake to view trial as a pathological event, resulting from settlement miscalculations of the parties. The system is designed to provide trials."[6] What can account for the continued support of trials and the jury trial? Why is it important, in explaining our legal civil process to the legal community of another country or to undergraduate or law students, to explain the American trial and the American jury? Why is the American legal system still designed around the driving force of a possible jury trial?

The answer usually given is that although trials are relatively few, lawyers negotiate the settlement of civil cases "in the shadow"[7] of possible trials. It is often the threat of trial, its costs, and the very unpredictability of results that precipitate settlement. The contradiction of trials has been aptly expressed, "[o]ur culture portrays trial — especially trial by jury — as the quintessential dramatic instrument of justice. Our judicial system operates on a different premise. Trial is a disease, not generally fatal, but serious enough to be avoided at any reasonable cost."[8]

The picture of trials is the predominant cultural icon of the American legal system. By contrast to the civil law tradition of discontinuous trials, the common law tradition is one in which one or more preliminary pretrial

---

2. Samuel R. Gross & Kent D. Syverud, *Don't Try: Civil Jury Verdicts in a System Geared to Settlement*, 44 UCLA L. Rev. 1, 1-2 (1996).

3. Richard L. Marcus, *Completing Equity's Conquest? Reflections on the Future of Trial under the Federal Rules of Civil Procedure*, 50 U. Pitt. L. Rev. 725, 726 n.11 (1989).

4. Gross & Syverud, *supra* note 2, at 2 n.2 (citing Theodore Eisenburg et al., *Litigation Outcomes in State and Federal Court: A Statistical Portait* 7 (May 7, 1995).

5. Leonidas Ralph Meacham, Judicial Business of the United States Courts: 2003 Annual Report of the Director 150 tbl.C-4. (Administrative Office of the U.S. Courts, 2003).

6. Ed Cooper, Reporter, Minutes of Advisory Committee on Civil Rules 20 (Oct. 21-23, 1993) (discussion on amending Rule 68 to increase sanctions for failing to settle), *cited in* Judith Resnick, *Many Doors? Closing Doors? Alternative Dispute Resolution and Adjudication*, 10 Ohio St. J. on Disp. Resol. 211, 261 n.200 (1995).

7. Robert H. Mnookin & Lewis Kornhauser, *Bargaining in the Shadow of the Law: The Case of Divorce*, 88 Yale L. J. 950, 950 (1979), in which the phrase "bargaining in the shadow of the law" was evidently coined.

8. Gross & Syverud, *supra* note 2, at 3.

meetings set the stage for and culminate in a single trial at which the evidence is received sequentially and orally through witnesses. The oral, uninterrupted telling of the dispute renders the American trial uniquely poised for drama and display. And so, even though trials are infrequent, the image and specter of trials are ingrained in our culture and continue to be the driving force on how we structure our civil litigation process.

The emphasis on jury, as distinct from judge, trials marks America apart from even other common law countries such as England or Canada. While approximately half of American civil cases that do go to trial are tried before a lay jury, presided over by a judge, other common law countries have abolished the civil jury for all but a few cases. Some opponents of the civil jury cite its abolition in other legal systems as evidence "that civil juries are outmoded. Indeed, the use of civil juries has declined significantly in Canada and Australia and has effectively disappeared in England, their country of origin."[9]

But the jury trial has played an important role in the history of our country, both by virtue of what was tried and decided and by providing a forum in which many of America's most storied citizens rose to fame, often from humble origins — from Abraham Lincoln to Clarence Darrow. Perhaps Abraham Lincoln is the most noteworthy example with his rise from poverty to successful trial lawyer to President of the United States, followed by his tragic assassination. Stories of Lincoln's oratory to civil juries are legendary; they are the staple of American folklore.

Yet, the civil jury is not simply a prelude to settlement or an historical footnote. Much of present day American civil process cannot be understood without noting its antecedents in and the influence of the jury trial. It is the civil jury that has shaped how we present the narratives of our disputes and at the same time, tempered the rigid application of rules in our dispute resolution process. The law of evidence, the directed verdict, summary judgment and the new trial motion, and "remittitur" and "additur" (terms that we will define later), for example, are all rooted in the jury trial. And so, despite the paucity of jury trials and in spite of the increasing complexity of civil cases, lay juries remain vibrant in the American courts and important in our understanding of civil procedure.

Most importantly, the story about trials and civil juries in America is a story about America's fear of abusive official power. Civil juries are the check on officialdom and tangibly represent American civil process concerns with re-distribution of power. With their common sense, civil juries provide community values in civil disputes and lend added legitimacy to and acceptance of our legal system. Civil juries are so ingrained in the American culture of democracy that the right to a jury trial is written into our constitution as a fundamental right.

We have emphasized throughout this book the importance of viewing the civil process as a part of the socio-economic-political makeup of a country; we stressed that one cannot evaluate civil procedure rules without articulating the goals of the legal system. Studying the right to civil jury trial in the United States and the jury trial itself, exploring the arguments for and against the jury trials, and noting the multiple methods judges have devised to control juries all force us and any student of procedure to confront the

---

9. *Developments in the Law: The Civil Jury,* 110 Harv. L. Rev. 1408, 1411 (1997).

critical question: What should one's country be trying to achieve through its civil adjudication process? In America, legal authorities and commentators continue to have dramatically different views on this question; and these views come to the fore in the debate about civil trials and civil juries.

WHAT IS AN AMERICAN TRIAL?

The American trial is a continuous event. When a judge sits without a jury, there can be more interruptions, but a jury trial (with jurors pulled from home and work) must be continuous without interruption from the time it begins until it ends with a final jury verdict. This, of course, is different from a civil law system in which the discovery and trial phase of the case are not severed and in which the judge periodically asks for more documents or oral testimony, that is reduced to documents.

In the United States, the trial itself is where the evidence is admitted or rejected. For the most part, if the evidence is not admitted at the trial it cannot be considered by the trial judge or by subsequent appellate courts on appeal. Most of the testimony in a jury trial is taken orally, with witnesses under oath in court, rather than through written summaries of what a witness has previously said. A stenographer is present at most civil trials of consequence and transcribes in verbatim manner every word formally spoken by the judge, lawyers, and witnesses.

In the American trial, the ideal role for a judge is said to be a "referee." She usually does not ask questions. As befits an adversary system, as party controlled as the American process is, it is the lawyers who decide what theory to present and what evidence to adduce. The judge presides over the choosing of jurors; administers the oath to jurors and witnesses; rules on objections to evidence; rules on motions to terminate the case ("directed verdict" or "judgment as a matter of law" as described in Chapter 8) and other motions; and instructs the jury as to the law. Increasingly, however, as discussed in Chapter 7, the judge in federal courts also acts as a case manager.

In most trial courts, the judge wears a black robe and sits at an elevated desk, a symbol of authority in the courtroom. There is often at least one court official, often called a "bailiff," who is charged with keeping the courtroom quiet and peaceful. Sometimes the trial judge — and almost always there is only one — has a judicial clerk who researches the law at the judge's request.

The American trial is quite formal. Ordinarily, trials proceed in the following manner. First, if it is a jury trial, the jury is impaneled (that is, selected by the parties' lawyers). With or without a jury, the plaintiff's lawyer makes an opening statement, giving the judge or judge and jury the theory of the case and what she expects to prove with the evidence. The defendant's opening statement follows in a similar manner. Then the plaintiff's lawyer calls her witnesses one by one. The bailiff or judge administers an oath that the witness will tell the truth. The plaintiff's lawyer then directs the testimony by asking the witness questions. The defendant's lawyer can make evidentiary objections to the questions and the judge will rule on the objection by either sustaining the objection (meaning that the witness is instructed not to answer) or overruling the question (meaning that the question is sound and the witness must answer).

When the plaintiff's lawyer is finished with each witness, the defendant's lawyer may cross-examine the witness, trying to impeach the witness (detracting from her credibility) or trying to obtain evidence from the witness that is helpful to the defendant's case. In cross-examination, the questioning lawyer can lead an adverse witness, meaning that the lawyer has more freedom to control the witness by phrasing questions that suggest the answer sought. For instance, in the Cherryum poison drink case, the defendant's lawyer on cross-examination might ask Lee: "Isn't it true, Mr. Lee, that in the last 12 months after you drank the Cherryum, your dizziness and head aches have subsided?" On the other hand, Mr. Lee's own lawyer, on direct, could not ask him: "Mr. Lee, the Cherryum really tasted like poison, didn't it?" Instead, on direct examination, she would have to ask a more open-ended, nonleading question: "How did the Cherryum taste when you first swallowed it?"

After the direct and cross-examination of each witness, the lawyer who called the witness can then re-direct, followed by questions on re-cross-examination. In many jurisdictions, cross-examination can only cover matters that were covered in the earlier direct examination, and re-direct is limited to cover new matters that appeared as a result of the cross-examination. After the plaintiff's lawyer has called all her witnesses and the opponent has had the opportunity to cross-examine these witnesses, plaintiff's lawyer will say "I rest," meaning that she has finished. The defendant's lawyer will normally move for a directed verdict (called "judgment as a matter of law" in federal courts) if she thinks that the plaintiff's lawyer has failed to introduce evidence sufficient to permit a reasonable jury to find that every element of plaintiff's cause of action is true (thus testing the production burden of the plaintiff).

If the directed verdict motion is denied, the defendant's lawyer will then put on its case just as the plaintiff did. The plaintiff's lawyer will be able to cross-examine the defendant's witnesses one by one, in the manner previously described. After the defendant rests, either the defendant or plaintiff may move for a directed verdict. Of course, the plaintiff can only win a directed verdict if the judge finds that the jury must believe every element of a cause of action of the plaintiff's claim (in other words, if as a matter of law the plaintiff has met both her production and persuasion burdens).

If all directed verdict motions (or motions for judgment as a matter of law) have been denied, what happens next is the closing arguments. The side without the burden of proof, usually the defendant, will begin the closing argument to the jury, followed by the plaintiff. In closing argument, the lawyer reviews the evidence and explains to the jury why that evidence should lead to a verdict favorable to her client. The lawyers may not come out and say "I believe my client is honest and has told the truth, and therefore you should believe my client and we should win." Rather, the lawyer must argue the evidence and may explain why certain witnesses are not credible and why the evidence should lead to a certain conclusion. Both lawyers will usually talk to the jury about what instructions of law they anticipate the trial judge will give the jury, so that the jury knows what law to apply as the closing argument is given.

After both lawyers have "closed," the judge will instruct the jury orally on the law to be applied. She will tell them that although they must decide factual issues and some issues of applying law to fact (such as whether the bottling company in the Cherryum case act "negligently"), they must take the law as instructed by the judge. The jury is usually told in a civil case that they cannot change or ignore the law even if they do not like the law. The judge will also explain to the jury the burden of proof. In other words, for the plaintiff to win, she must convince the jury by a preponderance of the evidence that each element of the cause of action is true. Stated another way, for the plaintiff to win, she must convince the jury that it is more likely than not that each element is true. As to each of plaintiff's causes of action, the judge will explain what each element legally requires. For instance, in a negligence case, there will be instructions on the meaning of duty (if that is at issue), unreasonable care, cause-in-fact, proximate cause, and permissible damages. There will also be an explanation of each of the elements of the defendant's affirmative defenses and that the defendant has the burden of proof on affirmative defenses.

The jury will also be instructed that they are not to speculate on questions that the judge disallowed nor should they in any way punish the lawyer or her client for making objections. Traditionally, the judge will give the jury a verdict slip to fill in with an "x" next to "for the plaintiff" or "for the defendant," and if they find for the plaintiff, they should also fill in the amount of damages that they find. This is called a "general verdict." At the beginning of the case, the judge will have appointed a foreperson of the jury, and the judge will instruct the jury that the foreperson is in charge of the deliberations and filling in the verdict slip. Depending on the jurisdiction, the judge will tell the jury whether they have to be unanimous in order to reach a verdict (the rule at common law). In some jurisdictions, contrary to the rule at common law, verdict is reached if it is five out of six in a six-person jury, or ten out of twelve in the more traditional twelve-person jury.

The jury deliberations are secret, and a bailiff or another official court officer makes certain that no one disturbs the deliberations. The jurors are normally provided meals during the case and throughout deliberations, as well as a small daily stipend. They may ask written questions of the judge, such as for a repetition of a portion of the judge's instruction or to have a portion of a witness's testimony repeated to them or given to them in transcript form. If exhibits have been entered in the trial (such as photographs or official reports), they are given to the jurors for examination in the jury room. Jurors are to deliberate until they reach unanimity or the requisite amount of agreement to sustain a verdict. If ultimately, even after the judge's urging, they cannot reach a verdict, then it is called a "hung jury," and the case will have to be tried again to a new jury unless the case settles.

Once the jury returns a verdict, it is read by the foreperson in open court. Subsequently, there may be motions for "judgment notwithstanding the verdict" or for a new trial, as described in Chapter 8. The clerk of court will enter a judgment on the official docket of the case in accordance with the verdict. It is from this final judgment that appeals can ordinarily be taken to an appellate court.

As can be seen, the present day civil jury has a large role in determining the facts of a case at the end of trial. That has not always been the role of a juror. Initially, the English jury developed as a means by which lay people in the community helped Norman judges by providing them with information jurors had of the dispute. Prior to the late 1500s, it was unusual to have witnesses testify in court. By the late 1500s, it became common for witnesses to appear in court and the jury's own "knowledge" played a minor part. By the end of the 1600s, the jury was allowed to have no information except what was offered in court, a complete reversal of function.

Once the jury became composed of lay people who were to sit "as impartial triers of issues on the basis of facts set forth to them by the testimony of witnesses," rather than as the provider of information, some systems of rules became necessary for the conduct of the trial.[10] Rules of evidence began to play an increasingly prominent part in trials, particularly jury trials, in ensuring that the untrained juror is insulated from irrelevant or inflammatory information. English, and later American, evidentiary rules were developed through the experience of judges in trying cases, rather than through orderly, systematic development. A closer look at the law of evidence in turn reveals the ambivalence that the Anglo-American legal system has historically had with respect to jurors. "Experienced judges" believed:

> that the jurors, untrained in valuing evidence, must have guidance. Somewhat was given them, to be sure, by the judge's comments, or "summing up." But more than guidance were needed, to prevent the jurors from being misled by irrelevancies, or by biased or fraudulent testimony, or by their own emotions, sympathies, and prejudices.[11]

Evidentiary rules were designed to keep out various kinds of evidence such that truly "rational, safe, and valuable tidbits" get through to the jury.

There developed four types of evidence admissible in court: oral testimony in open court, testimony by prior deposition, writings or "documentary evidence," and "real evidence," such as an article of clothing or a gun. There was also a series of elaborate rules to exclude certain evidence from trial. Evidence must be relevant, in the sense that it is logically related to proving a fact or issue that is part of the plaintiff's claim or the defendant's defense. Irrelevant evidence is excluded. Written documents and real proof must be authenticated. In other words, pieces of evidence must be shown to be what they purport to be. If a document is signed, there must usually be evidence of who signed it. Witness' testimony must represent the witness's own knowledge, rather than hearsay — what another has told her.[12]

Over time, exceptions and accretions developed for most of the rules, and the rules of evidence became more elaborate and numerous in the United States than in England. Added to the complexity, each state has its own evidence rules, although there is relative homogeneity amongst the states.

---

10. Professor Tracy lists four major criteria: 1) the case should be presented in an orderly manner; 2) waste of time and confusion should be avoided by limiting evidence to the issues before the court; 3) evidence should have some authenticity before the jury is given it; and 4) in the interests of policies, some communications should be protected as confidential, such as communications between lawyer and client and priest and penitent. John Evarts Tracy, Handbook of the Law of Evidence 2 (1952).

11. John H. Wigmore, Wigmore on Evidence: A Students' Textbook 4-5 (Foundation Press, Inc. 1935).

12. *Id.* at 4-6.

In 1975, the Federal Rules of Evidence were enacted to govern in the federal courts and simplified the rules to about 60 relatively short rules. Though they constitute the law of evidence only in the federal system, their influence has been much wider, with most states' evidence codes following the organization and substance of the Federal Rules of Evidence.[13]

THE INSTITUTIONAL ROLE SERVED BY THE AMERICAN JURY: ITS ADVOCATES AND CRITICS

Evidence law is not the only area exemplifying the American ambivalence toward the civil jury. Judge Learned Hand noted the American inconsistency in trusting jurors "as reverently as we do, and still surround[ing] them with restrictions which, if they have no rational validity whatever, depend upon our distrust."[14] Another observer suggested that through procedures such as directed verdict, judgment notwithstanding the verdict, and evidence exclusionary rules "we recognize . . . that the jury is the weakest element in our judicial system, and yet we pander to it as a sacred institution. . . . We treat the jury as a sacred institution, and we regard it, in all ways in which our regard can be measured, as wholly incompetent for the purpose for which we establish it."[15] The four quotes at the beginning of this chapter provide but a sampling of the hundreds of quotes, articles, and books either lauding or condemning the American jury. The debate is not too difficult to summarize, and it is likely that the reader could come up with most of the arguments.[16]

The jury system remains an enduring part of the American legal system not only because it is mandated by federal and state constitutions, but also because it serves an important role in the American democratic process. Dating back to the colonial and revolutionary periods, jury supporters saw the jury as not merely a sound method of dispute resolution, but also as a critical component of American governance. From the earliest period of the American colonies, the jury was considered a democratic barrier against the arbitrary power of royal English judges imposed on the colonists. Political theorists of the constitutional period thought that the jury provided the needed democratic balance of power against the royal judiciary. Later antifederalists retained the American jury to protect against those federal judges with life-time tenure, whose authority can be powerful and difficult to curb in both federal and state courts. The American Constitution includes a provision for a right to jury trial in any criminal proceeding brought in any federal court, and retained the jury for civil cases "at common law." In the civil context, the Seventh Amendment

13. Roger C. Park, David P. Leonard, & Steven H. Goldberg, Evidence Law, A Student's Guide to the Law of Evidence as Applied in American Trials 10 (2d ed., Thomson West 2004).

14. Learned Hand, The Deficiencies of Trials to Reach the Heart of the Matter, in 3 Lectures on Legal Topics 89 (1926), *cited in* Mark S. Brodin, *Accuracy, Efficiency, and Accountability in the Litigation Process — the Case for the Fact Verdict*, 59 U. Cin. L. Rev.15, 16 n.8 (1990).

15. Boston, *Some Practical Remedies for Existing Defects in the Administration of Justice*, 61 U. Pa. L. Rev. 1 (1912), *cited in* Brodin, *supra* note 14, at 16 n.8.

16. An excellent article on this topic is Paul D. Carrington, *The Civil Jury and American Democracy*, 13 Duke J. Comp. & Int'l L. 79 (2003).

preserved the federal judge's prerogatives when she is exercising power inherited from the English Court of Chancery in "suits in equity."[17]

The American jury not only performs a check on the judiciary, it also provides some check on the legislature. By providing community input, the jury assures that legislation straying far from community norms is brought back into the fold in actual application in individual cases. Because many disputes are mixed questions of law and fact, community input on community norms is important. The most obvious example is "negligence" or "unreasonable care," but even such issues as "discriminatory intent" or "anticompetitive motive and effect" may gain from community input, which helps to moderate the sometimes harsh application of formal law to concrete individual contexts. The jury system thus serves a functional institutional role, in preserving the accountability not only of judges, but also of the legislature, in the democratic process.

In addition to serving as an institutional check, the jury system has also been applauded as a form of civic education important to democracy. Early nineteenth-century observations by the Frenchman, de Toqueville, suggest that the jury was an important way of educating the population about law and democracy. Serving on a jury gives each citizen a personal stake in governance and makes the decisions reached by civil adjudication legitimate and acceptable to the population at large. This is supported by strong empirical evidence that jurors by and large take their responsibilities very seriously and that most jurors leave the courthouse with a sense of satisfaction in performing this public duty.[18]

Other rationales also developed for the use of the jury over the course of time. In the nineteenth century, as charges of corruption were brought against judges, the jury of 12 appeared a more habitually honest and reliable means of dispute resolution. It is difficult to bribe 12 jurors or even one lay juror, without the risk of discovery. Jurors also help diffuse the pressures faced by individual judges in politically sensitive cases. In a very real way, the jury acts as a lightening rod for the judiciary. When unpopular decisions are rendered, they are rendered by 6 or 12 lay people, who are not professionals and are not permanently connected to the government, thus insulating the judiciary from some of the political attack it would otherwise encounter and ensuring a certain amount of judicial independence.

Moreover, as many have pointed out, multiple heads are better than one. The jury provides a number of different experiences and viewpoints, as opposed to the monolithic vision of a single judge. Judges who hear the same type of cases repeatedly may become jaded and have preconceptions based on previous cases. Jurors, by contrast, are prone to listening to the evidence with a fresh ear. In a jury trial, the lawyer must focus on which issues are most important, as well as being able to explain more complicated questions

17. The use of juries only in civil cases at common law appears to have origins in the economic circumstances at the time. It was meant to protect foreign debtors who would bring cases in equity to enforce contracts and mortgages and would therefore prefer royal judges. *See* Matthew P. Harrington, *The Economic Origins of the Seventh Amendment*, 87 Iowa L. Rev. 145 (2001).

18. *See* Harry Kalven, Jr. & Hans Zeisel, The American Jury 3-11,149-62 (U. Chicago 1986); Shari S. Diamond, What Jurors Think: Expectations and Reactions of Citizens Who Serve as Jurors, in Verdict: Assessing the Civil Jury System 282 (Robert E. Litan ed., Brockings Institute 1993).

in a simple, clear way. Judges, in turn, must be clearer and more precise in their understanding of the law for they must explain that law to the lay jurors.

Where much of the argument in favor of the jury concentrates on its contribution to ensuring a balance of power and democracy, as well as to the civic education of the jurors themselves, jury opponents or detractors concentrate on costs, efficiency, accuracy, and predictability values. Jury trials do tend to take longer than when the judge sits alone, the usual figure being about one-third more time, because the evidence must be more fully explained to the lay audience.[19] The jurors must also be compensated for their time and travel expense, although the amount is usually quite small by American standards, such as $30 or $50 per day. Jurors must be provided lunch, and if they deliberate during the morning or evening, also breakfast and dinner. If jurors are sequestered, then there is also the expense of hotels. Court personnel must be assigned to protect the privacy and secrecy of their deliberations.

But the most scathing criticisms are leveled at the inability of jurors to understand and apply the law and be unprejudiced, unbiased fact finders. Critics complain that lay people are easily swayed by emotions and that they tend to be pro-plaintiff and anti-corporations. Critics charge that jurors give irrationally high damage awards because they feel sorry for a plaintiff, dislike the defendant, and know that the defendant, which is often a business, either has the money or is insured to cover for compensation. Pro-business critics tend to focus on the large punitive damage awarded by juries against corporations; some civil rights lawyers believe that lay jurors tend to carry with them prejudices against minority plaintiffs in discrimination suits.

Many feel that jurors are especially inappropriate and ineffective in more complex cases because of the number of issues or the complexity of the problems involved, which often include technical and scientific evidence. Critics also claim that juries are frequently composed of the unemployed, uneducated, and the elderly who are most likely to be at home and have time to serve as jurors, but who may not be most suited to deciding complex disputes. Additionally, with the growth of "jury consultants," jury sampling, and other innovative techniques, lawyers claim the ability to shape a potential jury pool through challenges in the selection process and skew the community input that jurors are theoretically bringing into the case.

Probably the most infamous example cited by jury detractors as the epitome of a so-called runaway jury is the large punitive damage jury award to a woman who suffered burns from dropping a hot cup of McDonald's coffee on herself. But as jury supporters pointed out in response, a more complete look at the story showed that:

> What was often ignored in these accounts of the case was that the eighty-one-year-old woman's injuries were very serious, that McDonald's had known about the problem of its exceptionally hot coffee, but had declined to warn consumers

---

19. Stephen J. Adler, The Jury: Trial and Error in the American Courtroom 43-47 (Times Books 1994).

or to change the temperature at which it served its coffee, and that the trial judge subsequently reduced the $2.7 million punitive damage award to $480,000.[20]

In fact, it turns out that Mrs. Liebeck, the plaintiff, was hospitalized for eight days and required skin grafts. McDonald's policy was to serve coffee 15 to 20 degrees hotter than its competitors and had in fact received 700 complaints about its hot coffee during the previous five years ("some involving serious burns") but did not consider changing its policy. "[In] the aftermath of the case, McDonald's lowered the temperature of its coffee."[21] Perhaps the anecdote really shows that the jury, the jury trial, and the punitive damages worked exactly as they should in curbing corporate misconduct.

Indeed, some empiricists have argued that anti-jury sentiment is largely based on myths and distortions.[22] Michael Saks, for example, concluded that "[e]ven a fleeting acquaintance with the relevant literature suggests that a wide gap separates the public's stereotypical beliefs about its civil justice system and its own role as jurors in that system, from the empirical facts about the system."[23] Contrary to the myth that "jurors are biased in favor of plaintiffs, out of sympathy toward victims of injury, while judges are much less prone to finding liability," both older and more recent research show that in most types of cases "there is no difference between judge and jury findings."[24] In fact, in the most publicized cases, namely medical malpractice and product liability, judges appear to be more favorable to plaintiffs than juries are.

Further, in contrast to the myth that "[j]urors give awards that are too large, and certainly larger than the awards given by judges or other experts,"[25] recent research has shown that while jury awards might overcompensate in pain and suffering,[26] they considerably under-compensate plaintiffs' future economic losses.[27] Professional boards, meanwhile, give considerably higher awards than juries, and arbitrators and jurors give "remarkably similar awards." Jurors then may not differ substantially from awards given by professional decision-makers.

Finally, as to the myth that juries routinely award far too high punitive damages, the data indicates that, "the amounts awarded do not appear to have grown out of proportion to the harm done and seem to be an amount reasonably calculated to punish the particular wrongdoer."[28] In the infamous McDonald's hot coffee case, the $2,700,000 punitive damage award was

20. Nancy S. Marder, *Juries and Damages: A Commentary*, 48 DePaul L. Rev. 427, 428 (1998).

21. The facts and the quoted material are from Gross & Syverud, *supra* note 2, at 5.

22. For a summary of empirical research on the civil jury, *see* Valerie P. Hans & Stephanie Albertson, *Empirical Research and Civil Jury Reform*, 78 Notre Dame L. Rev. 1497 (2003). They, like others find that the evidence shows jurors usually act responsibly and that "problems with the civil jury are overstated." *Id.* at 1522.

23. Michael J. Saks, *Public Opinion About the Civil Jury: Can Reality be Found in the Illusions*, 48 DePaul L. Rev. 221, 229 (1998).

24. *Id.* at 229-230.

25. *Id.* at 230.

26. Kevin M. Clermont & Theodore Eisenberg, *Trial by Jury or Judge: Transcending Empiricism*, 77 Cornell L. Rev. 1124, 1126 (1992); *see also* Neil Vidmar & Jeffrey J. Rice, *Assessment of Noneconomic Damage Awards in Medical Negligence: A Comparison of Jurors with Legal Professionals*, 78 Iowa L. Rev. 883 (1993).

27. Valerie P. Hans & Neil Vidmar, Judging the Jury 160-162 (Plenum Press 1986).

28. Saks, *supra* note 23, at 231.

apparently chosen by the jury to be equal to two days' worth of coffee revenue for McDonald's — hardly an irrational amount.[29]

Perhaps the strongest data for those who enthusiastically support juries is that judicial attitudes toward the civil jury "show virtually unanimous support for the institution."[30] Because judges are the group that most frequently see juries in action, and they have repeated opportunity to compare what juries do with their own sense of the merits of cases, their support, jury supporters argue, counts as a very high recommendation indeed.

JUDICIAL CONTROL AND THE RIGHT TO JURY TRIAL

The jury trial has been constitutionally protected since the beginning of the United States. After the American Revolution, each of the original 13 colonies, on attaining statehood, provided citizens with the right to a jury trial in both criminal and civil cases. In fact, the majority of representatives in several states said that they would not vote in favor of the federal constitution absent a Bill of Rights. The Bill of Rights, as the first ten amendments to the Constitution, became law in 1791 and included a right to a jury trial.

The Seventh Amendment to the Constitution guaranteed the right to jury trial in federal court in civil cases as follows:

> In suits at common law, where the value in controversy shall exceed twenty dollars, the right of trial by jury shall be preserved, and no fact tried by a jury shall be otherwise re-examined in any Court of the United States, than according to the rules of the common law.

The Seventh Amendment preserved the right of trial by jury in the civil cases only for "suits at common law." Federal judges retain their prerogatives to try cases when they are exercising their authority inherited from the English Court of Chancery in "suits in equity."

The Supreme Court of the United States has had to interpret what it means to "preserve" the jury right for "suits at common law." Two types of tests have been developed. The first, the historical test, looks to whether one was entitled to a jury in the type of case at issue in England or the United States in 1791, the year the amendment became effective. In more recent cases, some of the Justices have instead said that the type of remedy is the most important test of whether the lawsuit in question is one "at common law." Consequently, if the primary remedy sought is monetary damages, the traditional common law remedy, as opposed to injunctive relief, the province of equity, then these Justices would grant the jury right, even if the strictly historical evidence is murky.[31]

---

29. Gross & Syverud, *supra* note 2, at 5.
30. Valerie P. Hans, Attitudes Toward the Civil Jury, in Verdict: Assessing the Civil Jury System 262 (Robert E. Litan ed., Brookings Institute 1993), *cited in* Saks, *supra* note 23, at 235.
31. *See, e.g., Chauffeurs, Teamsters and Helpers, Local No. 391 v. Terry*, 494 U.S. 558, 565 (1990) (Marshall, J., plurality opinion in pt. III-A).

One of the constitutional questions about juries that the Supreme Court has had to repeatedly resolve relates to their composition and the extent to which lawyers can control their composition. In both state and federal courts, ordinary citizens are usually selected on a rotating basis from voting lists or automobile registrations and summoned to appear for jury service. Unless they have a valid excuse, they can be punished for failing to obey a court order to appear as a potential juror. These potential jurors are part of what is called a jury "panel" or "pool." From those in the pool, a clerk will randomly pick names of those who will be considered by the judge and lawyers to form the actual jury for the case.

In federal court, usually immediately before the jury is to be selected, the lawyers will be given a list of those potential jurors in the pool with some basic information, including their names, addresses, occupations, and spouses' occupations. With this information, the lawyers, and increasingly the judge, will conduct what is called a "voir dire," in which the potential jurors are asked a number of questions. The judge will have told the potential jurors a little about the case and given them the names of the parties and lawyers. If the judge determines, usually by questioning the potential jurors one by one, that any of them should be rejected for "cause," then she will excuse such a person. "Cause" would include such matters as knowing one of the attorneys or one of the parties or having been a party to a similar case to the one before the court or expressing some inability to listen and have an open mind about the case. The attorneys are also permitted to ask that a juror be excused for cause.

In addition to "for cause" objections to jurors, each party is given a number of what are called "peremptory challenges" to potential jurors. With the peremptory challenges (the number of which is typically three for each party in civil cases), the lawyer need not state her reason for challenging a potential juror. The rationale for the preemptory challenge was, and continues to be, that parties will think the trial is fairer if they can remove a potential juror for any reason, no matter how irrational. An attorney may simply have an intuitive feeling that a particular juror would not look favorably on her client's case. It is this peremptory challenge that has proved to be most controversial in the United States.

Some lawyers automatically "peremptorily" challenge any potential juror of the opposite race of their client, on the suspicion that a juror of a different race would be prejudiced against their client. Particularly in criminal cases, it was not uncommon for a black defendant to be tried in front of an all white jury and usually a white judge. In response to this use of the preemptory challenge, the Supreme Court has held that preemptory challenges on the basis of race is a violation of the right of potential jurors protected by the equal protection clauses of the United States Constitution.[32] In 1994, the Supreme Court overturned the use of sex-based peremptory challenges as well.[33]

But it has not proven easy to ascertain when an attorney has actually based her peremptory challenge on the forbidden grounds of race or sex. Attorneys are quite clever at giving the court nonrace or nonsex based reasons.

32. *See, e.g., Batson v. Kentucky*, 476 U.S. 79 (1986), *Powers v. Ohio*, 499 U.S. 400 (1991), and *Edmonson v. Leesville Concrete Co., Inc.*, 500 U.S. 614 (1991).
33. *J.E.B. v. Alabama*, 511 U.S. 127 (1994).

The Supreme Court has articulated a three-part test to determine whether a peremptory challenge is race-based:

> First, the party opposing the strike must show the circumstance surrounding a particular strike creates a prima facie case that the proponent of the strike challenged the potential juror on the basis of race. For instance, a party may satisfy this part of the test by proving that the opposing party excluded all members of a cognizable racial group. Second, the burden shifts to the proponent of the challenge to provide a race-neutral reason for exercising the strike. Third, it is then incumbent upon the party opposing the strike to prove to the court that use of the strike was motivated by purposeful discrimination.[34]

But commentators are not convinced that this test, as applied in actual cases by the courts, in fact ferrets out those instances in which a peremptory challenge was race-based, because the reason given by a party exercising the challenge need not be "persuasive, or even plausible."[35] The Supreme Court has upheld a peremptory challenge to a prospective black juror that was in part based on his having long, curly hair, a mustache, and a goatee-type beard that the challenging lawyer said looked "suspicious to me."[36]

According to empirical studies, people from minority groups remain underrepresented in both the jury pool and the jury as finally constituted.[37] This may be true for a number of reasons, including the presence of racial bias in the use of peremptory challenges. Lists from which prospective jurors are picked and the criteria in some states to be a juror, such as local residency requirements and standards, often require the ability to read, write, and speak English, a requirement that weeds out new immigrants from different countries. Some now believe that the best ways to achieve more racially balanced juries, critical for achieving the appearance and reality of legitimacy, include taking affirmative steps to increase the number of minorities in the initial jury pools or eliminating peremptory challenges altogether.

CURRENT DEBATES REGARDING JURIES AND TRIALS

There are several debates currently taking place in the United States in which avid juror supporters and detractors continue to passionately disagree — jury size, whether unanimity is required, and appropriate control of the jury. Thoughtful observers of the American experience with the jury believe that there has been an steady erosion of the right to trial by jury in recent years.

In a series of decisions in the 1970s, the U.S. Supreme Court "set aside 600 years of settled common law tradition and two centuries of constitutional history, including the reversal of its own precedents to the contrary, in holding

34. Betson v. Kentucky 476 U.S. 79 (1984).
35. *Purkett v. Elem*, 514 U.S. 765, 768 (1995).
36. *See id.*
37. Deborah A. Ramirez, *The Mixed Jury and the Ancient Custom of Trial by Jury de Medietate Linguae: A History and a Proposal for Change*, 74 B.U. L. Rev. 777, 780-781 (1994).

that both criminal and civil juries smaller than 12 do not violate constitutional requirements . . ."[38] Although at common law jury verdicts were required to be unanimous, the Supreme Court held in 1972 that the Fourteenth Amendment does not require a unanimous verdict in a state criminal case.[39] Astute observers of the federal courts think that the current Supreme Court would also not require unanimity in civil cases if the practice were challenged and brought before it today.[40]

Reducing the size of the jury and requiring less than unanimity for a verdict may dramatically weaken the value of the jury system. The reduction of the size of the jury can increase the unpredictability of verdicts and rewards. Empirical data also suggests that a reduced size jury also reduces the likelihood of minorities being on a jury, renders it more difficult for a dissenter to express her views because she is less likely to have allies, and reduces the collective memory and experience of the jury. Others believe that the unanimity requirement makes for more thorough evaluation of the evidence, makes minority views more likely to be aired, and results in a verdict that is more legitimate in the eyes of the jurors, the parties, and the public.[41]

The Supreme Court, while upholding the Seventh Amendment right, has also permitted a good deal of jury control by judges. Some examples are the use of extensive instructions to the jury or highlighting in her summary of the evidence what the judge deems is important. Jury control can also be seen in the use of "remittitur" or "additur" in which the judge will allow a motion for a new trial unless the plaintiff agrees to a decrease in the amount of the jury verdict (remittitur) or the defendant agrees to an increase (additur). Judges also increasingly use a series of questions to be answered by the jury, rather than the historic use of the general verdict, in which the jury merely says whether it finds for the plaintiff or the defendant.

Finally, judges have also used "bifurcation" or "trifurcation," to separate out and stagger the issues in a given case for trial and consideration by the jury. If a case is bifurcated for trial, the evidence may be heard first on one single element, usually liability, and only if liability is found would the trial continue on to the question of damages. Some juror supporters believe this makes the trial an antiseptic experience and denies the jury the right to hear the entire context of the case at the same time.[42] Others argue, however, that such jury control mechanisms are efficient and help the jury focus only on what is logically relevant. They claim, for instance, that it would be improper for a jury to consider the extent of damage in assessing whether there has been negligence or causation.[43]

The most profound jury-control mechanisms are perhaps summary judgments, motions for "judgment as a matter of law" (previously called directed verdicts), motions for judgment notwithstanding the verdict that occur after the

38. Michael J. Saks, *The Smaller the Jury, the Greater the Unpredictability*, 79 Judicature 263 (1996).

39. *Apodaca v. Oregon*, 406 U.S. 404 (1972).

40. Charles A. Wright, Law of Federal Courts 675 n.5 (6th ed., West 2002).

41. Saks, *supra* note 23, at 446-447.

42. Roger H. Transgsrud, *Mass Trials in Mass Tort Cases: A Dissent*, 1989 U. Ill. L. Rev. 69 (1989).

43. *See* Meiring de Villiers, *A Legal and Policy Analysis of Bifurcated Litigation*, 2000 Colum. Bus. L. Rev. 153 (2000).

jury has rendered its decision, and motions for a new trial in which the judge can grant a new trial if she thinks the verdict is "against the weight of the evidence." Chapter 8 discussed the expanded use of summary judgment, as embodied in the Supreme Court's trilogy of cases in 1986. By using summary judgments and judgments as a matter of law liberally, judges are turning what may be a factual issue into a legal one and thus expanding their ability to control or supervise juries by taking the issue away from the jury. For example, when a judge determines whether there is a sufficiency of evidence to permit a jury to decide on an element of the case, the judge may be making judgments about the evidence that would normally be made by the jury.

For some Justices of the Supreme Court, the directed verdict motion (now called motion for judgment as a matter of law) was an unconstitutional intrusion on the Seventh Amendment's "right to trial by jury as at common law." In 1943, Justice Black, a passionate believer in the jury trial, joined by Justices Douglas and Murphy, dissented in *Galloway v. United States*.[44] In *Galloway*, the plaintiff, a former enlisted man in the army during World War I, sought benefits under an insurance policy for disability. The majority upheld the directed verdict against the plaintiff and analyzed the evidence, witness by witness, and explained why several of them were not credible.[45] Justice Black vigorously dissented with a prediction that foretold the trend to come:

> The founders of our government thought that that trial of facts by juries rather than judges was an essential bulwark of civil liberty. For this reason, among others, they adopted Article III, § 2 of the Constitution, and the Sixth [right to trial by jury in criminal cases] and Seventh Amendments. *Today's decision marks a continuation of the gradual process of judicial erosion which in one hundred fifty years has slowly worn away a major portion of the essential guarantee of the Seventh Amendment.* (emphasis supplied).[46]

Prior to the invention of the directed verdict in 1850, a defendant in a case such as *Galloway* could either move for a new trial or demurrer to the evidence. The former would give plaintiff an opportunity to cure the defect in its paucity of evidence, while the latter would bind the defendant to the facts as admitted. Under the directed verdict rule, by contrast to the demurrer to the evidence, a defendant can make the motion without risk, and put in its own evidence if the motion is denied. The *Galloway* majority's decision in upholding the directed verdict, according to Black, had materially intruded on a jury's prerogative. The modern directed verdict gave defendants two opportunities to avoid the

---

44. 319 U.S. 372 (1943).

45. The majority even rejected a childhood friend/witness because he was unsure how many times he had seen the petitioner in the years in question and that the friend didn't take account of plaintiff's being in a hospital in France with influenza just before he came home. The majority totally discredited a medical witness who, based on several meetings with the plaintiff and on written records, had testified that the plaintiff had tendencies toward insanity when he joined the army and had become totally and permanently disabled during his military service. The doctor testified that the particular insanity was consistent with having lucid, relatively normal periods without aberrant behavior. The doctor's testimony was discredited, the majority said, because the doctor did not have knowledge of the plaintiff's activities for at least five years. The doctor's testimony, according to the majority, coupled with the plaintiff's attorney's failure to call plaintiff's wife to testify, showed a gap in testimony that was too great to permit the inferences drawn by the plaintiff's medical expert. *Id.*

46. *Id.* at 397.

jury (once as directed verdict, the second as j.n.o.v.) and with the adoption of a less restrictive "substantial evidence" test in granting directed verdict.

If the *Galloway* dissent bemoaned this erosion of the right to trial by jury in civil cases and regretted that the Court had not restrained its own power in a directed verdict,[47] what would they have said about the more recent developments? Of a jury now reduced to six people and the erosion of the unanimity requirement? What about the efforts to take cases away from the jury with the easing of standards in granting judgment notwithstanding the verdict and summary judgment? And what about the greater control of juries with special verdicts in lieu of the general verdict, the bifurcation of issues, heavy-handed case management, and judicial urging of settlement?

SOME CLOSING THOUGHTS ON JURIES

For us, the questions surrounding the right to a jury trial in the United States force one to confront the fundamental question of the goals of a civil litigation system. If litigation were solely to resolve commercial disputes, then perhaps a system with professional judges, such as those found in civil law countries, would be more efficient and generally more desirable. However, if civil litigation encompasses the resolution of broad political and social issues, as well as the litany of personal rights and injuries, such as many of the cases brought in the United States courts, then a jury system with its citizen participation may be critical. Civil juries can provide a needed community voice, insulate judges from political pressures, and most importantly, secure a level of legitimacy such that even controversial decisions are accepted.

The right to a jury not only reflects a different view towards the jury, it also reflects a different view towards judges. Jury proponents in the United States believe that our judges are not as neutral, objective, unemotional, and unprejudiced as jury detractors assume. This skepticism rings especially true for judges in a legal system in which they are politically appointed or elected, as they are in the United States and in which class and politics play a role. Eighty percent of the state judges in the United States face election, and their selection and election have become highly politicized. Vast sums of money are raised by interested people and lobbying groups to support judges in their election campaigns.[48] It is difficult to believe that such judges and their decisions are totally immune from the politics and pressures inherent in this process.

By contrast, jurors in the United States are not continuous participants in the legal system. They are drawn by lottery from the community and their political views are generally unknown. They are not employees of the

---

47. For the view that Black sorely underestimated the earlier power of judicial control of juries through such mechanisms as heavy handed instructions and the use of very specific and limiting substantive law, *see* Ann Woolhandler & Michael G. Collins, *The Article III Jury*, 87 Va. L. Rev. 587 (2001).

48. A recent lengthy front page article in the New York Times has these telling headlines: William Glaberson, *Fierce Campaigns Signal a New Era for State Courts — Escalating Cost of Races — Battles for Ideological Control That Critics Call Damaging to Judges' Impartiality*, N.Y. Times A1, column 3, (June 5, 2000).

government nor do they face elections that are frequently heavily contested. Lawyers and judges do not know who the jurors will be in advance of trial, rendering corruption of decision makers less likely. The unpredictability of a jury's composition and the freshness of juries provide safeguards in the civil litigation system.

Additionally, jury detractors may have a much different view of the civil dispute process than jury proponents. Jury detractors in the United States may believe that single factual issues can be disengaged from all the other factual and legal issues, that most facts can be found to be true or false, and that the law is sufficiently clear so that a judge can just apply the law to those facts. They focus on accurate fact finding, precise and predictable law application, and efficiency: How long does it take and how much will it cost?

Jury proponents meanwhile have a different and perhaps more skeptical view about the civil litigation process. They are unsure as to whether most facts are actually found true or false and whether true reality can ever be discerned, because human memory and perception fade and the human proclivity is to see life in terms of self-interest. Also to be considered are the temptation to lie (or self-deceive) when the stakes are high and the understandable attempts by lawyers in an adversary system to arrange facts in a way that will achieve the result they seek. Furthermore, jury proponents see the legal standards adding to the ambiguity, with such amorphous legal standards as "unreasonable care," "proximate cause" or "foreseeability," In light of these ambiguities, a diffused decision-making process may be better than a decision by a single judge.

One final issue tends to separate jury enthusiasts from jury detractors, relating to the nature of the trial itself. Those who are skeptical of the jury trial would like to make the event a more logical and substantially less dramatic enterprise, as trials are in many civil law countries. It would certainly seem to be more efficient to separate out issues, such as liability from damages, and to proceed to damages only if liability is found. It is also sensible to ask the jury a series of questions, rather than asking them for a general verdict, so that the jury is prevented from considering "extraneous" matters. With jury answers to a number of specific questions, the appellate courts would be better able to review and reverse if the instructions were not followed and the answers were inconsistent. These arguments, for the most part, relate to matters of efficiency and logic, both undeniably important considerations.

However, given the myriad of factors that go into a legal dispute, efficiency and cold logic may not be the primary concern. In fact, for the reasons we have already discussed and because of the policies in evidence law (such as excluding privileged communications), it is often, if not usually, difficult to know exactly what happened between disputants. Under these circumstances, at least for us, it makes sense to let the decision maker, whether judge or jury, witness a drama like a trial in which a story unfolds. The drama permits the dispute resolver to take into consideration the facts in a holistic manner, the law as best as it can be communicated, notwithstanding its ambiguity and uncertainty, and then to reach the best judgment possible, given the facts and the law.

Ultimately, juries are important in the United States Constitutional framework because they add legitimacy to our process by engaging a wider spectrum of the population. They counterbalance life-tenured judges or judges who must face election, by providing community input and permitting dialogue between many citizens. And in permitting every citizen an opportunity to partake in resolving disputes, citizens are educated in the values of democracy, law, and governance. The jury trial also exposes the juror to other types of people in the community whom the juror would not ordinarily meet, giving each juror the opportunity to discuss an important matter — the fate of the parties — with other citizens. In a highly individualistic society as the United States where consensus on social norms may be lacking, democratic participation in the judicial process takes on added meaning.

We think it is important in a democracy to engage citizens, as jurors, in this process of examining facts, law, and fairness. It is also important to have a group of citizens, called lawyers, who spend a lifetime telling real life stories in their full richness to both judges and lay juries. These same lawyers, who professionally help citizens resolve their disputes, must deal with tragedy, hope, facts, law, policy, emotions, morality, and justice; and they must explain this complex mix of what it means to be human to others.

The real question for us is how to improve the jury system rather than to eliminate it. Reform is needed to make the jury pools and the selected jurors more representative of the population at large. Perhaps jurors should and could be more active participants in the trial, such as allowing them to take notes and to ask some questions, which historically, jurors have not been able to do. The rationale was that they should concentrate solely on hearing the story unfold; jury deliberations should not include arguments over whose notes are most accurate; and jurors should not commit themselves to a position before the case was over. There is now some evidence that jurors find it helpful to take notes and to give written questions to judges to propound to witnesses and that these steps do not have undesirable consequences.[49]

In sum, what we have defended in this chapter is a system that incorporates a complex mix of values — the desire to balance accurate fact finding, predictable law application, community participation, community education, judicial expertise and experience, with attorney advocacy and creativity. It is a system pervaded by an overall sense that life's disputes do not come in neat, tidy packages and that their resolution is not merely a matter of logic. In the end, a combination of judge and jury makes sense for the United States. Those in other countries may well find that the values they nurture call for different solutions.

49. Larry Heuer & Steven Penrod, *Increasing Jury Participation in Trials Through Note Taking and Question Asking*, 79 Judicature 256 (1996).

The Quest for Finality: Preclusion, Appeals, and Enforcement of Judgments

> The Common Law, which utterly abhors infiniteness . . . is always
> accompanied with rest and quietness, the end of all humane laws.
> Ferrer's Case, VI Coke 7 (1599)

No other area of civil procedure demonstrates more clearly the tension between the desire for resolution and the search for justice than the topic of finality. Every functioning legal system must balance this tension by providing sufficient routes to revisit and correct errors, while eliminating such routes when efficiency and repose are unduly threatened, even at the expense of preserving errors. The legitimacy of a legal system commands that its judgments, right or wrong, be ultimately obeyed and enforced.

This chapter examines this final phase of litigation. We cover three different aspects of finality: the effect of final judgments on later lawsuits (now called preclusion law), the appeals process, and the enforcement of judgments. As we have emphasized all along, litigation steps are interrelated. When a plaintiff's lawyer thinks about commencing suit she must simultaneously think about what she wants to ultimately achieve through judgment at the end of the litigation. The concerns of finality are intricately connected with concerns of other areas of procedure as well. For instance, federalism and due process concerns underlie the parameters for a binding final judgment. For a judgment to be final and binding on a defendant, there must be personal jurisdiction over the defendant or her property that meets due process muster, as well as due process notice and the right to be heard. When judgments are found to be valid, federal law commands all courts, state and federal, to respect the final judgments of other courts, state or federal. All courts must give "full faith and credit" to the judgments and not allow relitigation of previously litigated claims.

Throughout this book we have pointed out the tension between broad narrative and confining rule. Ironically, as civil procedure became more flexible and all encompassing with the Federal Rules of Civil Procedure, finality doctrine became more strict and nonforgiving: The definition of what could not be relitigated by a later litigation expanded in scope. With the easing of commencement of suit, joinder of parties and claims, and discovery rules, courts logically decided that the initial lawsuit should also preclude more in subsequent litigation involving the same claims or issues than under previous procedural regimes.

Finality doctrine also impacts allocations of power in ways that are not obvious. You will discover that several aspects of appellate rules, when combined with the effects of the Federal Rules of Civil Procedure, have resulted in the distribution of power downwards from the appellate courts to the trial court judges and the lawyers.

TWO TYPES OF PRECLUSION AND THE LURE OF FINALITY

Most, if not all, judicial systems require that at some point an adjudicated decision end the disputed matter and that the adjudicated decision be appropriately enforced. In the Anglo-American system, the common law doctrine of res judicata (also called preclusion doctrine) operates to ensure, absent the unusual, that once a lawsuit is decided, it remains decided. Preclusion principles prevent the continual relitigation of matters already decided by insulating the final decision from relitigation in a second trial court. A case once decided can only be reviewed pursuant to an appeal process (unless the judgment is voided because of fraud or some other unusual occurrence), and not by relitigation of the same claim or issue by filing a new action.

This binding judgment prevents or *precludes* (and thus the term *preclusion*) the relitigation of claims and issues that have already been adjudicated in a prior lawsuit as between the same parties or those in close association with them (called "in privity"). Once a case is final, it is important that the judgment is enforced rather than relitigated. Lack of enforcement undermines the authority of the rendering court and the legal system itself. It is difficult to respect a court whose judgments are empty promises.

Res judicata, a Latin term meaning "the thing adjudicated," generally refers to the overall doctrine of preclusion — that is, the binding effect of a judgment entered in one action on a subsequent proceeding. Unfortunately, there is a bit of linguistic confusion in this field of law. While the term *res judicata* refers to the entire field of preclusion law, the preclusion doctrine has two strands: claim preclusion and issue preclusion. Claim preclusion is also sometimes called res judicata. So res judicata has two meanings: the entire field of preclusion law and the subtopic of claim preclusion.

Claim preclusion prohibits the relitigation of claims, and issue preclusion precludes the relitigation of previously decided issues between the same parties and those in privity with them (we will soon define "privity). Just as claim preclusion is sometimes called res judicata, so too issue preclusion has a second name. Historically, it was called "collateral estoppel." A party to a second suit was "estopped" — prohibited — from relitigating an issue decided between the same parties or those in privity with them in a prior action, even if the entire claim was not barred. The term *collateral* refers to raising an issue in a second or a collateral case, rather than directly in the initial litigation.

The American Law Institute Restatements of Judgments prefers the terms "preclusion" and "preclude" rather than res judicata and collateral estoppel.[1] "Res judicata," it calls "claim preclusion," and "collateral estoppel" is "issue preclusion." For the most part, preclusion law is not found in statutes. Rather, preclusion has evolved through case law and primarily state common law. Not having statutes to rely upon in this field, many state courts now turn to the Restatement Second of Judgments for guidance in their preclusion law. We will similarly use the terms "claim preclusion" and "issue preclusion" in the remainder of this chapter.

The rationale of finality underlying claim and issue preclusion rests in both public and private considerations. By producing binding decisions and preventing inconsistent decisions, these principles of preclusion increase reliability, predictability, and consistency in the judicial system. Without preclusion, multiple trials could yield different results on the same dispute and thereby encourage disregard for unfavorable verdicts, as parties could seek constant relitigation until a favorable verdict is reached. Such inconstancy and inconsistency would promote disrespect for judgments in particular and the judicial system as a whole.

Preclusion prevents vexatious litigation. The maxim, *nemo debet bis vexari pro una et eadam causa* (no one should be twice vexed for one and the same cause), has long stood in Anglo-American jurisprudence. As aptly pointed out in England by Lord Coke in 1599:

> ...otherwise great oppression might be done under colour and pretence of law; for if there should not be an end of suits, then a rich and malicious man would infinitely vex him who hath rights by suits and actions; and in the end (because he cannot come to an end) compel him (to redeem his charge and vexation) to leave and relinquish his right, all of which was remedied by the rule and reason of ancient common law...[2]

If finality were not sacredly guarded, a plaintiff could continue to sue even with nonmeritorious claims. A defendant would be unfairly forced to defend the suits continuously, settle a new case, or pay the judgment. This one chance to have your case heard removes the possibility of harassment of otherwise innocent defendants through successive unworthy lawsuits. Furthermore, as there are no second chances, parties are apt to take the first trial seriously and less likely to take frivolous positions.

The doctrine of preclusion, it is thought, then promotes efficiency.[3] The principle of claim preclusion operates to require that when a party brings a lawsuit, she bring all possible causes of action within the scope of her lawsuit for relief. In so doing, the principle of claim preclusion encourages efficiency in the legal system by prohibiting a party from splitting her lawsuit into several successive lawsuits, each time raising a new theory of action or a new type of injury. For example, a party who was injured in an automobile accident and

---

1. Restatement (Second) of Judgments § § 13-33 Rule 27.0 (1982). We describe the American Law Institute and its Restatements in Chapter 6.

2. *Ferrer's Case*, VI Coke 7 (1599).

3. Later in this chapter we question the extent to which preclusion doctrine in fact adds or detracts from efficiency.

suffered multiple injuries might (in the absence of preclusion doctrine) file separate lawsuits for each injury and separate lawsuits on different theories, one for speeding, one for drunk driving, one for faulty brakes, and the like. With the operation of the preclusion doctrine, however, a plaintiff must combine her lawsuits in a single litigation.

The doctrine must, on the one hand, encourage efficiency by freeing courts to resolve other disputes, fairness by barring vexatious suits, and legitimacy by avoiding inconsistent judgments. Yet finality must also be fair to the individual litigant. And so the requirements for when claim and issue preclusion apply also reflect the Anglo-American concern for procedural fairness, sometimes over and above substantive correctness of outcome. So long as a party has had the opportunity to be heard on that issue or claim, he or she will ordinarily be barred from relitigation regardless of the equities in final outcome.

Claim and issue preclusion are not self-executing. The person who wishes to rely on either doctrine must raise it. For instance, a defendant who wishes to raise claim preclusion should allege it as an affirmative defense in her answer and then file a motion with the court requesting that the second lawsuit be dismissed on claim preclusion grounds. Similarly, a defendant or plaintiff wishing to use issue preclusion must raise it by motion. A grant of that motion will deem the issue adjudged in a previous lawsuit and now binding on the parties in the subsequent litigation.

In the United States, the rules of preclusion vary somewhat from state to state. The state common law principles of preclusion apply in state courts as well as in the federal court that sits in that state, with the exception that federal courts hearing federal question claims will follow federal common law principles of preclusion.

CLAIM PRECLUSION

While the case law principles of preclusion lack the clarity that statutes might have provided, they nevertheless operate rather rigidly and formally. They will bar relitigation of claims and issues, regardless of whether the original decision was correct.

Generally speaking, the requirements of claim preclusion are as follows: 1) the claim advanced in the second action must be within the "same scope of cause of action" or within the same claim, to use Federal Rule language, as those advanced in the first action; 2) the second action must involve the same parties or parties in privity as the parties in the first action; and 3) there must have been a final judgment rendered on the merits of the case in the first action. As you can see, these requirements deal more with the procedural fairness rendered in the first action than with its substantive correctness. Review for substantive correctness lies within the province of appeals and the appeals courts, not with preclusion.

We will discuss each criterion in the reverse order. The third criteria — that there must be a final judgment on the merits — is understandable as necessary for the efficiency of the legal system. The "final judgment on the merits" requirement means that all regular proceedings on the claim must be concluded with no outstanding issues remaining before the judgment can be deemed final, binding, and preclusive of any relitigation. It would be inefficient to apply preclusion and bind a party to a nonfinal ruling that may be changed as the litigation proceeds at the trial level. Note, however, even if the judgment is on appeal, it will normally be considered final for claim preclusion purposes. This is true for the federal courts, while the state courts are divided. This is because the appeals process can take years to complete and it would be unfair to the winning party to allow the losing party to start another lawsuit on the same cause of action.

The final judgment on the merits requirement also means that the claim must have been decided on the merits, and not on some procedural technicality. The definition of "on the merits" is broader than one might expect. For example, a default judgment for failure to file an answer to a complaint, seemingly procedural, has often been construed as a final judgment on the merits. Otherwise defendants could ignore complaints and fail to appear in court with impunity. On the other hand, if there has been a dismissal based on lack of subject matter jurisdiction or a failure of personal jurisdiction or venue, this would ordinarily not be considered on the merits. In these instances, the plaintiff has not had the opportunity to present the merits of her case, making claim preclusion unfair.

The second requirement of claim preclusion is that it can only be raised as between the same people who were parties in the first case or persons in privity with them. Here is where due process comes into play. Parties may not be bound by a judgment if they had not had the opportunity to litigate the action, and so, similarly, they should not be bound from bringing a later action on the same claim. However, if the party were not the actual party in the first action, she may still be bound if there is sufficient identity of interests between her and the actual party in the initial case. The courts have worked out three major areas in which privity applies, although they occasionally use more flexible tests to extend the doctrine.[4]

One example of privity is when there is a successor in interest. I cannot sue you for trespassing on my property, lose, and then assign my cause of action to a new buyer who sues again for the exact same trespass. A second area covers representative parties, such as trustees and executors; if a trustee loses a lawsuit, a beneficiary cannot bring a suit for the same cause of action. Class actions are another example: Members of the class, who have not opted out, are bound by the victory or loss of the named class representatives. The third example of privity is when a party who controls the litigation, such as an insurance company, it will be bound by a final judgment in which the insured was a party. Liability policies typically give the insurer the right to control the litigation.

The criteria of "same scope of action" for claim preclusion is perhaps the most controversial. What is the scope of the prior action that will preclude the subsequent action? The idea behind same scope of action is that the prior judgment ends litigation not only as to every ground of recovery that was

---

4. For example, sometimes privity is used to reach "a wide range of commercial relationships." Jack H. Friedenthal, Mary Kay Kane, & Arthur M. Miller, Civil Procedure 721 (4th ed., West 2005). Some courts have also expanded privity through a concept called "virtual representation." *See, e.g.,* Jay Tidmarch & Roger H. Transgrud, Complex Litigation and the Adversary System, 229-232 n.5 (Foundation Press 1998).

actually presented in the action, but also as to every ground that might have been presented. The concept is that the entire original action is barred from relitigation by the first judgment; the first judgment precludes subsequent actions when they are the same.

What you have read previously about the history of American civil procedure is relevant to understanding the breadth of claim preclusion. Under the old British writ system, it was relatively easy to determine whether the first action was identical to the second because only one writ could be used for each action. With the elimination of the writ system, the Field Code system required the plaintiff to plead facts underlying "a cause of action." In order to ascertain whether what was then called res judicata applied, the courts would explore the breadth of the cause of action sued upon; whether the second case was merely a different argument subsumed under the initially brought cause of action (for example, bad brakes and failing to stop are two theories of the same cause of action — negligence) or whether it was a new cause of action altogether (breach of warranty against a manufacturer would be a different cause of action from negligence, although both arose from the same accident).

Under this traditional view, it is said that a plaintiff cannot split her cause of action with different recovery theories. The traditional view focuses on whether the primary right or type of injury is the same in the first action as in the second action. As a practical matter, the traditional view often applies a "same evidence" test to determine whether the same body of evidence is used to support the two claims. If so, then, the two claims are the same, constituting the same scope of action, and the second action is precluded by the judgment from the first. It is unclear, however, how much of an overlap in the evidence there must be. An alternative test applied by the traditional view is the "destruction of prior judgment" test to assess whether any decision in the second action would contradict the judgment in the first action. The same evidence test and the destruction of prior judgment test have different rationales. While the destruction of prior judgment test is concerned with maintaining the integrity of the first judgment, the same evidence test is motivated by the goals of efficiency and judicial economy.

The Federal Rules of Civil Procedure led to a more expansive view of the meaning of same claim for preclusion purposes. The term *claim* in modern civil procedure has two different meanings. Claim as used in preclusion is distinguished from the word as found in Fed. R. Civ. P. 8(a) "a claim showing that the pleader is entitled to relief" or as in Fed. R. Civ. P. 12(b)(6) "a claim upon which relief can be granted." A claim entitling one to relief under the rules is another way of saying that the pleader has a viable cause of action if she can prove its elements. This gives the claim a meaning identical to or at least similar to the Field Code's "cause of action." When used as such, the Federal Rules of Civil Procedure permit and even encourage joinder of claims (in other words, joinder of different causes of action) in a single litigation, whether or not these claims arose out of the underlying dispute.

On the other hand, the term *claim* standing alone is often interpreted to mean the underlying story that gave rise to multiple causes of action, rather than meaning any one or more of the multiple causes of action. This broader interpretation given to claim is consistent with the more modern "transactional" view to litigation. With liberality in pleadings and joinder, many courts have also come to interpret the word "claim" in claim preclusion consistent with the transactional view to encourage parties to join together their causes of action arising from the same set of circumstances in a single litigation or be forever barred. It is said that the pleader cannot split her claim.

Under this more modern transactional view to claim preclusion, the same scope of action requirement refers to all rights of plaintiff to remedies against defendant with respect to the underlying transaction that gave rise to the litigation.[5] When courts say that the pleader cannot split her claim, they are usually referring to the broader sense of the entire transaction or set of circumstances or occurrences giving rise to liability. They are using claim in the sense of the underlying dispute that gave rise to the lawsuit. The relevant factors to consider are "whether the facts are related in time, space, origin, or motivation, whether they form a convenient trial unit, and whether their treatment as a unit conforms to the parties' expectation or business understanding or usage."[6] If so, the causes of action constitute one claim and must be brought in a single litigation, rather than in successive separate lawsuits.

As applied to the case of Lee v. Cherryum, the plaintiff, Albert Lee, may bring a negligence claim against the Cherryum Bottling Company for providing the tainted soda. Whether he wins or loses, he will be precluded from bringing a subsequent case against Cherryum Bottling Company based on the same negligence. This would be true whether one uses a traditional same evidence or modern transactional approach to claim preclusion. Also, once Lee's case reaches final judgment, it will not matter if he later becomes sicker than he thought; he will not be able to sue later for new, different, or greater damages.

Furthermore, if Albert Lee neglected to bring his claim of breach of implied warranty in the first proceeding for ingesting the toxic soda, he will definitely be precluded from bringing it in a second proceeding under the modern, transactional approach. The breach of implied warranty claim is deemed to be within the same claim as the product liability claim; both arise from the same set of circumstances. He might even be barred under the traditional approach, because of the substantial overlap of evidence, but this result is less clear because negligence and breach of warranty are different causes of action.

However, under either approach, if Albert Lee were hit by a Cherryum delivery truck two weeks after ingesting the toxic soda, he would not be precluded from bringing a second claim against Cherryum Bottling Company for that accident. That second claim was not related to the first claim, nor could it be said to fall within the same transactional claim as the first bad soda case. Of course, under the liberal federal joinder rules, Lee could, but is not required to, join this unrelated cause of action against Cherryum Bottling Company in the initial case (Rule 18). If he did include the delivery truck accident claim in his initial complaint and a final judgment on the merits were

---

5. You have already encountered this transactional approach when you read about Rule 20 joinder of parties, compulsory counterclaims (Rule 13), and supplemental jurisdiction.
6. Restatement (Second) of Judgments § 24, cmt. b.

rendered, he would then be barred from bringing it in a later case under the principles of claim preclusion.

Claim preclusion applies whether the first case is won or lost. Some courts say that when the plaintiff wins, all of her claims arising from the same transaction are merged in the remedy given in the case. If the plaintiff loses, some courts use the term *barred* rather than *merged*. Whether barred or merged, plaintiff cannot split her claim.

Claim preclusion also precludes not only the claim that was litigated, but also defenses that might have been raised. Claim preclusion operates to prevent a defendant from raising any new defenses in any subsequent litigation to enforce a final judgment. The idea is that the first judgment is conclusive of all defenses that the defendant might have asserted, as well as those that were actually put forward in the first litigation. Additionally, if a defense were raised in the first action, most jurisdictions will also prohibit defendant from using that defense as a basis for a separate claim in a second lawsuit, if this lawsuit will undermine or nullify the judgment in the first action. Rule 13(a) of the Federal Rules provides the same result by requiring the defendant to bring compulsory counterclaims or forever lose them.

In sum, if the claim in a second case is deemed to be within "the same scope" as the first case, and the parties are the same in the first and second action, or in privity, and there has been a final judgment rendered on the merits in the first action, then the doctrine of claim preclusion (res judicata) will apply to bar the second action. The shorthand is: Do not split a claim.

ISSUE PRECLUSION

In contrast to claim preclusion (res judicata) that prevents relitigation of claims, issue preclusion (collateral estoppel) ends controversy over issues, usually a factual one or a mixed question of law and fact (such as negligence or breach of contract). When an issue has been fully litigated between parties or those in privity with them, issue preclusion operates to preclude relitigation of that particular issue in any later action. Unlike claim preclusion that precludes subsequent suits only if they are deemed to be the same claim, issue preclusion precludes relitigation of issues in later lawsuits on any claim (even if the second action involves a totally different claim as the first one). The potential reach of issue preclusion is therefore both more narrow and broader than claim preclusion in the sense that while it applies only to specific issues, it can be applied in any subsequent action.

The requirements for issue preclusion are: 1) the same issue of law or fact; 2) the issue or fact to be precluded (not relitigated) must have been contested, adjudicated, and essential to the judgment; and 3) in much current case law, the party against whom issue preclusion is asserted must have been a party or in privity with a party in the prior action. Historically, this third requirement was a bit different and called for mutuality of parties, that is, the same parties, in both the first and second cases, but, as you will see, mutuality is in retreat and the entire requirement has become somewhat complicated.

Let us look at the requirements in order. Practical considerations determine whether issues in two actions are the same. They typically include straightforward factors such as factual identity, legal standards, and the nature of the burden of proof (civil vs. criminal) for the issues in two actions.[7] As a result, the passage of time (between similar events) may render issues not identical and prevent issue preclusion from barring the litigation of these issues in a second separate action.

The courts exercise a good deal of common sense. In the well-known, if not notorious, *O.J. Simpson* case, the famous former professional football star was accused of murdering his wife. He was found "not guilty," and set free. In American criminal cases, the government must prove its case "beyond a reasonable doubt," which is a stringent burden of proof. In typical civil cases, the plaintiff need only prove all of the elements of a cause of action it relies upon by "a preponderance of the evidence." In other words, all the plaintiff has to convince the fact finder of is that it is more likely than not that each element is true. The family of the murdered widow in the O. J. Simpson scenario was allowed to bring a subsequent civil case against Simpson without the criminal case having any preclusive effect.

This is true for a number of reasons. First, the deceased's family was not a party to the first case and could not be barred by preclusion law for they did not have their due process day in court; the government is the plaintiff in criminal cases. Second, the civil case is a different claim than the criminal case (one brought by the family of the deceased wife based on tort law, and the other brought by the state based on violation of criminal law), so there cannot be claim preclusion. Third, since the burden of proof on plaintiffs in a civil case is less stringent than the criminal case, Simpson could have won in the criminal case but lost in the civil case.

Even if the plaintiffs were parties to the first case, they might prevail under the less demanding civil standard. However, if the reverse were true — that is, if Simpson had been found guilty in the criminal case, the plaintiffs probably could have used issue preclusion to preclude him from denying that he had intentionally killed his wife — an example of nonmutual offensive collateral estoppel, a concept to which we will soon turn. The same issues would have already been litigated in the earlier criminal case and Simpson had his day in court regarding them. Had he been found guilty, it would have been under the more stringent criminal burden of proof standard. If he was found to have been guilty under the more stringent "beyond a reasonable doubt" standard, one can fairly assume that he would also be found liable by the lesser "preponderance of the evidence" standard.

Turning to the second requirement, the issue must have been "fully litigated and essential" to the final judgment in the first action. Implicit in this requirement is that the second court must know how the issue was actually litigated and that the issue was essential to the verdict. The idea is that if an issue was not essential to a judgment, the fact finder may not have concentrated on it and taken it seriously. It would be unfair to preclude the party if he may not have paid much attention to it and failed to litigate it aggressively. Judicial efficiency also dictates this result. Otherwise, parties would in effect be forced to litigate

---

7. Friedenthal, Kane & Miller, *supra* note 4, at 699.

every issue (even nonessential ones to the litigation) simply to avoid the application of later issue preclusion. This would be inefficient to the legal system and unnecessarily costly to the parties.

While seemingly straightforward, this "necessary and essential" criterion is frequently a point of contention. Jury decisions are often general verdicts that do not delineate specific findings of fact. Parties in a second action seeking to raise the issue preclusion defense will have to demonstrate that the fact-finder did address and decide a particular issue and that it was necessary to reaching the verdict. Of course, if a jury or judge makes a special finding of fact that is necessary to the result, then issue preclusion is easy to determine.

A general jury verdict for a *defendant*, however, does not educate a later court as to what issues were actually found believable by the jury in the first action. The jury might have found that plaintiff failed to prove any one of the various elements of her case or that the defendant has proven her affirmative defense. A general jury verdict for the *plaintiff*, by contrast, is usually more instructive and conducive to issue preclusion. In order for a plaintiff to win on a cause of action, she must prove each element of her case. In a general jury verdict for the plaintiff, then, the court can justifiably assume that the plaintiff has proven each element of her case and that the jury believed each element of the cause of action. In that instance, there may be an issue preclusive effect as to those elements, at least among the same parties to the first case and those in privity with them.

The final requirement of issue preclusion deals with who may assert the doctrine. The traditional rule, the rule that still remains in some jurisdictions, is called "mutuality." That is, only parties who were parties in the first action (or those in privity with them) may mutually use or be bound by issue preclusion. Mutuality requires symmetry and provides that a party can't use issue preclusion against another if the party itself is not bound by the judgment.

For example, in the *Cherryum* case, assume that Albert Lee had shared his can of Cherryum with another gardener, Tony Smith, who also got sick but has not yet brought suit and also that the manufacturer, Cherryum, Inc., was found by a jury in the Lee litigation, on a special question on the issue, to be negligent in making the syrup used in the can in question. Tony now sues Cherryum, Inc., in a second action. In a jurisdiction requiring mutuality, because Tony (not a party in the prior action) is not bound by the judgment in the earlier action, Tony could not bind Cherryum with the prior finding of negligence and could not preclude Cherryum, Inc., from denying that it was negligent in this later litigation.

However, in those states that have replaced "mutuality" with the "non-mutuality" requirement, asymmetry reigns. Tony could take advantage of Albert's victory in the prior suit (particularly if there was a good reason why Tony did not join in Albert's suit), and preclude Cherryum from denying negligence, even though Tony was not in the prior suit and could not be bound by any adverse findings from that suit. Nonmutuality jurisdictions placed their focus on due process and deemed that because Cherryum was a party in the prior case, Cherryum already had its day in court. It is fair to bind Cherryum, but not Tony, to any findings from that suit. Due process requires that Tony be given his day in court.

The mutuality requirement is not without its fans.[8] Some argue that nonmutuality unfairly burdens parties, such as Cherryum, Inc., in our example, with broad preclusive effect if it loses, but it is not given the advantage of expanded preclusion if it wins. In our example, Cherryum, Inc., can only achieve a partial victory by defeating Albert, but it could be burdened with potential multiple losses if it loses the first case. Cherryum would have to bear the burden of that adverse issue finding in subsequent lawsuits brought against it by new plaintiffs. Mutuality advocates point out that ours is a party driven system in which each party is autonomous and independent. Why should Tony (or his lawyer), who has not done the work, get the benefit of Albert's victory when he was never at risk in the first case? Moreover, nonmutuality in this type of case encourages parties to lie in wait, not join in the first litigation; if mutuality were the rule, it is more likely that Tony would have joined Albert as a plaintiff in the initial case.

Nonetheless, the case law has been moving in an anti-mutuality direction. Starting in the 1940s, jurisdictions have increasingly rejected the "mutuality" requirement for issue preclusion, based primarily on efficiency grounds. When an issue is precluded in subsequent litigation, it need not be relitigated time and again, wasting parties and court resources. Beginning with the California Supreme Court's 1942 decision in *Bernhard v. Bank of America National Trust & Savings Association*,[9] the gradual but persistent desertion of the mutuality rule culminated in the 1972 U.S. Supreme Court decision in *Blonder-Tongue Laboratories v. University of Illinois Foundation*.[10]

In *Blonder-Tongue*, the plaintiff sued defendant unsuccessfully for patent infringement.[11] The patent was held invalid. In the subsequent suit by the same plaintiff against another alleged infringer, the Supreme Court said that the plaintiff was bound (issue precluded) on the question of the patent's validity — that is, the defendant in the second action need not defend that issue.[12] The patent was to be taken as invalid, even though there was a lack of mutuality of parties. In other words, if the initial decision had found the patent valid, the second defendant would not have been bound by that determination because it had not had its day in court in the prior suit. Yet, it could take advantage of the previous invalid patent finding. This is an example of using issue preclusion defensively, that is, by the defendant, or in the law school tongue-twister parlance, "nonmutual defensive collateral estoppel." The Court invoked the rationale of preventing court congestion and the misallocation of resources.[13] It would be inefficient to require a defendant, simply because of the mutuality principle, to present a complete defense to a claim that the plaintiff has fully litigated and lost in a prior action.[14]

---

8. *See, e.g.*, Anne Bowen Poulin, *Prosecutorial Inconsistency, Estoppel, and Due Process: Making the Prosecution Get its Story Straight*, 89 Cal. L. Rev. 1423 (2001) (arguing that mutuality should extend to criminal cases for consistent prosecutions between criminal defendants); Michael J. Waggoner, *Fifty Years of* Bernhard v. Bank of America *is Enough: Collateral Estoppel Should Require Mutuality but Res Judicata Should Not*, 12 Rev. Litig. 391 (1993) (in the civil context).

9. 122 P.2d 892, 895 (CA 1942).

10. 402 U.S. 313 (1971).

11. *Id.* at 315-317.

12. *Id.* at 330-334.

13. *Id.* at 329.

14. *Id.* at 347.

Important to reiterate, in mutuality as well as in nonmutuality jurisdictions, issue preclusion can only bind parties who were parties in the first action — or those in privity with them — and who had the opportunity to defend and litigate that issue. The due process requirement dictates that one who has not had an opportunity to litigate an issue as a party in court (or one who is in privity with such a party) cannot be bound by a lawsuit in which they were not a party.[15]

After the *Blonder-Tongue* decision, the U.S. Supreme Court tempered the offensive (but not the defensive) use of nonmutual collateral estoppel in the federal courts — that is, issue preclusion asserted by the plaintiff. Tony Smith precluding Cherryum, Inc., is a good example of "offensive nonmutual collateral estoppel." With the slow erosion of mutuality, scholars rose to its defense by pointing out the anomaly of nonmutuality in the multiple lawsuit scenario in which a party who defended the first suit successfully but lost the second suit would, despite her initial victory, be estopped from denying liability in all subsequent actions.[16] Others noted that while defensive nonmutual collateral estoppel promotes efficient administration of justice by encouraging the plaintiff to join all the defendants in a single action, the offensive use of collateral estoppel leads to inefficiency by giving plaintiffs incentive to abstain from the initial litigation and wait to use issue preclusion in a later litigation, if the first decision is helpful to them.[17] Moreover, by eliminating the mutuality requirement the courts have in effect encouraged parties in the initial litigation to litigate more issues to avoid being later bound by preclusion doctrine. Such results introduced greater inefficiency into the system, rather than the alleged efficiency.

The Supreme Court showed its awareness of the potential problems of offensive nonmutual collateral estoppel in the 1979 case of *Parklane Hosiery Co., Inc. v. Shore.*[18] In *Parklane*, the plaintiff, the Securities Exchange Commission, in the initial case without a jury was able to prove and enjoin the defendants from issuing false and misleading proxy statements.[19] A private claimant subsequently sued Parklane Hosiery in a second law suit for damages based on the same misstatements and sought to preclude Parklane from denying that it had issued false and misleading statements.[20] The Supreme Court permitted this offensive use of issue preclusion by plaintiffs on the facts of the case, despite a spirited dissent.[21] Although allowing the preclusion, the Supreme Court pronounced several caveats to govern future preclusion law in federal courts.

According to *Parklane*, four additional factors should be considered in the nonmutual use of offensive collateral estoppel (that is, use by a plaintiff who was not a party in the first action): 1) could the nonparty have joined in the

---

15. *See Hansberry v. Lee*, 311 U.S. 32 (1940).
16. Brainerd Currie, *Mutuality of Collateral Estoppel: Limits of the Bernhard Doctrine*, 9 Stan. L. Rev. 281, 285-286 (1957).
17. Michael Kimmel, *The Impacts of Defensive and Offensive Assertion of Collateral Estoppel by a Nonparty*, 35 Geo. Wash. L. Rev. 1010, 1025, 1034 (1967).
18. 439 U.S. 322 (1979).
19. *Id.* at 324-325.
20. *Id.* at 325.
21. The dissent pointed out that application of preclusion here denied the defendant a right to jury trial on the issue of these alleged misstatement. *Id.* at 337-356 (Rehnquist, J., dissenting).

prior litigation? 2) was the subsequent litigation foreseeable at the time of the first suit so defendant had every incentive to defend the action vigorously? 3) is the judgment being relied on consistent with prior judgments against this defendant so that there is no fear of the inconsistent prior verdict phenomenon? 4) are there any procedural opportunities available to the defendant in the second action that did not exist in the first, so that a different result might ensue if the issues are retried?[22] For example, was the defendant unable to engage in full discovery or to call witnesses in the first case?

The *Parklane* factors ensure that only decisions rendered on issues that have been fairly adjudicated can be binding in subsequent litigation. The Court was concerned with fairness to the defendant who may not have foreseen additional potential future lawsuits, and therefore, did not vigorously litigate her claims in the first action. The factors also seek to ensure that plaintiffs do not "lie in wait" to take advantage of another's favorable judgment. The *Parklane* treatment of mutuality is federal law. State jurisdictions vary substantially on their treatment of mutuality.

It is unclear whether the rejection of the mutuality doctrine and thereby, the broadening of issue preclusion, has actually resulted in greater court efficiency. One could make the argument that the combination of liberal joinder devices, particularly the class action, combined with nonmutual offensive collateral estoppel (issue preclusion utilized by subsequent plaintiffs) would have the result of expansive lawsuits with the potential to bind more future litigants. Liberal use of preclusion law for mass tort cases, such as asbestos or tobacco, might seem the perfect place for such savings of time and money. But the inherent requirements of issue preclusion render its liberal application unlikely.

For example, assume that Albert Lee and his wife won their case against the manufacturer, and further that thousands of other drinkers of Cherryum now want to sue, claiming that the drink was poisonous to them as well. It may be difficult for them to use issue preclusion against Cherryum, Inc. First of all, if the Lee case resulted in a general verdict for the Lees, it may be uncertain exactly what the jury found. Maybe they did not think the Cherryum manufacturing process was negligent, but that simply one batch was problematic because of a disgruntled employee who was beyond the control of Cherryum. Issue preclusion cannot be used unless one can identify what issue was actually decided.

Even if one knew exactly what the jury decided, there may still be distinctions rendering issue preclusion inapplicable. For example, even if the jury decided that the syrup was negligently manufactured, the fact that one batch of syrup is negligently manufactured proves nothing about other batches. How do we know that the can in a later suit was from the same batch? And even if we do know it was from the same batch (which itself will be a jury issue in a subsequent case), and the court is willing to issue preclude on negligent manufacture, there will still have to be a trial on whether the new plaintiff drank from a can containing that batch, whether the new plaintiff had been warned, whether the drink caused the harm, and the extent of the harm.

22. *Id.* at 331-333.

In the asbestos arena of thousands of cases, it has been even harder to use nonmutual offensive collateral estoppel. Similarly, even though there have been dozens of tobacco cases, including many class actions, brought by injured smokers and others, offensive nonmutual issue preclusion has not played a role in limiting the claims.

As the courts have pointed out, each asbestos litigation is substantially different. What a manufacturer knew about asbestos at one point in time is not precisely what it knew at another time. The failure to warn one plaintiff does not mean that another plaintiff was not warned or did not find out about the danger of asbestos on his or her own. Moreover, how the asbestos was used in a particular case (for instance, was it encapsulated by a protective seal) can alter many of the issues in subsequent cases, including unreasonable care, causation, and harm.[23] Furthermore, asbestos manufacturers have won many lawsuits. Even if we knew precisely what one jury found in a particular case, it would be unfair to preclude the manufacturer by utilizing a case in which it lost, when it has frequently won on the same issue.

The federal nature of our court system also clouds the use of preclusion. Subsequent courts usually look to the first court, the court that rendered the judgment to find the applicable preclusion doctrine. If the first court still requires mutuality for issue preclusion, then the second court normally will be bound by that limitation. Moreover, even if the first court has eliminated the mutuality requirement, the state tort law applied in the first case may be quite different from the state tort law to be applied in the second case. In that situation, the issue of negligence decided in the first case will arguably be different from the issue in the second case and therefore issue preclusion should not apply.

Even in class actions that the defendant has won, members of the plaintiff class have still been able to sue in a subsequent lawsuit arising from the same set of circumstances. In a case in which a class of African-America employees sued an employer for a pattern of discrimination against all the black employees, and the plaintiffs lost, the United States Supreme Court let individual employees later sue for individual discrimination against them: The fact that there is not a pattern of discrimination against a racial group does not prove that a specific individual did not suffer discrimination.[24]

Rather than reducing litigation expenses, preclusion law may have in fact contributed to increased litigation expense. The breadth of claim preclusion means that plaintiffs often include every possible cause of action because they do not want to later be precluded; the breadth may cause greater litigation of issues by defendants who wish to avoid later preclusion. And perhaps some cases are now brought that would not have been launched except for the advantages given by preclusion law. To avoid the possibility of issue preclusion in multiple subsequent suits, defendants may be forced to settle rather than face a losing judgment.[25] This advantage to plaintiffs may in fact encourage more plaintiffs to sue in search of settlement. Moreover, the sophisticated

23. For an analysis of why it is difficult to justify nonmutual offensive collateral estoppel against asbestos manufacturers and how many issues remain even if collateral estoppel was permitted, *see, e.g., Hardy v. Johns-Manville Sales Corp.*, 681 F. 2d 334 (5th Cir. 1982).
24. *Cooper v. Federal Reserve Bank of Richmond*, 467 U.S. 867 (1984).
25. Note, *Exposing the Extortion Gap: An Economic Analysis of the Rules of Collateral Estoppel*, 105 Harv. L. Rev. 1940, 1956-1957 (1992).

arguments about the breadth of both claim and issue preclusion themselves cause expense and require trial and appellate courts to consume valuable time. In class action cases that seek to bind members of the class, the second court permits hearings on whether the first court protected the interests of class members through diligent representation.

At this point, we probably do not have to remind you how complicated civil procedure is in the United States, how interrelated each aspect is, and how difficult it is to anticipate the results of procedural change. The Federal Rules brought with them ease of pleading, broad joinder, and liberal discovery. Preclusion law broadened in response, with claim preclusion capturing more subsequent suits than merely precluding the same cause of action. Court congestion and litigation expense encouraged nonmutual use of issue preclusion — so long as the party to be precluded had its day in court. But a combination of due process concerns, fairness, federalism, and lawyer creativity instead limited the potential benefits of nonmutual preclusion and may in turn have added to litigation expense. Trying to combine both fairness and efficiency in a court system is clearly not an easy task.

APPELLATE REVIEW OF FINAL JUDGMENTS

Challenges to the substance of final judgments may be appealed and reviewed pursuant to an appeals process to a court at the next level of authority. The federal courts and most states provide for a three-tiered court system, with an appeal as of right to the intermediate court. These intermediate appellate courts review decisions made by trial courts and administrative agencies. Appeals to the highest court are often only with permission of the court.

In the federal system, circuit courts of appeal review decisions from the district courts in their region.[26] The U.S. Supreme Court reviews decisions from the circuit courts of appeal and on federal matters, decisions from the highest state courts. While appeal to the circuit court is of right, appeals to the U.S. Supreme Court must be by leave sought through a petition of certiorari.[27] The courts of appeal may certify questions of law for guidance from the Supreme Court, but that is rarely done.[28] The party seeking a federal appeal is usually required to give notice of the appeal within 30 days after the final judgment below is rendered. The Federal Rules of Appellate Procedure, passed in 1967, govern the federal appellate process, but many states have also adopted procedures similar to the federal rules.

The role of the court of appeals is to review the decision rendered by the trial court, not to retry a case. The appellate court will review the decision for appropriate applications of law and egregious error in findings of fact, but an appellate court will be unlikely to overturn a trial court's findings of fact. This

26. As discussed in Chapter 1, there are 12 regional courts of appeals and a thirteenth court of appeals called the Court of Appeals for the Federal Circuit. The Court of Appeals for the Federal Circuit hears appeals from the Court of Federal Claims (that hears contract claims against the United States) and other specialized appeals.

27. 28 U.S.C. § 1254(1).

28. *Id.* § 1254(2).

again distinguishes the Anglo-American common law system from civil law countries where the right to a first level review means that the appellate court can review a trial court decision for factual as well as legal accuracy and even retry cases and accept new evidence (although the modern trend is to limit this right).[29] Because a trial in the common law system is a single, continuous event with live testimony and a jury, it is not easy or efficient for the court or the parties to retry cases. And because the appellate judge was not present to hear and judge the credibility of the live testimony, the appellate judge is reluctant to overturn a trial judge's findings of fact when the review is on the record alone.

On appeal, the review is therefore based on a closed record from the court below. There will be no new evidence or testimony presented, although in rare instances an appellate court will take judicial notice of a noncontroversial fact. The review is primarily to correct issues of law or egregious errors in factual findings that are revealed in the trial record. Thus, on a trial court's findings of fact, the standard of review is quite deferential (and even more so if the jury was the fact finder). The appellate court will only reverse the findings of fact if they were "clearly erroneous." If there was egregious error in a jury trial, the appellate court must remand the case for retrial, rather than substitute the reviewer court's decision for that of the jury.

For conclusions of law, the appellate court is less deferential to a trial court's findings and may review the question *de novo*. Such legal questions include erroneous instructions on the law to the jury, evidentiary rulings (if material to the outcome), or the judge's decision on a motion for a judgment as a matter of law. As to decisions within the "discretionary" powers of the trial court, these are reviewed only for abuse of the trial court's discretion. Moreover, under the "harmless error" doctrine, mistakes by the trial court are not a ground for reversal unless they caused a substantial harm.[30]

BRIEFS AND OPINIONS

It is the appellant's (the party seeking appeal) lawyer who must put together the record on appeal in the first instance. This record usually consists of a verbatim transcript of relevant portions of the trial proceeding, any relevant exhibits, as well as relevant motions filed in the case. The record is then transmitted to the court of appeals to be filed by the clerk of the court. Both appellant's and appellee's (the party opposing appeal) lawyers will also submit written papers, known as briefs, advocating their positions on appeal. Contrary to the name, most briefs are usually long, 30 to 40 pages in length, and sometimes longer. A brief will contain a summary of facts and arguments of law, as well as a table of legal authorities that the lawyers deem relevant. An appellate court will rely on these relevant legal authorities in its review.

29. Peter E. Herzog & Delmar Karlen, Attacks on Judicial Decisions, in Civil Procedure 50-89 (Mauro Cappelletti, ed. Martinus Nijhoff Publishers 1973).
    30. 28 U.S.C. § 2111.

The appellee will submit an opposition brief, but the appellant gets the final word by submitting a reply brief.

Judges receive the briefs and trial record well before oral arguments; nine weeks is typical. With the assistance of law clerks who often summarize documents for judges, appellate judges assess the legal arguments and consider the questions they still have. There will usually be a hearing at which lawyers present oral arguments. Lawyers typically have 30 minutes per side to present their arguments. Judges often interrupt with questions.

Judges normally sit in panels of three in intermediate appellate courts, such as the circuit courts at the federal level. The panel affirms, reverses, or modifies the lower court decision by majority vote. At the Supreme Court level, both state and federal, all of the judges usually hear the oral argument. Written decisions are almost always issued on appeal cases. In fact, this is the only form of communication between an appellate judge and the trial court as to any case on appeal. A single judge of the panel will be assigned to write the first draft of the opinion. The draft will be circulated to the other judges for revisions. A judge disagreeing with the decision can, and often does, write a dissenting opinion to register her disagreement. Some opinions are short; others can be longer than 30 pages, sometimes exceeding 100 pages. The electronic media has helped to expedite the publication of opinions. Most appellate decisions are posted online on the date of issuance, where the public can get access to the opinion immediately.

Appeals in the United States federal appellate courts have increased dramatically during the latter half of the twentieth century. Federal appeals increased from 3,899 in 1960 to 49,671 in 1996.[31] A major reason is the expansion of federal rights and the creation of more federal causes of action, and hence, more cases brought in the federal district courts. There is some evidence, though, that a significant amount of the increase has been an increase in the percentage of specific types of cases appealed; cases brought by prisoners and civil rights cases are appealed at a substantially higher rate than other types.

The U.S. courts of appeals have borne the brunt of this wave because they are the "breakwater against which the tidal wave of appeals spend themselves,"[32] before reaching the Supreme Court, which has discretion to reject petitions. Courts have tried to shorten the process of appeals by instituting shortcuts to a hearing, denying oral arguments in some cases, limiting the time for oral arguments, and requiring shorter brief requirements. In 1994, the federal courts of appeals heard oral arguments in less than one-half of the appeals that they decided.[33]

31. Judicial Conference of the United States, Committee on Long Range Planning, Long Range Plan for the Federal Courts 15, table. 4 (Washington, D.C.: Committee on Long Range Planning, 1995). Excluding prisoner civil rights cases and three other categories of cases, the study found that the rate of appeals held steady through the period 1977-1993 at 9 percent. Carol Krafka, Joe Cecil, and Patricia Lombard, Stalking the Increase in the Rate of Federal Civil Appeals 29, fig. 8 (Washington, D.C.: Federal Judicial Center, 1995). *See also* Daniel J. Meador and Jordana S. Bernstein, Appellate Courts in the United States 122 (West Publishing Co., 1994).

32. Meador & Bernstein, *supra* note 31, at 26.

33. Oral arguments can be denied under local rules when a three judge panel unanimously agrees that it is not necessary after an examination of briefs and record. Fed. R. App. P. 34(a)(2). *See* Thomas E. Baker, Rationalizing Justice on Appeal: The Problems of the U.S. Court of Appeals 7 (West Publishing Co., 1994).

Other recent proposals under consideration to alleviate the backlog of appeal cases include restructuring the circuits to a smaller number, which would reduce the disharmony among them.[34] Another idea is to create a two-tiered intermediate court system as in some state court systems, with the second tier having discretionary review to reduce the number of petitions to the United States Supreme Court.[35] Some appeals court judges have apparently responded to the high numbers of appeals by reducing the number of written opinions. Instead, these judges issue decisions that simply affirm, reverse, or remand the case without explanation. Since the United States is a common law country that relies on written opinions for guidance and modification of legal doctrine, some scholars fear that the declining use of published opinions may mean the concomitant decline of the common law system.[36]

THE FINAL JUDGMENT RULE

In most circumstances, an appeal may only be taken when the proceedings below are completed and a final judgment is rendered. This jurisdictional requirement is known as the "final judgment rule." There are complications to the determination of finality. Once again you will encounter the pernicious possibility of surprising consequences. First, let us look at the structure and the doctrine.

Title 18 U.S.C. § 1291 provides for appeal to the courts of appeals only from "final decisions of the district courts of the United States." For purposes of § 1291, a final judgment is generally regarded as a decision by the district court that "ends the litigation on the merits and leaves nothing for the court to do but execute the judgment."[37] The final judgment rule avoids piecemeal appeals and conserves the resources of the judiciary. If finality is not present, the appeals process may not be necessary because the case may settle or the issue may become moot as a result of the trial. Furthermore, allowing for appeals prior to the final judgment could lead to delaying tactics and harassment.

A final judgment is the final legal pronouncement of the judge's decision in a case or, if there is a jury, the final rendition of the jury verdict entered by the judge or clerk. A final judgment can also sometimes be entered early in the case as a result of dispositive motions, such as a judgment dismissing the case because the complaint states no cognizable claim under the law or after discovery as a summary judgment, if the judge concludes that there are no disputed factual issues and a party is entitled to judgment as a matter of law.

34. *See, e.g.,* Martha J. Dragich, *Once a Century: Time for a Structural Overhaul of the Federal Courts,* 1996 Wis. L. Rev. 11 (1996).
35. Meador and Bernstein, *supra* note 31, at 128.
36. *See, e.g.,* Martha J. Dragich, *Will the Federal Courts of Appeals Perish if They Publish? Or Does the Declining Use of Opinions To Explain and Justify Judicial Decisions Pose A Greater Threat?,* 44 Am. U. L. Rev. 757 (1995).
37. *Catlin v. United States,* 324 U.S. 229, 233 (1945).

Even after parties have settled, they will often agree to enter the agreement as a consent judgment or a consent decree with the court.

There are some judge-made exceptions to the final judgment rule. One exception is the collateral order doctrine. Under it, the appellate court will grant immediate review if there is a conclusive order to a disputed matter that is separate from the merits of the litigation and if review after final judgment is likely to be too late and ineffective.[38] Such collateral orders include a denial of defendant's motion to require security for bringing suit,[39] denial of a motion to dismiss based on a claim of absolute immunity from suit,[40] and an order requiring disclosure of documents as to which attorney-client privilege and work product protection was claimed.[41] Another judicially carved exception to the final judgment rule is those instances in which immediate appeal is allowed to avoid irreparable injury to the parties.[42]

In a case with multiple claims or parties, the trial court under Fed. R. Civ. P. 54(b) may make a ruling disposing of fewer than all of the claims or parties. In that instance, the ruling may be immediately appealed if the trial court makes "an express determination that there is no just reason for delay" and "an express direction for the entry of judgment." Thus, under Rule 54(b), a district court can authorize appeal of certain decisions by picking out appropriate rulings for appeal and labeling them as such. In addition, Fed. R. Civ. P. 23(f) grants courts of appeals discretion to hear interlocutory appeals (appeals before final judgment) of the granting or denying the certification of a class action, since the effect of class certification is so determinative in a litigation.

There are further statutory exceptions that allow appellate review of interlocutory decisions. These include interlocutory orders regarding injunctions, writs of mandamus and prohibition, and court certified questions. Under 28 U.S.C. § 1292(a), an interlocutory appeal may be taken with respect to injunctions. Injunctions are orders from the court prohibiting a party from certain action or mandating a party to take certain action. Injunctions generally require immediate action by parties; delays from appeal might pose exceptional hardship.

An immediate appeal may also be taken of writs of mandamus. Writs of mandamus are extraordinary orders requiring or prohibiting certain actions by public officials.[43] These orders may be immediately appealed, since they are in fact a new proceeding regarding not the controversy between the parties of the litigation, but rather, a controversy between a party and the court. Early appeal may also be granted on a request from a lower court for clarification on a controlling question of law as to which there is substantial ground for difference of opinion. In that instance, immediate appeal may materially advance the ultimate termination of litigation.[44]

---

38. *See Cohen v. Beneficial Industrial Corp.*, 337 U.S. 541 (1949).
39. *Id.*.
40. *See Mitchell v. Forsyth*, 472 U.S. 511 (1985).
41. *See In re Ford Motor Co.*, 110 F.3d 954 (3d Cir. 1997).
42. *See Forgay v. Conrad*, 47 U.S. 201 (1848).
43. *See Kerr v. U.S. District Court*, 426 U.S. 394, 402 (1976) ("the remedy of mandamus is a drastic one . . . [and] only exceptional circumstances amounting to judicial 'usurpation of power' will justify the invocation of this extraordinary remedy").
44. 28 U.S.C. § 1292(b).

Generally speaking, in the federal court, the judgment under appeal retains its preclusive effect while the appeal is pending.[45] However, the state courts are divided on this question, with some state courts postponing the claim preclusion defense in the second action until the appeal in the first action is determined. The more modern approach is to use a practical rather than a formal or technical concept of finality in deciding whether claim preclusion applies pending appeal.[46] As to enforcement of the judgment, enforcement may be stayed or halted in the court below pending an appeal. Usually, the stay is conditioned on the applicant's giving a bond.[47]

HIDDEN ISSUES OF POWER

It would be a mistake to leave the appeals process without noting its connection to other aspects of civil procedure and civil litigation generally. It is often said that civil law judges exercise more power in litigation than American common law judges operating in a lawyer-controlled adversary system. But as we have explained, American trial judges have more power than at first meets the eye, particularly in light of recent trends toward greater judicial case management. Further, in a very thoughtful article, Professor Stephen Yeazell points out that while the civil procedure rules have moved the courts in the direction of favoring the pretrial process over trials, the appellate rules have not correspondingly adjusted. The combined effects of a smaller percentage of trials, more discretionary motions involving discovery and joinder, the requirement of final judgment rule, and the great deference shown to trial court determinations by appellate courts have led to the surprising result of placing greater authority in lawyers and trial judges than ever before.[48]

Although the number of appeals has substantially increased, appeals have not kept pace with the increase in filed cases in the lower courts; and further, appeals have tended to leave large areas of trial judge discretion and lawyer conduct not reviewed in any realistic way by appellate courts. The vast bulk of civil litigation now occurs without trials, with most of the process (joinder, discovery, and settlement) in the hands of litigation lawyers whose activity is not initially monitored by any judge. When discovery or joinder disputes do reach a trial judge, they will usually be nonreviewable until final judgment is entered. As such, appeals courts have no opportunities to review critical pretrial steps in the vast majority of cases to review. Even if an issue does reach an appellate court, the "substantial error" rule (no reversal for "harmless error") and "abuse of discretion" doctrine will usually mean that the trial court

45. James Flemming, Jr., Geoffrey C. Hazard, Jr. and John Leubsdorf, Requirement of Finality, Civil Procedure, § 11.4 (4 th ed. Little Brown and Co. 1992).
46. *Id.*.
47. Fed. R. Civ. P. 62(c)-(e).
48. Stephen C. Yeazell, *The Misunderstood Consequences of Modern Civil Process*, 1994 Wis. L. Rev. 631 (1994). Yeazell uses the word "misunderstood" rather than "unintended" because it is difficult to understand the full intent of the drafters of the Federal Rules of Civil Procedure. They did know that they were adding to trial court discretion and lawyer latitude. We use the word "surprising" also in the attempt to avoid speculation at this point on the drafters' intent. In Chapter 3, we do discuss the complex array of "intents" in some detail.

determination will stand. Consequently, in Yeazell's view, and on this he is quite persuasive, the last 50 years have resulted in a huge shift of power from the appellate judges to trial judges, who rarely preside over trials, and trial lawyers, who rarely try cases.

MOTION SEEKING RELIEF FROM JUDGMENT

Once a judgment is deemed final, the normal route to review its validity is through the appeals process. As you have read, trial judges can and have exerted influence on jury verdicts, through such techniques as instructions and special questions presented to the jury. Judges can even determine verdicts on their own by granting motions for judgment as a matter of law, even after a jury verdict has been rendered or by granting new trials. But once a judgment is deemed final, appellate review is by far the major mode of revision.

There is, though, one limited way in which American lawyers can attempt to persuade a trial court to change its trial judgment — that is, by bringing a motion to vacate the judgment or in the language of Fed. R. Civ. P. 60, a motion seeking relief from a judgment or order. The language in this rule is somewhat broad, perhaps leading one to believe that vacating (voiding) judgments rivals appeals in rendering judgments insecure. For instance, Fed. R. Civ. P. 60 starts this way:

> On motion and upon such terms as are just, the court may relieve a party or a party's legal representative from a final judgment, order, or proceeding for the following reasons: (1) mistake, inadvertence, surprise, or excusable neglect; (2) newly discovered evidence which by due diligence could not have been discovered in time to move for a new trial under Rule 59(b); (3) fraud (whether heretofore denominated intrinsic or extrinsic), misrepresentation, or other misconduct of an adverse party; . . .

This litany of basis for reopenings of judgments is apparently relatively broad when compared with civil law systems. Given the more extensive scope of appellate review available to litigants, civil law systems narrowly circumscribe the opportunity to correct final judgments without bringing the matter before a higher tribunal.[49]

However, despite the broad language of Rule 60, in practice case law has severely limited each of the categories. A substantial number, and perhaps most, of the cases in which a judgment is voided under this rule is when there has been a default judgment where the motioning party has never entered any evidence in the case and has not "been heard." Even in cases of alleged fraud, the courts usually require clear and convincing evidence, and the "fraud or misconduct must be so serious that it prevents the . . . [moving party] from 'fully and fairly' presenting his or her case."[50]

---

49. Peter E. Herzog & Delmar Karlen, Attacks on Judicial Decisions, in Civil Procedure 19-25 (Mauro Cappelletti, ed. Martinus Nijhoff Publishers 1973).

50. Fleming James, Jr., Geoffrey C. Hazard, Jr. & John Leubsdorf, Civil Procedure, 787 (5th ed. Foundation Press 2001).

In sum, although the Federal Rules are in many ways extremely liberal (as compared to the procedural regimes of other countries) in such matters as party control, pleading, joinder, discovery, and permitting jury trial, the system goes to great length to protect and enforce final judgments rigidly. The expansion of breadth for claim and issue preclusion is one example of the respect given to final judgments. Other examples include the stringent "clear error" or "material error" standard applied by appellate judges in reviewing trial court rulings upon appeal, a standard so difficult to meet that it has often resulted in upholding a trial court ruling even when there is some legal error. The number of cases in which an appellate court proclaims that the trial judge has made a mistaken evidence ruling and then affirms because somehow the appellate judges surmise the error was "harmless" is truly legion.

The cramped reading of Rule 60 criteria for vacating judgments is but another example of the rigid position in America against reopening or altering final trial court judgments. Such respect is backed by enforcement as well — enforcement that is ensured through a panoply of sanctions and aids to execution.

ENFORCEMENT OF JUDGMENTS

It is widely believed that most judgments in the United States are enforced by voluntary compliance. Polls show that Americans have a high degree of confidence in judges and juries in civil cases. Voluntary compliance may be good evidence of a public's confidence and respect in the legitimacy of any judicial system.

A strong and highly trained legal profession is certainly critical to this legitimacy, but the common law system also reinforces this public confidence in a number of other ways. Written and published judicial decisions promote this public confidence by requiring appellate judges not only to comply with the law (although, the law is frequently sufficiently unclear to give judges great leeway), but also to explain their decisions in writing, thus making their reasoning transparent and subject to public scrutiny. Even trial judges, when acting as fact finders, must make written findings based on the trial record. Strict adherence to procedural fairness throughout the adjudicatory process makes it more likely that even losers will abide by an unfavorable decision; at a minimum, they have had their day in court.

Important to note, however, voluntary compliance in actual money payments, at least in jury award cases, means only a partial recovery. In a study of 198 jury awards of $1 million or more that occurred in 1984 and 1985, plaintiffs received the original jury award in just slightly more than a quarter of the cases.[51] On average, the final aggregate disbursement to plaintiffs was 57 percent lower than the original verdict.[52] Most jury awards were renegotiated

---

51. Ivy E. Broeder, *Characteristics of Million Dollar Awards: Jury Verdicts and Final Disbursements*, 11 Just. Sys. J. 349, 350, 353 (1986).
52. *Id.*

and reduced by parties post-verdict. This was apparently still true in 2001, as indicated by a study of medical malpractice cases in Pennyslvania that were closed between 1999 and 2001.[53] In these cases, jury verdicts were adjusted by post-verdict negotiations or by what is called high-low agreements in which parties agree before verdict that if a jury reached below an amount, then plaintiffs still got the agreed upon low amount and if the jury verdict is above the agreed upon high amount, it is reduced to the previously agreed "high.[54] High-low agreements serve to check what defendants perceive as runaway juries, and also encourage voluntary compliance, albeit with lesser returns for the plaintiff. They also insure that plaintiffs receive some recovery, even when the jury finds against them.

Backing enforcement are various legal methods available to the courts to compel obedience with judicial orders. The power of courts to enforce judgments comes from the Constitution and statutes, as well as from inherent powers that judges believe they possess. Article III of the Constitution extends federal judicial power to "all Cases, in law and Equity, arising under this Constitution, the Laws of the United States, and Treaties made, or which shall be made, under their authority." The Supreme Court has described judicial power as "the power of a court to decide and pronounce a judgment and *carry it into effect* between two persons and parties who bring a case before it for decision."[55] (emphasis added)

A judgment must be final before it can be enforced. Once final, judgments from courts of one state are recognized and enforceable by courts of another state. The Full Faith and Credit Clause of the U.S. Constitution requires each state to give recognition and enforcement to valid judgments from other state courts. It requires that "Full Faith and Credit shall be given in each State to the public Acts, Records, and judicial Proceedings of every other State."[56] By statutory enactment, the U.S. Congress also extended that requirement to the federal courts by mandating that a judgment issued in any state or territory shall be recognized and enforceable in all federal courts.[57] Federal common law requires that state and federal courts enforce all valid judgments of federal courts. As the Supreme Court explains:

> The very purpose of the full-faith and credit clause was to alter the status of several states as independent foreign sovereignties, each free to ignore obligations created under the laws or by the judicial proceedings of the others, and to make them integral parts of a single nation throughout which a remedy upon a just obligation might be demanded as of right, irrespective of the state of its origin.[58]

The procedure for the enforcement of a judgment by a court of another state generally requires the filing of a new and formal action on the judgment to

53. Neil Vidmar, *The American Civil Jury for Auslander (Foreigners)*, 13 Duke J. Comp. & Int'l L. 95, 120 (2003). This is true especially in malpractice and tort cases.
54. *Id.* at 122.
55. *Muskrat v. U.S.*, 219 U.S. 346, 356 (1911); Black's Law Dictionary 849 (Henry Campbell Black 6th ed. West Group 1990) (defining "judicial power").
56. U.S. Const. art. 4, § 1.
57. Evidence; Documentary, U.S. Code, vol. 28, § 1738 (1948).
58. *Milwaukee County v. M.E. White Co.*, 296 U.S. 268, 276-277 (1935).

obtain a new judgment in the second state for execution. While the Full Faith and Credit Clause ensures that the court in this second action will not reopen the underlying case and reconsider the judgment, the procedure for filing this new action can be costly. There is, though, a special federal statute for the registration of judgments between federal courts that has alleviated the process somewhat.[59] Similarly, some states have adopted the Uniform Enforcement of Foreign Money Judgment Acts, which simplifies the procedure for the execution of judgments between state courts of different states.[60] Both of these statutes alleviate the need to file a formal action on the judgment by replacing it with a simple registration procedure.

Judgments can take the form of a dismissal, a judgment for money of a determinate amount, or an order requiring or prohibiting some kind of action by one party (an injunction). For example, in the case of *Albert Lee v. Cherryum Bottling Co.*, if the Massachusetts federal court, either through a jury verdict or judicial finding, finds any defendant liable, a judgment will be entered for the plaintiff, Albert Lee, for the damages found by the judge or jury. If the lawsuit were litigated as a class action brought against Cherryum, Inc., as well as Cherryum Bottling Co., on the grounds that the Cherryum secret concentrate was defective, the court could issue an injunction restraining both the manufacturer and the bottler from distributing the defective product.

AID TO ENFORCEMENT: GARNISHMENT AND ATTACHMENTS

For each type of judgment, whether damages or injunctions, there are a variety of enforcement methods and sanctions. In the United States, there is no separate judicial division responsible for enforcement. Rather, it is the judge who handled the case who will supervise enforcement in the first instance. Sometimes, as in the well-known school desegregation cases, the judiciary can even call upon the executive branch, through the military, for assistance.[61]

The law surrounding the execution of judgments is primarily state law based. Unless a federal statute provides to the contrary, the federal courts will use whatever statutory procedures are available in the states in which they are sitting. Flexible procedures also exist to assist the judgment creditor (the person owed money as a result of a judgment) in enforcing the judgment, including discovery for that purpose. Fed. R. Civ. P. 69(a).

State statutes provide for a number of devices for execution of judgments, depending on the nature of property that the judgment is directed at. Typically, executions are simply papers issued from the clerk of the judgment court authorizing a sheriff to seize or to assert dominion over the property of the judgment debtor. Some state jurisdictions provide that the attorney for a

---

59. Pending Actions and Judgments, U.S. Code, vol. 28, § 1963 (1948).
60. *See* Jay M. Zitter, *Construction and Application of Uniform Foreign Money-Judgments Recognition Act*, 88 A.L.R.5th 545 (2004).
61. *Swann v. Charlotte-Mecklenburg Board of Education*, 402 U.S. 1 (1971); *Green v. County School Board of New Kent County*, 391 U.S. 430 (1968); *Brown v. Board of Educ.*, 349 U.S. 294 (1955).

judgment creditor can issue the execution papers. The sheriff need not physically take the property. Rather, it can simply be a verbal or written declaration by the sheriff to the judgment debtor.

If the property is real property, the judgment typically must be filed with an official of the county in which the property is located, constituting a lien on the property. The property may also be seized and sold in a public auction held by the sheriff's office, and the proceeds from the sale can be turned over to the judgment creditor in satisfaction of the money judgment. Perhaps you remember such a sheriff's sale in *Pennoyer v. Neff*, the foundation case for personal jurisdiction that you read about in Chapter 5. Public policy dictates that some property is exempted from seizure, such as the family home or artisan's tools.

Execution, called "garnishment," may also be directed against property held by a third party.[62] Under these circumstances, the sheriff will issue a restraining notice to the third party prohibiting the third party from transferring the property. If the execution is against the judgment debtor's employer for the judgment debtor's wages, a notice will be sent to the employer ordering the employer to withhold wages. Federal law provides, however, that no state or federal court may order the withholding of wages that will leave the income less than 75 percent of the judgment debtor's (the person who owes money as a result of a judgment) take home pay or 30 times the minimum hourly wage, whichever is greater.[63]

Since a court cannot issue an execution order against property not within its jurisdiction, plaintiffs will normally seek to have judgments enforced by a court in a jurisdiction in which the defendant's assets are located. As stated earlier, if the assets are in a different state and the judgment originated in federal court, the judgment creditor can register the judgment order for enforcement in that state by mailing a certified official copy to a court of that state. Thus, if Cherryum Bottling Co. has assets in New Hampshire in the form of a bank account, real estate, or otherwise, then the judgment may be sent to a New Hampshire court for enforcement. Once a writ of execution is sent to the courts of New Hampshire, Plaintiff Albert Lee can have the assistance of New Hampshire law enforcement to enforce this order by seizure and sale of the property in satisfaction of the judgment.

CONTEMPT OF COURT

Perhaps a court's most powerful weapon in aid of execution is its contempt powers to punish for disobedience. For example, if Cherryum Bottling Co. refuses to comply with the order to desist from bottling drinks with the Cherryum secret concentrate, the court can invoke its contempt powers and issue civil and criminal penalties against Cherryum. Unlike execution or garnishment, the sanction of contempt operates against the person of the

---

62. Friedenthal, Kane & Miller, *supra* note 4, Execution and Levies, Sec. 15.7 at 745.
63. Consumer Credit Protection Restrictions on Garnishment, 15 U.S.C. § 1673 (1968).

contemnor, rather than his property. Contempt powers of the court can be in the form of fines or in extraordinary cases, imprisonment.

A court's contempt powers have roots in the early equity courts of English law. Under early English law, disobedience of a court order was deemed contempt of the King. In the United States, under the Judiciary Act of 1789, federal courts were granted the same powers possessed by the English Courts "to punish by fine or imprisonment, at the discretion of said courts, all contempt of authority in any cause or hearing." However, the Judiciary Act did not define contempt or the nature of the punishment; this led to some abuses by judges who used contempt power to punish citizens for public criticism of their decisions. In 1831, federal legislation was enacted to proscribe the classes of conduct for which the courts might thereafter punish as contempt of their authority. Contempt of court now includes 1) misbehavior in the presence of the court, 2) misbehavior of court officers in official transactions, and 3) disobedience or resistance to any lawful writ, process, order, rule, decree, or command of the court.[64]

The power of the court to enforce its orders begins the moment the court's powers are invoked through the commencement of any case in the court. Contempt will be upheld even if the underlying order of the trial court exceeds that court's jurisdiction and the underlying order is later set aside on appeal. In other words, while seemingly harsh, an order of the court must be obeyed and contempt sanctions will be imposed for its disobedience until the court order is vacated or set aside on appeal.

Contempt may be civil or criminal, depending on the nature of the disobedience. Civil contempt is said to be remedial and the proceedings are for the benefit of the complainant, while criminal contempt is to vindicate the authority of the court. Civil contempt proceedings are intended to coerce compliance with the court order, to compensate for losses sustained by noncompliance, or both. By contrast, criminal contempt is punitive and its purpose is to punish for an already completed act of disobedience. If a party does not obey an order, the court may order fines and incarceration either as a civil contempt to compensate the plaintiff for damages due to defendant's noncompliance or as criminal contempt to punish the defendant's noncompliance. Whether the sanction is civil or criminal will depend entirely on its purpose and the proceeding surrounding its imposition, rather than in its form as fines or imprisonment.

In *Gompers* v. *Bucks Stove & Range Co.*, the Supreme Court explained, "[p]roceedings for civil contempt are between the original parties and are instituted and tried as a part of the main cause. But on the other hand, proceedings at law for criminal contempt are between the public and the defendant, and are not a part of the original cause."[65] Thus, civil contempt benefits a private litigant and follows civil procedure. Criminal contempt vindicates the public interest in law obedience and follows criminal procedure. Having said that, it is often the case that the line between the two is blurred.

Civil contempt is initiated by motion of a party, not the government. The proceeding is viewed as an extension of the existing civil case. However, the

---

64. Power of Court, 18 U.S.C. § 401 (1948).
65. 221 U.S. 418, 445 (1911).

burden of proof for civil contempt is slightly different than the burden of proof in ordinary civil cases. Civil contempt is proven by "clear and convincing" evidence, which is higher than "preponderance of the evidence" for civil cases generally, but lower than "beyond a reasonable doubt" standard for criminal cases.[66] Because this is a civil and not criminal case, a showing of intent is not necessary for a finding of civil contempt.

Coercive sanctions are treated as civil only if the party in contempt is afforded the opportunity to purge the contempt by compliance with the underlying order. The idea is that the court's power is used for remedial and not punitive purposes, by coercing the defendant to do what he had refused to do.[67] Therefore, these sanctions may be in the form of a repetitive fine or imprisonment for an indefinite period of time until the defendant complies. However, the fines may be so large as to compel compliance but not so large as to constitute punishment. Similarly, imprisonment may continue only so long as the court is satisfied that imprisonment might produce the intended result. Otherwise, imprisonment should be terminated. One prominent example of civil contempt and its use even against political figures, is that of Susan McDougal, a former business associate of then President Bill Clinton, who was jailed for 18 months for her refusal to testify against the President in an ongoing criminal investigation being conducted by independent counsel Kenneth Starr.

Unlike civil contempt, criminal contempt is a public litigation to vindicate the authority of the court. It is instituted as a separate action and prosecuted by the government (in the federal courts, by the U.S. Attorney's Office) much like any other criminal case. This means that a criminal contempt proceeding must provide all the due process protections and safeguards as would be provided to criminal defendants. This includes the right to counsel: the person accused of contempt, if indigent, is entitled to court appointed counsel in cases in which imprisonment is the potential penalty. Since criminal contempt is penal in nature, the prosecuting authority must demonstrate intent and willfulness as a part of their case.[68]

Although criminal contempt, like civil contempt sanctions, can result in either fines or imprisonment, criminal contempt sanctions differ from civil contempt sanctions in a number of ways. For example, compliance with the underlying court order cannot form the basis of purging one from criminal contempt sanctions. Criminal contempt is punitive, imposed solely for the completed act of disobedience. Furthermore, if the criminal contempt sanction is a fine, the fine is to be paid to the court rather than to the plaintiff. The public interest served is to vindicate authority of court and to deter further disobedience, rather than to benefit the plaintiff. However, the power to punish criminal contempt, like civil contempt, should be limited to "the least possible power adequate to the end proposed."[69]

66. Paul Coltoff, et al., Contempt, 17 C.J.S. Contempt § 90 (2004); Joel M. Androphy and Keith A. Byers, *Federal Contempt of Court*, 61 Tex. B.J. 16 (1998).

67. Lawrence N. Gray, *Criminal and Civil Contempt: Some Sense of a Hodgepodge*, 13 J. Suffolk Acad. L. 1, 78-79 (1999).

68. *Id*. at 83-85.

69. *Anderson v. Dunn*, 6 Wheat. 204, 231 (1821).

In sum, each method of enforcement requires some form of court involvement. An order such as garnishment requires the least judicial involvement, such as an order to a bank. Attachment and seizure orders require the court to work with local enforcement authorities. Finally, with the contempt order, the judge is intimately involved with state and federal enforcement authorities.

Contempt powers have played a vital role in protecting the authority of courts and judges. Contempt and the power of the court to enforce its orders played an important part in United States history. It was a turning point for the rise in federal powers when armed national guards were called upon to enforce federal court orders to desegregate the schools during the civil rights movement of the 1960s. The enforcement of these federal court desegregation orders was done, in some instances, in direct opposition to local authorities and police. This enforcement of federal court orders was an integral part of the expansion of federal governmental powers in the United States.

FINALITY AND JUSTICE

Valuing finality and ensuring the enforcement of judgments, at times even over and above substantive justice, is by no means the norm in all countries. For example, appellate courts in some countries outside the United States decide all issues *de novo*, both factual and legal, or at the least, can accept new evidence.[70] Still other systems provide even more leeway in allowing for the reopening and review of judgments beyond the appeals process.

Perhaps the fact that American courts have rested such responsibilities on the lawyers and that so much time and money is often expended at the trial level has led to a sense at the appellate level of "enough already — let the decision stand." Then, too, the jury system in the United States, as well as the emphasis on orality (that is, testimony being taken in open court, rather than by written documents), means that appellate judges, who are limited to reviewing the decision on the record and cannot assess the credibility of witnesses, are loathe to interfere with trial court factual determinations. It may further be that the high quality and independence of trial court judges at the federal level and in many states, as well as the trust in the system engendered by the lay jury and adversarial party-controlled participation, have allowed our appellate judges to be more deferential to trial court findings. By comparison, civil law systems chose to place confidence on professional judges and rely on government financed, judge-responsible fact finding resulting in a broader

---

70. *See, e.g.*, Charles H. Koch, Jr., *The Advantages of the Civil Law Judicial Design as the Model for Emerging Legal Systems*, 11 Ind. J. Global Legal Stud. 139 (2004) (noting that an emerging legal system would be better suited with a civil system — for instance France's — due to a corps of knowledgeable jurists who could review findings of fact de novo); Konrad Zweigert & Hein Kotz, Introduction to Comparative Law (Tony Weir trans., 3d ed. 1998) (regarding Italy's judicial structure); John C. Reitz, *Why We Probably Cannot Adopt the German Advantage in Civil Procedure*, 75 Iowa L. Rev. 987 (1990).

scope of first level review, but a strict line against reopenings of judgments after the review.

How extensive we allow later attacks of judgments beyond the appeal is certainly related to our trust and confidence in the competency of the decision maker. Thus, for example, in China, where the legal system was only reinstated in the late 1970s and judicial workers are still inexperienced, the liberal reopening of judgments may be necessary to correct inaccurate outcomes. The Chinese legal system (exemplifying formerly socialist legal systems) has a process called "adjudication supervision," by which the prosecutor and parties, as well as the court president can petition for a reopening of judgments at any time.[71] An internal committee called the judicial committee, composed of court president, chief judges of each division, and chief prosecutor for the court, will review the petition. If granted, the case will be retried. This procedure has led to successive reopening of judgments in which outcomes were changed for both correct and, what look to some, incorrect reasons. It has also led to opportunities for reopening judgments to suit changing political winds and increases unpredictability in the legal system.

Then, again, it may also be that in cultures in which individualized substantive justice is prized over procedural justice, and in which the lower courts are viewed as suspect, reopening of judgment is welcomed with more tolerance and liberality. In the United States, our faith in the adversary process and the judge and jury at the initial trial level and our belief in procedural justice as the best route to ensure substantive justice may help explain our relatively rigid stance in favor of finality and against reopening of judgments.

Any legitimate civil adjudication system must provide the appearance as well as reality of seeking and achieving justice in the individual case. Courts should seek to "get it right" in the sense that they try diligently to discern the underlying events that gave rise to the dispute, to apply known law to the facts, and to fairly adjust the law when it is uncertain. But litigation is expensive to the participants and society. There are always endless number of ways that the court could be a bit more certain of the result, be it through amended pleadings, additional discovery, one more witness at the trial, longer closing arguments, more extensive briefs, more time for oral argument on appeal, retrial, multiple appeals. Where a court's resources are not unlimited, every resource that is spent on one case is denied to another. And so, in civil litigation, as in so many other aspects of life, "the perfect is the enemy of the possible." Perfection in the individual case is in tension with the needs of society at large. Denying perfection in one case may make it possible for larger numbers of litigants to seek and obtain some type of justice in their individual cases.

One final case, we hope, will help illustrate for you the central tension that has pervaded all aspects of this chapter on preclusion, appeal, and execution. This is a tension that in some respects inheres in each stage of civil litigation, both in America and elsewhere.

The year was 1963. The place was Birmingham, Alabama. At that time, Birmingham was considered among the most, if not the most, racially

---

71. *See* Margaret Y.K. Woo, *Adjudication Supervision and Judicial Independence in the People's Republic of China*, 39 Am. J. Comp. L. 95 (1991).

intolerant and racially segregated cities in the United States. The city had repeatedly defied federal court orders granted in civil litigations to integrate public facilities, including its schools, allowing blacks and whites the same access to these facilities. For months, the Southern Christian Leadership Conference had considered strategies for attacking Birmingham's segregation. The leaders settled on peaceful demonstrations, including boycotts of white services and goods, commencing with a parade on Good Friday, April 12. On April 3, a representative of the demonstrators approached Theophilus Eugene "Bull" Connor, the notoriously racist commissioner of public safety, to request a parade permit. According to one account:

> Connor replied: "No, you will not get a permit in Birmingham, Alabama to picket. I will picket you over to City Jail." On April 5 – one week before Good Friday – Connor replied to a second, telegraphic, request for a parade permit with another refusal. The demonstrators proceeded with their protests.[72]

On April 10, Connor obtained an ex parte injunction from a state court judge forbidding the civil rights leaders, including the Reverend Martin Luther King, Jr., from encouraging or taking part in the parade and demonstrations. King and others, knowing from past experience that the Alabama state courts would not do them or their cause justice, that appeals would delay once again their justifiable protests, and that for important symbolic reasons, these demonstrations must take place on Good Friday and Easter Friday, went forward with their plans on both days. The state court judge who had issued the injunction found King and several other demonstrators guilty of criminal contempt of court for their disobedience and sentenced each of them to five days in jail and a $50 fine. While in jail, Reverend King wrote his famous letter from Birmingham City Jail. In this letter, King argued that some societal acts and judicial decisions are so inherently unjust that they cry out for civil disobedience. "We can never forget," King wrote, "that everything Hitler did in Germany was 'legal' and everything the Hungarian freedom fighters did in Hungary was 'illegal.' It was 'illegal' to aid and comfort a Jew in Hitler's Germany."[73]

King and the others who were held in contempt appealed to the Alabama Supreme Court. The Alabama Supreme Court refused to consider the constitutional attacks on the initial injunction and affirmed the contempt imprisonments and fines. The Alabama Supreme Court held that one must obey even an unlawful injunction until it is altered or reversed by appeal; one's recourse is appeal, not noncompliance.[74] The United States Supreme Court agreed. In *Walker v. City of Birmingham*, the United States Supreme Court affirmed in a 5-4 decision.[75] Justice Stevens, writing for the majority, allowed that "[t]he generality of the language contained in the Birmingham parade ordinance upon which the injunction was based would unquestionably raise substantial constitutional issues concerning some of its provisions...The

72. David Luban, Legal Modernism 218 (U. Mich. Press, 1994).
73. Martin Luther King, Jr., Letter from Birmingham City Jail, in A Testament of Hope: The Essential Writings and Speeches of Martin Luther King, Jr. 289 (James M. Washington, ed. 1986).
74. *Walker v. City of Birmingham*, 181 So.2d 493, 502-503 (Ala. 1969).
75. *Walker v. City of Birmingham*, 388 U.S. 307 (1967).

breadth and vagueness of the injunction itself would also unquestionably be subject to substantial constitutional question."[76] But appeal would have been the correct course of action for King and the others, not disobedience:

> The rule of law that Alabama followed in this case reflects a belief that in the fair administration of justice no man can be judge in his own case, however exalted his station, however righteous his motives, and irrespective of his race, color, politics, or religion. This court cannot hold that the petitioners were constitutionally free to ignore all the procedures of the law and carry their battle to the streets....[77]

A stinging dissent written by Justice Douglas, and joined by Chief Justice Warren and Justices Brennan and Fortas forcibly argued that on the facts of this case, an erroneous and unconstitutional ruling of a court should not have to be obeyed. The Alabama injunction and the ensuing contempt order, they argued, were "patently impermissible prior restraints on the exercise of First Amendment rights."[78] Alabama could have arrested King and the others for violating the statute, rather than contempt for violating a court order, and in that instance the alleged violators could have raised their constitutional issues as a defense. In the dissent's view, the state of Alabama used its contempt powers improperly and was illegally depriving King and the other protestors from raising their constitutional objections.

Lest for a moment you have found the issues in this chapter — res judicata, appeal, and enforcement — to be dry, procedural technicalities, we end with what David Lubin wrote about this 1963 controversy in Birmingham, Alabama:

> Both *Walker* and the [King] *Letter* address an ancient question, a question that more than any other defines the very subject of legal philosophy: that, of course, is the question whether we lie under an obligation to obey unjust legal directives, including directives ordering our punishment for disobeying unjust directives. All political philosophy, from Plato's *Apology* and *Crito* on, is driven by this question: all our political hopes and aspirations are contained in the descriptive and argumentative materials we use to answer it.[79]

When should finality trump the search for justice in the individual case? No system has the perfect answer, and perhaps, no system should.

---

76. *Id* at 316-317.
77. *Id* at 320-321.
78. *Id.* at 349.
79. Luban, *supra* note 72, at 220.

EPILOGUE

As with all comparative studies, our gaze outward inevitably turned inward. From our initial task to explain American civil litigation to civil proceduralists in China, we evolved to a better understanding of our own legal system. Through this process, we realized that we are witnessing a moment of significant change in the American legal system. After years of expansion, American civil process peaked in its breadth and depth at mid-twentieth century. At the time of this writing, retrenchment of civil litigation is in full swing. While we cannot predict the course or the pace of this retrenchment, we hope we can at least capture the character of American civil procedure at this very critical juncture.

We have tried to present American civil procedure from several vantage points: the procedural doctrine that has evolved over time; the practical implications of that doctrine; the social context in which the doctrine grew, is used and abused; and the global context of how other systems may have made different choices. It is now up to you to take away lessons of your own.

There are a few final thoughts we can share from what we have learned, however. In spite of our years of litigating in our own country and writing about and teaching civil procedure, we remain amazed at how pragmatic the American legal system is and how change within the system is often a "bottom up" phenomenon generated by those who use the system rather than simply a "top down" dictate of law and policy makers. And the reforms are more often pragmatic and incremental and less often grand scheme. It is these characteristics, we believe, that will keep American civil process vibrant.

American lawyers, like American legal culture, are adversarial, pragmatic, and result oriented. If they practice in the private sector, they aggressively seek clients and very much strive to win, both for themselves and for their clients. Many, if not most, are competitive in the extreme and success-driven. They use legal doctrine, often in creative ways, to achieve the ends their clients want. If you have read carefully, you will have seen this pragmatism and instrument-alism running through virtually every topic we covered — from the strategic use of jurisdiction to engaging in discovery, from selection of juries to the making of closing arguments.

One object of fascination is that this same pragmatism and drive to win may have in recent years moved the legal system in the direction of less formalism, less discovery, and more mediation. There has been a flight from the courts, at least a flight from trials. While one explanation may be the desire for a more cooperative society, the more likely is that lawyers, in large measure through the prodding of their clients, have made the practical and rational judgment that the risks and costs of full, non-mediated, no-holds-barred litigation are too high. The corporate drive to utilize contractually driven mandated binding arbitration might have no altruism behind it; the goal is saving costs. While the other currents driving ADR may have a softer edge, the true driving force may be that corporate clients are getting more out of mediation and arbitration than litigation.

The other characteristic of American civil procedure is its "bottom up" trajectory of change. As we have reiterated, procedural doctrine does not drop full-blown from heaven. It is shaped by culture, manipulated by those within the culture, and is simultaneously part of the wider culture with an inevitable political dimension. In the American context, civil procedure has been shaped at the ground level by lawyers, judges, and even litigants, and driven by iconoclastic conflicting images of lawyers as both saviors of individual liberties and "ambulance chasers" of profits.

A favorite metaphor of those who urged the creation of the Federal Rules of Civil Procedure was that procedure should be a clear bridge or open tunnel that lets the substantive law and the underlying facts flow through without distortion. This is a false metaphor. Procedure will influence what cases are brought, how cases are settled, and what cases are won. Thus, for example, ease of pleading means that some frivolous cases will sneak through but also that other meritorious cases will be brought and more discovery will be needed. Heightened pleading requirements, meanwhile, will mean that some frivolous cases will be barred, but also that other meritorious cases will not be brought and if brought, less discovery will be necessary.

If facts and law are more elusive than the description of "a clear bridge or open tunnel," then the mechanical application of law to known facts, once called "mechanical jurisprudence," is inapplicable The reality is that numerous filters are provided by the quality of the lawyers, the beliefs and the capacity of judges, the compromises inherent in the procedural, substantive, and evidentiary rules, the honesty or mendacity of the clients, the perceptions and misperceptions of witnesses, and the vagaries of the juries. Within that fluidity, law navigates. While legal doctrine frequently, perhaps usually, does not alone dictate results, any lawyer will attest that the law, both procedural and substantive, is highly relevant to the advice they give and the results they achieve in civil litigation. The facts are even more relevant.

And so, civil procedure is not a bridge or tunnel; it is not a machine. Procedure is part of a complex process that includes procedural rules; substantive doctrine; the attempt to find out what happened that precipitated the dispute; application of law to facts (legal analysis); clients and their needs, fears, perceptions, and ability and willingness to pay; lawyers, their training, their fees; witnesses; an adversarial and market driven culture; judges, their backgrounds and socialization, and modes of selection; evidence rules with their compromises around issues of privacy and fears of lay juries; juries, with their strengths and weaknesses; and loads of other variables of which we may be unaware. It is a process that reflects and is impacted by the many competing goals and complexities of human nature and the human condition.

Procedure, substance, access and cost of lawyers, quality of lawyers, composition of the judiciary and juries all interact in subtle and not so subtle ways to influence results. But that does not mean that societies cannot strive for more neutral processes. It does mean that whatever the process, process will inevitably skew the results. This is not because lawyers, judges, and legislators who draft procedural rules and statutes are incompetent. Rather, it is because how a society resolves its disputes, which law suits are treated, how much discretion is given to judges and lawyers ultimately have socio-economic-political consequences.

A credit to the American legal system is that many of the procedural changes have come from with the legal profession itself and from those seeking to utilize the courts. From discovery to class actions, procedural rules are often generated by judges, litigants and/or lawyers in individual cases that bubbled upward until they become an accepted and widespread doctrine. The present day retrenchment in civil process is a retrenchment that originated within the wider legal culture towards the use of litigation itself.

One thing we have learned in teaching in China and in writing this book is that critical legitimacy issues are more important than the specific procedures adopted in any country. The central question faced by any system of civil adjudication is whether the population at large trusts the system. The system cannot be perfect. There are too many variables and too much dispute as to what "perfect" justice would be. But if the population does not trust the legal system, then that system is, in our view, a bad system. A society with an untrustworthy, unreliable, inefficient system of dispute resolution will ultimately have a corrosive effect on the reality and perception of the legitimacy of government. A system with a "bottom up" trajectory for change, we believe, is one important method of securing legitimacy for a system that is trusted by the populace.

We tend to take some things for granted in the United States — that defendants will usually appear in some court; that the majority of judges will not be bribed or subject to corrupt influence (although, as all humans, they will have prejudices beyond their control); and that judgments, absent bankruptcy, can be collected in whole or in part. These assumptions are part and parcel of a legal system that is largely accepted by the population. Admittedly, the current influence of political contributions on judicial elections at the state level can lead to the reality or appearance of bias on the part of the judiciary. At the federal level, heated political battles over appointment have perhaps resulted in judges with stronger political views. And the still predominantly white male composition of the federal judiciary subjects the legal system to challenges of discrimination. But the jury system, procedural rules, and the training, experience, and habits of thought of lawyers and judges, percolating from below, will, we hope, continue to provide some checks on abusive power.

At the beginning of the twenty-first century, some new developments in modern American civil adjudication tantalize us as to what the future may bring. Their implications, for us at least, are unclear; and some of the developments may have aspects that are troubling. First, as we have pointed out repeatedly in the text of this book, the percentage of trials compared to terminated civil cases has materially been reduced; probably fewer than 2 percent of terminated cases are tried. Because settlement and ADR resolutions are usually predicated on what would happen at trial, we may end up in some situations with virtually nothing to provide intelligent predictions. Moreover, the paucity of trials drastically reduces the part played by lay people in the process of dispute resolution. Fewer witnesses and parties are taking the stand, and fewer lay people are acting as jurors. Lay participation has always been an important ingredient in providing a check on the judiciary and engendering "bottom up" changes to the process.

Second, and related to the first, is the incremental importance of written advocacy and reduction of oral advocacy as trials decrease. Today, motions and appeals are decided more on briefs and less on oral arguments. Writing tends to be less dramatic than oral advocacy. Perhaps, this is a good turn, as, for example, orality is not necessarily a critical feature in many civil law countries. Yet, in the United States where the political and legal systems are built on an oral tradition and open court, this may mean fewer lawyers who can engage at a high level of excellence in public oral advocacy, which over time can reduce their effectiveness in politics and other public functions. We are further concerned that judges will not have to look litigants in the face, rendering their decisions less directly related to the human experience, and that more outcomes are agreed to in the secrecy of private negotiations. Trials and open court hold judges publicly and privately accountable — publicly in making law accessible and comprehensible to the public and privately in forcing judges to look directly at the people whose lives they are profoundly influencing.

If the first two developments are worrisome, the latter two developments may provide at least part of a practical solution. Procedural rule makers are increasingly turning to numeric limits in their attempt to reign in the expense and time of civil litigation. At both the state and federal levels there are now limits on numbers of interrogatories and depositions, as well as the length of time for oral depositions. Some courts even impose time limits on trials. Many states and some federal courts are developing a fast track for simpler cases, in which there will be less discovery and earlier trial dates.

This development of using numeric limits and setting earlier trial dates may encourage lawyers and clients to try a larger percentage of cases. This in turn may allow judges to act more as judges in the traditional sense and less, in the words of Judith Resnik, as "managerial judges." For reasons we have explored throughout this book, we would applaud such a development. In short, the adjudication of cases in open court through trial by jury is consonant with our country's democratic values and adds legitimacy to the judicial branch specifically and to government generally.

Not to be ignored is the astonishing growth of ADR (apart from private settlements between lawyers). The data is thin on whether ADR in fact provides savings of time and money. We do not know whether the decrease in both the percentage and aggregate number of trials is attributable to ADR. An increase in granted summary judgments, the complexity of cases, the costs of litigation, and the effects of case management may be more important variables in this "vanishing trial" phenomenon. But we do know that the numbers of arbitrations and mediations have dramatically increased. We know that businesses have inserted huge numbers of binding arbitration clauses into their form contracts, and lawyers are finding it increasingly desirable to negotiate with the aid of mediators. Over time this should mean clients are hearing their lawyers present their cases more frequently before neutral "mediators" and arbitrators than when negotiation is solely between lawyers. It may be that lawyers are gaining experience with new types of oral and written advocacy and with a new type of negotiation — negotiation aided by neutrals that is not unlike public trials.

Ultimately, there is one cluster of problems in American civil procedure that seems so far to defy solution. Despite the bubbling up of procedural change, what should be the nature of procedural rules and who should draft them — courts or the legislature? The more practical variation of this question is how we systematically reign in a legal system in a way that is not unfair to those with real grievances. One could greatly reduce discovery for all cases, but this would be unfair to some plaintiffs in some types of cases that need discovery. One could use more judicial case management, but particularly the state courts lack the personnel to accomplish this. Moreover, case management increases judicial discretion that some lawyers and their clients greatly distrust. One can use numeric limits, as we have discussed. This may work well for smaller cases. Or one could try to hone the procedures in advance for certain types of cases. This would be substance-specific procedure: different pleading requirements, amounts of discovery, and other procedural attributes for different types of cases.

But substance-specific procedure entails its own problems. It is difficult to categorize cases. A simple discrimination case, for instance, can have elements of tort, contract, employment, and statutory law. A tort case can be small, medium, large, and anything in between. Even more difficult to solve is the problem that when one starts to design procedures for particular types of cases it becomes more obvious how politically charged the decisions are. Pleading requirements or the amount of discovery permitted in discrimination, products liability, or securities cases will help determine results.

These decisions sound like they belong in the legislature and not the judiciary, as they may be most accountable to public sentiments. But legislators have not proven to have the staying power or expertise in procedural rule-making that gives one confidence they would do a very good job. Moreover, legislators, in drafting procedures for one type of case, tend not to integrate those procedures with the general procedures that govern all cases. How to get the judiciary and legislature to cooperate in a sensible way to coordinate change has, for the most part, proven elusive.

We in the United States are still struggling with how best to choose judges, how best to draft procedural rules, how best to utilize juries, how best to construct a procedural system that meets the needs of the people as well as the institution. We have tried to show the pros and cons of our system. We provided a good deal of empirical data, but empiricism will not yield normative solutions; value-laden decisions need to be made. Perhaps the next generation of lawyers in our country and abroad will find successful approaches that respond to the needs of their citizens and their cultures. What fascinating challenges lie ahead for all of us? We wish you, as we wish for ourselves, the best of knowledge, judgment, and luck. You and we will need all of those — and more.

INDEX